N'

D0773062

west point

A BICENTENNIAL HISTORY

west point

A BICENTENNIAL HISTORY

Theodore J. Crackel

UNIVERSITY PRESS OF KANSAS

© 2002 by the University Press of Kansas

Published by the University Press of Kansas (Lawrence, Kansas 66049), which was organized by the Kansas Board of Regents and is operated and funded by Emporia State University, Fort Hays State University, Kansas State University, Pittsburg State University, the University of Kansas, and Wichita State University

Library of Congress Cataloging-in-Publication Data
Crackel, Theodore J.
   West Point : a bicentennial history / Theodore J. Crackel.
      p. cm. — (Modern war studies)
Rev. ed. of: Illustrated history of West Point. 1990.
Includes bibliographical references and index.
   ISBN 0-7006-1160-6 (cloth : alk. paper)
   1. United States Military Academy—History.   I. Crackel, Theodore J.
Illustrated history of West Point.   II. Title.   III. Series.
   U410.L1 C69 2002
   335'.0071'173—dc21   2001008230

British Library Cataloguing in Publication Data is available.

Printed in the United States of America

10   9   8   7   6   5   4   3   2   1

The paper used in this publication meets the minimum requirements of the American National Standard for Permanence of Paper for Printed Library Materials Z39.48-1984.

For Mary-Jo

Contents

Illustrations

Preface and Acknowledgments

There is a poetic power in the Highland setting where West Point reposes and in the river that the post commands. It perhaps derives from the incongruous path the Hudson has chosen—rising some three hundred miles from the sea in a tiny, high Adirondack lake and behaving for much of its course as a river should until, just above West Point, it leaves its valley and slices east through the granite Highlands in a narrow, twisting, picturesque gorge of its own making. And then, the much-shortened run to the sea.

Perhaps instead that poetic power derives from the ancient granite Highlands through which the Hudson courses and which loom over West Point, framing it so majestically. Here, wrote Washington Irving, "gigantic Titans" waged "impious war with heaven" and piled "cliffs on cliffs" and hurled "vast masses of rocks in wild confusion."

For hundreds of millions of years, these ancient mountains have been beveled by erosion and weathering; most recently they were shaped by the great ice sheets of the glacial age. Acting as enormous graders, these glaciers smoothed and rounded the northern slopes and summits of the Highlands. But the southern slopes—those that loom over West Point—were left irregular and precipitate and strewn with the loose boulders and debris that gave rise to names like "Rock Hill" and "Stony Lonesome."

West Point: A Bicentennial History is the story of this place—or, more precisely, of the school that was built there, the United States Military Academy. It is first and foremost the history of that institution, and as such it is the tale of the people—the officers and cadets—and the Academy they molded and remolded. But any history of this institution is also a chronicle of the physical place and the evolution of the striking Tudor-Gothic architecture that has defined it for the last century and a half.

West Point: A Bicentennial History is a careful, new look at West Point. It is essentially a chronological history, in which a number of themes can be traced from beginning to end—cadet and faculty life, institutional governance, curriculum, and growth and expansion. Because of the ebb and flow of many other events and issues, and the discontinuities of war and peace, there is some overlap in the story's telling. In some chapters it was necessary to go back and trace themes that could not be fully developed earlier. More often, issues are revisited from chapter to chapter.

Because this is the story of West Point and the Military Academy, the narrative only rarely ventures beyond the boundaries of that post. When it does, it is only to examine directly related topics such as policies and decisions made in Washington that affected the school. Similarly, graduates, individually or collectively, are seldom pursued beyond the gates, and their professional lives are chronicled only as they relate to West Point—shining the light again, for example, on those who return to the Academy as members of the faculty or as Commandants or Superintendents.

West Point: A Bicentennial History had its origins in my work on Thomas Jefferson's founding of the Military Academy, which appeared first in article form in 1981 and then as a chapter of *Mr. Jefferson's Army* in 1987. More immediately, this work is a major revision and enlargement of an earlier history of West Point, written over a decade ago for the USMA class of 1940—*The Illustrated History of West Point*—which became that class's fiftieth-anniversary gift to the Academy. The current volume features new research and new perspectives in every chapter. This is particularly true of the last chapter, which was expanded to cover the period from 1990 to 2001, enabling me to reexamine the events of the 1970s and 1980s. The new publication also gave me the opportunity to include the notes that identify my sources.

I have added to this work, as Appendix A, a listing of all of the Academy's Superintendents, Commandants, Deans, and heads of academic departments. I have done so not only because of the utility of this information but because all of them deserve notice, and I was unable to introduce every one of them in the text in some meaningful way.

The research that underpins this book was done during three periods: 1980, 1988–1990, and 2000–2001. In the process of preparing and writing a work such as this, one accrues numerous debts of gratitude. I want to express my thanks to the many individuals at West Point who aided me in one or more of the periods of research. In particular, I owe a great debt to Suzanne Christoff, the USMA Archivist and Director of Special Collections, and to Alan C. Aimone, Susan Lintelman, and Alicia Maldin of her department. Also, my thanks to Judith Sibley, who was with the USMA Archives during my first round of research, Frank Martini, the history department's highly skilled cartographer, and Mike Moss and David Reel from the West Point Museum. All went far beyond the demands of duty in attending to my many research needs. Their ability to ferret out an elusive book, document, or quotation or to steer me to a new and critical source never ceased to gratify and amaze me. Particular thanks are also due to Steve Grove, USMA Historian, whose annual reports (when that series was still being produced) were models of lucidity and precision. His interviews of departing senior officers are an invaluable resource and a unique window onto events. His knowledge of the Academy's history and his generosity in sharing it made my work much easier.

I am also indebted to a number of persons who consented to speak with me of their own experiences—some in 1990, others in 2001, and a few who helped me on both occasions. They include Brigadier General Thomas E. Griess, Brigadier General Elliott Cutler, Brigadier General and Mrs. Sumner Willard, Mrs. George Lincoln, Major General Chester V. Clifton, and General William C. Westmoreland. I also owe a great debt to the numerous persons at West Point, in Washington, and elsewhere who agreed to speak with me on background. My understanding of many past and current issues depended on these conversations. General Griess and Colonel Robert Doughty, Professor and Head, Department of History, read and commented on the last chapter. Their critiques not only pointed out errors but often caused me to reassess my interpretation of events. Although I sometimes chose to retain an interpretation that they might disagree with, their assistance was invaluable.

I owe a multiple debt to my wife, Mary-Jo Kline, a librarian and a remarkable historian and documentary editor who helped me chase down obscure facts and information. I also benefited mightily from her well-hewn editorial skills as she read, corrected, and commented on every chapter. Throughout, she asked questions about West Point that had never occurred to me. She made this a markedly better book. Needless to say, the choice of materials presented, of stories told, and of interpretation of events herein, as well as any errors or omissions, are entirely my own responsibility.

Introduction

The history of the United States Military Academy (USMA) is more than the story of a military school on the Hudson River. In fact, the Academy's history is a reflection of the nation it serves, for West Point has mirrored the broader movements of American society. To understand West Point is to better understand the country its graduates are sworn to protect and defend.

This phenomenon was true from the beginning. The Military Academy was born in 1801 as part of a broader plan by Jefferson to recast the federal government. Coming to grips with Jefferson's motives in sponsoring such a school (after long opposing one) is essential if one is to comprehend what Jefferson was all about.

The interplay of society and school continued in the next decades. The Academy added "civil" engineering to its curriculum in the 1820s in response to the nation's growing preoccupation with internal improvements and the needs of a geographically expanding young nation.

In the decades before the Civil War, Northern and Southern cadets experienced firsthand the growing sectional tensions as the nation moved toward disunion. Perhaps no other institution in the nation felt the rending of the union as profoundly as did the Military Academy—where time and again friends parted knowing they would next meet on opposite sides on some battlefield. And, no institution healed more publicly during and after Reconstruction.

The admission of African-Americans by the Academy again merely reflected American society as a whole. They were admitted during Reconstruction and shunned during the years of Jim Crow. Then black cadets were cautiously admitted again in the 1920s and 1930s after a Black Renaissance and growing white revulsion at lynch law rule. Finally, they were admitted in greater numbers after President Harry S. Truman ordered the integration of the armed services. Likewise, the conscious and conscientious recruitment of ethnic minorities (and later women) for the Academy in the decades after World War II reflected the growing movement for equality for those groups in the last half of the twentieth century.

West Point is better suited than any other institution of higher learning in the United States to serve as a window onto these phenomena in American life because it is so broadly representative of American society—geographically, socially, and economically. Even before 1828, when Secretary of War James Barbour began the practice of seeking nominations for appointments from each member of the House of Representatives (and 1843, when Congress codified the arrangement), the corps of cadets was already becoming diverse in social, economic, and geographic terms.

The first cadets appointed by Jefferson were from regions as widely separated as Vermont and Missouri (some two decades before the latter became a state). Over the next dozen years, cadets arrived from Georgia, North and South Carolina, Virginia, Maryland, Delaware, Kentucky, and the District of Columbia, from the Northwest Territory, Indiana, Ohio, Pennsylvania, New Jersey, and New York, and from Connecticut, Massachusetts, New Hampshire, and Maine (still a district of Massachusetts). Moreover, the cadets appointed by Jefferson (and later by Madison and Monroe) were from a far more diverse social and economic background than the first cadets appointed by Adams.

When this practice became policy in 1828, the Academy soon became nearly as perfect a republican institution as the Congress itself, and possibly more democratic. In the face of criticism of elitism in the early 1840s, the Academy began to examine the economic and social status of cadets' parents. The results showed that the majority of cadets came from families of either moderate or reduced circumstances, although some came from the ranks of the affluent and others from among the indigent. This record of the circumstances of parents was kept every year from 1842 to 1910 and continued to show this general pattern. It is no wonder that the Military Academy has so accurately reflected the nation it serves.

West Point is the caldron that created the vast majority of America's senior military leaders from the sons and now daughters of farmers, shopkeepers, laborers, and bankers. *West Point: A Bicentennial History* examines how that came to be so. It is the history of that institution at age two hundred and the story of the dedicated military academics who found a home at West Point and who, generation after generation, have made the school what it is. It is the story of how they have endowed the select of America's youth with dedication to its motto: duty, honor, country.

The nation has repeatedly called on the graduates of the Military Academy, and they have responded to every summons. They have fought and led with distinction in each of the nation's wars, beginning with the War of 1812. Since the early days of the Civil War, they have provided the Army's senior leadership—Grant, Sherman, Sheridan, Schofield, Hugh Scott, Tasker Bliss, Peyton March, Pershing, MacArthur, Patton, Eisenhower, Bradley, Maxwell

Taylor, Westmoreland, Creighton Abrams, and H. Norman Schwarzkopf, to name but a few. There are also those graduates, little known, who died young in defense of their country—Lieutenant Henry Hobart, class of 1811, killed in action at Fort George in 1813; Lieutenant John Center, class of 1833, killed in 1837 in the Florida Indian Wars; James Woods, class of 1844, killed 1846, Monterey; John Sweet, class of 1860, killed 1862, Gains Mill; Thomas Wansboro, class of 1896, killed 1898, Cuba; Francis Dougherty, class of April 1917, killed 1918, Meuse-Argonne; James Browning, class of June 1943, killed 1944, Battle of the Bulge; Louis Storck, class of 1951, killed 1952, Korea; James Gaiser, class of 1968, killed 1969, Vietnam—and many more who lived longer but gave their lives on the field of battle.

Others have contributed outside the Army and have provided America with leaders in all walks of life—in business, agriculture, the professions, and government. They built the railroads that made this a continental nation; they have been explorers, scientists, professors, bishops, and presidents. And, year in and year out, their contribution expands as new classes of graduates make their mark.

CHAPTER ONE

West Point in the Revolution

Today the terms "West Point" and "United States Military Academy" are synonymous in most peoples' minds. It was, however, a combination of strategic considerations, accidents of history—during and at the end of the war—and the imperatives of creating a new military peace establishment that resulted in their eventual coalition. The strategic importance of the Hudson River was immediately obvious; he who controlled the river also controlled communications between New England and the southern and central colonies, nay, states. West Point proved the most satisfactory place at which to deny the river to the British, and once the decision was made to fortify the site, the river never again fell under their sway. At war's end, the very extent of the fortifications and facilities at West Point, and its proximity to the main Army in and around Newburgh, meant that it would take on an additional life—that of a major military arsenal. The warehouses were being emptied of supplies and filled with weapons, the magazines with powder. It was during this time, in 1783, as the nation considered the nature of its peace establishment, that West Point was first spoken of as a site for a national military academy. And, at war's end, West Point was one of only two posts that continued to be garrisoned.[1]

Early in 1775, already concerned that the conflict around Boston would spread, the Provincial Congress of New York warned: "If the enemy persist in their plan of subjugating these States to the yoke of Great Britain, they must, in proportion to their knowledge of the country, be more and more convinced of the necessity of their becoming masters of the Hudson River, which will give them the entire command of the water communication with the Indian nations, effectually prevent all intercourse between the eastern and southern Confederates, divide our strength, and enfeeble every effort for our common preservation and security."[2]

The importance of the Hudson River had become clear in nearly a century of colonial wars, including the War of the League of Augsburg, known in America as King William's War (1689–1697); the War of Spanish Succession, known on this side of the Atlantic as Queen Anne's War (1702–1713); the War of Austrian Succession, or King George's War (1744–1748); and the Seven Years' War, or the French and Indian War (1754–1763). Time and again the Hudson Valley was to be a theater of war in these conflicts. The Indians raided settlements along the river's banks, the British sailed up its course to invade Canada, and the French moved down it to strike the English colonies. In this, an important pattern was established; the Hudson River–Lake Champlain corridor had become an established north-south highway of war.

The river's value was clear to the British from the beginning. In its simplest form their strategy in the Revolution called for them to strike north from New York and south from Lake Champlain to seize control of the crossings of the Hudson and cut communications between the two sections of the country. Isolate troublesome New England, and the rest of the colonies would soon come to their senses, it was commonly thought in Great Britain.

The river's importance was just as obvious to the American Patriots, and, fortunately, the Highlands provided them nearly ideal positions from which to defend the river. The ridges and valleys running perpendicular to the course of the river also served to protect and shelter the lines of communication between the two sections of the country, which, of necessity, had to cross the Hudson. A defense of the river in the Highlands was a foregone conclusion.

The Continental Congress agreed that the Hudson must be held, but, without resources of its own, it handed the problem back to the New York Assembly. On May 13, 1775, the New Yorkers sent Christopher Tappan and James Clinton to the Highlands to select a site or sites for fortifications and to report their estimates of the cost.

In surveying the region, three principal sites were considered. The first was at the Dunderberg, but here the width of the river weighed against selection. Next was Anthony's Nose, where the river was narrow and the banks on both sides were extremely rugged, particularly the near-vertical nine-hundred-foot peak to the east that gave the location its name. The main disadvantage here was that communication with the interior was difficult, particularly from the high ground on the west overlooking the mouth of Popolopen Creek, where fortifications would have to be built. This would add to the difficulty of construction, but more important, this was a real concern in case the post would need reinforcement under attack.

The third site, West Point, enjoyed all the advantages offered by the others, with few of the disadvantages. In addition, vessels passing there had to make a sharp, ninety-degree turn to the west, sail a quarter of a mile, then make another right-angle turn to the north as they continued upriver. These bends were the sharpest of any along the Hudson, but they were not the only hazards that a ship had to face at West Point. The river there was the narrowest in the Highlands, and the tidal effects the greatest; at ebb tide the current here was swifter than at any point south of Albany. Moreover, that channel was noted for treacherous winds that could cause the loss of headway and other steering difficulties for any sailing ship trying to negotiate it.

The lands along the Hudson River that would ultimately constitute the military post of West Point were granted by a succession of English governors over a period of a half century. The first of these grants included much of the land on the level of the Plain and to the north and went to Charles Congreve in 1723—a total of 1,463 acres. The next parcel, to the south of Congreve's land and extending essentially to Highland Falls, was granted to Gabriel and William Ludlow in 1731. The third, a small parcel of 332 acres adjoining the first two on the west, was conveyed to John Moore in 1747. These encompassed most of the original post.

John Moore, who had first purchased his "West Point" property in 1747, was a wealthy man and one of the most prominent citizens of New York. He liked the region so much that he purchased the adjacent Congreve land and combined it with his own. On the latter section, in a low, level valley on the banks of the Hudson opposite Martalear's Rock (soon to be known as Constitution Island), he built a large summer home. A road behind the house led from the river up the steep hill to a plain that overlooked the Hudson and thence to New Windsor. Moore's tenant, a Dutchman named Daniel Coovert, tilled the acres immediately around the house and on the Plain. The lands included, recalled Coovert's granddaughter, "a pretty good sized cornfield" in addition to land on which the cattle were pastured.[3]

The Moore family spent many of their summers there in the cooler and more healthy climes of the Highlands. When John Moore died, his son, Stephen, inherited the property, and it remained for years a family retreat. Upon reaching maturity, Stephen accepted a commission in a British regiment that was posted in Canada. It was not until 1765 that he left the army and retired in leisure to his house and lands at West Point. If he made any efforts from that time on to farm the land, he must have abandoned them in short order, for by 1777 the Plain was overgrown by scrub pine ten to fifteen feet in height.[4]

In reporting the results of their survey, Tappan and Clinton recommended that the river should be defended at West Point and Constitution Island. They reported their findings to the New York Assembly on June 10, 1775, but two months passed before anything more was done. It took a warning from General Washington of a suspected enemy raid on New York City to provoke action. Although a false alarm, the news caused the New Yorkers to appoint commissioners who were to erect the fortifications on the Hudson.

Construction by committee was attended by all the problems and difficulties anticipated by any such effort. But the committee did obtain the services of Bernard Romans, who had studied surveying and cartography and had been an official surveyor for the British for a number of years. Romans brought not only training but also experience to the undertaking. He had been with Ethan Allen and Benedict Arnold at Fort Ticonderoga earlier that year and had helped plan and conduct needed repairs at that important post. Despite his training and experience, however, Romans focused his efforts on fortifying Martalear's Rock and largely ignored West Point proper—an unfortunate choice.

Romans and the commissioners quickly settled on a plan. Romans drew an elaborate design calling for a "grand bastion" or principal fort, supported by a series of smaller fortifications. To control the river the plan relied on the fire from five blockhouses supported by several additional batteries in the principal fortifications. The entire system of defense was to be placed on Martalear's Rock except for one blockhouse and battery that would be erected at West Point. To Romans the most critical of the fortifications was the central fort, called Fort Constitution, for which the island ever after has been known. It was there that he began work in the fall of 1775. Remnants of these first works—now called Romans's Battery—can still be seen today. Construction material and cannon had begun to arrive at the island by early October, but progress was slow, and it was soon clear that Romans's fortifications would not be completed by winter.

There were a number of military defects in Romans's plan, but the first and most serious was that Constitution Island was dominated by the higher ground across the river at West Point. The small blockhouse and battery that was to be placed there would simply have been insufficient to prevent the enemy from taking the heights that overlooked Constitution Island. There they could place artillery that would dominate the positions below. Moreover, the artillery on Constitution Island was poorly positioned. Ships sailing north, for example, would be exposed to only a few of the guns until they had passed the crucial first bend in the river and were again under way. The real value of the river's S-turn at West Point was that ships would lose all their headway as they negotiated the first bend. In Romans's plan the fire of most guns was masked as a ship approached and entered the turn. Most of the cannoneers in Romans's "grand bastion" would have had a vessel in their sights for only a few moments as it regained speed, racing to the second and less difficult turn.

These considerations and the slow progress at Constitution Island prompted the commissioners to reconsider fortifying the Popolopen site opposite Anthony's Nose. Indeed, even Romans raised this possibility. By early 1776, the emphasis had shifted from Constitution Island to the Popolopen. From that time until disaster befell these positions in October 1777, the Patriots placed the main effort in defense of the Highlands on the fortifications and water obstacles in this area. The yet uncompleted works at Constitution were furnished with a small garrison, but all construction stopped.

By April 1776, work was under way at Fort Montgomery, on the north bank of Popolopen Creek. To supervise that effort the commissioners chose a new engineer, Captain William Smith, to replace Romans. Three months later, when the British occupied New York, even greater urgency was attached to the site. By autumn, however, twin forts—Montgomery and Clinton—had been erected on the high ground on either side of the deeply ravined Popolopen Creek, and a chain was stretched across the river to obstruct navigation. Because of design and structural weaknesses, however, the first chain soon broke, but it was replaced by the next spring.

Washington, quartered at Morristown for the winter of 1776–1777, was apprehensive about the defenses being built in the Highlands and expressed particular concern about the overland approaches to the rear of Forts Clinton and Montgomery. But, because of what seemed impossibly rugged terrain to the rear of these forts, nothing was done to secure them from such an attack. Even the delegation that Washington sent to survey the area—including Major General Nathanael Greene and Brigadier Generals Alexander McDougall, Henry Knox, George Clinton, and Anthony Wayne—reported in May 1777 that "the enemy will not attempt to operate by land" because the terrain was "so exceedingly difficult."[5]

As the Patriots attempted to fortify the Hudson, English officials had adopted an intricate scheme for capturing the vital river valley. If successful, the British would sever New England from the rest of the states and paralyze the American effort. The main invading force was to proceed down the Lake Champlain route from Canada under an actor-playwright-soldier, General John Burgoyne—"Gentleman Johnny" Burgoyne, as he is popularly known. If needed, General William Howe's troops in New York could advance up the Hudson to meet Burgoyne near Albany. A third, much smaller force would attack toward Albany from the west by way of the Mohawk Valley. As Burgoyne began his move south, however, Howe marshaled the main British army for an attack on Philadelphia. Washington, who had begun to shift his forces toward the Hudson, hastily retraced his steps and positioned his army to defend Philadelphia. Defeated in two pitched battles, at Brandywine Creek and at Germantown, Washington abandoned the city to the British and retired to winter quarters at Valley Forge.

Meanwhile, Burgoyne's southward march to Albany had stalled in front of Saratoga. At that point, General Sir Henry Clinton, who had been left in

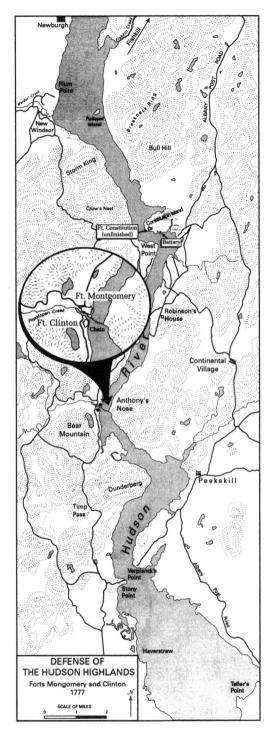

DEFENSE OF
THE HUDSON HIGHLANDS
Forts Mongomery and Clinton
1777

SCALE OF MILES
0   1   2

Department of History, United States Military
Academy.

New York and had just received reinforcements from England, decided to attack up the Hudson in the hope of relieving the pressure on Burgoyne. Sir Henry devised a sophisticated plan based upon advice of a Loyalist colonel, Beverly Robinson, whose home on the Hudson was just below and opposite West Point. The plan called for an attack with three divisions. The first, a diversion, was a feint toward the east bank, which would concentrate Rebel units there. Then Clinton would land the balance of the force at Stony Point, sending them west through the rugged Highlands. Ultimately he would split this force, marching one column around Bear Mountain to attack Fort Montgomery from the rear and the other parallel to the river to attack Fort Clinton from the south.

On October 5, 1777, General Clinton put this plan into effect, landing a force at Verplanck's Point on the east bank of the Hudson, thus threatening Peekskill and forcing General Israel Putnam to deploy his troops in response. Early the next morning, having deceived Putnam, Clinton went ashore on the west bank at Stony Point, as planned, with the bulk of his forces. Adding to the deception, a heavy fog covered the operations and delayed the discovery of Clinton's real intentions.[6]

Clinton's men, including some four hundred Loyalists led by Robinson, then marched into the difficult Highland terrain to take the northernmost fort. The trek led through narrow defiles and up nearly vertical cliffs, but they were unopposed. As the hours passed and the anticipated attack on the east bank never materialized, George Clinton, the new governor of New York, finally realized that the real objective was Fort Montgomery and its opposite number named in his honor. He quickly appealed to General Putnam for aid and dispatched some light forces to delay the British advance, which he now realized would come from the west. The American force discovered the British behind Fort Montgomery, but it was too late. The Americans were quickly beaten back. The two separate British columns then fixed bayonets and attacked. In less than half an hour, both forts fell.

The next day, October 7, 1777, Sir Henry had the chain cut and sent his representatives in a boat, under a flag of truce, to request the surrender of Constitution Island. There, nervous and undisciplined sentries opened fire on the approaching emissaries. Indignant at this breech of battlefield etiquette, the British returned the following day in twenty-two flatboats loaded with troops and supported by artillery from three galleys. Determined to take the works by storm, they found that the Patriots had retreated the night before. Although they had burned their barracks, the defenders had left in such haste that they had not even spiked the cannon. The British then occupied the island, and for a time, at least, control of the river passed into their hands.

Hardly pausing to consolidate his position, Sir Henry continued up the Hudson. He was, however, too late. It was just above Kingston that he learned of Burgoyne's surrender. Clinton, whose forces were not strong enough to hold the Highlands against the victorious General Horatio Gates, feared that he might be cut off from his base in New York, and so he withdrew. He razed the Highland fortifications that he had captured and relinquished the area and retired to New York on October 20.

When Patriot forces reoccupied the ruined fortifications, they faced the choice of rebuilding or beginning anew. Washington's chief engineer in the Highlands, Lieutenant Colonel Louis de la Radiere, of France, favored refortifying the Fort Montgomery–Fort Clinton area. Israel Putnam, who commanded the region, favored a new start at West Point. Another commission from the New York Assembly was appointed to assess the problem. That body sided with Putnam, and on January 12, 1778, he announced that the river and the Highlands would be defended at West Point.

Putnam immediately began to assemble the troops that would do the job. On January 27, a brigade under Brigadier General Samuel Holden Parsons crossed the ice on the river and occupied the heights. Wrote Sergeant Simon Giffin, "[We] marched over the Rever on the ise [and] marched back again for thar was no Place to Loge theor on the West side of the Rever." Major Samuel Richards, who marched the regiment over the first day, was one of only a few who remained there overnight, but from that day forward West Point has been continuously occupied by elements of the United States Army. For the next several days the troops crossed the ice to West Point to build their lodging. By January 30, the huts had progressed far enough to shelter the men, who camped on the west side of the river. "We mad a hut," wrote Sergeant Giffin, "that 15 of us Lay Prity worm considering the wether being so very cold."[7]

As the work at West Point began, Peter Townsend of the Sterling Ironworks of Warwick, New York, was asked to forge the new chain. Townsend, however, had not yet received payment for the chain that had been lost at Fort Montgomery and would not fire his forges until the earlier debt had been paid in part. Finally an agreement for manufacturing the chain was signed on February 2, 1778. The type of chain that Townsend had built and that Thomas Machin had installed at Fort Montgomery the year before was considered satisfactory, but the new chain would be even stronger, with links made from iron bar 2¼ inches square instead of the 1½-inch bar used in the earlier links.

The new plan for guarding the river was uncomplicated: the river would be blocked by a chain and boom stretching from Constitution Island to West

Point at the point where any ship would strike them with little momentum after negotiating the first turn; shore batteries on the west side of the river would both protect the chain and boom and engage approaching enemy ships. Some of the guns in the fortifications on the Plain above the river could also engage the ships, but the primary purpose of these emplacements was to deny the heights to the enemy and thereby protect the rear of the water-level batteries.

In mid-January, the French engineer Radiere traced the outline of a new fort on the plateau at West Point. Radiere envisioned a classic Vauban fortress—an extensive, permanent, scientifically designed fortification that could withstand a prolonged siege. Putnam, the commander of the Highlands, favored a smaller, temporary field fortification. In Putnam's view there was neither sufficient time nor money for anything more elaborate.

This lack of agreement had produced only "perfect chaos," noted Parsons, whose troops had first occupied West Point.[8] Undaunted by the problems he faced, however, Parsons had quickly determined that his first priority was to obtain the materials and equipment necessary to build the defenses—whatever they should be. Timber and rock were immediately at hand, but he did not have the teams of horses necessary to haul them. These he immediately requisitioned, and within days the teams arrived and work began in earnest. Problems remained, but Parsons was not one to await their resolution idly. He lacked money, tools, and equipment but could use his troops to cut timber and build the fascines (cylindrical bundles of sticks or brushwood) that would be used to strengthen earthen parapets. In less than two weeks, over 1,000 pieces of timber had been cut, and 1,000 to 1,500 fascines had been prepared.

The exact nature of the fortifications at West Point, however, still had not been determined. Parsons, like Putnam, was convinced that Radiere's plan was too extensive, but his attempts to convince the Frenchman that the works should better fit the time and money available were no more effective than had been Putnam's. Finally the Board of War stepped in and ordered that the decision be left to Governor Clinton. When Clinton sided with Putnam and Parsons, Radiere departed West Point.

Parsons wasted no more time. The next day, March 12, 1778, he broke ground and began construction of the fort on the heights overlooking the river and its water-level batteries. Perhaps the new works, built of timber, earth, and fascines, would not be able to withstand a classic siege with a prolonged pounding by artillery, but he reasoned it was better to have a functioning position from which the garrison and militia could fight and maneuver than to have half-finished—and indefensible—fortifications when the British arrived. Moreover, it now appeared that the chain would be emplaced in April, and the fortifications to protect it had to be ready.

Using every available man, militia and Continental alike, Parsons spurred on the garrison. He understood clearly that the main purpose of Fort Arnold, as he called the new fortification, was to protect the water batteries and chain from attack at the rear. From that he concluded that his first construction priority should be the west and south walls and the southwest bastion. Parsons now moved with energy and reported to Washington that he hoped to have the key elements of the fort "in some State of Defense" by the end of March. For the first time since the British sojourn up the Hudson the October before, there were visible signs of progress toward defense of the vital river. Parsons, however, was still short of tools and supplies, finances were precarious, and—most important—he did not yet have the required cannon. In addition, the militia whose enlistments were expiring had yet to be replaced.

However, Parsons soon found cause for renewed optimism. On March 25, the first guns arrived. In celebration he ordered a salute fired that evening— the first cannonade fired at West Point. Meanwhile, other changes further brightened the picture. General McDougall, a New Yorker, was sent to take command of the Highlands from the absent (and locally unpopular) Putnam. McDougall's instructions from Washington emphasized the importance of the work and promised needed support. Moreover, with McDougall came Colonel Tadeusz Kosciuszko, a Polish officer who had been sent to supervise construction at West Point in place of Radiere.

McDougall might correctly have observed that the Hudson was still defenseless, but in fact Parsons had made tremendous progress in only a few weeks. Although neither the chain nor the fortifications were completed, and the full complement of cannon had not yet arrived, much had been accomplished. Parsons continued to exhort the garrison, and guided by Kosciuszko the progress continued.

Radiere's plan had called for two water-level batteries. Kosciuszko concluded that these were insufficient and added two more. Now, with two positions south of the point, one at the point, and the last near the terminus of the chain, any ship attempting to crash the chain would be exposed to a continuous cross fire.

Parsons and Kosciuszko worked well together. Kosciuszko approved of the changes Parsons had already instituted in size and type of construction of Fort Arnold, and he drew new engineering plans to reflect them. He also agreed with Parsons that the surrounding hills presented a potential threat, and therefore that the south and west walls of the fort should receive priority. Located as Fort Arnold was, with the east face overlooking a cliff that rose more than one hundred feet out of the water and with the north side facing similarly difficult terrain, work on these latter two walls could be deferred. Not so on the west and south. These walls averaged nine feet in height and were to be twenty feet thick at the top of the parapet; the bastion would be another thirteen feet high and just a bit less thick than the wall upon which it sat. Immediately in front of the walls was a ditch thirty-two feet wide at the top and twenty-four feet at the bottom. The depth of the ditch was actually determined by the volume of dirt and rock needed to build the walls behind it.

To protect the rear walls of the fort, Kosciuszko planned for eight cannons, positioned in such a way that they would provide a cross fire in front of the walls of the fort to discourage any infantry assault. The gate, located in the western curtain, was also protected by guns on each flank. The remainder of Fort Arnold was rather simple in design and would require a minimal amount of time to construct. The main function of the north and east walls was to provide a stable platform from which the fort's guns could aid the water batteries in denying the river to the enemy. Here, Kosciuszko built only a low parapet 2½ feet high and four to six feet across, except for an irregular bastion at the northeast corner, which was to be nine feet high.

The new plan also called for a storehouse, powder magazine, guardhouse, commissary building, well, and a single barracks capable of housing the garrison of six hundred men. In the latter, rooms were to be nineteen feet by nineteen feet, containing nine bunk beds, each thirty-six inches wide. With two men assigned to each bed, every room would accommodate thirty-six men. The barracks was built just to the west of Fort Arnold and soon became known as Long Barracks. (Years later, this structure would become the first cadet barracks of the Military Academy.) The storehouse and commissary were located on the low ground between the point and the Moore House.

The emphasis placed on the sides of Fort Arnold facing the mountains shows an awareness of the danger of an enemy attack from the rear and an appreciation of the heights that overwatched the new fort. Both Kosciuszko and Parsons were rightly apprehensive. Less than six months before, the British had seized the forts on the Popolopen from the rear. Moreover, Kosciuszko had been at Fort Ticonderoga when it had been lost to the British. He had warned that if the enemy placed cannon on nearby Mount Defiance, Ticonderoga would be indefensible, but the commander had paid no attention. When Burgoyne's forces dragged their artillery up those steep slopes to fire down into Ticonderoga, the fort was indeed lost.

With construction of the main fortification now under way, Kosciuszko and Parsons turned their attention to the land approaches to the new fort. To cover the southerly approach, three smaller fortified positions were ordered constructed along a low ridgeline that rose abruptly from the plain and ran almost due south to a point along the heights adjacent to the river to a point about halfway between Buttermilk Falls and West Point, where the ridgeline tapers off. These positions—known today as Fort Meigs, Fort Wyllys, and Fort Webb—were placed so that the first two could fire on any body of troops trying to approach West Point via the river heights. At the same time, Forts Wyllys and Webb could cover a gully that leads from the Highlands to the southwest corner of the Plain at West Point. Constructed primarily of wood and earth, these fortified positions, manned by infantry and artillery, would provide depth to the overall defenses and deny that ridge to the enemy.

While Parsons and Kosciuszko had been reorganizing the work at West Point, McDougall had been inspecting his new command. His first visit to West Point followed immediately on an investigation into the loss of Forts Montgomery and Clinton. With what he had learned there, he approved the new plans for fortifying the ridge to the south of Fort Arnold and, in addition, ordered work to begin fortifying the higher ground to the west. On April 11, work began on the latter—Fort Putnam.

The principal purpose of Fort Arnold was to dominate the Plain upon which it was built and thereby protect the rear of the water batteries and chain. Additionally, it would help prevent the enemy from seizing the southern ridgeline on which Forts Webb, Wyllys, and Meigs were being constructed. Wyllys and Webb could be supported by cannon fire from Fort Putnam, and Meigs by mortar fire. All in all, this system of fortifications was intended to withstand at least a ten-day siege—to hold off the British while the local militia was assembled to relieve the forts, or until the Continental Army could march to the rescue.

Actually, the militia was expected to perform four major functions in the defense of West Point: first, it was to play a significant role in the construction of the fortifications; second, it was expected to furnish a significant part of the garrison; third, the citizen-soldiers would provide the bulk of the garrison's maneuver units, and the outposts and pickets connected with the defense of the post; finally—in the absence of the Continental Army—they would have to raise any siege that the garrison might suffer.

West Point's primary mission, of course, was to hold the river. The chain and the four water batteries would be the main means for accomplishing that. Fort Arnold assisted by protecting the rear of the batteries and by serving as their magazine. In April, when the river began to thaw, the chain was delivered, assembled, and eased across. On April 30, it was secured in a small cove on Constitution Island. Thereafter, until 1783, the chain was removed each winter and reinstalled the following spring.

April 1778 had proven one of the most productive months in the defensive development of West Point. The river was blocked, and the water batteries, as well as Fort Arnold, were in a sufficiently advanced state to resist any sudden assault of the enemy. At the same time, the works being constructed in the hills behind Fort Arnold would give the post an even better chance of holding out against a British assault until help could arrive. Most of the earlier weaknesses in the plans for the defense had been eliminated with the changes incorporated by Parsons, Kosciuszko, and General McDougall. Now only the failure to provide for the defense of the chain's anchor point on Constitution Island remained a serious flaw.

Life at West Point soon settled into an unrelenting repetition of fatigue duty as construction continued into the summer. Long hours and the heat and humidity of the season took their toll on both the rate of construction and morale. A drunken riot on June 29 caused Parsons temporarily to bar the local dram sellers. Parsons, who—despite the excellent results he had achieved— had never been happy with his assignment, now decided to seek a change. Washington's first visit to West Point the next month provided Parsons with the opportunity to request reassignment. The general obliged him and assigned a new post commander, Colonel William Malcom.

Malcom found much yet to be done, though Kosciuszko assured him that with sufficient manpower the works could be completed in a short time. The new commander tightened discipline and exhorted the available workers to double their efforts. Stonemasons were sought to face and strengthen the fortifications, and Kosciuszko began the bombproof magazine inside Fort Arnold. Workers were in such demand, however, that Malcom even accepted Governor Clinton's offer to use jailed Tories from the state's overcrowded prisons to work as forced labor.

In late August, Washington ordered his Chief Engineer, General Duportail, to examine the works at West Point. His report, though critical of some details of Kosciuszko's works, was generally favorable. Duportail, however, did strongly encourage the construction of fortified positions covering the eastern terminus of the chain on Constitution Island. With that, Washington approved Kosciuszko's work but ordered construction of the works on Constitution Island that had been recommended by Duportail.

By autumn, life at West Point began to settle into a somewhat less demanding routine. The men lived either in huts laid out in two long rows on the Plain or in the two-story Long Barracks, which had been constructed that summer.

A less demanding routine, however, did not mean laxity. The post commander enforced strict discipline in all things—particularly the mundane. When the laundry women began to inflate their prices, he imposed a ceiling on their charges. When some of the men resisted using the latrines that had been dug, he again acted. "The necessary [is] to be covered every evening . . . and every man in garrison [is] ordered to make use of them only—if any dirty fellow is detected [violating] this so necessary a regulation, he shall be ignominiously punished."[9]

Still, there were respites from duty and fatigue. Military balls were held, and young women from the local environs were invited. "The Dutch Girls are generally pretty well looking and entertaining," wrote one Continental soldier, "but have large ankles." These girls, he continued, were "fond of Dancing, Riding in Slays etc, for which they have become famous."[10]

The spring of 1779 began uneventfully enough, and as navigation became possible on the river, the chain was once more installed. Construction on the fortifications slowed for want of materials, and also because of maintenance demands on the existing fortifications, which were now beginning to deteriorate.

Meanwhile, in New York City, Sir Henry Clinton began to look north again. He hoped to force Washington into a decisive battle by seizing or at least threatening West Point. This scheme, however, depended on reinforcements from Europe, which Sir Henry expected momentarily. Confident that these troops were only days away, he launched his first attack at Stony Point and Verplanck's Point—the two ends of the critical King's Ferry. Initially the plan was successful. On May 31, Sir Henry occupied Stony Point and cut off one of the main Patriot lines of communication across the river. But then his plan hit a snag—the expected troops from Europe failed to arrive. Washington now reinforced the Highlands, and any further British advance up the Hudson was blocked. When Washington surmised that the British were not strong enough to continue, he ordered Stony Point retaken. The task was given to Brigadier General Anthony Wayne. At West Point, with the help of Baron Frederick von Steuben, Wayne quickly trained his force. On July 16, in a brilliantly executed attack, "Mad" Anthony Wayne's Light Infantry recaptured the position.

During the balance of the spring and summer of 1779, the fortifications at West Point were expanded to their fullest, though construction on these works continued into 1780. Kosciuszko now called for a series of redoubts along the ridges immediately to the south and west of that position, forming an outer ring of defensive positions that would further protect Fort Putnam and West Point from attack from the west. This outer ring of redoubts on the west side of the river was complemented by construction of additional works on the east bank. First was a redoubt on Constitution Island ordered by Washington; built roughly in the center of the island, it could block an attack on the chain from the east. In addition, three redoubts on the east side of the river were constructed on the ridges east and south, completing an outer ring of protection to the main works and chain on both banks of the Hudson.

With most of West Point's fortifications completed or under construction by mid-1779, it was time to evaluate and scrutinize the post's capabilities. In late August, General Duportail conducted another inspection and prepared a lengthy report. The basic object of any attack, he concluded, would be the destruction of the chain. Washington's engineer weighed several methods by which the British might achieve that end and concluded that only bombproof shelters to better protect the troops were now needed. These, Duportail believed, would assure "the defense of this mountain, as much as it is necessary to do it, in view of the number of troops the enemy can sacrifice to the attack of West Point."[11]

Thereafter, until the end of the war, the engineering effort would be confined to improvements and maintenance necessary to keep the works in serviceable condition. The earlier decision to build only temporary field fortifications rather than the more expensive and time-consuming permanent works now meant a constant struggle to maintain the facilities. It explains the constant complaint of inspectors who always found the works in a state of decay and decline.

The "Black Year" of 1780 began at West Point with one of the worst blizzards ever known in the Hudson Valley—a bad omen, as the year was to prove. It is said that the temperature dropped so fast that boats froze fast in the river and their occupants had to return to shore as best they could across the new ice. The soldiers at West Point, gripped by the subzero temperatures, huddled behind closed doors as the howling wind swept away the tents of those still encamped on the Plain. That storm lasted for three days, during which the garrison simply struggled to survive. With the extreme cold, heating fires were a necessity but also a danger. Men trying to keep warm sometimes built their fires too high or did not tend them carefully. Buildings were burned on the Plain, and bombproof shelters in the redoubts were set ablaze. Finally, on January 5, the snow and cold abated somewhat, but the winter continued colder than usual—the worst of the war.

The weather and a shortage of rations fostered discontent as well as misery among the troops. Not long after the storm abated, some one hundred men from the 4th Massachusetts Brigade mutinied and set off for home with their arms. Though orders were issued to bring them back dead or alive, the

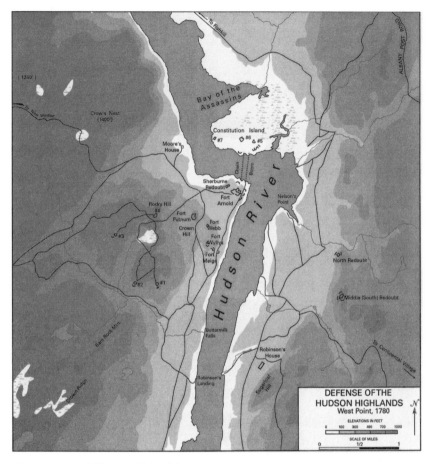

Department of History, United States Military Academy.

mutineers, when captured, received comparatively lenient punishment; most were ultimately pardoned, though some thought to be ringleaders received up to a hundred lashes.

The warmer weather of spring and then summer brought the task of rebuilding and repairing the damage caused by the weather and fires. The passing months also brought a succession of new commanders, including, in August, Benedict Arnold.

Arnold was no newcomer to the Hudson theater of the war.[12] Three times before he had fought along the Hudson-Champlain corridor: at Fort

Ticonderoga, en route to Montreal, and at Saratoga. But this time, the once heroic patriot was planning treason. He knew well the strategic value of West Point and long before arriving at the post had concocted a plan to surrender it to the British—thus hastening the end of the war and ensuring a British victory.

The seeds of this treason had been sown in Philadelphia during the late winter of 1779 and had progressed through a year of intermittent negotiation with Sir Henry Clinton in New York. Unable to conclude a satisfactory agreement, however, Arnold finally took a new tack and began to scheme to win the command of West Point, a prize the British could hardly resist. His plan worked. On June 15, Arnold, using an assumed name, wrote Major John André (Arnold's contact in Clinton's headquarters), indicating that he expected soon to assume command at West Point, and once again sent a letter to the British. It was surprising, he said, that "a Post of so much importance should be so totally neglected." Rocky Hill, which commanded the outer fortifications, was "defenseless from the back," he said, adding, "[you] may land three miles below and have a good road to bring up heavy Cannon to Rocky Hill." Arnold's letter was carefully phrased. Although the works were "well executed," they were "wretchedly planned"—implying the post could be seized even if at full strength, if the British knew the weaknesses and had assistance from within.[13]

By August 1780, when Arnold took command at West Point, the deal had been struck. If the post, its arms, its stores, and its garrison should be handed over, the sum of £20,000 was to be paid to Arnold. With his ultimate escape in mind, he chose to live in the Robinson House, opposite and downstream from West Point. He also made arrangements for Peggy, his young wife, and their infant son to join him there.

At West Point, Arnold busied himself showing all the marks of a commander intent on improving the defense of the post. Still, upon closer inspection, his activities actually promoted the decay of the existing fortifications and the delay of further works by focusing efforts and energies elsewhere. He directed the repair of buildings but increased the number of guards, thereby decreasing the number of laborers available.

On the night of September 21, after a year and a half of secret correspondence, Arnold and André met for the first time at Verplanck's Point. Precisely what passed between them during that meeting is not certain, but Arnold did pass to André several papers pertaining to the defenses of West Point, and their conversation ran on so long that approaching daylight made it impossible for André to return to the British ship *Vulture*, which had brought him to the rendezvous.

Arnold then made arrangements for André to be escorted back to British lines and provided a pass that should have seen him through. The Briton shed his scarlet uniform jacket, replaced it with a civilian coat, and set out in the late afternoon with a single escort provided by Arnold. The pair was stopped late in the day by a detachment of militia, whose local commander told them that it was too dangerous to continue after dark and suggested that they remain there for the night.

The next day, André's party was on the road again before daylight, but after breakfast his escort informed him that he would have to cover the last fifteen miles to White Plains on his own. This was a no-man's-land in which bandits operated freely in the uniforms of the militia of both sides. His escort having departed, André struck out alone, but when he heard a report that rebel horsemen had been seen on the road ahead, he turned west toward Tarrytown. At about ten o'clock, as he approached a bridge just above that town, he was halted by three militiamen. Expecting to encounter only Loyalists in that area, André revealed that he was British. When he learned that the militia were Patriots instead, André produced the pass that Arnold had signed, but to no avail. A search revealed the papers dealing with West Point in his boot, and his fate was sealed. He would ultimately be hanged as a spy.

André's captors, perhaps motivated more by the hope of reward than by patriotism, delivered their prize to Lieutenant Colonel John Jameson at North Castle, who sent off a message to Arnold explaining the circumstances of André's capture. At the same time, however, he sent the papers concerning the defense of West Point to General Washington.

Arnold was more fortunate than André. The dispatches revealing Arnold's treachery reached Washington only after the traitor had been warned and had escaped, although not a moment too soon. Washington, who was actually en route to Arnold's headquarters at Robinson House, was always just ahead of couriers dispatched to bring him the news. Word of Washington's imminent arrival reached Arnold just minutes after he learned that André had been captured, and that word of the affair had been sent on to the commander in chief. Arnold departed a mere thirty minutes ahead of Washington's arrival, but the latter still did not know of the attempted treachery. By the time Washington learned the truth, Arnold was safely aboard the *Vulture*.

Washington, having missed Arnold at his headquarters, proceeded to tour West Point, expecting to find the commander there. He was alarmed by what he saw: half-empty magazines, shoddy barracks, crumbling parapets, and a sinking chain. Once the general received the evidence of Arnold's perfidy, these deficiencies loomed even larger. As his aide, Alexander Hamilton, warned, "Arnold has made such dispositions with the garrison as may tempt the enemy in its present weakness to make the stroke this night," It would be prudent, Hamilton advised the commander in chief, "to be providing against it."[14] Washington had come to the same conclusion and immediately began deploying his forces to foil any possible attempt by the British to seize West Point. Washington now personally assumed responsibility for the Highlands, and riders dashed in all directions to spread the alert and issue his orders.

For some hours the troops at West Point remained entirely unaware of events. In fact, a celebration of sorts took place on the plain that evening as one of the officers provided a fireworks display. It was not until almost midnight that the post received Washington's warning. Immediately the garrison was roused, and by two o'clock in the morning the forts and redoubts were fully manned. The troops spent the next several days on alert. Water casks were filled, provisions distributed, and all available troops were sent to man the defenses.

The alert lasted for five days, and for some time afterward a heavy guard was continued and detachments were positioned south along the river at the site of old Fort Montgomery and at the cove above Buttermilk Falls (now Highland Falls) to ensure early warning. Soon the state of alarm subsided and a calm settled on West Point. Then, again, the focus of war shifted away from the Hudson. And henceforth, Fort Arnold would be known as Fort Clinton.[15]

In the spring of 1781, Washington had hoped to retake New York, but success required the help of the French. As it turned out, however, the opportunity to cooperate with both the French army and fleet against the British came not at New York against Sir Henry Clinton but at Yorktown, Virginia, against Lord Charles Cornwallis. In June 1781, Washington began to move southward toward the crucial battle that would end the war.

After the brief period of concern following Arnold's attempted treachery, West Point was largely stripped of troops, since Washington's main army lay between the river fortress and Sir Henry Clinton's forces in New York. West Point was left under the care of ingovernable and undisciplined militia. When Washington's forces began to move to Yorktown, West Point was once more exposed to the British in New York, and the proper garrisoning of the post once more became a concern. Washington, however, had no intention of leaving the Highlands as completely vulnerable to the British in New York as they had been in 1777. This time, he provided a considerable force—seventeen New England regiments, a legion of horse, a regiment of artillery, and as many state troops and militia as could be retained in service.

Still, General McDougall, again in command of the region that included West Point, complained loudly about the number and quality of soldiers he was being given. His complaints were redoubled when Washington sent him the Corps of Invalids.

"The bringing forward the Corps of Invalids from Philadelphia and Boston," Washington wrote, "was a matter of necessity and not choice; we must therefore submit to some inconveniences and put them to duties of the lightest kind." Washington felt compassion for this wretched regiment. Its ranks were filled with soldiers who had survived both the rigors of battle wounds and the even more dangerous subsequent treatment by eighteenth-century surgeons. To a degree, he held himself responsible for their condition, and before they were ordered to march to West Point, he wrote their colonel, Lewis Nicola, directing him to pay the greatest attention "to the convenience and accommodation of this body of veterans, both on their march and in quarters." The trek would have its reward, Washington pointed out, for the men might benefit from "the pleasant and healthy situation of [West Point] which is remarkable for the salubrity of its air." Moreover, he added, they would benefit from "the accommodations of a stationary post." And, of course, there was "the importance of trusting its defence to a body of tried men." "All," Washington concluded, "point out very forcibly the propriety of employing your Corps as a part of the garrison."[16]

The Corps of Invalids had been created by act of Congress in June 1777: eight companies, each authorized five officers, eleven noncommissioned officers, four musicians, and one hundred men; all of whom had wounds that made them unfit for more active service. The corps had been employed at light garrison duties and as guards at magazines and arsenals. It had small detachments at Boston, Rutland, Easton, Trenton, Fishkill, and West Point, but the largest contingent and the headquarters were in Philadelphia.

The law that created the Corps of Invalids required that, in addition to their regular duties, the officers of the corps were to assist with recruiting and training newly appointed junior officers. To prepare the Invalids for the latter mission, Congress had specified that the "Subaltern Officers [of the Corps of Invalids], when off Duty, shall be obliged to attend a Mathematical School, appointed for the purpose to learn Geometry, Arithmetic, vulgar and decimal fractions and the extraction of Roots." Toward this end, one day's pay each month was to be withheld from the officers of the corps for the purpose of "purchasing a Regimental Library of the most approved Authors on Tactics and the Petite Guere."[17] Despite the intent of Congress, there is little to suggest that these deductions or purchases were ever made, or that the Invalids devoted any effort to instructing new officers or, for that matter, ever attempted to prepare their own officers for that task. The corps seems to have done little more than execute its garrison and guard duties, and if the complaints of commanders are any measure, their performance of these duties was marginal at best.

The consolidation of the Corps of Invalids at posts in the vicinity of West Point was largely complete by late July, and Colonel Nicola established his headquarters at nearby Fishkill. "A number of these unfortunate men," wrote Colonel John Lamb, Chief of Artillery at West Point, "are capable of doing no duty but eating their rations." But, he conceded, "it is no doubt a piece of refined policy to bring these maimed men from a distant post, to present them to our soldiery, who have sagacity enough to infer, that after losing eyes, hands and feet, in the public service that their patriotic sufferings will be amply rewarded."[18] To the local garrisons, however, the Invalid Corps was simply a burden. Just a year later the War Office noted the "miserable state" in which the corps existed, "the very great expense" that attended it, and "the very little service received from it." Benjamin Lincoln, then Secretary at War, suggested to the Congress that the "really meritorious and debilitated officers and men" should be provided for otherwise.[19]

With the departure of Washington and the main body of the Army, life at West Point settled back into a tedious routine. "Time rather hangs heavily," wrote one officer. One day was much like another. Drummers mounted the parapet of Fort Clinton at 8:30 sharp in the morning and beat "The Pioneers' March," which called the men to work on the fortifications. "Roast Beef" signaled an hour's lunch, and then the drums recalled the men to work. Later "Retreat" and then "Tattoo" ended the day's labor. So went the days until near the end of October, when the rumor of victory over Cornwallis energized the camp. The story's confirmation sent the men into a violent, joyous celebration. Among the officers General McDougall led the festivities; like the other ranks, they drank, shouted, sang, and danced with abandon in a celebration that lasted three days.

In the spring of 1782, with peace only a formality away, Washington brought the Continental Army back to the Hudson Highlands and established his headquarters at Newburgh, just above West Point. That winter the troops were housed at the sprawling New Windsor Cantonment and at sites all around West Point.

While the Continental Army waited for the war to end officially, there was enough time to relax and celebrate. One occasion, in particular, offered itself—the birthday of Louis Joseph, the dauphin, or heir apparent, to the King of France. This was certainly the grandest celebration held at West Point during the war. But it was more than a salute to the French dauphin; it represented Patriot appreciation and gratitude—Washington's in particular—for French support during the war. It was also, of course, a celebration of America's victory and, even more to the point, of the anticipated disbanding of the army—to be followed by the return of the men to their homes and families.

For the celebration, a grand pavilion 220 feet in length and 80 feet wide was built, supported by 118 pillars made of tree trunks. The whole was covered with boughs or branches of trees and was decorated with evergreens and garlands of flowers. It is reported that five hundred gentlemen and ladies took part in the magnificent festival. Thirteen toasts were announced, each by the firing of thirteen cannon; a military band played, and Washington himself led the dancing that evening. The highlight for the guests and the troops, who were encamped encircling the post on both sides of the river, was "a general *feu de joie*," itself announced by thirteen cannon, in which thousands of troops discharged their arms into the air. This was "immediately followed," we are told, "by three shouts of acclamation and benediction for the Dauphin, by the united voices of the whole army on all sides."[20]

With the approach of a formal peace, the army was progressively dismantled. Because of its proximity to the main army, West Point soon took on the appearance of a major military arsenal. Thousands of stands of arms and hundreds of cannon were moved into its warehouses, and barrel upon barrel of gunpowder was brought there for storage. Unfortunately, West Point had been built as a defensive post, not an arsenal. As early as mid-1782, Henry Knox complained to Washington about the inadequate facilities, especially powder magazines.[21]

Plans, however, had already been made by Secretary at War Benjamin Lincoln to add a magazine at the post. "The very exposed state of our powder at the several Magazines on the Hudson, and the insufficiency of the Magazine at West Point . . . has induced a determination to build a magazine either on West Point or Constitution Island," wrote Lincoln to Timothy Pickering, the Quartermaster General.[22] Washington was convinced that the Constitution Island site was the better choice, and preliminary construction began there in August 1782. Shortages of men and materials, however, soon doomed that effort.

In the meantime, West Point had become a major focal point for the demobilization, but the same lack of men and materials that had plagued the work on Constitution Island also operated there. Knox wrote Lincoln in July 1783, "I should have been happy to . . . erect an arsenal and two magazines, had it been possible to have obtained the necessary workmen from the troops for the purpose." Unfortunately, he wrote, "the march of troops from this post almost as soon as they arrived prevented my even knowing whether they had an artificers or not."[23]

By mid-autumn 1783, Congress had ordered the army reduced to one regiment of 500 men. The next summer the number was reduced even further. Major John Doughty, who then commanded West Point, wrote Knox, saying that "this arsenal lies still, all the workmen being discharged." There were not even adequate facilities "so that the arms might be racked," he lamented.[24] Further progress would be slow, and even that would await the creation of a formal military peace establishment.

In March 1783—as the new nation considered the nature of its peace establishment—Benjamin Lincoln submitted a plan to the Continental Congress that included provision for five magazines or arsenals: one each at Springfield, Massachusetts; at West Point; at Carlisle; at New London, Virginia (near Lynchburg); and at Camden, South Carolina. At each, he added, "a military academy should be established and suitable buildings be erected to accommodate the pupils," and "officers of abilities and information" should "superintend the instruction of the scholars in the mathematics and such other branches of education" that would be required "to form a perfect engineer–artillerist–dragoon and Infantry officer."[25] A military academy—or even several such academies—was a common aspect of the plans drawn up by those who were asked to think about the future military needs of the new nation.

With Lincoln's proposal in hand, the Congress appointed a committee to study the requirements for a peacetime military establishment. Alexander Hamilton, who chaired the committee, sought Washington's views. The general, in turn, solicited the opinions of a number of trusted officers, including Generals Steuben, Knox, Heath, and Huntington and Colonels Pickering and Gouvion. Each of these men incorporated in his recommendation provision for one or more military academies. Gouvion and Pickering, on the one hand, called for a more narrow technical school to prepare officers for artillery and engineers, and recommended that it be located at West Point. Knox, Heath, and Huntington, on the other hand, envisioned a somewhat broader academy (or set of academies) that would prepare officers for all branches, even for the militia.

Steuben at first declined to respond at length to Washington, though he did suggest the "the establishment of military academies and manufactures for the United States is a matter of great consequence."[26] But Steuben was already in the process of providing his detailed recommendation directly to Lincoln. In that plan he proposed a broadly based, three-year program of study for up to 120 young men—80 cadets of infantry, 20 of cavalry, and 20 of artillery and engineers.[27]

Though Washington considered carefully the counsel he had received, his ultimate recommendations were much more modest than those of his advisers. After noting that Steuben's recommendations must already have been laid before the committee, he concluded that he would be satisfied, for the present, if provision was made "for instructing a certain number of young gentlemen in the Art of War particularly in all those branches of service which belong to the Artillery and Engineering Departments."[28] As it turned out, achieving even that modest goal was difficult, as the years ahead would amply prove.

CHAPTER TWO

The Founding of the Military Academy, 1784–1801

Interest in creating a military academy came early in our nation's history; John Adams suggested such an institution at the outbreak of the Revolutionary War. Washington and his generals favored a military school, and Alexander Hamilton repeatedly proposed one. John Adams actually came very close to establishing a military academy late in his presidency, but it fell to Thomas Jefferson to create the institution—much to the chagrin of historians who have had difficulty squaring his actions with his words.

In December 1783, after General Washington had delivered his farewell address and resigned his commission, General Henry Knox took command of the remnants of the Army, most of which were encamped in the vicinity of West Point. Knox retained command until June 1784, when the Army was almost wholly disbanded.

Alexander Hamilton, who worked to fashion a military peace establishment, had concluded that Secretary at War Benjamin Lincoln's proposal for multiple arsenals and academies would be too expensive. "The benefits of such institutions," he remarked, "rarely compensate for the expense." In any case, he wrote, "such institutions can only be the object of future consideration." Hamilton did, however, follow Washington in proposing training and instruction for the artillerists and engineers at the posts where they were stationed.[1] But, in 1784 the Continental Congress was so divided that nothing came of any of the proposals for a peace establishment. Faced with the inability to create an effective peacetime force, it decided to disband the Army. Only eighty officers and men were retained—twenty-five at Fort Pitt and fifty-five at West Point—all under the command of brevet Major John Doughty, who was the senior remaining officer of the United States Army.

Meanwhile, at West Point, the winter of 1784–1785 was bitterly cold, and the small force there suffered extremely as winter winds swept down the ice-covered Hudson. But when the weather improved, there was more than enough work to keep the small detachment busy. As soon as the sun came out, they labored to preserve the stores of powder, drying it and repacking it in new kegs. When the weather would not allow that work, there were cartridge boxes—hundreds of them—that required mending and oiling, and thousands of small arms that needed repair.

In 1785, after the Army had been expanded by levying the militias of several states, Major George Fleming took command of West Point. Under Fleming, the old arms, powder, and camp equipage of the army were preserved and stored, or condemned and sold, as rapidly as circumstances permitted. The committee on the War Department reported in 1788 that about five thousand arms had been repaired at West Point and were now ready for service. About ten thousand more awaited repair, it reported, but as a matter of economic necessity, the work was "going on at that post on a small scale." Nonetheless, the immense quantity of powder stored in the magazines at West Point was well cared for and reported to be in "excellent order." There were also a large number of cannon and mortars, and although these were generally fit for service, their wooden carriages and platforms were so deteriorated that they were largely useless. In addition, the structures there—built of "wood and materials unseasoned"—were reported to be "going fast to decay."[2]

The fortifications were also decaying. Fort Clinton, the committee reported, had "been Slightly built for a temporary purpose" and had "decayed in such a manner" that unless substantially repaired it would "soon become a heap of rubbish." In fact, the decay had progressed so far that the artillery had been dismantled from the redoubts in 1787, at which time a large number of guns had been sold for old iron. The committee estimated that at least $10,000 would be required to repair the fortifications, redoubts, and buildings at West Point—an amount they knew was beyond the financial capability of the young nation. Moreover, this sum did not include the cost of purchasing the land itself.[3]

In late 1779, Stephen Moore, who owned the land upon which the fortifications and facilities of West Point had been built, presented a petition to the Continental Congress asking payment for damages to his property as well as compensation for the timber that had been used to build barracks and fortifications. In December 1779, the Congress had ordered the Quartermaster General to estimate the damages due Moore. His report had concluded that Moore was owed $292,000 in Continental script. On February 7, 1780, Congress issued an order to the Treasury in favor of Moore for $10,000 and also a draft on the governor of North Carolina for an additional $30,000—partial payments toward satisfaction of the larger estimate of damages.[4]

In July 1783, Moore petitioned both for the balance due him on the earlier estimate of damages and for the value of the additional wood and timber taken in the years since the last payment. In addition, he requested that a reasonable annual rent be established and paid. In September the committee considering his request proposed that a new estimate of damages and a fair annual rental be determined. To do so they approved a three-person commission—one member chosen by the Superintendent of Finance, one by Moore, and the third by the first two—which revised the estimate of damages downward a bit and suggested a rent of $437 per year. The rent apparently was paid, but nothing further was done to satisfy the balance of the debt.[5]

In June 1786, Moore again asked for payment of the balance due to him, and again the committee appointed to reexamine his claim recommended that the Board of Treasury pay it. The finances of the young nation, however, would not admit an immediate payment, and again the claim languished.[6]

Congress, in the meantime, considered the purchase of West Point and ordered a report by Henry Knox, the Secretary at War, on the military value of the post. Knox was unequivocal: "In case of an invasion of any of the middle or eastern states by a marine power the possession of Hudson's River would be an object of the highest importance as well to the invader as to the United States." West Point, he continued, was "of the most decisive importance to the defense of the said river."[7]

West Point offered numerous advantages, Knox reported: the narrowness of the river at that point, the "peculiar bend or turn of the river" there, the high banks on both sides of the river, the "demonstrated practicability" of fixing a chain at that point, and the difficulty of investing the fortifications that overlooked the river batteries and the chain. "A regular siege of West Point properly garrisoned and furnished," he concluded, "would require a large army, vast war-like apparatus and much time." This would allow the militia adequate time to "draw forth their utmost force" for West Point's relief.[8]

Knox went on to note that some might regard West Point as an interior post, though "the reverse is a fact, as may be proved by a slight consideration of the facility with which it can be approached by water." Vessels coming in from the sea that arrived at Sandy Hook in the evening could reach West Point before the next morning, for the river could easily be navigated at night. West Point, he concluded, was vital "and as such ought to be guarded at the common expense of the Union with at least one company of troops." This cost would be small, he argued, in contrast to the "humiliating and distressing consequences" of allowing Great Britain or any other marine power to find the post defenseless. "Your Secretary," he concluded, "being convinced of the importance of retaining West Point as a military post until the United States shall possess a navy," strongly recommended its purchase.[9]

On August 3, 1786, the Congress approved the purchase and authorized the Board of Treasury to negotiate an equitable price with Moore. Again, however, the effort came to naught. In 1788, the committee on the War Department reported that "owing to the absence of the said proprietor," the purchase had not yet been effected. Then the turmoil that surrounded the adoption of the new Constitution and the change in form of government again delayed resolution of the issue.

In May 1790, Stephen Moore approached the new government and again asked for compensation. His petition was referred to Alexander Hamilton, the new Secretary of the Treasury, who submitted a report on June 10. Hamilton quoted Knox's 1786 report at length and added that he, too, was convinced that the land should be purchased. Hamilton put forth two reasons in addition to its strategic value. First, "where the public safety requires the permanent occupancy of the property of an individual for the public use," purchase was the most equitable solution. Second, outright purchase was more economical in the long run.

Now Congress acted with dispatch. A bill introduced on June 15, authorizing the purchase of Moore's land, was agreed to by both houses before the end of the month and signed by Washington on July 5, 1790. The price was fixed at $11,085. On September 10, 1790, Stephen and Griselda (Grisey) Moore, his wife, signed the deed transferring West Point to the United States of America.[10]

For a decade following 1784, the garrison had generally consisted of a single, understrength company whose primary task had been the security and servicing of the stores there. Then, in 1794, when the Corps of Artillerists and Engineers was created, it was headquartered at West Point, and its battalions and companies were stationed there until its establishment was complete. Most of the captains and lieutenants were assigned or appointed almost immediately, but the nomination of field-grade officers—a lieutenant colonel and five majors—was delayed and fell to Timothy Pickering, who succeeded Henry Knox as Secretary of War in January 1795.

Pickering filled the senior ranks of the new Corps in the next month, giving three of the five appointments to foreign officers who had formal training in engineering and artillery: a lieutenant colonelcy to Stephen Rochefontaine and majorities to Louis Tousard and John J. U. Rivardi.[11] The two other majorities went to Henry Burbeck, an Artillery captain, and to Constance Freeman, who, like Rochefontaine, Tousard, and Rivardi, was chosen from outside the existing Army. Major Burbeck and his battalion were sent almost immediately to the western frontier, and Major Freeman was assigned to detached duty as an inspector of fortifications. Pickering, however, planned to utilize the three foreign officers at West Point.

When Congress had created the new Corps in 1794, it had authorized the purchase of books, instruments, and apparatus that would be required for its training.[12] Pickering explained his intentions relative to this training to the Congress: "To become skillful in either branch of their profession," he said, "will require long attention, study and practice." That could only be accomplished by "the foreign officers who have been appointed with a special reference to this object"; it was important "to keep the corps together for the present"—its mission permitting—in order that "its principal station may then become a school for the purpose mentioned." All that was now needed, he said, was the addition of "a geographical engineer and draughtsman."[13] To fill this role he provided a "temporary engineer." Pickering knew that the young American officers might chafe at serving under foreigners, but he was convinced that this was the best available solution if the artillerists and engineers were to be properly trained.

Tousard and Rivardi began training the assembled artillerists and engineers in June 1795. They began with the officers, noncommissioned officers, and just two men from each company and drilled them in the maneuver and exercise of field pieces. Soon they were drilling full gun crews.[14]

Rochefontaine spent little time at West Point until January 1796. Then, in February, he introduced a more formal and demanding regimen of training for the more junior officers of the Corps. Instruction was conducted in a room of the old provost prison, which had been converted to an officer barracks. Classes were scheduled six days a week from eleven o'clock to noon and from four to five o'clock. In the morning, the instructors explained the different principles of fortifications and guided studies in texts provided. In the afternoon, the officers were to draw plans of fortifications based on the morning's instruction. In the evening, Mr. Warin, the "temporary engineer," was available to demonstrate the principles of drawing to those who needed this instruction.[15] In March, when milder weather allowed company drill to be resumed, the schedule of officers' classes was reduced to three mornings per week—Tuesday, Thursday, and Saturday.

Unfortunately, Rochefontaine's effort to instruct his officers was undercut by his own poor relationship with them. His classes had hardly started when the officers of the Corps held an evening meeting and drafted a protest against him to the new Secretary of War, James McHenry. The cause, in part at least, was the difference between Rochefontaine's stern manner and that of the more lenient Tousard, who had been in command of the artillerists and engineers at

West Point for some months before Rochefontaine arrived. The officers resented Rochefontaine's efforts—particularly his "wishes to innovate" and efforts to "render the duty hard and disagreeable"—referring, of course, to the daily classes which he had instituted, and which he insisted they attend.[16]

This experiment in military education largely came to an end in April, just a few months after it had begun. What had not been undone by the officers' resentment was finished when the officers' barracks where classes were held was burned. "The want of a proper place to meet with the gentlemen upon theoretical instruction Since the Destruction of the officer Barrack," Rochefontaine wrote, "has led me to Exercise oftener in the Field upon Manoeuvers of Field pieces and Infantry."[17] Though he sought new quarters for the classroom, instruction was conducted only infrequently from that date.

Not long after the fire, Rochefontaine's relations with the officers deteriorated so badly that he became embroiled in a duel with one of them, Lieutenant William Wilson. The underlying factor in this dispute was the general dissatisfaction just noted, but the proximate cause was an epithet Wilson hurled at Rochefontaine, followed shortly by an altercation in which the colonel struck the younger officer with the hilt of his sword. Rochefontaine related the story of what followed:

> The agreement after we met was, that in order to avoid the formality of a Duel, we should settle the dispute by a Rencounter with two loaded pistols each and a Sword. The fires were to be given at pleasure and the distance be such as it Suited the two adversaries. The first fire went off almost at the same time on both sides. My second pistol went off unaware and I remained against my antagonist who had yet a Loaded pistol against me. He came up to me within three steps and misfired. It is a general rule in such occasions to lose the chance when the pistol has not gone off, yet my adversary cocked up and missed his fire a second time. In order to prevent his firing a third time, I fell on him to try to prevent him from cocking his piece, but he did it notwithstanding, and his pistol missed fire again, the muzzle touching my breast. The two witnesses came up then and separated us.[18]

Unfortunately, this result satisfied neither Wilson nor the other officers, who then publicly denounced Rochefontaine. The minds of the officers were completely set against him, Rochefontaine complained. Though he was by now a United States citizen, he lamented, "I am still looked upon as a stranger." "It may be to the general advantage," he concluded, "to place a man drawn out of the U.S. at the head of a Corps officered by American Gentlemen."[19]

Rochefontaine remained at West Point until he was discharged in 1798, but by the summer of 1796 he had wholly abandoned his effort to train his officers. Two of the three battalions of Artillerists and Engineers were reassigned in the summer and fall of 1796—three companies were detached to the westward and southward, and five others were sent to the sea coast. Pickering concisely summarized the result of Rochefontaine's efforts: "The officers have made very little improvement." Moreover, he confided in 1798, "We have been totally disappointed in our expectation of finding instructors in the Foreign officers appointed to command." The problem was "the disgust conceived by the captains and subalterns of the corps against their field officers, especially Rochefontaine."[20]

Some historians have mistakenly attempted to establish a linkage between the school Rochefontaine briefly conducted and the later military academy. The best evidence to the contrary is that the immediate contemporaries did not see any such ties. Washington's last annual message in December 1796 made a cogent case for the establishment of a military academy, without reference to the on-again, off-again school at West Point. "However pacific the general policy of a nation may be, it ought never to be without an adequate stock of military knowledge. . . . [F]or this purpose an academy where a regular course of instruction is given is an obvious expedient." Later, in 1799 and again in 1800, when more formal military academies were proposed, there was no reference to expanding on the training that had been attempted in the Corps of Artillerists and Engineers. That was not the model on which they hoped to build, for it was to have been nothing more than a temporary expedient.[21]

In 1796, Thomas North opened a grog shop just outside the boundaries of West Point. North may have been encouraged to do so by the larger number of troops that were stationed there after the creation of the Corps of Artillerists and Engineers. If so, he must have been disappointed by the departure of many of them only months after he opened his business. Still, off-duty soldiers gathered there and drank. North was not a man to encourage moderation, so his establishment gave rise to frequent disorder in the garrison. It also caused friction between the soldiers and the local lads who also gathered there. They had "a hostile disposition towards the Soldiery," noted Captain John Steele, who in 1800 commanded the only artillery company remaining at West Point. "There is scarcely a public day of any sort that they don't assemble [at North's], and endeavor to raise a disturbance with the Soldiers," he wrote.[22]

In April, Captain Steele placed North's premises off limits and ordered guard patrols to enforce his directive. On July 4, 1800, a particularly large crowd had gathered at North's, and when Steele sent a patrol to check for soldiers among them, the guards were disarmed and beaten. Word spread quickly among the garrison, and before Steele could gain control, his men had stormed the establishment. Those inside retreated upstairs and from there held off the troops with the weapons they had taken from the patrol.

When Steele had regained control of his men, he formed them up in front of North's place and ordered the surrender of those within. When they refused, Steele ordered an artillery piece brought forward and leveled it at the front door. That prompted those inside to reconsider. They surrendered forthwith.[23]

The idea of establishing a military academy dated back to the beginning of the struggle for American independence. In November 1775, John Adams had asked Henry Knox, formerly a Boston book dealer, for the names of those officers who were "best acquainted with the Theory and Practice of Fortification and Gunnery," as well as "what Books are best upon those subjects."[24] Knox replied, "The officers of the army, are very deficient in the Books upon the military art which does not arise from their disinclination to read but the impossibility of procuring the Books in America." He especially recommended Marshal Saxe's *Memoirs upon the Art of War*.[25]

Adams considered Knox's reply and concluded that a military academy was essential. "I could wish," he wrote, "that the Public would be at the Expense not only of new Editions of these Authors but of establishing Academies for the Education of young Gentlemen in every Branch of the military Art."[26] It was in September, in the midst of recriminations concerning the defeat at Long Island, that Knox received Adams's letter. He responded, echoing Adams's call for a military school. "Military academies must be Initiated at any expense," Knox agreed. Without such a "radical Cure" from Congress, the army will continue to get "the same unmeaning puppies for officers with which she had been curs'd."[27]

A visit to Washington's encampment, in September 1776, by a committee of the Continental Congress gave Knox another opportunity to promote the idea. At the conclusion of that visit, Knox supplied the committee with detailed "hints for the improvement of the Artillery" advocating the establishment of a military academy "to be nearly on the same plan as that of Woolwich . . . a place to which our enemies are indebted for the superiority of their artillery."[28] The committee, in turn, did call for the establishment of an academy but suggested that it be located with a Continental laboratory or ordnance facility. The ordnance school founded at Carlisle, Pennsylvania, shortly thereafter was a response to that initiative. This establishment operated for nearly two years, from 1777 through 1779, but it was hardly the academy that Knox or Adams had envisioned. While in operation, the laboratory's school focused its efforts almost wholly on the fabrication and repair of weapons.

Despite Adams's efforts, and those of Knox and others, no military academy was ever created during the War for Independence. In fact, the creation of the Invalid Corps was as close as the Continental Congress came to a broader "school" for training the Army's officers. In theory, the Corps was (among many other things) to serve as a "school for propagating military knowledge and discipline." In reality, however, it never effectively served the ends of military education.[29]

With the adoption of the new Constitution in 1789, a truly federal military force finally came into being. Still this force was modest. While Congress struggled to define the nature of this military establishment—particularly measures to regulate the militia effectively—the Army, under the leadership first of Josiah Harmar and then of Arthur St. Clair, sustained a pair of humiliating defeats at the hands of the Indians in the Northwest. Of a force of some fourteen hundred, the majority of whom were raw recruits and militia, St. Clair contrived to lose almost seven hundred (half his strength) in a single disaster in November 1791.

Anthony Wayne, selected the next year by President Washington to command the new Legion of the United States, took special pains to drill his new command and to organize an effective supply service. These efforts yielded complete victory over the Indians at Fallen Timbers in the summer of 1794.

There remained, however, the problem of training officers, particularly in the technical branches of artillery and engineers. In November 1793, when Washington called a Cabinet meeting to discuss the contents of his fifth annual address, the issue of a military academy came up once again. Hamilton and Knox favored calling for one, but Thomas Jefferson opposed it on the grounds that the Constitution did not specifically authorize such an institution. Washington chose to leave the issue to Congress, suggesting only that officers needed "an opportunity for the study of those branches of the military art which can scarcely ever be attained by practice alone."[30] Congress heeded this advice. When it created the new Corps of Artillerists and Engineers in 1794, it also authorized two cadets for each of the companies and the purchase of books, instruments, and apparatus necessary for their instruction. No cadets were appointed under this authority, however, until the last days of the Adams administration, and even then there was no academy for them to attend.

Despite the early expressions of interest in a military academy, little of real substance was done to create one until 1798. Then Hamilton, nominal head of the Army, which had been dramatically enlarged that year in response to the threat of war with France, again began to promote the idea. In June, he wrote Oliver Wolcott and enclosed a list of measures that should be undertaken without delay. Among them was the establishment of "an academy for naval & military instruction. This is a very important measure and ought to be permanent."[31] In July, he wrote General Louis Lebeque Duportail, the former Chief of Engineers of the Revolutionary Army: "If it were not to intrude too much upon you, I would request you to favor me with a digested plan of an establishment for a military School. This is an object I have extremely at heart."[32] Du Portail's plan reached Hamilton late in the year. Hamilton shared the plan with Charles Cotesworth Pinckney but does not appear to have given it to McHenry.[33]

By that time, Secretary of War James McHenry had also taken up the cause, but he was inclined toward a plan that had been submitted by Louis Tousard—a proposal for the "Formation of a School of Artillerists and Engineers." Tousard, building on what he had learned at West Point during the Rochefontaine fiasco in 1796, suggested that an academy be created. His preference regarding location, however, was not West Point but either Carlisle or Springfield. The director of the new school, he suggested, should be a field grade officer, assisted by two captains who would teach artillery tactics. In addition, there would be a professor of mathematics and a professor of drawing, each of whom would instruct in the practical application of these subjects. Classes in mathematics and drawing would be held on Monday, Wednesday, and Friday mornings; artillery practice was scheduled for Tuesday and Thursday afternoons. On Thursday mornings, the director of the academy would lecture on the science of fortifications.[34] It was a simple and straightforward plan that appealed to McHenry.

By late spring 1799, McHenry had convinced President John Adams—who, some twenty years earlier, had been one of the first to address the need for a military school—that the administration should move to create such an institution along the lines suggested by Tousard. Not long after that, he submitted a long letter to the Committee of Defense that contained the essence of Tousard's proposal, but nothing came of it.

That fall, Hamilton again turned his mind to the project. "A regular Military Academy," he wrote James Wilkinson, was "indispensable." He promised that during the upcoming session of Congress the subject would command his "best exertions."[35] In November 1799, he submitted a new plan to the Secretary of War—a proposal to organize an academy of five schools. The first was to be the Fundamental School. All entrants, except those "who by previous instruction elsewhere may have been acquainted with some of the branches taught," would complete two years of basic instruction there. They would study "arithmetic, algebra, geometry, the laws of motion, mechanics, geography, topography and surveying, and the designing of structures and landscapes."[36]

A cadet's education after the Fundamental School would depend upon the branch of the military he was destined to join. Those to be assigned to the Corps of Artillerists and Engineers would devote an additional two years to the study of advanced mathematics and mechanics, the theory of gunnery, and ordnance topics, as well as fortifications and engineering. There was also to be a school for infantry and one for cavalry; and those scheduled for the naval service would be enrolled for two years at a naval academy—studying astronomy, navigation, seamanship, and naval architecture.

Hamilton's plan also provided for rotating members of the active Army through the academy (both commissioned and noncommissioned officers) for regular periods of further training. The staff of his academy would consist of six directors and eighteen faculty members, suggesting a student body of about two hundred cadets. The administration's position—prepared by McHenry and submitted to Congress by Adams on January 14, 1800—followed Hamilton's plan closely.[37] The most important deviation was McHenry's streamlining of Hamilton's infantry and cavalry schools into a single institution. Later, however, sensing that the proposal was in trouble, McHenry submitted a supplement to the bill, suggesting that only the Fundamental School (with its fifty cadets) and the School of the Artillerists and Engineers (also with fifty cadets) were needed at that time. McHenry also sought estimates of the cost of establishing such an institution from prominent engineers and architects—estimates that ranged from $39,000 to $80,000. The latter figure was submitted by Benjamin Henry Latrobe, who had prepared a plan and sketches of the large, classically adorned structure that could house this academy.[38]

But in an era of domestic crisis and the dislocation of public matters in general, the academy bill lay unattended in the military affairs committee until McHenry personally interceded with the chairman, Harrison Gray Otis. "I consider the measure of the last [greatest] importance," he said, "as it respects character, efficiency, utility and economy in every part and portion of our system of defense. . . . I ask for it your protection."[39] Under normal circumstances, the bill would have been in good hands, for Otis was a respected and well-connected member of Congress, but these were not normal times. Not only were fundamental party rivalries threatening to erupt into broader conflict, but all the branches of government seemed disoriented by the upcoming transfer of the government from Philadelphia to the new capital of Washington, in the equally new District of Columbia.

Otis, however, did manage to get the bill through committee and presented it to the House in March. The political current still ran strongly against the project. Republicans' attacks upon the Federalist military establishment, which they believed to be a threat to their political existence, and thereby to the nation, were gaining breadth and vigor. Even more important, the Adams Federalists, growing weary of Hamilton's domination, were beginning to lend support to the Republicans.[40]

As an early warning of the difficulties to come, the military academy bill was attacked on its first reading, and once again it languished. Otis, whom McHenry had asked to manage the bill, left Philadelphia in late March and did not return to his seat until Congress met in the new term in Washington late that year. Without his support, and without the votes of the Adams Federalists that he might have delivered, the bill died—the victim of both Republican concerns about a partisan Federalist military establishment and a growing split in the Federalist party. The vote, sixty-four to twenty-three, said more about the times than about the strength of opposition to the idea of a military academy.

As bleak as prospects appeared in early 1800, they took a turn for the better that summer. In early July, Hamilton wrote the new Secretary of War,

Samuel Dexter, Secretary of War (May 13, 1800–January 31, 1801). Painted in 1873 by Walter M. Brackett (1823–1919). Courtesy of Army Art Collection, U.S. Army Center of Military History.

Samuel Dexter, calling his attention to the need for a military academy and suggesting Bureaux de Pusy, a French émigré, to head it: "The institution of a Military Academy being an object of primary importance will I doubt not be zealously pursued. Whenever it shall take place, Mr. Du Pussy will be a most desirable Character to be at the head of it."[41]

Dexter, however, needed no encouragement, for he had already devised a way of circumventing congressional foot-dragging and opposition. Artillery and engineer cadets, as well as the books, instruments, and apparatus necessary for their training, had been provided for in 1794. In 1798, the Congress had authorized "teachers of the arts and sciences" for each of the two regiments.[42] All that was left to do, Dexter realized, was to bring these elements together in a single location. After discussing his plan with Secretary of the Navy Benjamin Stoddard, and with Colonels Tousard and Burbeck, who commanded the two regiments of Artillerists and Engineers, he laid it out for Adams:

I have the Honor of submitting to your consideration a sketch of a plan for the instruction of the Artillerists and Engineers. It already is very evident to me that they need all the means that the Law has provided for the purpose.

The law has provided for two Cadets to each Company of Artillery, making in all Sixty-four Cadets. It is provided by Law that four Teachers and two Engineers may be appointed by the President of the United States.

The Secretary of War is to provide, under the direction of the President of the United States, necessary Books, instruments and apparatus for the use & benefit of the Artillerists and Engineers.

If the President thinks proper to appoint two Teachers and an Engineer, the Secretary will take measure to induce young men to enter the service as Cadets, and he will collect them together and form a regular School. He will cause the Battalions to be instructed in rotation at some regular stations.

Should these measures be taken, the Secretary conceives it would be necessary that he should be authorized to assure the Cadets that in future Officers will be taken from the most deserving of their members, if any should be found fit for appointment.

The Secretary of the Navy thinks it would be highly useful to the navy that Midshipmen might be admitted into the School by courtesy.

I am induced to make this statement from an apprehension that the Corps really needing instruction, and the law having provided the means of it, it may be considered incumbent on the War Department to see that the Laws be executed. Teachers may easily be found: an Engineer, fit to be the head of the institution probably would not so easily be found. I am told that M. Bureau de Pusy, now resident in New Jersey, is a suitable man. He is highly spoken of by Mr. McHenry, General Hamilton and Col Tousard. Col Burbeck is now here; he and Col Tousard both are of opinion that it would be highly useful that something like the above should be done.[43]

Dexter's plan needed no additional congressional approval—beyond, of course, continued annual appropriations.

"I am very ready," Adams answered, "to appoint both cadets and teachers"; he then launched into a catalog of specific instructions. Dexter was to "take the earliest measures" to obtain the books, instruments, and apparatus that would be necessary and that were provided for by law. He was also to make inquiries "for proper characters" for teachers. The President proposed Captain William A. Barron as a teacher of mathematics. Barron, who had been commissioned a few months earlier in the Second Regiment of Artillerists and Engineers, had previously taught mathematics. Adams, however, rejected the Frenchman, Bureaux de Pusy, whom Dexter had mentioned as a possible head of the institution. "I have an invincible aversion to the appointment of foreigners, if it can be avoided," said Adams, recalling the unpleasant experience with Rochefontaine in 1796. It "mortifies the honest pride of our officers," he concluded, "and damps their ardor and ambition."[44]

Adams's response had barely reached Dexter when the Secretary fired back more details. In anticipation, he had already begun to consider potential instructors. But the only name he could yet add to Barron's was that of the engineer, Jean Foncin, an associate of de Pusy's.[45] In response, Adams agreed to appoint Foncin, but not ahead of Barron. "If you can find another American mathematician better than Barron, it is well," wrote Adams; "if not, we will appoint him first teacher." He nevertheless suggested that Dexter should continue to inquire about American mathematicians.[46]

The upcoming fall 1800 election soon diverted Adams's attention, but Dexter continued his search for acceptable faculty. In August, he began to make inquiries about Jonathan Williams, who was not a teacher but was well read in mathematics, the sciences, and natural philosophy. He was also not a soldier—despite brief periods of service with the Pennsylvania militia during both the Whiskey Rebellion and Fries's Rebellion—but his translation of two French military texts suggested more familiarity with these subjects than most American officers could boast.[47] In September, Dexter offered Williams a commission as a major, but he revealed neither his plans for a military academy nor the role Williams might play there. Williams declined in hopes of obtaining a civil appointment but did agree to have his recent translations of works on artillery and fortifications published for use by the War Department.[48]

Adams's loss of the November election ended all hope that the administration would be able to see the project through to maturity. What is more, a fire gutted the War Department's offices, bringing work to a halt. "All the papers in my office [have] been destroyed," wrote Dexter, as he began the slow process of restoring some measure of order to the day-to-day routine.[49] Finally, for the President, the tragic death of a son dampened any enthusiasm he might yet have had for affairs of state.

Still, early in 1801, Dexter turned once more to the effort, although it must have been clear that little could come to fruition before the Adams administration left office. He renewed the offer of a commission to Williams and this time was somewhat more direct about his plans. Williams accepted. "I have been indefatigable," he wrote, "in brushing up all my former mathematical knowledge and adding to the stock." In addition, Williams wrote, he had begun to gather a personal library on military engineering and had started work on a program of lectures on subjects he thought essential to the young men he soon hoped to be instructing.[50]

As his term ended, Adams filled a number of the vacancies in the cadet ranks. But in the midst of an orgy of appointments made in the last days of the administration, this was an act of political expediency—if not spite—rather than an effort to revive the earlier plans for an academy with which his administration had, however haltingly, been engaged.

Adams departed Washington on March 4, 1801, only hours before the inauguration, leaving the military school's fate in the hands of a new administration, which, past actions being the guide, seemed likely to dismantle any work that had been done. By all rights, proponents of the school should have expected little. In Washington's cabinet, in 1793, Jefferson had argued that proposals to create a military school were unconstitutional.[51] More recently, in 1800, an academy bill had been vigorously attacked by the same Republicans who now controlled the executive branch and dominated the Congress.

Contrary to all expectations, however, the new administration acted quickly to establish the school, and did so with an energy and facility that had escaped Adams, McHenry, and Dexter. The decision to create a military academy came in the early weeks of the new administration. The first evidence of their intentions came on April 11, barely a month after the new administration had taken office, when the new Secretary of War, Henry Dearborn, offered the position of teacher of mathematics to George Baron, an Englishman who was at the time residing in New York.[52] He outlined the duties, salary, and benefits and indicated that "West-Point on the Hudson, will probably be the position for the school."[53] Four days after offering to hire Baron, Dearborn notified the commander at West Point of the plans "to establish a military school" there.[54]

The choice of West Point was a simple one. The post was already associated with the Corps of Artillerists and Engineers, which would be the Academy's most immediate benefactor. The Corps had been stationed there in 1794, as it was recruited, and major elements had continued there until at least 1797. Even when those units were dispersed, there was at least one company left to garrison West Point's decaying fortifications and help maintain the stores of powder and weapons. Establishing the Academy without going to Congress first, as Dexter had conceived and as Jefferson and Dearborn planned, required placing the school at an established post. West Point was one of a few choices available. Carlisle had been abandoned, and the Springfield Arsenal, which had not been formally established until 1794, was little more than a few storehouses and offices. It was not a decision that Dearborn troubled over. Later, in December 1801, when he was drafting

Henry Dearborn, Secretary of War (March 5, 1801–March 7, 1809). Painted in 1873 by Walter M. Brackett (1823–1919). Courtesy of Army Art Collection, U.S. Army Center of Military History.

the administration's new peace establishment bill, he saw no reason to consider any other site for the formal academy the new law provided. In fact, all information Dearborn and the administration had at that point indicated the new school, under Baron, was progressing well.

Soon after choosing West Point as the site of the new school, the administration selected Jonathan Williams to superintend it—the same Jonathan Williams whom Adams had recently commissioned with this role in mind. Williams was a nephew of Benjamin Franklin and for a time had been secretary to the old sage in Paris. He was a lay scientist and an officer of the American Philosophical Society. Jefferson had been acquainted with him in both capacities for a number of years. They had corresponded occasionally, in reference to both Society business and scientific endeavors. Williams was a moderate Federalist, but if Jefferson harbored any concerns about his politics or loyalty, Williams made every effort to dispel them. In a solicitous letter to the new President just after the inauguration, Williams took pains to assure him that his recent appointment to the Army by Adams had no political basis.[55] Dearborn ordered Williams to Washington in April and after a brief interview offered him the appointment as Inspector of Fortifications. Williams at first declined, but when it became clear that in this role he would head the new military school at West Point, he changed his mind.[56]

By mid-May, the plan had been given full shape: a Superintendent had been selected; curriculum considerations had been addressed; measures had been taken to engage a qualified faculty; and facilities were being prepared for students and staff alike.[57]

Lieutenant Colonel Louis Tousard, newly appointed Inspector of Artillery, reported that $1,500 would suffice to prepare a mathematics room, a drawing room, quarters for the cadets, two mess rooms, and quarters for the officers, teachers, and surgeon, as well as their families.[58] Dearborn ordered work to proceed immediately, but he did not ignore Republican concerns for economy. "No expense must be ignored that shall not be actually necessary to render the . . . buildings comfortable outside painting [which] should be attended to on the score of economy."[59] Major John Lillie, who took command of the post in June, supervised the repairs. His young daughter, Mary Ann, was amused when he had the classroom benches painted green. But green paint was what was at hand, and economy ruled.[60] On July 2, less than four months after the administration had taken office, Dearborn ordered the cadets to West Point. They began to arrive there, as directed, in September.[61]

Dearborn and Jefferson had moved with a purpose and alacrity that suggests that the new academy was viewed as part of some larger plan—as, in fact, it was. Jefferson recognized the need for an adequate regular military establishment but feared the mischief a Federalist officer corps might cause.

Congressional sanction of the Academy was an element of the Peace Establishment Act of 1802 with which Jefferson initiated a political and social reform of the military establishment as a whole. That bill allowed Jefferson to discharge the most vociferous of his opponents in the Army and created new opportunities for Republican appointments at the lower levels. The institution at West Point on the Hudson provided one more means to further Jefferson's reformation of the Army, for it would admit, and train, the sons of the country's sturdy Republican stock.

It is interesting that the new administration had been able to move so much more effectively than the previous one in establishing the school. To begin with, of course, it built on the foundation created by Adams and Dexter, but the real explanation is bound up in the motive that impelled the administration to take these actions. There had been more than a decade of debate over the role—even the necessity—of a regular military establishment in American society. After having once suggested that the powers of the Constitution would not authorize the establishment of a military academy, it seemed strange that Jefferson would now move so purposefully to create one.[62]

Jefferson's creation of the Military Academy has, until recently, seemed a paradox. The Academy was a "Hamiltonian institution created by Jefferson," wrote one historian. It was "a curious turn of the wheel" or an "ironical" affair, wrote others—that Jefferson should create a military school. When obliged to account for Jefferson's motive in creating such an academy, most fell back on one or both of two related themes. It was either a national academy that emphasized science instead of the classics or a school that would provide trained engineers—military and civil—for the new nation. "[Jefferson] was eager," wrote Stephen E. Ambrose, "to found a national institution that would eliminate the classics, add the sciences, and produce graduates who would use their knowledge for the benefit of society. Within this framework Jefferson realized that a military academy had the best chance of success."[63] As Dumas Malone argues regarding Jefferson: "If little concerned about the professional training of army officers in time of peace, he fully recognized the usefulness of engineers in peace or war and valued the infant Academy chiefly for its potential scientific contribution." Some authors have placed more emphasis on the military nature of the school.[64] Others have stressed the peaceful benefits it produced—particularly from the engineers it trained.[65]

More recent reexaminations of Jefferson's relations with the Army, including my own *Mr. Jefferson's Army,* have shown these earlier efforts to rationalize Jefferson's founding of the Military Academy to be unpersuasive.[66] Jefferson simply did not consider the Military Academy at West Point to be

Thomas Jefferson. This portrait was commissioned by the officers and cadets at
West Point in 1821. Painted in 1822 by Thomas Sully (1783–1872). West Point
Museum Collection, United States Military Academy.

a key institution of scientific learning, though no doubt he would have liked to have seen one established. Similarly, formal engineering training was neither the sole nor the primary goal. In fact, an engineering curriculum (beyond the construction of crude field fortifications) was not even introduced until a decade after Jefferson left office. If Jefferson had intended West Point to be an important element of a national scientific school, he certainly would have chosen differently in terms of student body, faculty, and curriculum.

The extent of scientific training conducted at the Military Academy in its early years is easy to exaggerate. At times, in fact, the administration seemed to resist efforts to include any emphasis on science beyond the practical necessities of officership. For example, when Williams requested new books on science that might push the curriculum beyond the most basic treatment, he was put off by Dearborn with the excuse that scientific thought was changing so fast that these texts would soon be useless.[67] Also, as will be seen, the early faculty would be better characterized as laymen with interests in science and mathematics than as learned scientists or mathematicians such as were beginning to emerge in faculties at the better colleges.[68]

The early curriculum at West Point clearly showed the very limited extent of either scientific or engineering instruction that was to be offered at West Point. In 1802 and for several years thereafter, while other institutions were offering higher mathematics, astronomy, natural philosophy, and chemistry as a matter of course, the Military Academy offered only the rudiments of mathematics and military fortification.[69] Moreover, the Academy made no pretext of doing otherwise. The mathematics text—C. H. Hutton's *Mathematics*—made no pretext of reaching into the higher realms of mathematics. In many ways the curriculum was more like that of a secondary or even an elementary school than a college—and for good reason. A few cadets, upon arrival, could neither read nor write, while a larger number had only the most rudimentary skills in either arithmetic or grammar.[70]

By design, the instruction was to impart only the most basic, practical knowledge needed by army officers of that day: sufficient mathematics and practical skills to lay artillery correctly, to construct simple fortifications, and to make rudimentary maps. Jonathan Williams, the Superintendent, had loftier goals but found them consistently frustrated. He argued "that mere mathematics would not make either an artillerist or an engineer." But, though French and drawing were soon added to the curriculum, the administration resisted all efforts to alter the basic nature of the school.[71] It was not until the eve of the War of 1812 that the direction of the school began to change, and not until after Sylvanus Thayer became Superintendent in 1817 that it began to offer more than the rudiments of engineering.

Jonathan Williams was the first Superintendent of
the United States Military Academy. Painted in 1815
by Thomas Sully (1783–1872). West Point Museum
Collection, United States Military Academy.

At "the elementary school at West Point," reported a graduate of 1806,
cadets "so fortunate as to render themselves serviceable either in the artillery or engineers" must have done so by "their own industry, and not in the
education received by them at West Point, which was barely sufficient to
excite a desire for military inquiries and of military pursuits."[72]

The administration obviously envisioned the new Academy at West Point
as something more than a school for engineers. In fact, the cadets appointed
by Jefferson were almost uniformly given artillery rather than engineer warrants. A few of the best of these were later chosen to be engineers—particularly in the first few years as the Corps of Engineers was being completed.
Most, however, became artillerists, although the school did graduate men
into all the branches. The newly commissioned graduates were assigned
where they were needed—or, possibly, where they were best qualified to

serve. Of the fifty commissioned during Jefferson's two terms, fourteen were made engineers, twenty-seven were sent to the artillery, eight to the infantry, and one to the dragoons. (One additional cadet was graduated but not offered a commission.)

The efforts to explain Jefferson's founding of the Military Academy at West Point as a manifestation of his Enlightenment interest in science or engineering simply does not square with the evidence. Rather, the founding of the Military Academy needs to be seen as part of a more comprehensive Jeffersonian plan for the military establishment, which was itself part of a broader effort to break the Federalists' hold on the strings of government—the civil service, the courts, and the military. It was no coincidence that the formal sanction he sought for the Academy was contained in the administration's focused program of military reform, the Military Peace Establishment Act of 1802. The Army and the other elements of government responsive to the President were to be made more responsive to the views of the new administration. The creation of a Military Academy is no paradox when viewed as an element in the reform of the Army, and that is even more clear when the reform of the Army is understood as part of a broader reformation of the political establishment—a process necessary to safeguard the new, Republican regime.[73] The President's new school would prepare loyal young Republicans for commissioned service in his reformed army. Jefferson's announcement to Nathaniel Macon of a "chaste reformation" of the military establishment came just two days after the first formal report indicating the contemplated establishment of the Military Academy.[74] That juxtaposition was hardly coincidental. The Academy was to be an integral part of Jefferson's effort to Republicanize the Army.

At West Point, where the cadets who began in the summer of 1801 had all been appointed by John Adams, the change was soon noticeable. Joseph Gardner Swift, one of the Adams cadets, reported that after the new administration had come into power, "appointments to military office were made from families of prominent Democrats and of less Educated Persons than had been heretofore appointed."[75] The first cadet to be appointed by Jefferson was probably young John Lilly, who was offered a warrant at the end of 1801 and who appears to have started classes in January or February 1802. His father had been the Military Storekeeper at West Point until his death in September 1801, and the son, only eleven years old, was appointed largely out of sympathy for the family. Lilly left the Academy without graduating in 1805. Other Jefferson appointees joined in the summer of 1802, and more were added in each succeeding year. Drawn from Republican families and trained under officers carefully selected for the task, these young men, it was hoped, would form an officer corps that would be thoroughly attached to the republican principles they were sworn to defend.

Dearborn and the President were diligent in their efforts to select cadets from within the country's Republican ranks—just as proper political credentials were essential for any appointment made by this administration. Applicants whose recommendations came from Federalist sponsors stood little chance of nomination; recommendation by a High Federalist meant almost certain rejection.[76] The political affiliation of academy applicants (or of their families) was a common and important subject of mention in letters of recommendation. The files of the very early years are quite fragmentary, but those that exist are indicative. "His father . . . is a Republican and I am informed the young man is also," reported one correspondent.[77] "He is . . . of reputable parentage, the family have all be[en] considered as thoroughly attached to republican principles," wrote another.[78] You will not take exception to "his moral character, his education [or] his political creed," reported still another.[79] These young men were all offered cadet warrants, though not all accepted them.

Federalists, on the average richer and more likely to have obtained an education, held the upper hand. "The children of illustrious families," wrote John Adams, "have generally greater advantages of education . . . than those of meaner ones, or even those in middle life."[80] How was Jefferson to create a Republican army if Republican sons were unprepared for officership?

To break the upper-class monopoly in the officer corps, something had to be done to break the upper-class monopoly of education.[81] If the commissioned ranks were to become accessible to all classes of citizens, if the aristocracy of wealth and birth in the army was to be replaced with the aristocracy of virtue and talent, if men were to be included who lacked the advantages that wealth and position offered, then education and training would have to be provided that would equip them to lead.

The new establishment of Republicanism in the Army necessitated the academy that Jefferson created at West Point. His new military school would train men from the country's Republican stock for positions of leadership in his new Army.[82] For many it would provide the education they could not otherwise acquire. It was a key component in Jefferson's new military establishment. Its creation was a conscious, purposeful act of an eminently and consistently political man. This school would provide Republican sons with the fundamental skills they needed to officer Mr. Jefferson's Army.

CHAPTER THREE

The Early Years, 1802–1817

By the time George Baron, the first instructor, arrived at West Point in late July 1801, preparations for the new Academy were well under way. In May, Secretary of War Henry Dearborn had ordered that quarters be readied for the Inspector of Artillery, the Inspector of Engineers, an instructor in mathematics, and up to thirty cadets.[1] The post, which had recently quartered three of the army's four artillery battalions, was more than adequate to accommodate the new school.

Facilities at West Point in 1801 had not changed a lot since the Revolution. The Provost jail—built during the last years of the war and most recently used as an officers' billet (and classroom)—had burned and wartime huts and smaller barracks had been pulled down. Little else had changed.

The building chosen as the Academy was a small, two-story frame structure about the size of a country schoolhouse, erected sometime before 1780. It had served, at various times, as the post headquarters, as officers' quarters, and in other capacities. This building, situated on the western periphery of the Plain, was used for both recitations and chapel until 1815. (Sylvanus Thayer lived in the structure from 1817 until the Superintendent's new quarters were completed in 1820; it was razed not long after.) On either side of the Academy, officers' quarters nestled against steep slopes that reached up nearly four hundred feet to Fort Putnam. The most prominent structure on the Plain was Long Barracks, located just west of Fort Clinton's ruins. Refurbished in 1806, it housed the cadets for another decade. On the flats below the Plain, near the river, there were the ordnance storehouses, a small hospital, and a collection of smaller buildings, virtually all of which dated from the Revolution.

By the end of September 1801, the cadets thus far appointed had arrived, and classes began. George Baron initiated their instruction using Charles Hutton's *Mathematics*, a text he had brought with him.[2] Hutton's book soon became the Academy's basic mathematics text and remained so until 1823. Classes in mathematics—the only regular subject—began at eight o'clock and continued until noon. Each lesson was demonstrated at the blackboard and accompanied with a lecture from Mr. Baron upon its application. The afternoons were variously occupied in military exercises or field sports.[3]

Trouble arose for Baron almost at once. The junior officers at the post, who were also expected to attend the classes, refused to do so. One of these, Lieutenant William Wilson (who had clashed with Rochefontaine just a few years earlier), was likely the source of the trouble again. At first, Dearborn supported Baron. "If the Subalterns persist in their contumacy," he wrote, "their ignorance of the duties of an officer, and their culpable want of ambition shall be noticed in an exemplary manner."[4]

When Wilson and Lieutenant Lewis Howard took cadet Joseph Gardner Swift into their mess, Baron objected. He did not want the officers' arrogance and lack of discipline to infect the cadets, who until then had evidenced "good conduct," as well as "diligence and rapid improvement."[5] Wilson, however, persuaded Swift to resist the order. In response, Baron pronounced Swift "a mutinous young rascal," and when Swift confronted Baron and threatened to avenge this insult, the instructor fled to the Academy with the young cadet in close pursuit. Baron bolted the door in Swift's face and, from the window of the upper story, berated the cadet with coarse epithets that were returned in kind.[6]

"You may confidentially rely on my aid in support of your authority," Dearborn assured Baron at the end of October and then advised Swift to apologize or be dismissed. Wilson again counseled Swift to stand his ground. "The officers of the post deemed Mr. Baron's conduct to be so ungentlemanly and irritating," Swift recorded, "that an apology could not be made to him."[7] Dearborn, far from the scene of conflict, continued to support the teacher. "No officers of the Garrison," he wrote in early December, "except Officers attached to the School as directors will have any command or direction over the students."[8] By the time Dearborn's last letter arrived, however, the officers on the post had brought serious charges against Baron and placed him under arrest. His conduct, they alleged, was unbecoming to one of his position and responsibility: he degraded the officers to the enlisted soldiers, abused his wife and children, and made a "habit of collecting many Citizens of the lowest rank and the most depraved characters at his house."[9] When a New York paper got hold of the story, Baron's situation went from bad to worse.[10]

With George Baron's arrest in November, instruction at the Academy came to a halt. This was how matters stood when the new Superintendent, Major Jonathan Williams, arrived in mid-December. After surveying the situation there and considering the charges against Baron, he advised the Secretary of War that the instructor should be encouraged to resign. Dearborn concurred, but when Baron departed the post without tendering his resignation, the Secretary dismissed him.[11]

Williams took over the teaching responsibilities after Baron's departure in February and immediately began to modify the curriculum, adding geometry to the arithmetic and algebra already being taught. He soon discovered, however, that everything at the new Military Academy came under the watchful eye of the administration in Washington. To accommodate the teaching of geometry, he requested twelve sets of mathematical drawing instruments and put Dearborn on notice that it would "soon be necessary to have a good drawing Master." He also requisitioned the surveying and mapping instruments required in both fieldwork and practical exercises, as well as one hundred copies each of his translations of *Elements of Fortification* and Scheel's work on artillery.[12] The wheels of government procurement moved slowly, however, and in the spring, he found it necessary to renew these requests.

Instruction at West Point was interrupted again in March 1802, however, when Williams became ill. He took an extended leave in order to recover, retiring for a time with his family to their home in Elizabeth, New Jersey. Any disappointment at West Point that might have been felt at the suspension of classes was vanquished by news later that month of the passage of the Military Peace Establishment Act of 1802, which confirmed, *de jure*, Jefferson's *de facto* creation of the Military Academy. The Peace Establishment Act, formulated by the administration and introduced in December 1801, passed the Congress and was signed by Jefferson on March 16, 1802—the date celebrated ever since as that of the Academy's founding. The new Corps of Engineers created by the act was "to be stationed at West Point," where it would "constitute a military academy."[13]

The provisions of the act creating the Academy were carefully drawn to allow the President exceptional powers over this Corps of Engineers. The division of the Artillerists and Engineers into separate branches had been proposed by the previous administration in 1800,[14] but Jefferson and Dearborn saw a particular advantage in this arrangement and effected the change. The officers of this new Engineer Corps were all to be appointed by the President, and in this way were peculiarly beholden to him. Moreover, in creating this Corps, Jefferson was not bound by the traditional promotion by seniority, and he chose whom he wished with regard only to ability and compatibility with the new regime. This Corps, more than any other, belonged to Jefferson.

In selecting those who would conduct the affairs of the new Military Academy, Dearborn and Jefferson took care to avoid men with strong Federalist leanings. Nonetheless, the same shortage of qualified Republicans that had prompted the school in the first place also made it necessary to cast an especially broad net. Their first choice as an instructor, the now discredited Baron, was a Republican, but they soon found that they could not avoid choosing some who were moderate Federalists—"Republican

Federalists," Jefferson called them. Jonathan Williams, whom they selected to superintend the school, was one of these. More staunch Federalists, however, were not considered. The administration did not even bother to consider those who were tainted by strong loyalties to the Hamiltonian faction. It simply would not do to have strongly antiadministration role models for the young men.

Even before offering to allow Baron to resign, Dearborn had begun to toy with the idea of sending another mathematics teacher to West Point—Captain William Amherst Barron.[15] When he raised this possibility with Williams, the latter replied that he did not know Barron, but that "most assuredly a Teacher belonging to the Corps would tend to harmonize with the students and the officers of the Garrison."[16] Barron, like Williams, was a moderate Federalist. He was a Harvard graduate and had tutored there. Though the officer was unknown to Williams, his credentials were impressive, and, more important, he had served with the Artillerists and Engineers since he was commissioned in 1800. Barron was named an instructor of mathematics and ordered to West Point. He arrived there in early June 1802.[17]

And before Captain Barron had been ordered to West Point, the administration was considering a second mathematics instructor, Jared Mansfield. Mansfield came to the attention of the administration through the efforts of Abraham Baldwin, a Republican senator from Georgia. Baldwin, formerly from Connecticut, had been a student of Mansfield's and had been associated with him in Republican political circles there. But Mansfield had more to recommend him than mere politics. He had taught mathematics at Yale, and his new book, *Essays, Mathematical and Physical,* included a chapter, "Theory of Gunnery," that discussed the physics of projectiles. When Baldwin sent a copy of the book to Jefferson in January or February 1802, the President requested several additional copies.[18] In early April, while waiting for the books to arrive, Baldwin raised the issue of the new Military Academy with Mansfield. "A thought has occurred to me," he wrote. "My wish is that you should be their instructor, and I have no doubt it may be made worth your while."[19] Mansfield agreed, and in just a month he was appointed to the new Corps of Engineers and ordered to "repair with convenient dispatch to the post of West Point."[20]

In the spring, as he regained his health, Williams began again to address the affairs of the fledgling academy. He again requested the books and instruments that were needed. "I will consult the President, and will write you an answer," he was told by the Secretary of War in reply. A few weeks later the promised answer arrived. "You will observe the notes made by the President on the margin of your list," wrote Dearborn, who then instructed Williams to order the items that Jefferson had approved.[21]

When Captain Barron arrived at West Point in the late spring, Williams still convalesced at his New Jersey home. Based on the latter's written instructions, Barron opened classes again in June. Williams directed Barron to continue to use the Hutton text but to "proceed to theoretical and then to practical geometry, before the students acquire the higher parts of algebra." The Superintendent reasoned that it would be "a loss of time to wait until a student becomes a perfect algebraist, before he is even a theoretical geometrician."[22] When Williams returned to West Point in July, he was impressed by Barron and reported to Dearborn that the Captain was presiding over the daily duties of the Academy and that he "anticipated much Satisfaction in my dealing with him."[23]

Mansfield arrived in August and immediately joined in the instruction of cadets. Williams lectured occasionally on the construction of fortifications, and from time to time other engineer officers were available to assist. The burden of presenting instruction, however, fell mainly to Barron and Mansfield. With the latter's arrival, classroom hours were extended—now beginning each morning (except Sunday) at nine o'clock and continuing until two o'clock. Four afternoons each week, from four o'clock until sunset, the cadets met for field exercises.[24]

The number of new cadets that arrived as fall approached in 1802 disappointed Williams. "It would give me great pleasure," he wrote, "to have my full number of cadets [forty], composed of intelligent young men with a proper degree of Rudimental knowledge."[25] Williams was pleased with his assignment to direct the new academy but not at all satisfied with the progress he had yet made. "In all your conversations with the Secretary," he reminded Captain Decius Wadsworth, one of his engineers, "you will never . . . lose sight of our leading star, which is not a little mathematical School but a great national establishment to turn out characters which in the course of time shall equal any in Europe."[26] Wadsworth, however, warned his superior that, with the school still in its first year, the time was not yet right to press the administration for additional faculty. "The moment is not yet arrived for us to ask for them with a tolerable Prospect of Success," he argued.[27] But a month later, when Barron reported a conversation with Dearborn in which the latter seemed inclined to favor the Academy, Williams fired off a "digest report" on the needs of the Academy and the Corps of Engineers—in particular noting the necessity for teachers of drawing and French.[28]

Officers' quarters at West Point seem always to have been in short supply, and their assignment was a contentious issue from the beginning. For years, officers lived in the scattered quarters that had housed their predecessors in the regiment of artillerists and engineers. Many of these structures survived from the period of the Revolution.

Lieutenant Colonel Lewis Tousard, now the Inspector of Artillery, arrived in September 1801, some months ahead of Williams. Dearborn had earlier directed that houses be prepared for both men, but Tousard, the senior, got the largest and finest (relatively speaking). When Williams arrived, he had to accept the smaller and less desirable one, just off the Plain to the northwest, overlooking the ordnance warehouses and the river below. Disappointed, Williams approached Dearborn about having that house renovated; the latter replied that, although he could have repairs made, "It may be proper to mention to you in confidence that Col. Tousard will probably go out of service." The administration's Army bill, which formally established the Military Academy at West Point—and which was then under consideration by the Congress—also provided for a substantial reduction in the number of officers. This reduction was designed to allow Jefferson and Dearborn to rid the Army of many of the more vociferous Federalist opponents of the new Republican regime. Tousard, who was closely identified with the Hamiltonian faction, was one of those slated to go as soon as the bill became law. His quarters would then be available for Williams.[29]

The bachelor officers were quartered wherever space allowed. These quarters were described by a visiting French officer as "little houses, irregularly built," although better than the barracks available to French officers.[30] Here the bachelors organized themselves into informal messes. Lieutenants William Wilson and Lewis Howard, who formed the self-styled "artillery mess," and Lieutenants James Wilson and Alexander Macomb made a similar but separate arrangement.

The cadets likewise organized their own messes and accommodated themselves as best they could, but, reported one, they "were not comfortably lodged."[31] Some of the structures being used to house the cadets, Williams reported, needed to be pulled down. Long Barracks, he suggested, which was then used for the troops on post, could accommodate the cadets as well if renovated. The two wings of that building would suffice for the students, while the main section could be reserved for the artillery company usually assigned there. Williams suggested that with plastering and a few other repairs, sixteen good cadet rooms could be furnished, at least temporarily.[32]

As 1802 drew to a close, the officers and cadets faced the unpleasant prospect of another winter at West Point in the poorly heated frame buildings. Williams asked the Secretary of War to allow winter vacations that would "commence annually on the 1st day of December and terminate on the 15th day of March following." Dearborn concurred, and this practice continued until 1817, when new buildings more suitable for winter occupancy had been completed.[33]

Despite some problems, Williams had cause for satisfaction as the first term of operation came to an end, including the first graduation of cadets from the academy on October 12, 1802. Cadets Joseph Gardner Swift, Simon Levy, and Walter Armistead were examined in arithmetic, algebra, geometry, trigonometry, and the elements of fortifications. They all passed, and the first two were appointed Second Lieutenants of Engineers, thus becoming the first graduates of the Military Academy. Armistead chose to remain at his studies for a few more months before accepting a commission.[34]

Williams's relations with the administration had, in most respects, been quite happy. For example, his request for teachers of French and of drawing had met with quick approval and was presented to Congress early in the next session. In February 1803, the bill passed and was signed. Williams was cautioned against recommending for the post "intemperate men, foreigners, or men far advanced in years," but he found it impossible to meet all these criteria, and the choice was eventually made in favor of Francis D. Masson, a Frenchman, who was appointed to fill both positions.

Also significant in the fall of 1803 was Williams's creation of a national society to promote the study of the military sciences—the United States Military Philosophical Society. In November he assembled the officers of the Corps of Engineers and laid out his plan for an organization that would stimulate the collection and dissemination of useful military knowledge, particularly in areas not then supported by public funds.[35] The name clearly revealed the extent to which this new organization was modeled on the American Philosophical Society of which Williams had been an active member and officer. Williams was elected president, and Wadsworth, vice president.

Not everyone was as enthusiastic about the new organization as Williams. Wadsworth, the second ranking engineer officer, confided to Williams that he feared that the new organization was superfluous or even dangerous to the prospects of the Corps. "The organization of the Corps of Engineers, if the Act of Congress be attended to, did of itself constitute us a *military Philosophical or rather Scientific Society*," Wadsworth argued; the Corps being stationed at West Point, and its control of the military school there, "shew that it was the Intention of Congress to give us opportunity and the Means of Improvement in military Sciences." In promoting the interests of the new Society, he feared, the officers "might be suspected of wishing to change our Corps into something different from what was originally contemplated."

However, Williams's success in winning Jefferson's sponsorship of the organization had "diminished somewhat" Wadsworth's apprehension. "Independent of [the President's patronage]," he wrote, "I see no particular Advantage or necessity of" the association. With that patronage, however, he conceded, "I foresee many eminent Advantages to us as Individuals and as officers resulting therefrom." With that he pledged his support.[36] Under Williams's active direction the society soon embraced as members "nearly every distinguished gentleman in the navy and Union, and several in Europe." In 1807 the membership stood at about two hundred, including Jefferson, James Madison, James Monroe, John Quincy Adams, John Marshall, Benjamin Latrobe, and Charles Cotesworth Pinckney.[37]

If advance of military science had been Williams's only motivation in founding this new Society, Wadsworth seems justified in questioning its necessity. But there was more to it than that. A clue to his added motive may be found in the report of a chance meeting between Williams and Alexander Hamilton just days before Williams offered his plan for the Society. The two men conversed at length, reported Swift, who was accompanying Williams. "General Hamilton, Colonel Williams and General [Philip] Schuyler discussed the subject of the Military Academy, the colonel giving his ideas and purposes to encourage an enlargement of the present plan; General Hamilton approved."[38] This meeting and the support he received for his plans concerning the Academy may have suggested to Williams the desirability—even the necessity—of creating an organization that would encourage and harness broad support for the continued growth of the new institution.

The Society, however, offered little to its general membership, and it seldom met outside West Point—an objection raised by Timothy Pickering, who rejected an invitation to join. However, in 1808, when Williams was pressing the administration to transfer the Academy to the capital, he arranged a meeting of the Society at the War Department in Washington. Although the meeting was well attended, Williams failed to generate adequate support for his long-sought relocation of the Academy.

In essence, the United States Military Philosophical Society was little more than a creature of its founder, Jonathan Williams, and its fate was bound up with his own. When Williams resigned from the Army in 1803, the Society floundered. He revived it upon his return in 1805, but after he resigned permanently in 1812, it was disbanded within a year.

For Williams, all efforts were focused on two issues that dominated the years of his superintendence—the relocation of the Academy and its command by engineers. Removing the Academy to Washington was Williams's consuming desire. From the beginning, Dearborn encouraged him in the belief that the President favored the move but reminded him that Congress, having designated West Point as the site of the Academy in 1802, would now have to act to change it. In many respects Williams's failure to establish the Academy more firmly during his time as Superintendent was due to his desire to see the school moved to Washington. In 1808, Williams described the institution as "like a foundling, barely existing among the mountains," but his concern was less that it was a "foundling" than that it still existed "among the mountains."[39] Throughout his tenure he was reluctant to do anything that might foreclose a relocation, and so failed to initiate the buildings and improvements that the Academy so clearly needed to make it a permanent fixture.

The second issue, command at West Point, first came to a head in September 1802 in a dispute between Williams, now Lieutenant Colonel of the Engineers and Superintendent of the Academy, and Captain George Izard, who commanded the artillery company stationed at West Point. Dearborn had earlier decreed that the commander of troops should have no control over "matters relating to the academy," while the officer superintending the Academy should have no "command of the troops of the garrison."[40] Problems arose, naturally, in areas not so clearly delineated. The most immediate cause of friction was the requisition of supplies, which, Williams found, had to be made through the captain. If Izard disapproved the issue, as he sometimes did, he was in effect controlling affairs of the Academy. The real issue, however, was one of principle—of whether or not engineer officers could command other troops. Williams complained, "In effect, [by losing] controul over my requisitions, the Commanding officer of the Engineers, whatever be his nominal Rank, may become inferior even to a Subaltern."[41]

The issue was never resolved to Williams's satisfaction and was to remain a continuing source of irritation. "We still keep up personal appearances," wrote Williams, but he was humiliated by the arrangement. "It is not in the power of man to be consistent if he is to have *command* as a Lieut. Col. under the *controul* of a Captain." In December 1802, Williams asked Dearborn to reconsider the issue, with particular attention to the situation at West Point. The Secretary ignored his request, so in March of the next year Williams and Wadsworth drew up a set of demands—"points" which they "determined to be essential to their existence as Officers of the Corps." The first and most important was that engineer officers would have the same military authority as officers of the other corps. Of most immediate concern was the specific situation at West Point, which was "appropriated to the Corps of Engineers," and therefore ought to be commanded by an engineer (so long as the engineer was senior to other officers at the post).[42] Once again Dearborn simply ignored them.

When confronted directly, in June 1803, Dearborn answered in the negative, and Williams submitted his resignation. Dearborn asked him to reconsider but warned: "No change however can take place, in the principles earlier established to the command contended for." Williams was unmoved, and his resignation was accepted.[43]

Dearborn explained the position of the administration to Wadsworth, now the senior engineer: "It is the wish of the Executive that the Gentlemen who have received appointments in the Corps of Engineers should devote their Time and Attention exclusively to the Theory and Practice of their Profession. By this means," he added, "we may avoid the unpleasant Necessity of employing Foreigners as Engineers."[44]

The departure of Williams and his family from West Point broke up the small social circle there, wrote Swift. "Colonel Williams had been the friend and adviser of every one of us." The society at West Point was restricted at best; cut off as they were, the officers and their families were left to their own devices. This was particularly so in the winter, when ice closed the river, although in that season their numbers were sometimes enlarged. Often, the officers of the Corps of Engineers spent the worst of the winter months at West Point. There, despite the harsh weather, they enjoyed a revelry with old friends. But beginning in the early spring they would depart to supervise the construction of fortifications along the coast. Such seasonal losses were keenly felt—permanent losses even more so.

The different social origins of the officers and their wives sometimes caused temporary problems. Not long after arriving at West Point, Elizabeth Mansfield reported that the other wives were polite, but that they were "used to living in high style." They exhibited "a set of manners very different from our acquaintances in New Haven," she wrote a friend. "I see them seldom; tho I have been treated by them with the greatest attention. You know I was never no hand at visiting and I visit less now than ever."[45]

The loss of Williams and his family was compounded just a few months later when Jared Mansfield accepted the appointment as Surveyor General and moved to Cincinnati, Ohio. "Mrs. Mansfield," Swift recalled, "was a very intelligent lady, and her conversation not only agreeable but instructive to the young gentlemen who found a welcome at her residence."[46]

Upon Williams's resignation, command of the Corps of Engineers and the superintendency of the Military Academy devolved upon the next senior officer of the Corps, Major Decius Wadsworth. Until the spring of 1804, however, Wadsworth was heavily engaged in directing the extensive harbor fortification program then in progress along the Atlantic seaboard, and he found it difficult to find enough time to supervise Academy affairs effectively. The result was that actual control at West Point was left largely in the hands of the next senior engineer officer, Captain Barron.

By the spring of 1804, the Academy staff was reduced to only Barron and Masson, with the occasional assistance of Macomb, Swift, or Levy. Barron conducted instruction in mathematics and fortifications during the morning hours, and Masson taught French and drawing in the afternoons. Wadsworth returned to West Point in the late spring of 1804. He assisted when he could, but he was frequently ordered away on inspections, and in the fall, ill health caused him to take an extended leave of absence. In effect, Barron continued in charge of the Academy—with unfortunate results. "Never was West Point so in want of you as at this moment," wrote Macomb to Williams in October 1804. "Everything is going to ruin; morals & knowledge thrive little & courts martial & flogging prevails. The military academy instead of being the seat of knowledge & the place of application is fast turning into that of ignorance & idleness."[47] When Wadsworth submitted his resignation early the next year, Barron was left in full command. The decline at West Point continued.

Barron seemed to have difficulties on every front. There were charges of irregularities in his accounts and allegations that he had neglected his duties at the Academy.[48] His fellow officers complained that he "has become so strongly infected with the pride of Command, as to believe that He is competent to form, govern & instruct a Corps."[49] Moreover, there were rumors that Barron, a bachelor, kept a woman in his quarters.[50]

All of this caused Williams to reconsider his earlier resignation. Moreover, word from every side encouraged his return. Macomb had circulated a petition among members of the Corps asking that Williams be prevailed upon to return. "It has been hinted by the President," Macomb wrote Williams, "that your return to the service would be very pleasing to him."[51] In fact, the administration had kept the lieutenant colonelcy open in just such a hope.

General James Wilkinson, the Army's commanding general and a longtime friend of Williams, strongly encouraged a reconsideration. Wilkinson, in fact, wrote three separate letters to Williams—all dated March 29. "I am authorized by the Secretary of War," began the first, "to inform you that, if agreeable to you, the President will reappoint you to the Command of the Corps of Engineers." Dearborn, however, had attached a condition: "You are not to interfere with the discipline, Police, or Command of the Troops of the Line, but by [the President's] orders to which alone you are to be subject." In his second letter Wilkinson took pains to point out that "your right of Command is held in trust by the President, & will be conferred when it may be deemed convenient to the Public Service—in the meantime you are subject to his orders only." This accommodation did hold out the prospect of command at West Point but beyond that made little concession to Williams. Still, this was as far as the administration was willing to go. "If nothing else will do," Wilkinson advised, taking a more personal tone, "silence your Military Sense, look forward to a change for the better, & in the interval avail yourself of a *little sinecure*." In the last letter, which Wilkinson marked "confidential," he nurtured Williams's long-standing dream of relocating the Academy. "It is determined to remove the Corps from West Point," he revealed, "& you may, I am persuaded, regulate its Permanent fixture. The President prefers this place [Washington] & it is the most proper—but the Expense & the shew are objections. Baltimore, Fredreck Town, & Harpers Ferry have been spoken of."[52]

Thus encouraged, Williams acquiesced and rejoined the Corps on the terms offered. But before returning to West Point, he met in Washington with Dearborn to discuss affairs of the Academy and the Corps of Engineers at large. For the most part this discussion was unremarkable, but in a private conversation the Secretary told Williams of persistent rumors that Captain Barron was keeping a woman in his quarters. An explanation was required.

When he returned to West Point, Williams learned immediately that the Secretary's information concerning Barron had been correct.[53] Still, Williams's first impression allayed his suspicions: the young woman, Sarah Dobbs, Williams reported, was "of a very decent appearance & deportment." Even so, he called Barron to his quarters and "in a very candid manner stated the suspicions that such an appearance had excited." Barron insisted that Dobbs was only his housekeeper and a strictly virtuous young woman. "On the honor of a Gentleman and a Soldier," he proclaimed, "(except for dress & external open appearance) he knew not the sex of the person in question." Williams was inclined to accept Barron's explanation and to let the matter rest. Shortly afterward, however, when others at West Point openly questioned the virtue of the woman, Barron charged them with slander and demanded a formal hearing on the matter.

Testimony before the Court of Inquiry revealed that Sarah Dobbs and a second young woman, Margaret (Peggy) Gee, the housekeeper for another officer at West Point, had "committed every degree of prostitution" with young men of the post. Moreover, while serving as Barron's housekeeper, Dobbs had carried on illicit liaisons with cadets in her room. One cadet, in fact, mistakenly crawled through the wrong window and was discovered half in and half out of Barron's parlor. Barron threw a spitting box at the head of this unfortunate lad and then gave chase, but the cadet escaped. Both Dobbs and Gee—about sixteen years of age and daughters of local families—were expelled from the post and barred from returning.

Barron professed no knowledge of the activities of these young women, and Williams, "in order to preserve [the former's] reputation from the stain of suspicion," destroyed the records of the inquiry. "Barron loves solitude," Williams had written Swift earlier that year, "and at West Point he must this year have enjoyed it in supreme degree."[54] Williams, of course, was referring to the harsh winter they had just endured and had no inkling of just why Barron might have sought and valued his seclusion.[55]

"I have endeavored to put the academy on the best footing its present means would permit," Williams reported to Dearborn some weeks after his return to duty in April 1805.[56] That included a new daily schedule that added an hour of drill led by the adjutant, Lieutenant Macomb, before breakfast, and two hours of study in quarters each afternoon. This was followed either by some period of recreation—for which sports were recommended—or by practical exercises in gunnery, surveying, or engineering.[57] He also sought and obtained permission to establish a central cadet mess. "Both pay & rations," he informed Dearborn, "are swallowed up in food" in the separate messes. "They have nothing left for clothing," he noted. A single mess, managed by a steward, would operate on "little if anything more than the present Rations" and leave the cadets with the means to dress themselves. This not only would end the frequent appeals to the War Department for special help but also would provide meals that were "regulated in quantity & quality."[58]

With Dearborn's approval a general mess was established in August. The facility chosen was a large dwelling just south of the Academy building that had been occupied by Captain George Fleming, West Point's military storekeeper, who was relocated to the valley nearer his storehouses. The mess was supervised by Barron, who, despite the recent rumors of scandal linking him and his housekeeper, had been promoted to major. A baker by the name of Morrison, who had supplied the post with bread, was engaged as mess steward. The building, when reconfigured for its new use, contained not only the kitchen and mess room but also separate quarters for Morrison and his family, and for Major Barron. The size of the structure may be judged by the fact that each set of living quarters contained a parlor, bedroom, kitchen, and dining room.[59]

Williams also sought to obtain musicians for the Academy, but with little success. Music, he believed, would "take off the monotony & give a spur to the Military Spirit." A drum and fife were essential, he told Dearborn, but a band was highly desirable—so much so that Williams volunteered to find the instruments, if only musicians could be furnished.[60] To that argument the Secretary turned a deaf ear.

In June 1805, before moving his own family back to West Point, Williams again raised the issue of relocating the Academy. If this move was imminent, he told Dearborn, he would not relocate his wife and children. He would raise no objection, he said, if the decision was made to move the school to Washington, "but if any other place be thought of," he hoped to be allowed to "freely express all proper Sentiments."[61] Dearborn responded that he "was persuaded that whenever a new site for the academy is established" it would be Washington, but he could offer no assurances as to when that might be.[62]

Williams's desire to relocate the Academy was, in part, motivated by his and his wife's fondness for city life and society. It also reflected his conviction that the Academy would fare better if it were located under the eye of Congress and the administration. But his zeal to relocate was not shared by all of his subordinates. By 1806, most had come to regard West Point as the permanent home of the Military Academy. Barron, for example, sketched out an extensive building program that included a new academic hall, a mess hall, and a new laboratory. He also proposed the extensive renovation of the old Revolutionary War "Long Barracks." This "commodious tenement," wrote Barron, was now more than adequate to accommodate all who were attached to the Academy. In addition, Barron noted the need for a number of ancillary items: apparatus for the laboratory and for engineering, a complete military library, a clock and bell, and a morning gun.[63]

Williams, however, continued to hold out hope that the Academy would be moved to Washington, and he wished to do nothing that would jeopardize that possibility.[64] Expenditures on the scale that Barron recommended would almost certainly fix the location. To forestall this, Williams wrote Dearborn in May 1806 that he considered "West Point as a temporary Station for the Corps of Engineers & military academy." Short-term expedients, therefore, were all that he would recommend: repairs to make the first floor of the academy building suitable for temporary use and minor renovations of the old barracks to accommodate the cadets. He also renewed his request of the year before for musicians or even a band.[65]

Dearborn approved the temporary measures, ordering Fleming to proceed with the required repairs of the barracks, the Academy, and various officer's quarters. The Secretary added the mandate that "no greater expense would be laid out upon them than is absolutely necessary to render them comfortable."[66]

The issue of the permanent location of the Military Academy aside, Williams could have taken justifiable pride in many developments at West Point. The buildings were being put in order, if only for temporary use, and the Academy had graduated fifteen cadets in 1806—more than in all the previous years combined.

Late that year, however, Williams, who had been absent much of the time supervising the construction of fortifications, received new and distressing reports concerning Barron's conduct at West Point. In November, Macomb wrote that he had just been informed of "a thousand things which have happened & do happen at West Point in your absence." He reported that "Gees of *notorious fame* were the companions of your second officer and that those who were by your orders expelled from the Point were not only permitted to return but to take a seat at your second officer's table."[67] Williams was furious. "I shall . . . pursue the same steps I took relative to a former professor of Mathematics also named Baron who was disgracefully discharged," he wrote Macomb in return. Still, the matter required some discretion.[68] "This affair is a delicate & a very painful one," he wrote Dearborn. "There is a disgrace in publicity that [for the sake of the institution] I wish it were possible to avoid."[69]

In January 1807, when confronted with the charges against him, Barron admitted that it had been foolish to allow Peggy Gee to return and to remain for months at a time, but he continued to insist that otherwise he was innocent. This time, however, his protests were not enough. Barron was linked, by testimony of a number of officers and cadets not only to Gee—and Dobbs before her—but also to a number of women of questionable reputation whom he had allowed to frequent West Point. At first, Barron demanded another formal inquiry, but in March, when faced with the evidence arrayed against him, he agreed simply to resign and thus to put an end to the matter. The mess steward, Morrison, and his family, who were also implicated in the affair, were likewise required to leave West Point. After that, the general military mess that they had operated was closed.[70] Henceforth, the cadets were assigned to board in small messes arranged with local families—an arrangement that continued until 1813, when a central mess was again organized in the same facility.

Barron's position was filled by Ferdinand R. Hassler, who had been appointed in February 1807, anticipating the major's imminent departure.[71] Hassler, a Swiss mathematician, had an excellent reputation and was a significant addition to the staff. When increased demands on the engineers prevented Williams from effectively overseeing affairs at West Point, he ordered Captain Joseph Gardner Swift to West Point. Under Swift's direction the Academy ran smoothly during 1807. In part this reflected Williams's advice to Swift. The "leading principle," he told the young officer, was to require "a gentlemanlike deportment towards" the professors by all concerned, and "in this particular," he cautioned Swift, "the example of the commanding officer has more influence than any orders whatever."[72]

Of course, not everything went so well, and the example of the commanding officer did not penetrate to all members of the West Point community. An altercation in one of the new separate messes between a cadet and an enlisted waiter initiated a chain of difficulties. The culprit, Cadet Samuel Rathbone, struck the waiter repeatedly for failing to obey his order. For this inappropriate behavior Rathbone drew the ire of his fellow cadets, who decided to punish him by denying him all social intercourse—"sending him to Coventry." Any cadet who did not comply was similarly threatened with silence. Williams objected. As he explained, "Putting any one into Coventry . . . is done in armies only in cases where there is some personal disgrace of Character or Conduct, which renders a Man unworthy of Society, although not of a nature to be cognizable by Law." This case, Williams insisted, was cognizable by martial law and could be handled accordingly. Under this circumstance he would not allow "self erected Censors" to prevail. "Nothing of that kind shall ever be permitted on this Ground," he added, and forced the cadets to relent.[73]

The threat of war with England in 1807–1808 and the subsequent expansion of the Army produced an unexpected opportunity for Williams to renew his call for an enlargement of the Academy—and again to argue for its transfer to Washington. In fact, the President intimated to him that both would be welcomed.[74] Williams submitted the plan in draft to Jefferson and incorporated in the final proposal the suggestions of both the President and Dearborn. "It never can be supposed," he argued, that members of the Corps of Engineers were axiomatically "efficient elementary teachers." Instead, he proposed adding three permanent professorships that could be drawn either from the corps or from among civilian academics: a professor of natural and experimental philosophy, a professor of mathematics, and a professor of the art of engineering. In addition, the proposal added a total of five assistant professors and teachers who would usually be drawn from among the engineer officers. He also proposed occasional instruction in architecture, chemistry, and mineralogy to be given by visiting civilian professors, as well as training in riding and swordsmanship by a part-time instructor.[75] Assured that the move to Washington would be approved, he also recommended an appropriation "for the proper building, apparatus, library, &c." This, he argued, "being once well done," would "not [be] subject to repetition."[76]

In spite of a strong endorsement by the President, Congress provided no augmentation of the Corps of Engineers, no provision for permanent professors at the Military Academy, no appropriation for new facilities, and no action on the request to move the school to Washington. It did, however, increase the number of cadets authorized from 44 to 200.[77] With the expansion of the Army, the administration had requested that cadets be appointed for each of the added artillery companies, including the new light artillery. Congress went further and authorized cadets in all branches—artillery, cavalry, and infantry, a total of 156 new cadets. Interestingly, this growth in the Academy had little to do with plans and proposals that had been formulated at West Point. Rather, it reflected a response to the nation's growing troubles with England and, in a significant sense, an endorsement of the Academy that Williams had nurtured.

Neither Williams nor the administration was pleased with this result. For one thing, Williams's plans to relocate the Academy and reform its faculty had been ignored. For another, Dearborn had not asked for cadets of infantry and cavalry, and after they were authorized, he did not appoint any. He summed up the administration's concern at the beginning of the next session of the Congress in December 1808: the administration had appointed the new artillery cadets authorized, but "no other appointments of Cadets can with propriety be made until the site for the Academy is established and provision made for the reception of the additional number" now authorized. The administration then resubmitted Williams's proposals, but to no avail.

In the years that immediately followed, these proposals were resubmitted regularly by Jefferson and then by Madison, with similar results. Congress showed little interest in augmenting the Academy and no willingness to agree on any other location for the school—although many were proposed. It was not until the country began to move toward war in 1812 that any positive congressional action was forthcoming. That emergency provoked long-overdue reform, but even then there was no consensus about where the Academy should be located—and that effectively fixed the site at West Point.

In April 1808, Williams had been required to assume personal direction of the construction of the harbor defenses of New York City. He left Lieutenant Alden Partridge in day-to-day charge of the Academy and the thirty-five cadets who reported for duty at the commencement of the new term. As it turned out, Williams would never again resume immediate control over the Academy for any extended period.

Partridge, an 1806 graduate, had been retained at West Point after he was commissioned and was made an assistant professor of mathematics. He remained at the Academy for more than a decade—often in charge of its operation. It was a period of great turbulence, often (but certainly not always) attributable to Partridge.

Part of the turmoil arose from the constant coming and going of the Academy's small faculty. Christian Zoeller was appointed in 1808 as a teacher of drawing. This freed Francis Masson from his classes in this subject (he had, since 1803, been teaching both French and drawing) and allowed him to add instead instruction in military engineering. In 1809, Ferdinand Hassler, the mathematics instructor, resigned after just two years. His departure meant that Partridge alone had to carry the heavy load of mathematics instruction. His administration of the Academy was further complicated in 1810 when Zoeller resigned and Masson went abroad for a period of study, leaving his brother Florimond to assume his duties.

More uneasiness came from the repeated contests with the administration and Congress. Williams unburdened himself to Jared Mansfield, beginning with his old complaint: "The military academy is at present in a miserable state resulting from an Absurd Condition in its original creation *'that it shall be stationed at West Point'*. . . . My zeal is almost burnt out, and without the fuel of public patronage it will certainly be extinguished."[78] The school had enjoyed the regular patronage of Dearborn and Jefferson, but that was not to be the case with the new President, James Madison, and his first Secretary of War, William Eustis. Eustis was a veteran of the Revolutionary War, but he had been a surgeon—sometimes attached to General Washington's personal staff—not a line officer. Likewise, his service in the House of Representatives (1801–1805) provided him with little useful experience. Eustis brought neither talent nor inclination to the job. "We stand in need of the talents of a Knox or a Pickering as head of the War Department," opined a friend of Williams, shortly before the new administration took office.[79] Instead they got William Eustis.

Although Eustis has often been portrayed as hostile to the Military Academy—for he does seem almost to have destroyed it—there was an ambivalence (or ineptness) in his decisions that belied outright hostility. Rather, his actions reveal a lack of policy direction admixed with indecision and incompetence. At one moment he would seemingly attack the Academy, the next, he appeared to act in its behalf. In 1809, Eustis ordered troops of the line to West Point, crowding the cadets out of their barracks, and then toyed with the pay of the civilian faculty. Just months later he attempted to persuade Mansfield to return to West Point to teach—proclaiming the "importance of the institution."[80] The next year he established the first regulations requiring that cadets should have a solid background in reading, writing, and mathematics before appointment; then, just a month later, he dictated that all cadets serve an apprenticeship as privates in their companies before being considered for commissions. Although he was soon persuaded to reverse this decision, it reinforced the conviction that his intentions were malevolent.[81] A brief visit to West Point by Eustis in July 1810 did nothing to alter this impression.[82]

In November 1810, he reassured Williams of continued administration support for the institution, and then, within six months, ordered almost the entire corps of cadets away from West Point. After that, the Academy lay dormant for over a year (mid-1811 to early 1813)—at times with neither faculty nor cadets. Yet, as if to confound the critics, Eustis and the administration were all the while actively supporting a plan to augment the school along the lines laid out by Williams in 1808. And they pushed such a bill through Congress in June 1812.

This on-again, off-again support (or hostility) frustrated Williams and all those at West Point. "I totally despair," Williams wrote in 1810, "of any alteration that will raise the Academy to that state which the honor of the nation and the advantage of the Army indispensably require."[83] Even the augmentation of the Academy in 1812 could not rouse his spirits, for it failed his primary objective—moving the Academy to Washington. Nor did the administration's efforts encourage his trust in or respect for Eustis. There were, he wrote Swift, "many reasons I have to detest the domination of William Eustis." Williams would not be obliged "to respect a man for whom I cannot have a shade of respect," nor would he receive "orders founded in ignorance, and dictated with petulance."[84] Williams tendered his resignation in July 1812, and the administration accepted it. Eustis was forced out not long after.

President Madison appointed Joseph Gardner Swift, who had risen to be Williams's second-in-command, to the vacant colonelcy in engineers. Swift had been the first graduate of the Military Academy in 1802 and had spent the intervening years supervising the construction of harbor defense fortifications and occasionally teaching mathematics at the Academy. Now, despite being actively engaged in the field throughout the second war with England, he displayed a strong interest in reviving the school. The vehicle, of course, was "An Act Making Further Provision for the Corps of Engineers," signed into law by Madison on April 29, 1812. In many respects this act provided everything that the men of West Point had been seeking, and more—save the move to Washington that had been an obsession with Williams. In addition to the teachers of French and drawing already provided for, the act authorized a professor of natural and experimental philosophy, a professor of mathematics, and a professor of the art of engineering. Moreover, assistant professors were provided for each subject. The law further stated that cadets would thereafter be appointed "in the service of the United States" instead of as members of a specific regiment or corps. Now, cadets were to be organized into companies of noncommissioned officers and privates. They were to be encamped at least three months each summer. They were to be between the ages of fifteen and twenty upon admission and were to be well versed in reading, writing, and arithmetic. Each was to be given a degree upon completion of his examinations and then commissioned "in any Corps, according to the duties he may be judged competent to perform." Finally, the act authorized four musicians per cadet company and appropriated $25,000 for buildings, academic and engineering apparatus, and a library.[85]

In the fall of 1812, despite the initiation of hostilities with the British, the first concrete steps were taken to reactivate the Academy. Before leaving office, Eustis approved preliminary plans and contracts for a new barracks, a mess hall, and an academy building and approved recruiting a new faculty.

Swift reported to Monroe, the Acting Secretary of War, in December 1812 that "some of the Academic Staff, officers, and cadets are appointed" and that he intended to "commence the Military Academy prior to the 1st April 1813." Andrew Ellicott, one of the nation's foremost surveyors, accepted the professorship of mathematics. Ellicott brought a measure of national acclaim to the faculty; his precise astronomical observations and careful calculations had elevated American surveying and cartography to a new level of precision. He continued at West Point until his death in 1820. Partridge, in addition to his administrative duties, was made professor of engineering. Zoeller returned and was reappointed as drawing instructor. Florimond Masson, who had earlier substituted for his brother, was now appointed in his own right as instructor of the French language. Swift also persuaded Jared Mansfield to return to the Academy to occupy the chair of professor of natural

Joseph Gardner Swift. Gardner was Superintendent of the United States Military Academy from 1812 to 1814. Painted in 1829 by Thomas Sully (1783–1872). West Point Museum Collection, United States Military Academy.

and experimental philosophy. Mansfield accepted but postponed his arrival until August 1814—and came then only under the threat of dismissal.[86]

As Swift had promised, the school began to function again with the spring term of 1813. "I find [the Academy] in as good condition as could be expected after laying dormant so long," Swift reported to John Armstrong, Madison's new Secretary of War.[87] Still, he was not altogether satisfied with the organization of the Academy or with the changes that Williams had sought and the Congress had finally authorized. In 1808, he had made his own recommendations to Williams, and in many respects they went well beyond those of his superior. In addition to the mathematics, natural philosophy, and engineering that Williams had sought—and which the Congress provided in 1812—Swift recommended instruction in ancient and modern history, geography, morality, and, on a different plane, fencing and dance.[88]

In formulating this earlier plan, Swift was motivated by the belief that army officers had to be more than narrowly trained military technicians. His own experience convinced him that officers had to work closely with civil authorities—national, state, and local—and that these officials generally represented the best-educated and most socially influential segments of the population. Swift came from a respected New England family and was at ease in any company, but not all cadets enjoyed this advantage. This was particularly true of many of Jefferson's Republican sons.[89]

In 1813, Swift moved to incorporate his own ideas into the growing curriculum. He secured the assignment of Adam Empie as both chaplain and acting professor of geography, history, and ethics. The next year he obtained Pierre Thomas as swordmaster.

For the most part, however, his efforts ran afoul of both the demands of the ongoing war with England and the inclinations of Captain Alden Partridge, nominal head of the Academy during Swift's frequent, extended absences—just as he had been earlier under Williams. Qualified officers were needed immediately to meet the needs of an expanding Army. The War Department demanded that as soon as "a tolerable knowledge of books indicate the fitness of a young man for an Ensigncy and Lieutenancy" his name be transmitted to them, and that he be commissioned.[90] In any case, Partridge proved more interested in drilling the cadets than in providing classroom instruction, and here he utilized the musicians authorized in 1812. By 1816 there were eighteen musicians assigned at West Point, providing both traditional company music—fife and drum—and a small military band.[91]

By the end of July 1814—barely a year after the Military Academy had returned to full operation—thirty cadets had been commissioned. The course of study implied by the law of 1812 and expanded upon by Swift was set aside before it had even been put into practice.

A contract for the construction of the new buildings was signed in the fall of 1812 with builder Jacob Halsey and mason Thomas J. Woodruff. Final approval from the War Department, however, was delayed repeatedly as the war went from bad to worse in 1812 and 1813.[92] Construction was finally ordered to begin at West Point in the spring of 1814.

In the meantime, the old Long Barracks was once more renovated, and 100 of the 160 cadets then at the Academy were billeted there. The balance were quartered in other locations around the post. Classes had long since outgrown the original frame Academy and were held wherever space could be found—sometimes in the professors' quarters.

The new barracks and mess hall were ready to receive cadets by the spring of 1815, and the Academy building was finished later the same year. All three buildings were constructed of rough gray granite with slate roofs. The three-story barracks was a long, narrow building with modest wings at each end. Its core contained forty-eight small, two-man rooms for the cadets, while the wings at each end featured small suites generally used by the bachelor officers. This building, soon known as South Barracks, was located on the southern boundary of the Plain.

The mess hall, or refectory, was located in line with South Barracks, near the southwest corner of the Plain. It was a two-story building with mess rooms on both floors, a kitchen, and quarters for the steward. The mess hall was enlarged in 1823, when a larger kitchen was added to the rear of the original structure, with rooms on the second floor for the staff of the mess.

The two-story Academy was located between South Barracks and the mess hall. On the first floor were the engineering room, the chapel, and the chemistry laboratory. Above them were the Adjutant's office, the library, and the philosophical department. These three buildings established the continuing tradition of bounding the Plain on the south with the Academy's major edifices.

In December 1815, Swift reported to Monroe that the buildings had been completed and the Academy now needed a second barracks. In addition, he reported, they required new quarters for the Superintendent, the professors, and the other married officers—a total of six new sets of quarters. He also suggested a chapel and a new hospital.[93] Swift's request for an additional barracks was approved the next year, as were three sets of quarters, but the balance of the proposed construction was postponed.

Quarters for the officers at West Point were in such short supply during the early years that families were usually required to share houses. That custom was perpetuated by the construction, beginning in 1819, of duplex structures (referred to as "doubles"), which soon became the norm. The arrival of each new officer precipitated a crisis of greater or lesser proportions as arrangements had to be made to house them. When Jared Mansfield returned with his family in 1814, they were assigned to share a set of quarters with Dr. Samuel Walsh, the post surgeon—the same quarters, in fact, that they had held alone years before. Dr. Walsh had been told to clear the south part of the house, but, having guests, had not done so. When notified that the Mansfields had arrived, he rushed to the dock and told the professor that "he was sorry," but he could not admit them just then "as he had company, & could not spare any part of the house." When Mansfield insisted, Walsh angrily relented but heaped abuse on the professor, his family, and his servants. That ill-treatment continued for several days, until Mansfield threatened to have the surgeon arrested.[94]

The first new officers' quarters were located along the west edge of the Plain, on a line roughly perpendicular to that of the barracks, Academy, and mess hall. Contracts for the first three sets were made with John Forsyth of Newburgh in January 1817, and the quarters were completed late that year. The Superintendent's house and others were added just a few years later on the same line. The new quarters—two-story brick structures with eleven finished rooms—were "commodious and pleasant," wrote Elizabeth Mansfield. She complained, however, that the kitchen was located in the basement and often smoked intolerably, filling "every part of the house."[95] She also complained of losing the view afforded by her old quarters. "I should prefer keeping this [her old quarters] and having it put in repair," she wrote before moving, for the old quarters looked north up the Hudson, through the ancient gap the river had etched between the massive Storm King and Breakneck. "You can have no idea," she wrote, "of the beauty and grandeur of the scenery as you view it from this house in the summer."[96] Still, she moved.

The second barracks, somewhat larger than the first, was erected in 1817. It was located to the north and at a right angle with the earlier barracks and extended out into the Plain. This structure, known as North Barracks, was designed by Claude Crozet, who was assigned to the faculty in late 1816. It was four stories high, provided forty large, four-man rooms, and was constructed of the same rough gray stone as the earlier buildings. The mason was Thomas Woodruff, who had been engaged on the previous buildings; the carpenter, John Morse of New York City. The two barracks provided sufficient billeting for the entire corps of cadets for more than thirty years. These "public edifices" were "without any pretension to architectural embellishment, but solid and substantial," reported the *London Quarterly Journal*. Strangely, it was the aging Long Barracks that most pleased the eye of

North Barracks, 1817. An elevation drawn from the plans in 1885 by Cadet Albert D. Niskern (Kniskern), class of 1886. West Point Museum Collection, United States Military Academy.

that critic; although it was "entirely destitute of ornament," he opined that the wooden structure had "more architectural beauty of form than any other building on the Point."[97]

From 1807 to 1815, Lieutenant (and then Captain) Alden Partridge provided what continuity there was in the administration of the Academy. As the senior engineer officer at West Point, he assumed command during the frequent absences of the Superintendents—who at that time were also the Chiefs of Engineers. He had enjoyed the full confidence of both Williams and Swift. Having joined the faculty upon his graduation in 1806, he had spent his whole Army career at West Point.

Although he had held the title of professor of engineering since 1812, Partridge had little interest in purely academic affairs, preferring instead the more narrowly military subjects. "He was passionately fond of drilling," recalled one graduate, but he made even this interesting by "forming diminutive armies and fighting over renowned battles." These were "always accompanied by an intelligible and interesting lecture" showing "how fields were won." He was a rigid disciplinarian and sometimes prone to favoritism, but he was popular with the cadets.

Partridge was not, however, popular with his faculty colleagues. He was jealous of his prerogatives and first grew to resent being subordinated to anyone but the chief engineer and finally came to resent even that authority. Still, his accomplishments at West Point were not insignificant. The school, under his immediate supervision since 1808, struggled along beneath a burden of barely adequate appropriations, as well as wholly inadequate facilities and staff. But it had survived. By 1815, these problems were largely overcome, and Partridge was convinced that these successes were due primarily to his efforts.

Partridge soon embarked on a campaign to make himself the unquestioned master and guiding force of the Academy. In late 1814, he began by drafting new regulations for the administration of the Academy—regulations that would put him firmly in charge. Then, in early January 1815, without Swift's knowledge or permission, he carried the draft regulations to Washington and obtained the blessing of James Monroe, who had once again assumed the responsibilities of Secretary of War. There were four key provisions of the new regulations. First, a permanent Superintendent would report directly to the Secretary of War. Second, the Chief Engineer's authority and responsibilities relative to the Military Academy were restricted to a point where he became little more than an inspector for the Secretary of War. Third, the Superintendent was empowered to determine when cadets

Captain Alden Partridge was Superintendent of the United States Military Academy from 1814 to 1817. Painted by Charles Rosen (1878–1950). West Point Museum Collection, United States Military Academy.

were prepared for commissions, and which corps they should join. Finally, the authority of the Superintendent was to be unchallenged at West Point—even upon the assignment there of a more senior officer.

At West Point the reaction to Partridge's efforts was as immediate as it was predictable. Even while Partridge was seeking Monroe's approval of his new proposals, his colleagues at the Academy penned a joint letter to the Secretary denouncing him. They complained that he had failed to follow the practices prescribed in the act of 1812 either in examining new cadets prior to accepting them or in recommending those further along for commissions. He had made the process dependent upon "favor, or friendship," not qualification, they complained.[98] These objections, of course, were red herrings. The real issue was the faculty's desire for the power to influence events and refusal to be excluded from the decision-making process.

When Swift added his objections to Partridge's plan—and to Monroe's failure to consult with him—the Secretary suspended the new regulations "until General Swift's opinion can be known."[99] Though in general agreement with Partridge's proposals, Swift was emphatically opposed to those aspects of the regulations that stripped away his authority. "The Military Academy shall be under my control," he wrote Professor Ellicott, "or I will have nothing to do with it."[100]

When he heard of Swift's opposition, Partridge assured him that he had not intended to cause friction but strongly reasserted his own case. "I think Sir that the experience acquired in more than six years constant duty in it, and performing the duties of Superintendent for more than five years, ought to afford me data tolerably accurate to ascertain what will be for its advantage."[101]

Swift, however, prevailed, and the new regulations were amended, restoring the Chief Engineer's responsibility for, and authority over, the permanent Superintendent. On the basis of the amended regulations, approved February 21, 1815, Partridge was appointed Superintendent.

Partridge's elevation to the superintendency did little, of course, to eliminate friction with the faculty. "You must come and reside here," wrote Ellicott to Swift, arguing that "in my opinion it is necessary both for the reputation of this institution, and the welfare of our country." Partridge was "almost unrivalled in the management of Cadets," Ellicott admitted, but strongly intimated that his authority should be confined to that area.[102]

Mansfield, who chafed under Partridge's close supervision, shared Ellicott's opinion and actively led the opposition to Partridge at West Point. "Mr. Ellicott & myself have had the mortification daily of receiving visits from the Superintendent" he said. They were "inspected, watched & looked in with an eye of suspicion" that was calculated "to bring us into contempt with our pupils," Mansfield complained.[103]

Jared Mansfield was instructor of mathematics from 1802 to 1803, and later a professor in the Department of Natural and Experimental Philosophy from 1812 to 1828. Painted by Thomas Sully (1783–1872). West Point Museum Collection, United States Military Academy.

Mansfield, and to a lesser degree Ellicott, kept up a steady stream of complaints to members of Congress, the Secretary of War, and the President. By early 1816, the cumulative effect of criticism was beginning to tell in Washington. In February, President Madison informed Swift that he wanted Partridge's resignation. Swift, however, argued that such precipitous action would be unfair. When the issue was again raised by Secretary of War William H. Crawford, who had replaced Monroe, Swift argued that there were few officers qualified for the duty—and none who would voluntarily take the post. For a time the matter was allowed to drop.[104]

By late 1816, however, the administration made the final decision to remove Partridge. Swift, who had been his champion, was not consulted on this issue. In September, French mathematician Claude Crozet, a graduate of the Polytechnique School in Paris, was appointed to fill the professorship of engineering that Partridge had vacated in assuming the superintendency. In November, Brevet Major Sylvanus Thayer, class of 1808, who was in France inspecting the French military establishment and schools, was informed that he "had been designated by President Madison to be permanent Superintendent of the academy and that he was to return in the Spring of 1817 to assume that duty."[105] Thayer, then thirty-one years old, had served for two years as an assistant professor of mathematics. During the recent war, he had made a name for himself as an engineer, including his successful planning and execution of the defense of Norfolk, Virginia.

At West Point, where the officers were unaware of the administration's maneuvering, the lines between Partridge and the academic staff became ever more sharply drawn during the winter of 1816–1817. Only Swift's decision to take quarters at West Point kept the situation there in check. Partridge was seemingly blind to everything but his own desire to rule. He wholly misunderstood the cause of the opposition to him and completely misjudged its extent. In an effort to right matters, he repeatedly sought to increase his own control over affairs at the Academy—a course that only made matters worse. He could not understand the position or the attitude of the faculty and complained frequently to Swift of being thwarted by them. He could see no remedy but greater authority for himself and new and more stringent regulations for the governance of the school.

During the spring, as the situation deteriorated further, Swift departed for Washington to attend James Monroe's inauguration. Swift had great respect for the new President. Monroe has "done more for the Corps than ever has been done before put all together from 1802 to 1814," Swift had said.[106] But in Washington, Swift discovered that he had not been consulted on many key decisions dealing with West Point in recent months. Instead, Monroe had personally decided many issues. "Major Thayer may be ordered to West Point for the purpose of Superintending," Swift was now informed—the first he knew of Thayer's candidacy for the post. In addition, he discovered that the new President was going to visit and inspect West Point on an upcoming swing through the Northeast. While at the Military Academy, Monroe intended to make "such arrangements as may be proper for its future government." In the meantime, Swift was instructed, "no other alterations will be made in relation to it."[107] Swift's continued support of Partridge had seemingly cost him the confidence of the new administration in matters related to the Academy.

Monroe's stay at West Point lasted for three days, during which time he was introduced to the faculty and officers of the Academy and received orally and in writing their complaints against Partridge. Mansfield discussed the problem at length with the President, with apparent effect; Monroe ordered that a court-martial examine the charges brought against Partridge. In the face of the administration's clear determination to oust Partridge, Swift was now forced to withdraw his patronage.

Partridge was to be replaced by Thayer upon the latter's arrival at West Point. No one, however, informed Partridge, and that oversight led to unnecessary misunderstanding and bitterness.

CHAPTER FOUR

Sylvanus Thayer: Father of the Military Academy, 1817–1833

Sylvanus Thayer served as Superintendent of the Military Academy for sixteen years—under Presidents James Monroe, John Quincy Adams, and Andrew Jackson. With Monroe and his Secretaries of War, he enjoyed complete support from Washington, and in that eight years he made the little mathematics academy he had inherited into an engineering school of renown. His last eight years, however, were marked by increasing conflict with Adams and then outright hostility from Jackson. Despite this, Thayer instigated an academic program and succession of leadership at West Point so remarkable that they assured his lasting influence.[1]

Sylvanus Thayer arrived at West Point on July 28, 1817, and presented the orders placing him in command. The disbelieving Partridge departed on leave but refused to accept dismissal from his post.

Before coming to West Point, Thayer had been instructed that he should work closely with the faculty. President Monroe, on his recent visit, had spent several days listening to faculty members' complaints about Partridge's failure to consult with them, and he was in no mood for a repetition of that performance. To ensure that Thayer understood, George Graham, the Acting Secretary of War, dispatched written instructions that were delivered shortly after Thayer's arrival. Thayer was to consult with his faculty and submit recommendations based on their advice to the War Department concerning the division of cadets into classes, the courses of study each class should pursue, the texts that should be employed, and the number of assistant professors required.[2] The faculty in late 1817 included Jared Mansfield, Professor of Natural and Experimental Philosophy; Andrew Ellicott, Professor of Mathematics; Claude Crozet, Professor of Engineering; Christian Zoeller, teacher of drawing; and Claudius Berard, teacher of French. In addition, Thayer soon detailed Second Lieutenant George Gardiner, class of 1814, as instructor of infantry tactics and soldierly discipline, making him responsible for the interior police and administration of the Academy.

In obedience to his instructions, Thayer drafted a memorandum asking each professor to sketch out a program for his department, "specifying the branches to be taught, the time required for each, and the books which shall serve as guides." Thayer outlined a rough daily routine for the school: "principal studies" from eight o'clock to twelve-thirty or one o'clock, followed by French and drawing from two to four o'clock. In addition, he notified the faculty that in the future cadets should be admitted to the Academy only once each year, and that they should be arranged into regular classes and advanced to the next higher class only at the general examinations. He concluded on a reassuring note: "I have thus given you the outlines of my hasty and desultory reflection on some of the means of better organizing the instruction of this institution." But he had done so, he said, "not with an idea that the opinions here advanced are the most correct, but with the view to invite a discussion of the subject and to elicit your opinion thereon. This business is new to me and I rely with pleasure on the superior judgment of the learned professors."[3] Thayer's approach to the faculty stood in stark but welcome contrast to that of Partridge.

The difference was all the more clear when, on August 28, barely a month after his departure from West Point, Major Partridge returned. The cadets, who by now had been ordered back to West Point, welcomed him enthusiastically. A small group, waiting idly by the landing when Partridge arrived, rushed to meet him and escorted him noisily up the hill. There more cadets crowded around and wildly cheered his return.

Partridge immediately sought out Thayer and asked to be allowed to use his former quarters. Thayer refused, however, because the house had been cleaned and reassigned; it was now occupied by Captain David B. Douglass, Assistant Professor of Mathematics. The next morning Partridge renewed his request for his old lodgings, arguing that by virtue of his rank the quarters belonged to him. Again Thayer refused. Partridge then wrote out an order by which he assumed command of the Military Academy once again and handed it to Thayer. Thayer chose not to argue the point but merely observed that he would not resign of his own will. If Partridge insisted on assuming command in the face of the orders that had brought Thayer there, then the responsibility would be Partridge's. Thayer walked to his quarters and wrote out a quick report of the affair to Swift, the Chief of Engineers, who was then in New York. He mailed the letter, went straight to the wharf, and hailed the first sloop heading for the city.

Partridge ordered the corps paraded and listened in delight as the cadets cheered the order announcing his resumption of command. It was a short-lived victory, however. A few days later, Swift's aide-de-camp arrived at West Point with Thayer, and with orders restoring Thayer to command. Swift himself arrived shortly thereafter and soon ordered the usurper to Governor's Island. Partridge, however, tarried at West Point, using as an excuse the difficulty of

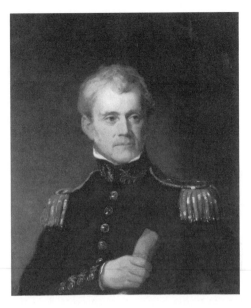

Sylvanus Thayer was Superin-
tendent of the United States
Military Academy from 1817
to 1833. West Point Museum
Collection, United States
Military Academy.

collecting his furniture and papers. When he did depart on the evening of
September 10, the cadets escorted him to the dock, shouting and cheering.
Right behind them marched the post band, which, against Thayer's explicit
instructions, joined in giving Partridge a rousing send-off. Thayer wrote op-
timistically to Swift reporting the affair: "All has gone well here since you left
us, and I have reason to believe that I shall have no more difficulties."[4]

At his court-martial, Partridge was found guilty of disobedience to orders and mutiny. He was sentenced to be cashiered, but in light of the "zeal
and perseverance" he had brought to "his professional duties," the court
recommended to President Monroe that the punishment be remitted. The
President accepted the recommendation for clemency and directed that
Partridge report to Swift for reassignment. Partridge, however, was too
embittered. He chose instead to resign. Throughout the rest of his life he
was relentless in his attacks on Thayer and the Academy at West Point.

As soon as Partridge departed, Thayer began to consolidate the reports he
had requested from the various members of the faculty. He soon prepared a
new plan of study, which was forwarded to Washington and quickly approved
by both General Swift and the Secretary of War.

The stipulation that Thayer obtain faculty concurrence in the recommendations he sent forward marks the true inception of the Academic Board

as it has existed until only recently—empowered by law, regulation, and tradition with the authority to establish the Academy's course of instruction and manage its academic affairs. Though Congress had specified in 1812 that the "Academical Staff" should confer degrees upon cadets who had completed their classes and identify those who should receive commissions, the board had never functioned in either capacity under Partridge. Thayer soon established the duties and composition of the Academic Board in the Academy's regulations—which were in turn approved by the Secretary of War. It was, wrote Thayer, the duty of the board "to report to the secretary of war, on the system of studies and instruction, proposing for his approbation such additional rules and regulations for perfecting the same, and such improvements in those already existing, as experience may have suggested." The board was made up of "the professors of natural philosophy, mathematics, engineering, [chemistry], and ethics; . . . the principal teacher of French; the teacher of drawing; the instructor of tactics, and instructor of artillery; [and] the superintendent [who] shall always be president."[5] The scope of the Academic Board's influence as defined by the regulations is remarkable, for in addition to its academic duties—curriculum, texts, examinations, merit and standing, degrees and diplomas—the board could recommend changes or additions to regulations that governed any area of the Academy, and make these recommendations directly to the Secretary of War. It was a dramatic change from Partridge's near-dictatorial regime, but it was also a remarkable sharing of power in any circumstance.

"On securing the command I made a new organization of the studies, and commenced a system of reformation which was indispensable and required rigorous measures which were not very pleasing to the cadets," Thayer wrote his brother-in-law, the Reverend Josiah Moulton, shortly after Partridge's final departure. The first step in instituting the new program was a general examination of the cadets. The results were revealing: a number of cadets had made little, if any, progress in their studies, though some had been at the Academy under Partridge for several years. A number of others were judged incapable of completing the course satisfactorily, and twenty-one were recommended for removal. "I am now continuing my course of reformation, have dismissed some Cadets, suspended others, and shall persevere until I produce that state of Military discipline which is as indispensable in an institution of this nature as in a regular Army."[6]

To those who remained, Thayer drove home the point that indiscipline and neglect of studies would no longer be tolerated.[7] He then ordered the faculty to prepare weekly reports on the progress of their classes—noting in particular those cadets who had neglected their lessons or who had not made suitable progress. In support of Thayer, General Swift informed the cadets bluntly that "implicit obedience was their only course" in response to the new regime, and he directed Thayer "to dismiss from the institution with promptness any offender."[8]

Instruction began again at the conclusion of the examinations in accordance with the curriculum Thayer and the faculty had devised. But difficulties were encountered almost immediately when Professor Crozet found that the cadets had not been taught descriptive geometry and therefore were not yet ready for the formal engineering program he had prepared. Immediate adjustments to the program were required. After quick consultations with Thayer and the Academic Board, Crozet revised his course to include instruction in that new branch of mathematics. There was no textbook available, but, said Edward Mansfield, son of Professor Jared Mansfield, "we had what was better. We had Claude Crozet, a large black-board and chalk, with the drawings of the Polytechnique Institute. We were compelled to adopt the old Greek method or oral instruction, and it is the best."[9]

In December 1817, Thayer ordered another round of examinations. The results were as good as could be expected, he wrote John C. Calhoun, the new Secretary of War. His only real disappointment was in the area of French language. He attributed the problem here to the need for an additional instructor, a position he had already been authorized to fill and for which he was seeking candidates.[10]

The new Superintendent had ingratiated himself with the faculty, but to cadets he remained "a most mysterious personage." In his early years as Superintendent, Thayer was not at all popular with the cadets—especially with those who had been at West Point under Partridge. "We had seen Capt. Partridge everywhere and on all occasions," wrote one graduate, but "Thayer we never saw."[11] They complained incessantly about the discipline and challenged his system whenever the occasion allowed—but to no avail. There were even personal affronts. Once, when Thayer was offering advice to a graduating cadet about his choice of corps—engineer, artillery, cavalry, or infantry—the young man cut him off, saying, "Major Thayer, when I want your advice I'll ask you for it!"[12]

In his first years as Superintendent, Thayer charged the lack of discipline among the cadets to Partridge. When he faced a seeming mutiny of the corps of cadets in 1818—orchestrated by the same cadets who had so joyfully welcomed Partridge back to the post the year before—he attributed their rebelliousness to Partridge's continuing influence. Then, in later years, he blamed the discipline problems on a lack of support from the Adams and Jackson administrations—particularly the latter.

The 1818 affair, however, had less to do with discipline itself than with how that discipline was administered. The central figure was Captain John Bliss, class of 1811, who had replaced Gardiner as instructor of tactics. His duties included both the tactical training of the cadets and the maintenance of order. In fact, it was Bliss's reputation as a strict disciplinarian that had made him attractive to Thayer. Unfortunately his heavy-handed methods were not well suited for controlling the high-spirited, bright, and articulate cadets, and predictably, he became a focal point of cadet discontent.

The issue came to a head on November 22, 1818, when one cadet deliberately marched out of step during a parade and repeatedly ignored Bliss's injunctions to correct himself. The captain flew into a rage, stepped into the ranks, and "violently seized by the collar, shook, jerked, and publicly damned" the offender.[13]

That night, in the barracks, the cadets elected a committee of five to present their grievances to Thayer. He met briefly with the committee and explained firmly that though they had the right to make complaints as individuals, they had no right to band together to present a petition. He then dismissed them without receiving their petition. When the committee persisted, drew up new charges, and again confronted Thayer, he placed the five under arrest and then ordered them off the post. "[Their] first object," wrote the Superintendent, "was to remove Captain Bliss, . . . and [they] even dared to threaten me with rebellion, in case of a noncompliance with their wishes."[14]

The young men took their case to the War Department and to Congress but got no satisfaction. After a year's suspension, President Monroe ordered the five cadets reinstated. Thayer, however, refused to allow them to attend classes, and the rest of their class graduated without them. Angry, the five cadets resigned as a body and went back to Congress in a last vain effort to prosecute their case. A court of inquiry upheld Thayer's action, and a congressional investigation came to a similar conclusion, finding that the cadets had been both wrong and mutinous. As for Captain Bliss, Calhoun concluded that he did not possess sufficient command of his temper and ordered him transferred.

Thayer had been quick to blame Partridge's influence for these problems, and on the surface he seemed to have some justification. Four of the five agitators had been Partridge cadets, and one, Thomas Ragland, had been a Partridge favorite. Moreover, other Partridge cadets had supported the five, including Cadet Andrew Jackson Donelson, who was encouraged in his actions by the uncle (and future president) for whom he had been named.

Bliss was replaced as Commandant of Cadets by Captain John R. Bell, class of 1812; he, in turn, was replaced by Major William J. Worth, who served from 1820 to 1828, but the effort to instill discipline did not slacken.

To better deal with the problem, Thayer issued a new set of 134 regulations that more fully defined and circumscribed cadet life. Among other things, the regulations forbade cadets to go beyond the walls of West Point; be absent from their rooms without permission; cook in their quarters; play cards; miss or misbehave at Sunday service; scuffle, duel, or issue a challenge; write or publish a newspaper article concerning the Academy; write directly to the Secretary of War; ask for or receive money from relatives or friends; wear civilian clothes; organize any society or hold meetings without permission; or take more than one newspaper or periodical without permission. But the rules also forbade corporal punishment and provided that cadets could not be dismissed, or kept in close confinement for more than twelve days, unless by order of the President.[15] The gentlemen were made to understand that it was their province only to listen and obey.

Cadet discontent smoldered and then blazed up again one winter night in December 1821. The cry "Fire!" sent the cadets scrambling from their beds to man the post's primitive pumper. The mess hall was ablaze, and before they could put out the fire, most of the roof was destroyed. Only after the fire had been contained was it discovered that, while attention was focused on the fire, a loaded cannon had been dragged from the artillery park, aimed at the Superintendent's quarters, and lighted. Serious injury and damage were avoided only because the slow match, or fuse, had burned out before it reached the main powder charge. The culprits were never identified.[16]

This incident only strengthened Thayer's resolve to enforce discipline. He obtained the assignment of two additional tactical officers (Lieutenants Zebina J. D. Kinsley, class of 1819, and Henry W. Griswold, class of 1815), moved them into the North and South Barracks, and charged them and the cadet officers with responsibility for reporting cadets who disobeyed the regulations. Cadets named on their "skin list" would report to the Commandant of Cadets each day in his office. The cadets, as gentlemen and men of honor, were expected to answer truthfully any and all direct questions concerning the reports. Where doubt existed, all a cadet had to do was deny the accusation, and the report was forthwith canceled. The punishment for those found guilty was the issuance of demerits, which had to be "walked off" on guard duty in the company area. As a result, lengthy judicial procedures were largely done away with. Although some guilty parties may have thus evaded punishment, the process worked because it appealed to a profound sense of honor in which officers and cadets took particular pride. It was, in effect, an early application of the Academy's venerated honor system.

Thayer's early belief that the lack of discipline among cadets stemmed from the leniencies of the Partridge era proved unfounded, however, for discipline did not improve as the last of the so-called Partridge cadets departed West Point. Thayer's most important device in his battle for discipline was dismissal, but that weapon was blunted when so many cadets were returned to the Academy by the President or Secretary of War because of the "youth" of the offender, or because the young man's previous conduct had shown no "vicious traits." In 1825, Thayer instituted another disciplinary device, the cumulative total of demerits—a measure that would highlight repeated misconduct. Thereafter the number of demerits given a cadet each year would play a part in computing his class standing, and soon Thayer obtained approval to dismiss cadets who accumulated more than two hundred demerits in any academic year.

After a drunken and near-riotous Fourth of July celebration in 1825, Thayer decreed that there would be no more alcohol served to cadets on the post for any reason. (Cadets had up to that time been allowed to have wine at the annual Independence Day dinner they gave for the officers on the post—an infraction of his rules that Thayer had chosen to ignore by leaving the post that day.)

Discontent with Thayer's emphasis on discipline grew through the next year and reached another climax on Christmas Eve 1826. The trouble began when Cadet Jefferson Davis and a number of other Southerners invited the corps to join them in partaking of some holiday eggnog. As the night wore on, drunkenness and disorder increased. Captain Ethan Allen Hitchcock, class of 1817, the Officer of the Day, attempted to intervene. He ordered the cadets to their rooms, under arrest, but most refused. He ultimately called for reinforcements, but the tactical officers were met by a barrage of stove wood, stair railings, and chair backs—anything that could be broken up. One cadet, Walter Guion, seized a pistol and attempted to shoot Hitchcock, but the weapon misfired. Then Guion and others loaded their muskets and vowed to defend themselves. Before the affair was over, North Barracks was almost completely wrecked. Nineteen cadets, including Guion, were finally dismissed, but Davis, who had honored his arrest, was spared.[17]

Thayer was never able to achieve the level of discipline to which he aspired. His efforts brought him repeatedly into conflict with the cadets, as well as with the Jackson administration, which he often saw as undermining his actions by returning to the Academy cadets whom he had dismissed. Still, he was unbending in his effort. Thayer was by nature aloof and even cold in his official dealings, yet he was scrupulously fair, honest, and evenhanded. He was always the gentleman. There was no meanness in him—even discipline was dispensed with kindness. But these were qualities that cadets often came to admire in him only after they had left the Academy. His colleagues found a warmth in him that was seldom evident to the cadets. "With all his strictness and apparent coldness on duty," Professor Albert Church later recalled, "he had a heart as big as breast could hold."[18]

Although it was spartan at best, cadet life was not all regulations and harsh discipline. The cadet rooms were generally crowded. There was hardly room enough to spread out the narrow mattresses on which the cadets slept, for in these days they had no bedsteads. The rooms in both barracks were ventilated only by the doors and windows and a large fireplace—before which many a late-night meal was illicitly prepared. The South Barracks, in particular, was cold in the winter. Cadets at their studies there were often obliged to sit at their tables before the fire with blankets at their backs, scorching on one side and freezing on the other. Those in North Barracks fared somewhat better, but even here the fireplaces provided the only source of heat.[19]

To prevent danger from fires, each room was furnished with a large sheet-iron fender, which it was the duty of the last person leaving the room to place before the fire. Fires from neglect of this regulation were frequent, though speedily extinguished by a quick-acting cadet bucket brigade.

The cadet mess, or "cadet commons," as it was sometimes called, was reestablished in 1813 under Isaac Partridge (an uncle of Captain Partridge) in the old storekeeper's quarters. It was moved into the new mess hall when that building was completed in 1815. About that same time, however, complaints of nepotism and profiteering led to the dismissal of the senior Partridge. Robert Nichols then took over the position and ran the mess successfully until he died two years later. Thereafter it was operated by a succession of contractors who were awarded the business upon submission of the lowest bids. In 1821, William Cozzens won the contract and continued for years in that role. Cozzens served the cadets very adequate, though plain, meals—some even pronounced it excellent fare.[20] He was known particularly for the quality and quantity of bread and butter he offered. "Give young men plenty of first-rate bread, butter and potatoes," he was heard to say, "and they will require little meat, and never complain of that."[21]

A few fortunate cadets were allowed to board with Mrs. Alexander Thompson. Her husband had been the military storekeeper at West Point beginning in 1806, and when he died in 1809, his widow and their three daughters were allowed to remain in their quarters just below the level of the Plain on the road to the dock. At that time there was no organized mess, and many cadets boarded with local families, including Widow Thompson's. When the central mess was reorganized in 1813, Mrs. Thompson asked to be allowed to continue boarding cadets because it was her family's only means of support. Partridge, the Superintendent, agreed. That permission was continued by successive Superintendents until the death of the last daughter in 1878. A place at the Thompsons' table soon became an envied honor, granted to only a dozen cadets annually. Not only was the fare at the Thompsons' excellent and vastly more varied than at the mess hall, but there was no requirement to march to and from meals, nor to bolt down one's food. Here cadets enjoyed the comforts and observances of a private family at a table at which Mrs. Thompson or one or more of her daughters was always present.

Other cadets who wished to escape the plainness of the mess hall diet might—although strictly forbidden to do so—visit the public house located just steps away from the southern boundary of the post and barracks. This establishment, first operated by Thomas North and then, after 1819, by Oliver Gridley, was situated just beyond the woodyard at the rear of the barracks and was easily reached through well-concealed openings in the plank fence that marked the post boundary there. "Scarcely a night passed," one graduate recalled, "in which one or more parties [of cadets] did not enjoy the excellent suppers set forth by this enterprising host."[22] North's—or Gridley's—was so close, in fact, that when a cadet was found absent from his room by an inspector, his roommate could simply slip through the fence and warn the offender. The errant lad could return to the barracks, report to the inspector within the authorized ten minutes, and then, if he dared, go back and resume his supper. But supper was not all that these innkeepers served; cadets in search of strong liquid refreshment also found it at this abode.

Thayer did everything in his power to stop these visits. He sent tactical officers again and again to Gridley's and made life extremely uncomfortable for the owner—so much so, in fact, that less than a year after Gridley had purchased the property, he agreed to sell it to the government. This was exactly what Thayer wanted, but after having convinced Gridley, he was unable to secure the appropriation necessary to complete the deal. Gridley continued in business until 1824, when funds were made available to purchase "Old Grid's" establishment and convert it into a cadet hospital. As a bonus, the government gained historic Fort Putnam, which was located on the farm.[23] Gridley, who was glad enough at first to be done with Thayer's harassment, soon came to believe that he had sold too cheaply and complained the rest of his life of the loss.

Gridley's loss proved to be Benny Havens's gain. Havens had once lived on the post near the dock and at times had boarded cadets, but now he was operating a tavern just below Buttermilk Falls—in modern Highland Falls—a mile or two south of the barracks. With Gridley's gone, Benny Havens's establishment acquired a new and loyal clientele. Some went for Benny's buckwheat cakes, oysters, and roast turkey, but those who had tried suppers both there and at Gridley's insisted that "Old Grid" had provided the better fare.[24] Still, Benny had other claims to fame, including his "hot flip"—eggs, well beaten, sweetened and spiced, in ale, the whole then heated by plunging a red-hot iron, or "flip dog," into it. Done properly—as Havens could do it—this brew had a delicious caramel-like flavor. To these attractions Benny added the bonus of his Irish wit, liberal credit, and a willingness to barter for almost anything a cadet might bring from the barracks. Havens's place was a favorite retreat of Edgar Allen Poe, who attended the Academy in 1830–1831 without graduating and, while there, found the tavern most congenial.[25]

Benny Havens enjoyed a monopoly of this business for years, and it made him famous. In 1838, Army doctor Lucius O'Brien became so fond of the establishment while visiting a friend at West Point that he composed some verses honoring it and its proprietor. Sung to the tune of "The Wearin' o' the Green," it soon became known as "Benny Havens, Oh!":

> Come, fill your glasses, fellows, and stand up in a row,
> To singing sentimentally, we're going for to go;
> In the army there's sobriety, promotions very slow
> So we'll sing our reminiscences of Benny Havens, oh!
>   Oh! Benny Havens, oh!—oh! Benny Havens, oh!
>   So we'll sing our reminiscences of Benny Havens, oh![26]

Over the years other bards have added more verses commemorating events in the lives of West Point, its cadets, and its graduates—the number now exceeds sixty.

Not all the cadets were inclined to spend their free moments at Grid's or Benny Havens's establishment. Some spent their leisure time hiking and climbing through the scenic Highlands that surrounded West Point. Some formed musical clubs and provided entertainments. Others, more academically inclined, formed literary and debating societies. The Amosophic Society was organized in 1816 and merged in 1823 with the Philomathean Society. In 1824, this recent amalgam merged with another newly formed club, the Ciceronian Society, to create the Dialectic Society—a cadet organization that remained an active part of the Academy for many years. These groups were organized for "improvement in debate, composition, and recitation" and offered cadets a welcome relief from the tedium of day-to-day life. Membership often included as much as 20 percent of the corps of cadets. Thayer and the faculty generally encouraged these clubs and usually provided meeting rooms—often one of the section rooms on the first floor of North Barracks—in which the societies' sometimes extensive libraries and collections could be maintained.[27]

As early as 1820, the Board of Visitors noted the need for a suitable hotel at West Point. The following year, when Cozzens took over the mess hall, he added to its operation (as far as space would allow) an officers' mess and rooms for visitors to the post. The expansion of the mess hall in 1823 made more space available, but when Gridley's tavern, which had accommodated some guests, was closed in 1824, even that larger facility was soon strained. "The floors of the parlours . . . are literally covered with the beds of the strangers that crowd here," wrote one guest.[28] The demand for facilities to accommodate visitors continued to grow, and in 1829 Thayer received approval to construct a hotel—a stone structure some fifty by sixty feet, containing sixty-four rooms—to be paid for from the proceeds of the sale of wood cut from public lands. William Cozzens was the first to operate the new West Point Hotel, and he continued to manage it for a number of years.

Throughout much of the 1820s, the officers had messed "very pleasantly" at Cozzens's, but when he took over the new hotel, he announced that he could no longer afford to keep up the mess without an increase in price. When the officers rebelled at this, the mess was broken up, and the officers were left to their own devices.[29] Some had their meals prepared in the basement of the Old South Barracks and took them in their rooms, while others went down to Mrs. Kinsley's to board.[30] However, after some unsuccessful agitation in 1832 to obtain a separate officers' mess, most of the officers gravitated back to Cozzens and took their meals at the new hotel.[31]

When President Monroe had visited West Point in the summer of 1817, he had listened at length not only to the faculty objections to Partridge but also to complaints about officers' housing. As a result, Thayer's first instructions from the War Department after arriving at West Point directed him to investigate the problem of housing as well as to coordinate a new program of instruction.[32] Aside from three new professors' houses that were just being completed, the hodgepodge of existing quarters for the faculty was both inadequate and badly in need of repair. Thayer's first response was to ask the Secretary of War to station a quartermaster at West Point and to furnish him with enough funds to do the most urgently needed work.[33] He was quick to add, however, that repairs alone would never solve the deficiencies in housing, and in December 1817 he requested funds for new quarters for the Superintendent and for three other new structures—two brick houses for professors and a stone duplex for teachers with families.[34]

The new Secretary of War, John C. Calhoun, was sympathetic to Thayer's request and discussed it with members of Congress. They wanted a "plan of buildings at West Point" showing their use that would support his housing request, he wrote Thayer in early January 1818.[35] Thayer responded with a report submitted later that month "designating the number and size of the apartments assigned to officers at West Point or occupied by them; together with information as to the number of rooms which . . . should be assigned to officers stationed there." That report was submitted in January 1818. "A reference to past expenditures for the repair of these Quarters will prove the expediency of replacing them by new & *permanent* buildings," he wrote, adding that he believed each professor should be provided a two-story house "40 by 27 feet" (at a cost of about $4,000 each) and that "every two teachers or assistant-professors having families" should get a similar house. In fact, the only adequate quarters on the post were three new brick single-family homes that had just been completed, and that were located at the southwest corner of the Plain. The unmarried officers, he noted, were adequately accommodated in the new barracks.[36]

After due consideration, Thayer's report and request for new housing were approved, but it was not until the spring of 1819 that the contracts were let for three more brick singles, including one for the Superintendent, and a stone double (or duplex), also for the senior faculty.[37] The three new brick houses were built along the west edge of the Plain, in line with and to the north of the 1817 quarters. The two new brick quarters—located on either side of the unfinished Superintendent's house—were completed in early November 1819. The set to the north was occupied first by Captain Bell (1819–1820) and then by Major Worth (1820–1829), successive Commandants of Cadets. It is still the home of the Commandant, and the oldest surviving set of quarters at West Point.[38] The Superintendent's house, which also survives, was finished the next year. The stone double, located a bit to the west of the old Rivardi quarters that had for a long period been occupied by the Mansfields, was also completed in 1820. The site, it is said, once held Revolutionary War barracks, but it is the view of the Hudson River that makes it special—the view that Mrs. Mansfield had so regretted leaving when her family was offered new quarters a few years before.[39]

In 1826, Thayer asked for another set of brick quarters for the professor of chemistry, and for two more stone doubles for assistant professors. When appropriations fell short of what was needed to complete all these structures immediately, he stretched the project out, beginning all three but completing only two in 1827; the last, one of the stone doubles, was finished the next year.[40] The three stone doubles—remodeled and enlarged repeatedly over the years and long since known as "Professors' Row"—have housed most of the Academy's most influential department heads. The brick professors' houses of this era—except the quarters for the Superintendent and Commandant—were demolished in the first decade of the twentieth century to make way for new barracks.

Thayer also installed running water in many of the buildings on the post by drawing from a mountainside reservoir through iron pipes. He also considered, but rejected, the notion of lighting the Academy with gas and heating it centrally by steam.[41] His purchase of the Gridley property not only had rid him of old Grid's troublesome establishment but also had provided land onto which the Academy could later expand without encroaching on the Plain—the borders of which Thayer had lined with trees.

The growth of the faculty under Thayer meant an enlarged social circle. "We have an addition to our society of several families," noted Elizabeth Mansfield in March 1818. "Among them are ten young Ladies" whose presence, she reported, had made it a gay winter. There were "regular assemblies, occasional balls, tea parties, sleighing parties, &c." And there were lessons for the ladies in music, French, and drawing.[42] Among the officers—particularly the married officers, whose larger quarters could accommodate such events—there were many parties to which everyone in this small society was invited. Of necessity, the entertainments were plain and inexpensive. The dancing consisted mainly of quadrilles, Spanish dances, and an occasional waltz, but the evenings always ended with the Virginia reel.[43] Card playing had been another favorite pastime among Army officers and wives, but when Thayer announced the ban on card playing among cadets, he strongly suggested that "all officers and families of this post" would in future "exclude card playing from their social parties."[44]

Thayer, though a bachelor, also entertained regularly—hosting "delightful" dinner parties and an occasional chess party. His years in France had made him something of a gourmet and a wine connoisseur, and he kept a first-rate wine cellar in the Superintendent's quarters. Thayer's entertainment of the many distinguished visitors who were drawn to West Point revealed a cultivated and urbane nature. He was perfectly at home with men of all callings, foreign and domestic—soldiers, statesmen, lawyers, physicians, divines, historians, poets, scientists, and merchants. "In expressing his ideas," wrote one officer, "his voice was low, distinct and very impressive; and when he spoke all present would listen with rapt attention." And yet he had a way of drawing out the best from each person with whom he spoke, making all feel comfortable in his presence.[45]

The officers at West Point also entertained and were entertained in turn by both the old Hudson Valley families and the newly rich, whose fine homes began to spring up on the river's banks. One of these was the wealthy and hospitable Gouverneur Kemble, who had built his mansion directly across from West Point at Cold Spring. On Saturday nights Kemble held regular dinner parties—usually affairs for men only—at which Thayer and the other officers were frequent guests. There they met and mingled with some of the brightest and most powerful men in America, including George Bancroft, Edward Everett, Hugh S. Legare, Washington Irving, Martin Van Buren, and many others.[46]

For some years prior to Thayer's arrival, the better cadets were drafted into the role of assistant instructors. For the chosen students this meant extra privileges, extra pay, and freedom from many of the more mundane aspects of cadet life. Thayer objected to the practice but was unable to avoid it altogether, although he did arrange the assignment of a number of young officers as assistant instructors. In the early years, newly commissioned officers were sometimes simply retained at West Point after graduation; in 1820, the Academy's new regulations required that these officers first serve two years with their regiments. With time on their hands, these young officers organized literary societies similar to those they had known during their cadet years. They "took great pains" in preparing their presentations, said Albert Church, and the weekly meetings "were of great interest and profit." Occasionally, the clubs opened their meetings to all the officers and ladies of the post, adding yet another pleasant dimension to the routine of daily life.[47]

Beginning in December 1817, the Academy conducted semiannual examinations that often lasted for a week or more. The winter examinations often began in mid- to late December and continued into January. For some years, the classes at the Military Academy had been divided into small sections for purposes of better instruction and daily recitation. After the examinations that concluded in January 1819, however, the Academic Board refined the procedure by adopting a "method of organizing the sections, according to the graduation of talent." This, they said, would "give sufficient scope to young men of genius," while ensuring that the slower cadets would also cover the essential material. Sectioning by demonstrated talent was, in itself, a simple matter, but the modification of the course of studies to accommodate the differences among the sections was another matter. The Academic Board spent the balance of the spring studying the problem, producing a concept of instruction geared to the capacities of the students. All would receive the most essential knowledge, while the better sections went progressively deeper into the subject.[48]

The twin pillars of the academic program were French and mathematics. Mathematics was the basis for training in engineering, and French was, at that time, the language of the advanced texts. In a cadet's fourth-class (or freshman) year, his studies were limited to these two subjects, with mathematics including algebra, geometry, and trigonometry. In the third-class (or sophomore) year, drawing was added to French and mathematics, which included analytical and descriptive geometry. Having completed the basic foundation, cadets moved on to the more technical sciences in their last two years. Second-class cadets studied natural and experimental philosophy (mechanics and physics), chemistry (beginning in 1822), and topographical drawing. Finally, in their first-class year, cadets arrived at the course toward which the whole curriculum had been aimed: engineering, to which was added instruction on the science of war, a smattering of rhetoric, and an introduction to the moral and political sciences.

Once this program had been installed and validated by the performance of cadets in their public examinations, both Thayer and the Academic Board resisted efforts to tinker with it. The board, whose primary function was the establishment and maintenance of the curriculum, was reluctant to make stark changes and grew ever more so over time. Incremental change through consensus was the way the board moved. The power of the board to resist even Thayer's efforts to institute change was clearly evident as early as September 1823, when the Superintendent proposed that they should "detach the subject of Grand Tactics, in the course of instruction, from the Department of Engineering and impose the duty on the Instructor of Tactics." The initial discussion of the proposal went on "for some time," but the board reached no decision and postponed further discussion until its next meeting, when the subject was further postponed and never reintroduced.[49] The strength of the Academic Board derived from its charter—found in law and Academy regulations—which placed the Academy's curriculum (and more) in its hands, and from three essential rules of operation: first, all decisions were to be made by a majority of the members present; second, no decision or opinion was to be divulged until regularly promulgated by the Superintendent; and, finally, no individual comments or opinions were to be divulged on any occasion. Whatever its internal differences and conflicts, the board spoke with one voice to the outside world.

There was one important exception to the Academic Board's ability to deflect change: the Academy was forced to add courses in civil engineering to what had been an almost wholly military engineering program. The impetus for this change lay largely outside the Academy. A growing interest in internal improvements in Washington and across the nation made the introduction of civil engineering inescapable—despite resistance from Thayer and the Academic Board. Even here, however, change came slowly and in measured steps.

The beginning of a national movement for internal improvements can be said to begin in 1818, when William Lowndes of South Carolina introduced four bills on the subject. The House of Representatives first declared that Congress had power to appropriate money for the construction of military and other roads, and for canals and other improvements of watercourses, but quickly reversed itself in the face of a veto. The next year, Congress invited Secretary of War John C. Calhoun (a fervent supporter of internal improvements) to submit a report outlining a comprehensive system of roads and waterways necessary for the defense of the United States. Calhoun replied that a judicious system of roads and canals, constructed for commerce and mail, would be an effective resource for the complete defense of the nation, and he expressed support for the use of Army engineers and Army troops to survey and construct them. In 1821, Rufus King, a member of the Academy's Board of Visitors, brought the issue to West Point. He proposed including civil engineering in the course of instruction. "If instead of confining the studies to mere military mathematics," he wrote, "the branch of civil engineering were taught, greater public benefits would be derived from this Academy." Wars and combats would be infrequent, King pointed out, "but the science, which may be employed in constructing canals, roads & bridges, is always in demand, and those who possess the same would meet with constant and profitable employment."[50]

Despite these hints, neither Thayer nor Crozet, Professor of Engineering, nor other members of the Academic Board made any move to broaden the engineering program by adding civil engineering. When Crozet departed West Point for the University of Virginia in 1823, he was teaching the same course he had been offering since the early curriculum reforms after Thayer's arrival in 1817—"permanent and field fortifications" and their "appendages," and "the different modes of attacking and defending fortified places."[51]

Even though Thayer observed in 1823 that if some of the graduates were ever unneeded in the military ranks, "they might be usefully employed as Civil Engineers either in the service of the General Government or of the States," he meant only that there was some natural transfer between the civil and military branches of the subject and intended no suggestion that the course then taught be broadened.[52] As late as 1825, he still argued against the introduction of "any new studies" into the Academy's curriculum. "Those who are not satisfied with the existing course of studies," he asserted, "have not reflected upon the nature and object of the Institution and have not considered that this is a special school designed solely for the purpose of a *military* education."[53]

David B. Douglass assumed the chair of engineering in 1823, just as the national debate on internal improvements took on new vigor with the introduction of the General Survey Bill. The issue was a heated one, but by year's end the mood of Congress was clearly in favor of an increased role for the federal government—and the Army. The bill, as it began to take final shape, would empower the President "to cause the necessary surveys, plans and estimates to be made of the routes of such roads and canals as he may deem of national importance in a commercial or military point of view, or necessary to the transportation of the public mails."[54] The legislation mandated the use of military engineers and federal participation in internal improvements.

At West Point the debate over this bill was watched with both concern and anticipation. Changes in the curriculum at the Academy would be essential if the mission and role of the Army were broadened. At the end of January 1824, the Academic Board directed Douglass to review his course.[55] Early the next month the bill was passed. Douglass, who was immediately appointed to the Army's new Board of Engineering for Internal Improvements, rushed to prepare a trial course in civil engineering, which he introduced immediately to the top section of his engineering class.[56] In June, he examined this section separately on the subject. "When we consider the rising demand in our country for civil engineers," the 1824 Board of Visitors reported, in response, "we must admit that the full endowment of this branch of study would be a great national economy."[57] Beginning that fall, Douglass introduced the course to the entire class.

With congressional prodding, the Academy had responded. But the Congress was not finished. The next year it signaled a desire to go further when it considered sending some cadets to Europe to improve their knowledge of civil engineering. Douglass suggested instead that he should be sent to Europe; upon his return, he argued, he could introduce what he learned into his new course at West Point. In the end, neither Douglass nor the cadets were sent. In 1827, Douglass raised the issue again. The Academy badly needed a textbook in civil engineering, he pointed out and promised that— if allowed fifteen to eighteen months abroad—he would complete one fitted precisely to the requirements of the institution.[58] Again he was disappointed, for it was his assistant, Dennis Hart Mahan, class of 1824, who was sent instead. Douglass had to content himself with self-study and the experience he could gain in private engineering engagements.[59] In this way, he began to introduce changes into the civil engineering course that progressively broadened it by adding material on roads, bridges, and inland navigation. Successive boards of visitors endorsed the changes, and in 1830 they noted with satisfaction that "a large portion of the cadets are destined to act as civil engineers."[60] The cadets had come to a similar conclusion but were possibly less sanguine about the pace of change. In 1829, they formed the American Association for the Promotion of Science, Literature, and the Arts for the purpose of improving their knowledge of civil engineering.[61] The civil engineering program continued to expand throughout the next decade, adding topics as contemporary interests dictated, including railroad construction, tunneling, and the creation of artificial harbors.[62]

Despite the Academic Board's apparent reluctance to introduce the new program, the Military Academy did move more rapidly than any other school in the nation in responding to the need for civil engineers. It was the first school of civil engineering and remained the leading center of such instruction until the Civil War.

Although Thayer might resist outside pressure to alter the curriculum, he welcomed public scrutiny of the Academy and its cadets. He saw it as a means of building public support for the institution. In the spring of 1819, as soon as the new academic program was in place, he asked a committee of the Academic Board to draw up a "systematic view" of the Academy's regulations and course of study and the cadets' "military and scientific duties." This would be useful, he thought, for the parents and friends of the cadets, "and [for] the public generally."[63]

Toward the same end, he revitalized the annual Board of Visitors. These boards were invited to look into details of academic activity and the physical plant and to report their findings to the Secretary of War. Each year a list of distinguished educators and men of science; leading officers of the Army, the Navy, the militia; and members of Congress—often men who had previously expressed hostility to the Academy—were invited to West Point as members of these boards. Thayer believed that criticism of the school arose largely from a lack of information or a prejudice that could be resolved by personal contact and observation. In support of Thayer's view, the boards' reports usually contained high praise of the Academy and its programs. Exposed to the beauty of the Hudson Highlands in June, the spectacle of martial music and dress parades, competent examinations, erect and correct cadets, the suave and gracious hospitality of the Superintendent, and the enthusiasm of the majority of their colleagues, the opponents of the school were won over to at least a toleration of the institution, while those who had been lukewarm to the Academy often became firm defenders.

Thayer believed that it worked to the Academy's advantage when the people saw the cadets. What better way to achieve that than by taking the cadets to the people? In 1819, he approved the first of several highly publicized summer marches: to Hudson, New York, in that year; to Philadelphia in 1820; to Boston in 1821; and to Goshen, New York, in 1822. The cadets proved popular with the people wherever they went, and the widespread publicity they received was almost universally favorable.

The most memorable march was the one to Boston in 1821. The corps of cadets departed West Point on July 20 on two transports, en route to Albany. From there they marched to Lebanon, Lenox, Springfield, Roxbury, and finally Boston. They returned through Providence, New London, New

Haven, and New York. In Roxbury, they visited Henry Dearborn, and in Boston's outlying Quincy they met John Adams. The cadets paraded for Adams, then each was presented to him. Finally the former President said a few brief words to the cadets and then fed them breakfast. In his remarks, Adams spoke to them of glory—the kind of glory personified by Washington: "no ambition of conquest or avaricious desire for wealth; irritated by no jealousy, envy, malice, or revenge; prompted only by the love of their country." He closed by congratulating them "on the great advantages you possess for attaining eminence in letters and science. As well as in arms. . . . These advantages, and the habits you have acquired, will qualify you for any course of life you may choose to pursue." The corps departed Boston on September 18 and arrived at West Point eight days later. Major William J. Worth, who commanded the march, reported, "The people had formed the most sanguine expectations of the Corps, and in no one particular I sincerely believe were they disappointed. By the general intelligence, soldierlike and gentlemanly conduct they seem to win all hearts."[64]

Adams was pleased by the cadets' visit. A few days later, in a letter to Thomas Jefferson, he commented that "the late Visits of the Cadets to several States seem to have made the institution popular." The Academy, he remarked, "is now brought to a considerable degree of perfection." He did not mention the honor the cadets had paid him with their visit. Perhaps to do that would have been to gloat, for he knew that the cadets were not scheduled to go to Monticello. He closed by asking if Jefferson thought a "similar establishment" for the Navy might now "be equally Usefull." Jefferson replied: "I think with you that there should be a school of instruction for our navy as well as artillery; and I do not see why the same establishment might not suffice for both." Jefferson, too, avoided any mention of the cadets' call on Adams, although he must have known of it from the wide press coverage that their march to Boston had received.[65] But neither did he share with Adams the fact that the officers and cadets of the Military Academy were also extending him an honor: commissioning his portrait by Thomas Sully— a full-length painting that would hang in the library at West Point.[66]

To a large degree Thayer's triumphs of the early 1820s were a reflection of the early support he received in Washington. This, however, would not continue indefinitely. During his first eight years as Superintendent at West Point, Thayer had enjoyed the full patronage of both President James Monroe and Secretary of War John C. Calhoun. Seldom had either man even questioned Thayer's efforts. On the contrary, when Congress cut the size of the Army in the early 1820s and considered abolishing the Academy, the administration swiftly came to its defense.

The years from 1826 to 1833, however, were marked first by decreasing support and finally by active hostility in Washington. In the last years of John Quincy Adams's presidency, the process of government was so consumed by controversy and rent by the realignment of political factions that Thayer had no hope of getting the administration to focus on the Academy's needs. In the summer of 1827, he went to Washington to speak with the President personally. Thayer confided to Adams his concerns about discipline and "the moral condition of the institution," noting in particular "that a habit of drinking had become very prevalent among [cadets]." However, when the discussion turned into a debate about the propriety of a naked admission physical, it was clear that Thayer's effort came to naught.[67]

In the election of 1828, a tidal wave of votes submerged Adams and swept Andrew Jackson into the presidency. Neither the new President nor his Secretaries of War, John Eaton (1829–1831) and Lewis Cass (1831–1836), were well-disposed toward Thayer. They were particularly unsympathetic to his attempts to maintain his desired level of discipline. Jacksonians looked upon the Military Academy as a haven for sons of the privileged, who would monopolize this avenue of access into the officer corps, denying entry to the ordinary citizen and producing an increasingly aristocratic military body.

Jackson's own attitude toward West Point was somewhat ambiguous. He once described it as "the best school in the world," but he clearly disapproved of Thayer's dismissal of cadets for what he saw as mere boyish pranks. The Superintendent, he believed, was unbending and autocratic, and Jackson's antipathy toward Thayer increased as the years went by.

As soon as the cadets discovered that appeals to Washington brought dramatic reprieves, even from the judgments of courts-martial, discipline declined even further. Reinstatements followed so rapidly upon dismissals that Thayer was driven to sending cases requiring extreme discipline directly to the War Department for action. Earlier administrations had occasionally reinstated cadets, but in the first two years of Jackson's presidency, seven of sixteen cadets sentenced to dismissal were reinstated. Bitterly, Thayer complained that the President was "in the habit of dispensing with the most important regulations of the Academy in favor of his friends." The chances of success if one approached Jackson, he calculated, were "three to one" in the cadet's favor.[68]

In 1830, Thayer's troubles were compounded by assaults upon the Military Academy from other quarters. First came a broadside from Alden Partridge, who published an attack on the Academy entitled *The Military Academy, at West Point, Unmasked: or, Corruption and Military Despotism Exposed*. The book was composed of three repetitive appeals (first to the Congress, next to the President, and finally to the American people), each warning that West Point was spawning a "military aristocracy."[69]

At about the same time, the Academy faced denunciation in the House of Representatives as a repository for the sons of the rich and influential who would monopolize the offices of the Army. The most outspoken opponent was frontier democrat David Crockett of Tennessee, who argued: "The institution was kept up for the education of the sons of the noble and wealthy, and of members of Congress, people of influence, and not for the children of the poor." He proposed abolishing the Academy entirely.[70] Crockett went further than most, but he was not alone in his hostility to the Academy.

Still, over the years, Thayer and his staff at the Military Academy had carefully cultivated a base of support in the Congress, and in the end, Crockett's words were more of an annoyance than a threat. Likewise, Partridge's bitter, but transparent, attacks did not attract a significant following.

With Jackson's reelection in 1832, Thayer concluded that he must have a showdown. He discussed the problem with Ethan Allen Hitchcock, the Commandant of Cadets. "We agreed," recalled Hitchcock, "that the evil influence was spreading. [Colonel Thayer] noticing it chiefly in the growing neglect of study, while I observed it principally in the tendency to disorder." They decided that, given Jackson's apparent hostility to Thayer, Hitchcock should go to Washington and seek a personal interview with the President. On November 24, Hitchcock met with Jackson, but the results only confirmed their worst expectations. Jackson spoke of the "tyranny" of Thayer. "Why, the autocrat of all the Russias couldn't exercise more power," he raged.[71]

Thayer suspected as much and, even before Hitchcock returned from Washington, wrote to Cass, the Secretary of War: "I am led to believe that there is something at this institution which does not altogether meet with the President's approbation, but I am at a loss to conjecture whether the dissatisfaction, if such really exists, relates to persons or things."[72] Thayer could have had little doubt about the real state of affairs, but his letter left the administration ample latitude in which to seek a solution, if it desired to do so. Hitchcock's report of his interview with the President, however, left no doubt that Jackson's antipathy was directed toward Thayer personally. Cass's response to Thayer's letter, though solicitous, did nothing to change that view. In January, Thayer put the administration to the final test by offering his resignation as Superintendent and asking to be reassigned to other duty. Though the administration delayed in responding, his resignation was ultimately accepted with no attempt to persuade him otherwise. Thayer would depart after the upcoming June examinations.

Even though Thayer lost his personal battle with Jackson, he was successful in a larger sense. The system he had installed at West Point endured. Certainly, some elements of that system had been conceived under Swift, such as the annual Boards of Visitors, the four-year curriculum, the semiannual examinations, and the small sections and daily recitations. Yet it was Thayer who had vitalized and adapted the system, and, even more, it was Thayer who had made it work. "He had brought order out of chaos," wrote historian James Morrison, "no trifling achievement considering the muddle he had inherited from Alden Partridge."[73] For his efforts, Thayer has become known as the "Father of the Military Academy."

But Thayer's legacy went far beyond the system itself, for he embodied what was to become known as "The Spirit of West Point." In every aspect of his person he represented rigid, impartial justice; uncompromising honor; impeccable honesty; literal, unquestioning obedience to orders; and towering intellect. "His comprehensive mind embraced principles and details more strongly than any man I ever knew," wrote one graduate. "His object was to make [cadets] gentlemen and soldiers. And he illustrated in his person the great object he sought to accomplish."[74]

In addition, Thayer's influence was perpetuated by his students, who dominated the school until long after the Civil War. Alexander Macomb, for many years the Chief of Engineers, had advised him that "for the sake of harmony" at West Point, professors should be selected from among those who had graduated and taught there—men "who would advance the interests of the institution and conform willingly to its discipline."[75] As the opportunities arose, Thayer willingly did so, thus filling the faculty with men of his own mold and making.

In 1827, the resignation of Dr. John Torrey as acting professor of chemistry gave Thayer the opportunity to appoint Lieutenant W. F. Hopkins, class of 1825, to that post. Mansfield's resignation the next year left vacant the most prestigious professorship at the Academy. There was, therefore, keen interest in the position. Douglass, who had been Mansfield's assistant for five years before accepting the chair of mathematics and then engineering, wanted the position and had a strong claim to it. He had been at the Academy longer than any other member of the faculty and had served as secretary of the Academic Board since its inception. Thayer, however, chose Lieutenant Edward H. Courtenay, who had graduated at the head of his class in 1821. Courtenay had served three years at the Academy as an assistant professor (assisting first Mansfield in natural philosophy and then Douglass in engineering) and was then assigned as assistant to the Chief Engineer in Washington. Courtenay assumed his duties as head of experimental philosophy on September 1, 1828, and was officially confirmed by the Senate early the next year.

David Douglass, disappointed by his failure to gain the more exalted assignment, resigned eighteen months later. To replace him Thayer chose his assistant, Dennis Hart Mahan. Mahan had been retained at the Academy upon graduation as an exception to the general rule that graduates must serve two years with their regiments before returning. He was first an assistant professor in mathematics and then, in 1825, the principal assistant to Douglass in engineering. In ill health in 1827, he had been sent to Europe to recover, as well as to study military and civil engineering.

In the midst of these changes in the academic staff, Thayer also chose a new Commandant of Cadets. In 1828, Major William Worth requested relief from the assignment and returned to his regiment. He had been Commandant since 1820 and suggested as his replacement Captain Ethan Allen Hitchcock, who had been his assistant. Hitchcock, only months earlier, had been relieved from his assignment at West Point at his own request, but when offered the commandantcy, he returned. He reported back in March 1829 and remained throughout the balance of Thayer's tenure.

By 1830, there were new men in charge of the Departments of Chemistry,[76] Natural and Experimental Philosophy, and Engineering, and a new Commandant of Cadets. Further changes later in the decade would only entrench the Thayer influence more firmly.

The examination of 1833 was one of Thayer's last official acts, and in an ironic sense, it typified his administration of the school. The classes performed handsomely—particularly the graduating class of 1833. They did so well, in fact, that Joel Poinsett, the president of the Board of Visitors, admitted that the examinations were the best he had ever heard, but he wondered aloud

This drawing portrays the examination of June 1868, but it accurately depicts the June examinations held from Thayer's time until then. Sketch by Theodore R. Davis (1840–1898) for *Harper's Weekly*, July 4, 1868.

how the class as a whole could have done so well without knowing before-hand the subjects upon which they would be examined. That remark was overheard by a member of the faculty who reported it to Thayer.

Thayer was incensed and would not allow the remark to pass. He imme-diately ordered Mahan to prepare a full synopsis of the subjects in his whole course. The class was then ordered back to the examination room, where Thayer explained that Poinsett's remark forced him to take the unusual step of reexamining the entire group. Poinsett objected and attempted to apolo-gize—insisting that his comment had been intended as a compliment—but Thayer would not be dissuaded. The injury done to the Academy and to the class, he insisted, could be repaired only by a thorough reexamination.

"The examination was resumed and continued with the deepest inter-est," recalled one of those who was reexamined, "each member of the class feeling that an appeal was made to his honor as well as his pride." When this examination was completed, "the highest compliments" were extended to the class by Poinsett and by the other members of the board. The class, the Academy, and Thayer had been vindicated.[77]

A few days later, on July 1, the class of 1833 graduated. Afterward, every member came to Thayer's office to say a personal farewell. That evening Thayer strolled down to the dock and awaited the arrival of the night boat to New York. When it had discharged its passengers, he stepped aboard. He departed West Point just as he had come, with little notice and no ceremony.

CHAPTER FIVE

Years of Growth and Fulfillment, 1833–1865

In the years between Sylvanus Thayer's departure and the end of the Civil War, the Military Academy at West Point came to maturity. Not only did the Academy take on the familiar Tudor-Gothic appearance that would define it ever after, but its sons served with distinction in the Mexican War and then garnered even greater acclaim in the War Between the States. It was a period that saw both growth and fulfillment at West Point.

"Your own late domicile," Dennis Hart Mahan wrote Sylvanus Thayer in late 1833, "is gradually putting off its bachelor habit, by such additions as single gentlemen do not always think of." The community at West Point was adjusting to a new Superintendent, Major Rene E. DeRussy, class of 1812. The quarters, which had known only the bachelor Thayer, was being shaped to the desires of Mrs. DeRussy.[1] The new Superintendent shed the aura of aloof dignity that Thayer had cultivated. He regularly invited cadets to his home for tea, where they conversed as equals with him, his charming wife, and other members of the faculty, and he encouraged other officers to do the same.

Although DeRussy had known Thayer, both as a fellow cadet and as an instructor, he was hardly a "Thayer man." Rather, he shared Jackson's conviction that Thayer's rigid discipline bordered on the tyrannical and that this was the real source of cadet misbehavior.

"Everything wears an unsettled aspect," wrote Mahan.[2] And well it might. Thayer's inability to get along with the Jackson administration had meant that a number of matters had simply been held in suspense—both in Washington and at West Point—until a new Superintendent was in place. Barely a month after arriving, DeRussy forwarded to the War Department the plan for a chapel, which had "been under consideration" at West Point for some time. "The details are not yet drawn," DeRussy noted, but he sent the general plan, noting that he was "anxious to begin the building immediately." Similarly, no plans had yet been drawn for a "building for exercises" originally proposed by Thayer, approved in Washington, and already partially funded. This structure was to provide an enclosed area for drill and exercises, a floor of section rooms, and additional quarters for the bachelor officers.[3]

Among the few accomplishments of DeRussy's superintendency was the completion of the chapel (1836) and construction of the new academic and exercise hall (1838). The chapel, a simple, rectangular Greek temple form, was typical of structures then being built in the Greek Revival style. To this was added impressive Doric columns and a portico. The interior was adorned with a large mural over the altar painted by Professor Robert W. Weir, head of the Department of Drawing (1834–1876), who in his years at West Point established himself as one of the important American painters of the century.[4] Constructed of marble, the chapel remained essentially unaltered until 1910, when it was moved to the West Point cemetery, where it stands today—the oldest public building at the Academy.

The new academic building, roughly 75 by 275 feet, and the largest building yet constructed at West Point, was built of stone and stucco. Three stories high, it featured a hipped roof and round-arched openings on the first floor that hinted at an Italian Renaissance influence. At the same time, the east front, opposite the chapel, was adorned with a two-story portico supported by six Doric columns similar to those of the chapel, giving the whole a rather nondescript appearance.

The area in which DeRussy made his most notable progress was in his relations with President Andrew Jackson. The new Superintendent was able to convince the administration that restoring cadets who had been dismissed for disciplinary reasons was counterproductive. "I had hoped that a lenient system of administration would be found sufficient for the government of the Military Academy," wrote the President to the cadets, "but I have been disappointed and it is now time to be more rigorous in enforcing its discipline." Henceforth, cadets who "will not demean themselves as they are required to do by the regulations . . . must suffer the prescribed punishments."[5]

Discipline, however, did not improve. The cadets' celebration of the New Year on January 1, 1837, was a case in point. Six of them pulled the reveille gun between the North and South Barracks and fired it. "The effect was great," wrote one of the participants, "only four windows on the west side of N. Barracks escaped having their eyes put out." They then hoisted the gun to the fourth floor of North Barracks and attempted to fire another salute to the New Year. Fortunately, more levelheaded leaders took charge of the situation before graver damage was done.[6] Discipline in the corps of cadets had seemingly collapsed under DeRussy.

Although DeRussy was more satisfactory to President Jackson than Thayer, he did not impress Martin Van Buren, who succeeded Jackson in March 1837. Van Buren had known Thayer for some years through

Gouverneur Kemble's Saturday night soirees and admired the officer, his methods, and the school he had created. Van Buren soon ordered his Secretary of War, Joel Poinsett, to find a new Superintendent. Poinsett, too, knew Thayer; it was he who had caused Thayer to reexamine the graduating class in 1833. Far from resenting that incident, Poinsett admired Thayer and was determined to reappoint him. Thayer, however, resisted so stubbornly that the Secretary finally agreed to look elsewhere but did extract a promise from Thayer that he would serve if no other suitable officer could be found. Thayer undoubtedly felt that his return would only invite fresh barrages from those partial to Partridge and other Jacksonians.[7]

The search for a new Superintendent went on for over a year; in the meantime, DeRussy stewed. "I long to resign the reins of this complicated and arduous Command into more able hands," he wrote Gouverneur Kemble, "and God knows, I will never envy the lot of the one selected for the Service; I have *seen* and *felt* enough of the difficulties attending the Superintendence of this Institution to be satisfied that nothing gratifying can grow out of it."[8]

On February 19, 1838, a fire heavily damaged the 1815 Academy building, which housed the engineering, chemistry, and natural philosophy departments, the post headquarters, and the library. The fire destroyed much of the building and wholly undermined its structural integrity. The records of the post headquarters were completely burned, but the apparatus of the various departments and most of the books in the library were saved.[9]

Poinsett immediately instructed DeRussy to draw up plans and estimates for the required rebuilding and to determine what temporary measures would be necessary until permanent buildings could be constructed. The Superintendent responded by forwarding the plans and estimates to Washington. DeRussy's plans called for two new buildings: the first for a library, an observatory and for natural philosophy instruction, and for offices for the Adjutant and Treasurer; the second to house the chemistry classroom and laboratories.[10] Meanwhile, plans were made to move the academic departments into the new exercise building just completed. The necessary renovations were finished and the academic departments installed just in time for the fall term of 1838. The library remained at the hotel, where the books had been placed when rescued from the fire.

In the meantime, the preliminary plans and estimates that DeRussy sent to Washington were examined with care. In appearance the new designs copied many of the features of the exercise building. Both the proposed two-story library and the one-story chemistry building featured low hip roofs largely hidden behind railings all around and arched openings on the first floor. Their designs had something of an Italianate appearance—harmonizing with the new academic building. Poinsett approved his plans, but DeRussy departed in September 1838, and the actual construction was left to his successor.

The administration's choice to succeed DeRussy was Major Richard Delafield, who had graduated at the head of the class of 1818. His had been the first class examined under Thayer. Unlike many of his classmates who were through and through Partridge men, Delafield had been won over by Thayer and his methods. The new Superintendent was an energetic officer with a large nose and a bustling manner. From the breadth of his activities the first month, it is clear that he arrived with a mandate from the administration to restore order and direction.

Not since the arrival of Thayer had a Superintendent shown so much energy. Delafield reviewed the Board of Visitor reports beginning in 1820 and immersed himself in a quick review of the professional subjects taught at the Academy. He recommended to the Academic Board the addition of geography and history and suggested dropping the second year of French. And he studied the plans that DeRussy had presented for the new library and the new building for the chemistry department.

Another fire, this time a relatively small one in North Barracks, gave Delafield an opportunity to call for the development of a more general plan that would address the Academy's multiple needs. He wrote to Charles Gratiot, the Chief of Engineers, saying that he would "bring the whole subject of buildings before the Department before commencing any new ones under existing appropriations." He promised that he would devise "an entire system" that would be "suited to the wants of the institution"—a system "that when adopted shall not be departed from."[11] When consulted about this, Thayer admonished Delafield "not to move a finger till a general plan for the entire new system shall have been matured & adopted."[12]

Of even more immediate impact, Delafield set about restoring discipline. He clamped down hard on those who frequented Benny Havens's congenial establishment and forbade civilians in the area to sell either food or liquor to the cadets. He punished infractions of the regulations with a heavy hand and ended DeRussy's practice of permitting students to attend officers' parties.

Not surprisingly, most cadets disliked Delafield. His tough, Thayer-like discipline was not administered with the compassion that had mitigated the harshness of the earlier Superintendent's rule. Neither was he popular with the other members of the garrison. What is more, his popularity did not grow over time. Most cadets and officers perceived him as mean and vindictive; his better side was seldom apparent.

Yet Delafield did have a better side. He sometimes showed genuine concern and compassion for the cadets and was open to new ideas, particularly when they might benefit cadets. John Tidball, class of 1848, claimed that Delafield saved him from dismissal on learning that the charges against him had been made by an unfair and spiteful tactical officer.[13] Delafield also acted in the cadets' behalf in other ways, and he was not afraid to break with tradition. He lengthened the period between parade and supper, thus allowing cadets more time to bathe, and he opened the library to cadets "all time when not on duty." He believed that it was irksome to cadets "to be confined in quarters the whole afternoon without employment." Of course, it did not escape him that at the library "they may innocently amuse, if not advantageously instruct themselves" and thereby reduce "the temptation to violation of the Regulations."[14]

Delafield broke with tradition in other ways, too. He replaced the side-button trousers that the cadets wore with fly fronts, much to the embarrassment of the ladies on post. Mrs. Delafield reportedly told her husband that "cadets thus dressed should not come in person to the house." Despite the protests of the wives, the style soon became regulation at West Point and throughout the Army.

Unquestionably, though, Delafield's greatest contribution was his influence on the architectual heritage of West Point. In November 1838, he appointed a board of three officers, Professors William H. C. Bartlett and Dennis Hart Mahan and Captain Charles F. Smith, to draw up a general plan for the needed buildings. To assist them, Delafield engaged the services of Isaiah Rogers, a New York City architect.[15] Rogers, who was noted for his work in Greek Revival architecture, had earlier designed the Astor House, a New York hotel, and was at the time supervising construction of the New York Merchants Exchange, one of his most significant works.

Delafield's architectural board made its first report in February, recommending that both North and South Barracks should be replaced in addition to replacing the old burned Academy building. The board also recommended relocating the buildings. "The present location of the barracks," it reported, "deprives the Institution of nearly, if not quite, one third of the plane [sic] for military manoeuvers."[16]

At about the same time, Rogers's first designs reached West Point. They reflected the Greek Revival style with which he was most closely associated. Delafield was dismayed: "They are in *no manner* suited to our wants, or the discipline of the corps—and would cost ½ a million. I cannot think of submitting them, being in principle worse than the existing buildings altho *very* elegant."[17]

Richard Delafield was Superintendent of the United States Military Academy from 1838 to 1845 and again from 1856 to 1861. Painted by Henry Peters Gray (1819–1877). West Point Museum Collection, United States Military Academy.

Disappointed with the Rogers plans, Delafield engaged a second architect, Frederick Diaper. Born in Devonshire, England, Diaper was also noted for his Greek Revival commercial and public buildings and for his Italianate residences. Interestingly, Diaper's first plan for the barracks, which he submitted in the spring, was in the "Gothic or Elizabethan" style.[18]

Delafield was so taken by Diaper's Tudor-Gothic designs that subsequently no other style of architecture received any serious consideration. On June 3, 1839, in a long report to Joseph G. Totten, the newly appointed Chief Engineer, he summarized the work that had been done to date. Enclosed with the report were the plans for the barracks and library that had been submitted by the architects. Of the plans for the barracks only Diaper's work pleased him, although even this design presented serious problems in the details. "Another design after this style of Architecture has presented itself to my mind," he noted, however, and promised to submit his own drawings "at the time of asking approval."[19]

Of the plans submitted by the architects for the library and department of natural philosophy, none were acceptable, Delafield reported. As a result, he offered his own design which he recommended for approval—a Tudor-Gothic plan that clearly reflected Diaper's influence. Delafield's plan met with the immediate favor of both Totten and Poinsett in Washington, and after some minor modifications by federal architect Captain Robert Mills of the Engineer Department, it was formally approved.

Delafield's preference for the Tudor-Gothic over the Greek or Classical Revival architecture that was then the accepted style in federal buildings is something of a mystery. It may have resulted from the interplay among that particular architectural style, the Academy's martial aspects, and West Point's unique geological and scenic features. Delafield hints as much when he characterizes Diaper's Tudor-Gothic design as "a style not only pleasing to the eye, but suited to the scenery."[20] Later generations of architects, following the same motif, would confirm this conjunction of style and setting with designs whose massive vertical walls seemed to spring from the rock itself—suggesting a unity between the natural and the man-made.[21]

The new library was begun in 1839 following the Tudor-Gothic lines proposed by Delafield. It was completed in 1841. The east wing contained the library of about twenty thousand volumes. The first floor of the west wing housed the offices of the Superintendent, the Adjutant, and the Treasurer. Above them were the lecture hall and apparatus of the natural philosophy department. The library's construction on the approved site necessitated tearing down two buildings that housed the ordnance shop and laboratory. A new ordnance compound with three stone buildings and a large yard enclosed by a stone wall, all similar to the Tudor-Gothic library, was constructed just beyond and below the northern boundary of the Plain. Construction of this compound, in turn, demanded razing three small buildings (the post office, the Thompsons' house, and a set of officers' quarters) that had occupied this flat area. When these three structures were pulled down, the Thompsons (and the small cadet mess they continued to operate) were moved into the old storekeeper's quarters, which sat slightly behind the line of brick professors' quarters. Construction on the compound began in 1839 and was completed early the next year.

Delafield began immediately to seek approval and funding for new barracks, but it was not until 1843 that he succeeded. Some of the delays may have been caused by renewed attacks on West Point in this period. "You see by the notice I sent you," wrote Cadet William Dutton that year, "that great efforts have been made to abolish the Academy. But so far from proving successful—a 'bill' *has passed both houses* to build a new barracks . . . that will cost at least 150,000 dollars." Dutton assumed, correctly it seems, that the willingness of Congress to approve such large expenditures was a sure sign that the institution at West Point was in no serious danger.[22]

Later that same year, with this appropriation in hand, a board of engineer officers met at the Military Academy to study the plans for the bar-

A View of the United States Military Academy in the mid-1840s. The artist
captured West Point in the midst of Superintendent Richard Delafield's rebuilding of the Academy. Delafield's library (1841) and the earlier chapel (1836) are
shown with the older barracks—North Barracks (1817) in the foreground and
South Barracks (1815) to the right of it. Watercolor by Augustus Köllner (1813–?)
ca. 1845. United States Military Academy Library.

racks and to consider the school's other requirements. They approved the
Tudor-Gothic style Delafield favored for the barracks—a plan that is generally attributed to him, although the design owes a clear debt to Diaper.
The board, however, recommended rejection of Delafield's scheme to lo-
cate the Academy's future buildings along the eastern perimeter of the Plain
overlooking the Hudson. It suggested instead that they be placed on the line
of construction—the academic building, chapel, and library—recently established along the south boundary. Delafield protested the board's action,
but Poinsett approved their recommendations. Construction finally began
in the spring of 1845, only months before Delafield departed.[23]

Delafield's West Point was becoming a "great stone castle," as one cadet
put it, and such it would remain. "It is not desirable that any scheme should
attempt to sweep the field clean and destroy architectural associations made

honorable by generations of great men," wrote Charles Larned, Professor of Drawing, in 1901, as a massive new wave of construction was being considered. "It is of the highest importance," he continued, "to preserve intact the structural sentiment which gives character and individuality to the Academy."[24]

The political attacks on the Academy that began in Thayer's superintendency continued periodically into the 1840s. They centered on two issues: West Point's monopoly on Army commissions, and the large number of resigning graduates. This clamor became so loud in 1838 that when Congress authorized new regiments, it specified that some officers were to be drawn from civilian circles. The same year, legislation passed lengthening the active service required of Academy graduates to four years. In 1843, when the Academy was again accused of being a breeding ground for an aristocratic officer corps, the institution began to collect data concerning the parents of each cadet. With that information in hand, friends of the Academy were able to demonstrate that the vast majority (156) of 194 cadets at West Point that year came from families in moderate circumstances, while 26 came from homes of reduced means, and 6 came from families that were considered indigent. Only 6 came from families of wealth.[25]

In truth, the Academy had never been in serious danger from these attacks. The institution had many friends, and even congressional critics usually ended up voting for West Point when its existence was threatened. Since 1828, when Secretary of War James Barbour began the practice of seeking nominations for appointments from each member of the House of Representatives, congressmen had come to value the opportunity to "appoint" cadets to the Academy. In 1843, Congress formalized the arrangement by authorizing House members to choose one cadet each at the Academy and to name candidates when vacancies occurred. In the absence of a more worthy rationale, this gave members a tangible motive for supporting the Academy against its enemies.[26]

Captain Henry Brewerton, class of 1819, succeeded Delafield as Superintendent on August 15, 1845. Brewerton's appointment generally coincided with the beginning of a period of growing maturity and assurance at West Point. Certainly, the period from the late 1840s through the end of the next decade was one in which Congress was more favorably disposed toward the Academy than in any earlier period. In this atmosphere Brewerton did much to add to the convenience of life at West Point. He graded the surface of the Plain, built the south wharf and the road leading to it, and enlarged the water supply. In 1850, he persuaded a telegraph company to run a line from

New York and to establish an office at West Point. Even more important, he carried on Delafield's general program of construction.

Brewerton assigned Captain Frederick A. Smith, class of 1833 and an instructor in practical engineering, to oversee the construction of the barracks. The west half of the barracks was completed and occupied in 1849, after which South Barracks was torn down. The east section of the new barracks and the sally port were completed in 1851 under the supervision of Captain George W. Cullum, also of the class of 1833. (Cullum would himself be Superintendent one day.) The occupation of the final section of the new structure was followed by the demolition of the decaying North Barracks. Other new buildings followed in quick succession: a mess hall (1852), stables (1854), and a riding hall (1855).

From 1829, when Cozzens stopped serving meals to the officers at the old cadet mess, until the fall of 1841, when Lieutenant Irwin McDowell, class of 1838, was assigned to West Point, no serious effort had been made to establish a true officers' mess. McDowell, however, "was full of the mess question." After graduation, he had been assigned to the northern frontier, where his regiment "came under the influence" of the British regiments opposite them. There his regiment formed the 1st Artillery Mess. It was "a very modest affair compared with those" it emulated, McDowell noted, still "the

Central Barracks (1849–1851). This structure was built to designs prepared by Richard Delafield, but Delafield's plans reflected the earlier work of architect Frederick Diaper. United States Military Academy Library.

mess life . . . had a great charm for me." When he arrived at West Point, he immediately began to promote the same kind of formal mess he had known in his regiment. He had little immediate success, making only one convert, Lieutenant Alexander E. Shiras, class of 1833. That conversion, however, was a critical one because Shiras occupied a two-story brick house immediately behind the mess hall—one of those completed in 1817. His quarters provided adequate space in which to organize and operate a small mess. Shiras invited McDowell to share these quarters, but, as McDowell put it, "we could not well set up a mess table on two legs only." To solve this problem, McDowell, the Academy's adjutant, arranged the immediate assignment to West Point of Lieutenant Henry C. Wayne, an 1838 classmate who had also been assigned to the 1st Artillery and "was as much an enthusiast" for a mess as McDowell.[27]

Upon Wayne's arrival, the mess was set going, being officially established on December 20, 1841, at Shiras's and McDowell's quarters. To purchase the necessary mess fixtures, they levied an initiation fee of one-third of a month's pay—married officers to pay half that rate. In keeping with the mess traditions they copied, they prescribed that "the dinner costume of the Mess shall be the full uniform prescribed by the General Regulations of the Army with the exception of the sword, sword belt and cap."[28] This meant that at dinner the members appeared in their swallowtail coats with high-standing collars, gold lace and epaulets—and a red sash at the waist. Delafield, the Superintendent, attempted to promote the mess by offering to use the Post Fund to purchase "a complete service of plate" if the majority of the young officers would join.[29]

The officers, however, demurred. "There was a decided hostility to the mess in the beginning," McDowell recalled. One reason for this, he suggested, was that the officers resented the initiation fee, fearing that they might not stay long enough at West Point to benefit from their investment. Yet another "very potent cause" of early disaffection was pointed out by Professor Henry Kendrick, class of 1835, who joined the mess in 1844. Kendrick insisted that the requirement that members dine in full dress uniform was the principal objection to the mess.[30]

McDowell, however, believed that Delafield was the principal problem; he had been at odds with the single officers for some time over the issue of quarters assigned them. But it is just as likely that McDowell himself was to blame, for in promoting the mess, he had antagonized many of his unmarried brethren. "I was enthusiastic, & perhaps I was not judicious, or did not take my measures sufficiently with reference to the fact that others did not see the question as I saw it," he later admitted.[31] In 1844, an influx of new officers to the Academy brought several new members to the mess. The next year, however, just days after the departure of McDowell and Delafield, a flood of new members joined, including a number who had earlier refused.

The additions of 1844 meant nearly a dozen resident members, and the West Point Army Mess, as it was now known, outgrew its original small quarters and was allowed to move into rooms in the west end of the cadet mess. At the same time, the membership petitioned for a separate, new mess building to be located along the line of brick officers' quarters. Though agreeing in principle that a mess facility should be provided, the Chief of Engineers and Secretary of War did not approve of locating it in the midst of family housing. Totten suggested several alternatives, including special provision for the officers' mess in the proposed new cadet mess. In 1852, larger and more elegant rooms designed specifically for the mess were provided in the new mess hall. That building also offered the Billiards Club on the floor above the mess. Many of the married officers who had not joined the officers' mess were drawn to the Billiards Club, and in 1859 the two organizations were merged.

After 1845, the mess became the center of social activity for the bachelor officers. They ate, drank, and entertained there. They took their seats at the mess table according to military rank—the senior officer present sitting at the head of the table. No discussion of the affairs of the Military Academy was allowed at the table "before the removal of the cloth." No card playing was allowed in the mess parlor, nor were dogs permitted in any of the mess rooms. Ladies were admitted only on special occasions. Visiting officers were extended the "civilities of the Mess," and their first meal—along with a bottle of wine of their choice—was paid for by the resident members. It was at the mess that the single officers entertained. Here they feted the new Superintendents, the new families on post, and the newly wedded officers and their wives.

There were, of course, other activities for the officers, including the Shakespeare Club and a chess club. But, just as the officers' mess was the focal point of their social life, the Napoleon Club was at this time the center of their intellectual recreation. Professor Mahan was president and assigned the Napoleonic campaigns to be discussed by each member. Officers were allowed six weeks to prepare the papers, and, finding ample authorities in both French and English at the library, they worked diligently on them. While he was Superintendent, Robert E. Lee gave the club a room in the academic building. Under Mahan's close supervision, the walls were painted with large maps of the theater of Napoleon's campaigns in Spain, Italy, and Germany. Here the officers submitted their analyses of these campaigns to the critique of Mahan and their other colleagues. Here officers would also sometimes bring cadets to lecture on a key battle or campaign.[32]

These outlets for the energies of the young bachelor officers stationed at West Point were all the more important because of the inadequacy of their assigned residential facilities. Quarters for single officers had been included in the plans for South Barracks, but as the number of instructors grew, these soon became inadequate. Thayer had planned quarters for the surgeon and a number of bachelors in wings of the cadet hospital that was completed in 1830. The surgeon and his family occupied one wing, and the unmarried officers the other. In 1834, however, the single officers were turned out of these rooms to accommodate a married assistant surgeon. Still, relief did seem to be in sight; planning was already under way for the exercise building, in which the whole upper story was intended for the single officers. They scarcely had settled into their new quarters in 1838, however, when the 1815 Academy was destroyed in a fire and their rooms were needed to replace the lost academic facilities. The single officers were once more forced out, and their quarters were transformed into a drawing academy and additional section rooms.[33]

Delafield, who inherited this problem, did what he could to accommodate the unmarried officers, but he could not keep them happy. Finally, exasperated with one officer's complaints, the Superintendent pointed out that, if the officer wished to be reassigned, he "apprehended no difficulty whatever . . . in finding an officer to succeed" him.[34] Henry Brewerton, who replaced Delafield in 1845, had more compassion. "It has been my desire and study to make this class of officer as comfortable as possible in respect to quarters," he wrote Totten, "well knowing that this has been a source of discontent heretofore, and that we could not expect to retain officers of merit at the Academy . . . unless this cause of complaint was to some extent removed." Brewerton made available to the single officers "some 20 or 30 fine rooms in the new barracks for Cadets," in addition to two former professors' quarters.[35]

Not everyone agreed that the bachelors were well served when billeted in the cadet barracks. Officers should be "free from the disagreeable contact of cadets and the noise and disturbance to which they are continuously exposed in the barracks," wrote Captain George Cullum.[36] Brevet Colonel Robert E. Lee, who replaced Brewerton in 1852, agreed and proposed constructing a building specifically for the unmarried officers. Early in 1854, he submitted handsome designs, which were approved, but Lee departed in 1855 before more could be done. John G. Barnard, who followed Lee, was wholly unsympathetic to the project. "I feel myself some doubt about the expediency of erecting" the quarters for the unmarried officers, he wrote Totten shortly after arriving, for "it adds nothing to the accommodation of married officers." He favored "the multiplication of cottages" for families rather than the new bachelors' quarters. "So long as the Corps of Cadets is not increased," he argued, "the unmarried officers . . . [can] find quarters in the barracks."[37]

Robert E. Lee, class of 1829, who succeeded to the superintendency on September 1, 1852, was the son of a Revolutionary War hero and a member of one of Virginia's first families. He had graduated second in his class and had gone on to serve with great distinction in the Corps of Engineers. Lee had compiled an outstanding record during the Mexican War and was considered by many the most promising officer in the Army.

George Washington Custis Lee, the new Superintendent's oldest son, was a cadet when the senior Lee arrived, as was a nephew, Fitzhugh Lee, son of brother Smith Lee.[38] As a consequence, Lee took a particular interest in the cadets, though he showed no partiality to his son or nephew. He invited cadets for informal visits on Sunday afternoons and arranged small dinner parties and more formal holiday affairs. On occasion the Lees used silverware that had belonged to George and Martha Washington, thus thrilling cadets and officers alike.

Lee was a man of dignity and grace, strikingly handsome, quiet, and patient. If he had a fault as superintendent, it was that he acted extraordinarily lenient with cadets: some who ran away and returned a few days later were given another chance; one who lied to the officer of the day was forgiven when he confessed and convinced Lee that he had learned a lesson. He was not by nature a disciplinarian and could not bring himself to become one. He simply could not understand why cadets would not obey the regulations. He himself had completed his four years at West Point without a single demerit. On a ride, Lee and his younger son, Robert, came upon three cadets far off limits. Spotting Lee, the cadets jumped a fence and disappeared into the woods. Said Lee, "I wish boys would do what is right. It would be so much easier for all parties."[39]

The lax discipline of the period ideally suited one cadet, James Abbot McNeill Whistler. The young man entered the Academy in 1851, following in the footsteps of his father, George Washington Whistler, who had graduated in 1819 and been an assistant teacher of drawing at the Military Academy from 1821 to 1822. James Whistler was to become one of the country's best-known artists, and even at the Academy usually led the first section in Professor Weir's drawing class. His fun-loving nature, however, often got the best of him. Although selected to take his meals at Mrs. Thompson's house, he lost the privilege when she caught him flirting with her maid one evening. On being asked what he was doing there at an hour when the house was off limits, Whistler replied, "I'm looking for my cat." Mrs. Thompson ordered him out and told him not to return.

Whistler's wit, which was sometimes biting and sarcastic, and his tendency to ignore his studies and his military duties repeatedly got him into trouble, but it was his habit of studying only what interested him that ended his career at West Point. During his examination in chemistry, Whistler was asked to discuss silicon. "I am required to discuss the subject of silicon. Silicon is a gas. . . ." he began. "That will do, Mr. Whistler," said the examiner. He failed chemistry and was dismissed. In later years, Whistler, who always retained an affection for West Point, would say, "Had silicon been a gas, I would have been a major general." Whistler later sent a copy of his book *Whistler vs. Ruskin: Art and Art Critics* to the Academy with the inscription "From an old cadet whose pride it is to remember his West Point days."[40]

Cadet life at the Military Academy had changed little in the days since Thayer had departed. Until 1849, at least, cadets occupied the same barracks, and until 1852 they ate in the same mess hall. The size of the corps of cadets had changed little from year to year, usually hovering at about two hundred. In 1846, cadet William Dutton described the "order" that dictated the arrangement of his barracks room. Except for the iron bedsteads, which had been introduced by Delafield (cadets who chose them paid a charge of twenty cents each month to defray the cost of their purchase), the order could just as well have been dated any time in the previous quarter century. It read:

> Bedstead—against door; Trunks—under iron bedsteads; Lamps—clean on mantel; Dress Caps—Neatly arranged behind door; Looking Glass— between washstand & door; Books—neatly arranged on shelf farthest from door; Broom—Hanging behind door; Drawing books—under shelf farthest from door; Muskets—in gun rack and locks sprung; Bayonets in scabbards; Accoutrements—Hanging over musket; Sabres, Cutlasses & swords—hanging over muskets; Candle Box (for scrubbing utensils)— Against wall under shelf nearest door & fire place; clothes—neatly hung on pegs over bedsteads; Mattress & Blankets neatly folded; Orderly Board—over mantel; chairs—when not in use under tables; Orderlies of rooms are held responsible for the observance of the above mentioned arrangement.[41]

Messing arrangements were also not much changed, though in these years contracting out had been replaced by the hire of a purveyor whose salary was independent of the number of cadets he fed. The purveyor was required to furnish a plain but substantial soldier's regimen. For breakfast there was "the remains of the meat of the former day's dinner, cut up with potato with considerable gravy," bread, butter, and coffee. At dinner the fare was roast beef, veal, or mutton, boiled potatoes, and bread—green vegetables and sweets were almost unknown at the mess. At tea, the evening meal, there were bread, butter, and tea or coffee, supplemented occasionally by cornbread and molasses. The menu changed daily but was repeated each week. For years the main complaints had been that cadets were forced to wolf down their meals in order to finish on time and that the food was boring. Under the purveyor system the quality of rations also began to slip further. When Secretary of War Jefferson Davis, class of 1828, brought a congressionally appointed commission to West Point in 1860, they heard a chorus of complaints about the food. These, in turn, were followed by some quick, if not wholly effectual, remedies. "They have caused an improvement in our mess hall fare until it now presents a respectable appearance," reported Cadet Tully McCrea shortly thereafter. "If the cleanliness only equalled the quality," he added, "I would be satisfied. But I see no change in that respect. Last night my coffee tasted so plainly of soapsuds, that had not been wrenched from my cup, that I could not drink it."[42]

Life in the classroom, too, remained little changed. Once the section entered the recitation room, the teacher called upon a cadet, who "immediately rises from his seat, [and] arms himself with a piece of chalk and sponge" before taking his place in front of the blackboard. "Thus armed, and standing in the position of a Soldier, the subject which he is required to demonstrate is announced to him." The cadet then faced about "toward the board and, while some other one is demonstrating, performs the necessary work." In turn, each cadet would be required to explain his work.[43]

Examinations in January and June were the culmination of this academic work. Failure in any subject was tantamount to dismissal. Cadets in the upper sections usually had little to fear, but those of the lowest section—the "Immortals"—suffered considerable anxiety. During the examination, each cadet would be called upon in turn to discuss one of the more important subjects of the course. Shortly before the examination, the instructor in each section listed the subjects to be examined on separate bits of paper, shook them up in a hat, and then drew them out one at a time, recording the subject on a roster of his students opposite each name in succession. For the "Immortals," getting a look at this list could mean the difference between life as a civilian and a career as a soldier. This prompted a rather peculiar distortion of the code of honor by which, as gentlemen, the cadets lived. While they considered it dishonorable to lie, or worse, to steal—including copying from another cadet's blackboard during a recitation or an examination—they seem to have seen nothing wrong with an attempt to acquire the examination in advance. Faculty members, particularly the younger officers, often seemed to wink at the practice—while at the same time doing all in their power to defeat the efforts. Cadets would bribe their way past servants, steal into an instructor's house in the wee hours of the morning, and even enter offices through ventilator shafts to get access to the lists. They were known to defeat locks and even to disassemble desks (and reassemble them when done) to copy these examinations. "You may think that is not altogether honest," one cadet admitted to his sweetheart after having recounted such an escapade, but he insisted that the end justified the means.[44]

Cadets could temporarily escape the harsh routine of the barracks and the section room by several approved means: the debating and literary societies, informal sports, hiking, reading, and occasional organized entertainments. Some, of course, engaged in unauthorized enterprises—such as "running it" to Benny Havens's or to Garrison's Landing across the river, or even into New York City. Drinking or even possessing alcohol, visiting local taverns, and departing the post under any guise were offenses that risked dismissal, but this did not deter the more adventurous. Members of the opposite sex were yet another reason cadets strayed beyond the limits; more than once they brought young trollops to the post and even into the barracks. This, too, of course, invited almost certain dismissal.

The Dialectic Society was long the only authorized debating group. It met on Saturday nights to read and critique members' papers and to argue topics that had been approved by the Superintendent. Over the years, these included: "Does the United States owe a greater debt to Thomas Jefferson or to Alexander Hamilton?"; "Should capital punishment be abolished?"; "Ought females to receive a first-rate education?"; "Should nations go to war to preserve the balance of power?"; "Whether universal suffrage should be allowed?"; and "Has a state the right to secede from the union?"[45]

Delafield had had earlier run-ins with that organization. In 1838, there had been "an animated discussion" concerning "the justice of lynch law." That debate had "got very warm" and "came very near merging into the discussion of abolition." Sectional aspects of the log cabin and hard cider presidential campaign of 1840 had also been reflected in Dialectic Society debates when the cadets asked, "Ought the South to prefer William Henry Harrison to Martin Van Buren at the coming Presidential Election?" Indeed, by the fall of 1842, the Dialectic Society had become such a divisive force that the Academic Board complained that it had "given rise to improper feelings" and recommended its "dissolution . . . as soon as circumstances will permit."[46] It is likely that Ulysses Grant was president of the society at this time, and he almost certainly held that office the next spring, when the society proposed to debate the question: "Has a state under any circumstances the right to nullify an act of Congress?" At this point, Delafield intervened, forbade the topic, and effectively disbanded the organization.[47]

When Superintendent Henry Brewerton replaced Delafield in 1845, he was asked by the cadets to revive the organization; he did so, but with the explicit warning that the society must be "governed by wholesome rules, and the discussion of subjects [must be] confined within proper limits." The society's subsequent restraint appears to have kept it out of trouble with the Academy's leadership, but at a cost. Unable to take on the central issues of the times, the society was nearly moribund by the late 1850s.

There were also unauthorized groups such as the Independent Roysterers Club, which had been secretly organized "to promote social intercourse" among its membership. The Roysterers were most active from 1840 to 1842, thriving on raucous but largely innocuous revelry in North Barracks and an occasional illicit foray to Buttermilk Falls. Though associations of this kind were generally short-lived, the Military Academy was seldom without one.

Except for Christmas and New Year's—which were celebrated by suspension of classes for the day and a feast in the mess hall—Saturday nights were the only times when cadets were allowed to attend entertainments. In the main, such activities included Dialectic Society productions, plays put on by the cadets, band concerts, and an occasional touring troupe.

Possibly the greatest change in the life of cadets in this period came with the introduction of horses and riding lessons in 1839. To accomplish this, Secretary of War Poinsett had to override the opposition of the Academic Board—the first significant action of this kind since the Academy was forced to add civil engineering in the early 1820s. Poinsett merely ordered that equitation be added to the program. To preclude foot-dragging on the part of the board, he dispatched a sergeant, five dragoons, and twelve horses to West Point. Most cadets, once they had become proficient, enjoyed riding, but not all. More than a few faced the prospect with nothing more than grim determination, experience having taught that the horse was likely to get the better of each encounter. But, for Ulysses Grant, otherwise an inattentive student, riding provided a chance to excel. He had grown up around horses and was the most daring horseman in the Academy. He once demonstrated his ability to handle his mount before the Board of Visitors and a large crowd of spectators. The riding master had one of the dragoons hold a pole parallel with the ground but at arms' length above his head—one end resting against the wall. He then signaled Grant, on York, his favorite mount, to jump it. The pair cleared the pole and landed "with a tremendous thud," amid a din of applause. At the demand of the crowd, Grant and York repeated the feat three more times.[48]

During the early years of this period, West Point's faculty, led by Dennis Hart Mahan (Professor of Engineering, 1830–1871), the senior member of the Academic Board, chose the best of Thayer's sons to head its departments:

William H. C. Bartlett (class of 1826), Professor of Natural and Experimental Philosophy, 1834–1871; and Albert E. Church (class of 1828), Professor of Mathematics, 1837–1878.[49] These men, along with Mahan, were the nucleus of West Point's intellectual vigor. But there were others who had also come under Thayer's influence and who would play important roles at West Point in these years: Jacob W. Bailey (class of 1832) and Henry L. Kendrick (class of 1835), Professors of Chemistry, 1835–1857 and 1857–1880, respectively. Of course, many of the Superintendents from 1838 to 1866 fell into this category—Delafield (class of 1818), Brewerton (class of 1819), Lee (class of 1829), Barnard (class of 1833), Alexander H. Bowman (class of 1825), and George W. Cullum (class of 1833).[50]

Thayer's influence was pervasive, but Mahan was the reigning spirit. It was Mahan who defended West Point in the press, Mahan who acted as confidential adviser to prominent public figures, and Mahan who exploited those connections to protect what he perceived to be the best interests of the Academy. Even more significantly, it was Mahan who guided the Academic Board for four decades and led it in its battles with the Superintendents who passed through West Point and with the Army hierarchy in Washington.

Mahan had a brilliant scientific mind—his *Course of Civil Engineering* was the leading text on the subject for decades—but he was more; he was

Dennis Hart Mahan. Mahan was professor of civil and military engineering from 1830 until 1871. West Point Museum Collection, United States Military Academy.

the nation's leading theorist of war. To his official title, professor of civil and military engineering, Mahan often added the words "and of the Art of War." His brief text *Advanced Guard, Outpost and Detachment Service of Troops with the Essential Principles of Strategy,* commonly known simply as *Outposts,* guided the military thought of two generations of America's professional soldiers. Still, his personality prevented him from winning the affection of cadets, for he was aloof and relentlessly demanding.

William H. C. Bartlett's interests were much narrower than Mahan's. The professor of natural and experimental philosophy concentrated on his own field, especially mechanics and astronomy. There he, too, achieved distinction. His *Elements of Analytical Mechanics,* first published in 1853, went through nine editions and was widely used in American colleges. Unlike Mahan, Bartlett was liked by his students, for he went out of his way to interest them in what he was teaching—sometimes assembling the entire class in the lecture hall to demonstrate a point with the laboratory apparatus. His subject was not an easy one for cadets, but he had a flair for skillful questioning that could lead even weak students to see the problem from a whole new perspective.

Albert E. Church, Professor of Mathematics, resembled Bartlett in devotion to a single academic discipline but lacked his colleague's ability to stimulate the interest of students. He gained scholarly recognition with a widely used series of mathematical texts. Church could be kindly and patient with a student who sought his help, but apparently he was not a dynamic classroom teacher because it was his subject in which the most academic deficiencies occurred. A sonnet by an anonymous cadet lamented the difficulty in which so many found themselves in Church's course:

> Of all the girls I ever knew,
>   The one I've most neglected,
> Is Called Miss "Anna Lytical,"
>   For her I've least respected.
> Oh! Anna! Anna Lytical
>   I'll never love you more
> For you, I fear, will cause my fall,
>   And make me leave the Corps.[51]

When the disproportionate percentage of academic failures in mathematics was pointed out to Church, his answer was that the institution should change the curriculum by eliminating some of the nonscientific subjects so that cadets could devote additional time to mathematics. Since the mathematics program—which dominated the first two years of the curriculum—

supported both engineering and natural philosophy, Church could count on both Mahan and Bartlett to join him on the Academic Board in resisting attempts to tinker with his program. In this, they were always successful.

Although the Academic Board was presided over by the Superintendent, its decisions were made by majority vote. The board, which had come to fruition during the Thayer era, was the most powerful entity at West Point. And, in matters over which the board had primacy, Mahan, Bartlett, and Church usually had their way. Throughout this period, the board enjoyed a large degree of autonomy; it designed instructional programs, selected texts, and passed on curriculum changes. And its members examined cadets, determined order of merit standing, recommended graduates for branches of the Army, and decided whether students found deficient at the semiannual examinations should be allowed a second chance.

But the Academic Board did more; it acted as a buffer between the academic program at West Point and those from without who would change it. Only twice between 1817 and 1854 was it defeated on major matters—in the 1820s over the introduction of civil engineering, and in 1839 when it was forced to introduce riding. In a hierarchical organization such as the Army, where obedience to the orders of superiors in the chain of command was ingrained, the Academic Board provided a means of resisting unwanted and disruptive tinkering. The board could usually "study" an issue until it simply disappeared. It could postpone action while one committee and then another weighed every aspect of the problem—until a troublesome Superintendent or Secretary of War let the matter slip or moved on. On the occasions when this failed, board members were often able to frustrate the implementation. In short, the Academic Board provided a mechanism by which essential institutional stability was maintained. Without it, each new Superintendent or Secretary of War could whipsaw the program as he saw fit. Given its charter, the Academic Board was often able to resist undesirable or ill-advised reforms. And when it could not, it was usually able to outlast its foe and ultimately reverse the decision. Though there might be internal rifts, those on the outside saw the board as a united bulwark.

The Academic Board was repeatedly called on to defend the scientific orientation of the curriculum and the heavy emphasis on mathematics. One of the first cases came in 1843 when a board of officers headed by Winfield Scott convened to study the Academy and took issue with what it considered undue stress on these subjects, calling for more practical military training. The Academic Board responded that all officers needed a basic knowledge of mathematics, science, and engineering, and that mathematical training developed mental discipline. Moreover, the board pointed out, only the upper sections went beyond the scope of courses taught in civilian colleges. "One of the most important objects of the Academy," the Academic Board argued, was "a thorough course of mental as well as military discipline." And this was best accomplished through "a strict sense of mathematical and philosophical study." The ideal vehicle to attain this was the curriculum they had developed—"the result of the experience of many years." "The officer whose mind has been thus disciplined" could serve effectively "in whatever station the interests of the service may place him." This argument was repeated whenever the curriculum came under attack and always seemed to disarm the critics.[52]

Proposals for curriculum change or revision, whether generated externally or internally, were the issues of great importance to the Academic Board. The regulations specified that no more than ten hours daily be devoted to academics, including both classroom time and study periods, and each department fully utilized every minute of its allocation. Meals, formations, and other duties occupied much of the remaining time, leaving cadets with barely two hours for recreation. Because that schedule was so crowded, a new course could be introduced only by shortening or eliminating an existing one. Even a slight modification of the curriculum required painstaking study, planning, and interdepartmental haggling. The sheer complexity of making change often militated against it.

In 1854, during Robert E. Lee's superintendence, the Academic Board faced another significant onslaught. For several years the Boards of Visitors had recommended the addition of courses in the humanities and an increase in military training. By the early 1850s, Totten, the Chief of Engineers in Washington, became a champion of the idea. Despite the Academic Board's insistence that there was no time in the curriculum for these subjects, the pressure grew. The Academic Board reported that the only way to include them was to extend the course from four to five years. This, the board members were certain, would be as unpalatable in Washington as it was at West Point. But Totten called their bluff and gained the support of Secretary of War Davis. To the chagrin of all at West Point, the Secretary ordered the Academic Board to inaugurate the five-year course in 1854. There was no easy way that Mahan or the board could resist, for this was their own recommendation. To ensure that the Academic Board carried out the intended reforms, Totten's implementing directive specified that none of the added time would be allocated to engineering, natural philosophy, French, drawing, or chemistry. Instead, the increase could be devoted only to adding new courses in Spanish, history, geography, and military law, and in augmenting existing programs in English and military training. It was the most significant defeat the Academic Board had yet suffered, or so it seemed at the time.[53]

Instruction in Spanish began in 1856, based on the program of studies drawn up and approved in 1854 for the five-year course. To teach Spanish, the board chose Patrice De Janon, the swordmaster, and named him professor of Spanish in 1857. With the exception of eighteen months, beginning in September 1863, when he was "out of service," De Janon was head of the department until his retirement in 1882.[54]

In 1858, the Academic Board petitioned a new Secretary of War, John B. Floyd, for a return to the old system. It argued that the five-year program was intellectually exhausting to cadets, but, more important, it diverted the time and attention of students from the scientific subjects. As far as the majority of the Academic Board was concerned, West Point should abandon the humanities, reduce military training to its pre-1854 status, and return to its old preserves: mathematics, science, and engineering. At first it appeared that the board had won; Floyd backed it and ordered the reinstatement of the four-year program. Then he reversed himself. Regardless, the five-year program was abolished at the outbreak of the war in 1861. By the war's end, its two principal supporters were gone—Totten had died, and Davis had defected. The program was never reestablished. The newly added courses were either dropped quietly or dramatically scaled back. The Academic Board had simply outlasted its opponents.

In the spring of 1855, Lee accepted a transfer from the engineers to the cavalry in order to gain a promotion. The law required that the Superintendent be from the Corps of Engineers. If Lee wanted the promotion, he would have to leave West Point. Jefferson Davis wanted neither to deny the Superintendent the promotion (which he was unlikely to receive for years in the engineers) nor to lose him from West Point. There was, however, no immediate recourse.[55]

Engineer Captain John G. Barnard, of the class of 1833, relieved Lee on April 1, 1855. In Barnard's case, the requirement that the Superintendent be an engineer had the peculiar effect of placing him over the more senior Major William H. T. Walker, an infantry officer, who was the Commandant of Cadets. An act of Congress the next year solved the problem by giving the temporary rank of colonel and lieutenant colonel to the Superintendent and Commandant of Cadets, respectively. Barnard's tenure as Superintendent was brief—lasting less than a year and a half—and generally uneventful. Richard Delafield was sent back to West Point in September 1856 to replace him.

When Delafield returned to West Point after an eleven-year absence, he immediately undertook another thorough review of the Academy's operation, much as he had at the beginning of his first tour. The most obvious problem was discipline, and Delafield was famed as a strict disciplinarian. After the lax years of Lee and Barnard, however, his efforts to restore order engendered considerable animosity. His manner of sarcastic reprimand further embittered cadets and officers alike, and his unwillingness to grant leave to cadets, however justified the need, caused some to question his judgment and even his sanity.[56]

Delafield's attempt to establish discipline was complicated by the times. Issues that had begun to divide the nation and would lead to civil war also affected the Military Academy. Most cadets made friends among cadets from the North and the South alike. Still, sectional feelings sometimes ran high. Cadets often reflected the feelings current in their home communities, and correspondence with family, hometown newspapers, and furloughs tended to keep that localist spirit alive. The Academy could not overcome all the sectional biases that its students brought with them.

Events and debates of the times also injected sectional feelings. The reaction to John Brown's raid on Harpers Ferry in October 1859 showed that clearly. Students and faculty at the Academy followed the news of Brown's raid, and of his trial and subsequent execution, with intense interest and furious debate. "In each scene of the tragedy West Point was deeply engrossed," recalled Morris Schaff, class of 1862. Still, Delafield kept a tight rein on that debate.[57]

Delafield, who was never particularly popular, had become something of a curmudgeon as he had grown older. Cadet John Pelham thought him "arbitrary" and "a hypocritical and deceitful man," and seemed to reflect the prevailing mood.[58] Mahan's daughter, Jane, thought him "a fine officer, but a martinet, and very imperious. We children were terribly afraid of him and ran away if we saw him coming."[59]

Until the mid-1850s, sectional sentiment at West Point only occasionally burst forth in open hostility. After that, however, sectional feelings grew steadily more intense and overt. Fights between Northerners and Southerners became commonplace. In the summer of 1856, Dodson Ramseur of North Carolina wrote home that he was looking forward with pleasure to punishing severely any miserable abolitionists in the new plebe class.[60] Emory Upton, who entered the Academy that summer, had previously been a student at Ohio's Oberlin College, a radical school that admitted both women and blacks. Upton, a staunch abolitionist, was the object of much attention from the Southern upperclassmen. In 1859, Ramseur's roommate, Wade Hampton Gibbes of South Carolina, made an offensive remark concerning Upton's supposed intimacies with African-American coeds at Oberlin. Upton demanded an explanation, Gibbes refused to give one, and Upton challenged him to a duel. They met that night with swords. As a crowd of cadets gathered on the first floor of the barracks, the two went upstairs into a darkened room. When the affair was finished, Upton had received a cut on the face—a scar he would carry the rest of his life.[61]

As the crisis approached, even the strongest ties of friendship became strained. A mounting bitterness seeped into the corps from every side. The political parties, harried and split by slavery, had named their candidates. Lincoln was the Republican standard-bearer, and the remnants of the Whig Party, out of which the Republicans had grown, nominated John Bell of Tennessee. The splintered Democrats nominated Stephen A. Douglas of Illinois, and then the defecting Southern Democrats nominated John Breckinridge of Kentucky. In October 1860, a month before the election, a group of Southern cadets decided to hold a straw vote at West Point. "A better scheme to embroil the corps and to precipitate hostilities between individuals could not have been devised," wrote Morris Schaff, class of 1862. When Lincoln received sixty-four votes, the Southerners promptly appointed tellers to interrogate cadets personally and discover the names of "the Black Republican Abolitionists" in the corps who had voted for him. The interrogations produced violent confrontations. Fistfights by the dozen broke out.[62]

The intransigence of the Southern cadets only intensified with the election of Lincoln on November 6. On the ninth, South Carolina called a Secession Convention. On the nineteenth at West Point, Henry S. Farley of South Carolina handed in his resignation—the first member of the corps of cadets to withdraw in response to secession. Before the end of the year, he was joined by most of the other South Carolina cadets, along with three from Mississippi and two from Alabama. Two other cadets resigned in January 1861, four more in February, and another four in March. A few officers also departed—the separations sometimes tearful occasions.

On January 23, 1861, Delafield was relieved by Captain Pierre G. T. Beauregard, class of 1838. Beauregard, a Louisianian, had been appointed in late December 1860 in the closing days of John B. Floyd's term as Secretary of War. Joseph Totten, longtime Chief of Engineers, nominated Beauregard in an attempt to thwart Jefferson Davis's renewed effort to open the superintendency to officers of all branches of the Army. Beauregard had a reputation for brilliance as an engineer and, just as important, had well-placed political connections. Totten hoped that the combination would make it embarrassing, if not impossible, for Davis and his allies to oppose his nomination—thereby defeating Davis's decision.

Beauregard, however, was relieved of his new command just five days after he assumed it. The new Secretary of War, Joseph Holt, was informed that Beauregard planned to resign as soon as his home state of Louisiana left the Union, and Holt fully understood the devastating impact of having a sitting

Superintendent resign to join the South. But before the Secretary could act, Louisiana bolted. Holt immediately ordered Delafield to reassume command at West Point, and the old Superintendent once again took up the now-familiar reins on January 28. He remained in command until March 1, when he was relieved for the last time by Major Alexander H. Bowman, class of 1825. Local reaction to Delafield's final departure can be summed up in this brief exchange: "Well Luke so the Major has gone," remarked an officer to Luke Scanlon, an old Irishman who worked in the academic building. "Deed Captain an' he has," Scanlon replied. "And it's many the dry eye followed him."[63]

On April 12, 1861, less than three months after being relieved at West Point, Beauregard ordered the Confederate shore batteries in Charleston harbor to open fire on Fort Sumter. The war had begun. The next day, the officers, professors, and cadets at West Point were ordered to take a new oath of allegiance, and those who refused were dismissed. By April 22, almost all those from the Southern states who would depart had withdrawn. Of the 278 cadets at West Point on November 1, 1860, 86 had been appointed from the Southern states. Of these, 65 were discharged or dismissed, or else resigned for causes connected with secession.

On May 6, the first class was ordered to Washington without graduation. It was commissioned and immediately assigned to units of the growing Union Army. The new first class, which had already spent nearly four years at West Point, immediately petitioned to be allowed to take the field as well. In June, they were hastily examined, graduated, and ordered to Washington. As soon as they were commissioned, they were assigned to train the "three-month" regiments then encamped around the Capitol.

At the outbreak of hostilities, the Military Academy immediately returned to the familiar four-year curriculum. The fourth class received mathematics and French, along with some English and geography. The third class continued the study of mathematics, French, drawing, and riding. The second classmen took natural and experimental philosophy, chemistry, drawing, and riding. The first class program consisted of military and civil engineering, the science of war, ethics, law, and mineralogy and geology. In addition, military science was taught in each of the four years. It was a curriculum remarkably similar to that of a decade—even two decades—earlier, and it remained fairly stable throughout the war.

Most features of the Academy's operation were thrown into turmoil in the early days of the war. Early in the conflict, the officer personnel of the academic and Commandant's staffs were in constant flux. In 1861 alone, thirteen officers applied for and received service in the field. The Superintendent, Alexander Bowman, complained in September that instruction in artillery and cavalry had to be totally suspended because of the absence of officers, horses, and guns. As the war progressed, able-bodied officers were replaced by those who were paroled or disabled or by appointees from civilian life, but these substitutes were not always qualified. Some fell short of the academic requisites, and others, whose wounds were slow to heal, were physically unable to carry out their duties fully. The turnover rate among these instructors was high, and extended absences were frequent. This often necessitated a return to the unsatisfactory expedient of employing cadets as teachers. It was not until the last months of 1865 that a sufficient number of qualified officers became available to restore a measure of stability.

Despite this, academic studies were continued without interruption during the whole course of the war—except for a brief period during the New York City draft riots in the summer of 1863. The Superintendent then dispatched a detachment of several officers and fifty-nine men to the city to help restore order—essentially the entire regular force at West Point. This left the cannon and powder magazines at the Academy unprotected at a time when rumors were rampant that the New York mob intended to march up the Hudson and seize the material. Though baseless, these fears caused the staff at West Point some anxious moments: ball cartridges were issued to cadets, guards were posted, and pickets with field guns were established at the South and North Docks and Gee's Point. This vigilance was maintained for several days and nights.[64]

Though far from the front, West Point followed each campaign and battle of the war with close attention. Spirits rose and fell with the fortunes of war. In the early years of the conflict, the President's calls for days of fasting and prayer were observed solemnly, but, as fortunes changed, the victories prompted thanksgiving and rejoicing. As victories began to pile up in the fall of 1864, one-hundred-gun salutes were fired in honor of the triumphs at Mobile Bay and Atlanta, and in December of that year a salute of thirty-six guns was ordered in honor of "General Sherman's gift to the nation of the city of Savannah."

Major Zealous B. Tower, class of 1841, replaced Bowman as Superintendent in July 1864, but Tower departed just two months later. He had graduated at the top of his class and afterward had stayed on to teach at the Academy. One of Tower's former students, Ulysses S. Grant, had only recently been made Commanding General of the United States Army. Interest in Grant, therefore, was high, and stories of Grant's cadet high jinks enjoyed great currency.

One tale involved both Grant and Tower. Cadet Franklin Gardner, later a major general in the Confederate Army, had acquired an old silver-cased watch about four inches in diameter. The watch was passed around as the cadets marched to mathematics class. Grant had the watch as they reached the classroom and merely stuffed it under his coat. As it happened, Cadet Zealous Tower, a first classman, was substituting for the absent instructor. Tower sent four cadets, including Grant, to the board to work out problems. Grant finished his work and was about to recite, when the old watch in his coat began striking—producing a muffled *bong, bong, bong*. Gardner had wound and set it. Cadet Tower first thought the noise was coming from the hall and ordered the door closed. The bongs only got louder. Grant stood unperturbed while the rest of the cadets struggled to maintain their composure. Before Tower realized where the noise was coming from, it ceased. Grant then proceeded with his recitation and took his seat. Only years later did Tower learn the source of the clanging.[65]

The wartime Superintendents, Alexander H. Bowman, Zealous B. Tower, and George W. Cullum, who replaced Tower in September 1864, were faced with numerous challenges, but none more troublesome than the criticism brought on West Point by the large number of cadets and graduates who deserted the Union. To make matters worse, the early performance in the field of many senior officers who had remained loyal was hardly inspiring. Something, critics proclaimed, was fundamentally wrong at West Point. The criticism was all the more troublesome because it was launched by Secretary of War Simon Cameron. In his annual report of 1861, he first singled out the militia and volunteers for praise and then assaulted the Military Academy. Its graduates were bound "by more than ordinary obligations of honor to remain faithful to their flag," Cameron argued. He blamed the defections on the disciplinary system at West Point, which, he insisted, failed to distinguish between immorality and simple violations of regulations. It encouraged cadets to substitute "habit for conscience." A number of Radical Republicans in Congress joined Cameron's attacks on the Academy. Some charged that early Union defeats and McClellan's lack of aggressiveness stemmed as much from lukewarm patriotism as from incompetence. Others simply echoed the old Jacksonian complaints: there was an aristocratic tone in the regular Army, and regulars, in particular West Point graduates, discriminated unfairly against militia and volunteer officers.

Edward Chauncey Marshall answered in 1862 with a small pamphlet entitled *Are the West Point Graduates Loyal?* After "a very *careful count*," he answered in the affirmative. The numbers, he said, "should give us renewed confidence in this noble nursery of soldiers, which was the child of the Revolution and was planned and formed by . . . the purest and best of the patriot sires of the Republic."[66] The champions of West Point won a critical battle in 1863 when they defeated a Radical effort in Congress to abolish the Military Academy. By then, however, the fortunes of the Union forces had begun to improve under Grant, William T. Sherman (class of 1840), and other graduates. This, coupled with the less-than-sterling performances of non–West Pointers such as Benjamin F. Butler, John C. Fremont, and Daniel E. Sickles, robbed the attacks of much of their impact. Moreover, it did not escape attention that the successes of the South had largely been engineered by West Point graduates. Even the final victory in 1865 did not completely silence the voices of hostility, and suspicion and new attacks resurfaced after the war.

Still, West Point had much of which to be proud. West Point graduates, taken as a group, acquitted themselves nobly in combat, just as they had earlier in Mexico and against the Indians. But there was a difference in the Civil War. Prior to 1861, no graduate had attained the rank of general officer in the line of the Army. In this war, graduates of the United States Military Academy stepped forward to lead the forces of both the North and the South. At the conclusion of the struggle, West Point graduates commanded all the armies in the field on both sides, nearly all the corps, and a majority of the divisions. Every important battle of the conflict had been commanded by a graduate on one or both sides—generally both. Of the sixty most critical battles or campaigns, all but six were commanded on both sides by graduates. Of the exceptions, a graduate commanded one side in every case, and was victorious on all but one occasion. Equally significant, if less visible, it was almost exclusively Academy graduates who performed the Herculean logistical feats that had sustained the largest armies the world had ever known—that, in fact, had made a new modern form of warfare possible.

This outcome served to validate the approach the Academy had employed since Thayer had taken the helm, and for many years it nurtured the institution in the belief that this was the approach that would best secure the future. For better or worse, the Academy would bask for decades in the glory of the accomplishments of its graduates in that titanic struggle between the North and South.

CHAPTER SIX

Basking in the Glory, 1866–1902

If the United States Military Academy seemed to bask in the glory of its graduates' accomplishments, it was not the result of any isolation from the world of education or any uncertainty of purpose, but rather the conscious and considered conclusion that West Point was already on the right course. The Academy's leaders were convinced that their emphasis on mathematics and the sciences developed mental discipline—the key to success regardless of what difficulties the future officer might encounter.[1]

During the winter of 1865–1866, a small group of second classmen conceived the idea of forming a billiards club of their own—an illicit one, of course, for no such thing was allowed to cadets by the regulations. The very idea of such an undertaking would have been unthinkable only a year before, but now the war was over, and a new standard of behavior seemed justified. In searching the barracks for a safe location, the cadets discovered a small auxiliary coal room hidden behind the huge coal bunkers in the cellar under "C" company. They bought the silence of the furnace tender, ordered a table from New York, and set about emptying and cleaning the new clubroom. They boarded up the window and filled the opening with tanbark to deaden the sound of the balls. They put in a stove, a card table, a half dozen chairs, four kerosene lamps with reflectors, a supply of pictures on the walls, a stock of pipes and tobacco, a keg of cider, a barrel of crackers, and a whole cheese— all the trappings of a first-class billiards room.

    The table was shipped to a willing party in the town of Garrison, and then, late one night, it was transported across the frozen river and up to the barracks, where it was carefully and silently carried down to the newly decorated clubroom. The secret was well kept for two or three months, then a voucher from the manufacturer came into the hands of the Academy's treasurer. Obviously, the cadets had purchased a billiard table! But where had they put it? The officers made several searches through the barracks, through the attic among the timbers and cobwebs, and through the expanses of the basement of the barracks—but not the coal bunkers, which were piled high in anticipation of winter. They even went so far as to search some of the houses in the vicinity of the barracks. The members were so careful that their comings and goings to and from the billiards room continued undetected. Meanwhile, the club was going full tilt, and the membership grew to about thirty.

The table was little used during the summer, but in the fall and early winter the members, now first classmen, once again enjoyed its privileges. Late one night in November, however, two officers who were returning from the mess spied some cadets stealing into the 6th division. Anticipating that they might discover the phantom billiard table, the officers followed the unwary cadets into the basement hall and watched them disappear into the coal bins. A door opened, and light flooded out into the passage, then the click of balls confirmed the officers' suspicions. The officers held a whispered consultation. Should they break in immediately or wait and share the fun with the other officers the next night? They decided to wait.

However, the officers' discovery had been observed, and their conversation overheard. Upon learning of their narrow escape, the billiard club members decided to yield in style. The room was put in order, the balls spotted on the table, and a note was left for the officers. Early the next evening, the lamps were lit, and the room abandoned for the last time. When the officers burst in, they found the neat and brilliantly lit room, and the billiard table they had so long sought. But try as they might, the authorities could find no clue as to the club's membership, and the matter was allowed to drop. The table was placed in the Commandant's quarters, where it stood for years.[2]

Billiards and other temporary diversions aside, cadets in the postwar era lived much as had their predecessors. The barracks built in 1851 had coal-fired boilers that provided steam heat—and the steam pipes were a useful means of signaling the approach of an inspecting officer. In time, gas lighting was added, and running water was installed in the basements to supply the boilers, though the barracks were still without baths or toilets. Baths, lavatories, and commodes were in a long, low building at the rear of the barracks known as the "cadet sinks." Cadets who did not bathe at least once a week were reported and punished. Clothes were washed twice a week at a central laundry, and cadets who did not turn in soiled clothes and linens likewise drew demerits.

Punishment still meant walking guard tours or "extras" on the "area." This entailed marching back and forth in a prescribed location behind the barracks in full uniform, with the rifle at shoulder arms. Some spent hours upon hours walking the area with nothing but the gloomy stone walls and fellow sufferers to gaze upon.

Of course, time did bring changes. Since 1808, the Thompsons—widow and daughters—had provided meals for about a dozen select cadets who enjoyed not only the excellent food and the opportunity to linger over it but

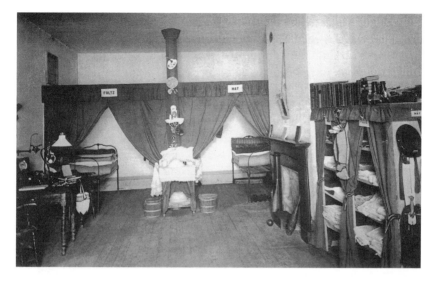

Cadet room in barracks, ca. 1879. United States Military Academy Archives.

also the homelike atmosphere of the Thompson household. In 1878, with the death of Miss Amelia Thompson, the eldest and last surviving Thompson daughter, this small, exclusive mess was closed. In earlier days, the Thompson house had been known as the military storekeeper's house. It was the last of the Revolutionary War structures on post and was razed soon after Miss Thompson's death. With it passed one of the oldest traditions at West Point.

In the years just after the war, it became the custom of the first class to celebrate the arrival of the year in which it would graduate. The New Year's celebration of 1876 was a particularly raucous affair. While some cadets sang songs at the top of their lungs, others rolled cannonballs along the floor of the barracks piazzas, and yet others set off firecrackers. They kept up the racket until being dispersed by the appearance of the tactical officers. When 1877 approached, these officers prepared to act, and they stopped the celebration almost before it began. The next year, the class of 1878 learned that the tactical officers were again organizing in advance to stymie the New Year's revelry. So confident of success were the officers that some had promised to give their lady friends an opportunity to see the midnight celebration and then to witness their dexterity in dispersing the celebrants. Learning of this, the class decided to forgo the usual pranks and fun. To the disappointment of the officers and the young women who had been invited to view the fun, midnight arrived and the area was quiet and deserted.

Two years later the "success" of an elaborately planned New Year's celebration of the class of 1880—and the aftermath—brought an end to such
affairs. Just an hour before midnight, when the barracks sentries were removed, the plan was put into effect. Small detachments were silently dispatched to man the reveille gun and the guns of the siege battery at Trophy
Point, and others were sent to a gun that had been smuggled onto the roof of
the barracks; the balance were given fireworks that had been smuggled onto
the post. At the last minute, the ground floor doors of the barracks were locked
from the inside. All was stillness; then the chapel bell signaled midnight.
Before the second chime could sound, the cannon were fired as if one. The
tactical officers, who were celebrating at the mess, came rushing toward the
barracks but were met by a barrage of Roman candles, rockets, and firecrackers. In the confusion, the cadets who had manned the guns returned
and were admitted to the barracks. By the time the "tacs" could gain entry
to the barracks and regain control, the corps members were all "asleep" in
their bunks—except the cadet officers, who were found bound and gagged.
In response, John McAllister Schofield, class of 1853, who had become
Superintendent in 1876, confined the entire corps to cadet limits (the immediate area of the academic buildings, barracks, and mess hall). He also
prohibited cadets from visiting the officers' quarters and ordered additional
officers into the barracks to see that discipline was maintained.[3]

In the wake of this demonstration, the class of 1881 passed up the obser-
vance of the New Year and, with the permission of the Superintendent,
sponsored a special entertainment at the traditional "open" meeting of the
Dialectical Society, just one hundred nights before graduation. One of their
number had convinced Samuel Langhorne Clemens, the humorist better
known as Mark Twain, to come and speak.[4]

Clemens became a frequent visitor to West Point, making at least ten visits
to the Academy between 1876 and 1890. He thoroughly enjoyed the company of the cadets and made it a standing practice to join them in the barracks away from the officers. Long into the night, he told jokes and stories
as the cadets roared with laughter. And, on these occasions, the tactical officers would obligingly overlook the noise and other infractions involved.[5]

At West Point, Clemens also befriended certain officers, particularly
Lieutenant Charles E. S. Wood, an aide to General Howard, and Colonel
Wesley Meritt, who replaced Howard as Superintendent. He visited whenever the opportunity arose. Clemens loved to saunter around the post, chew-
ing on a cigar and swapping stories with cadets, and he occasionally allowed
himself to be coaxed into a formal speaking engagement. In 1887, he helped
inaugurate the recently renovated cadet mess hall, where, much to the delight of the cadets, he read his "English as She Is Taught." The next day, he

accompanied Merritt to review a parade. Here, too, he drew mirth from the cadets, for he forgot to throw away his cigar before taking his place in line with the staff.[6]

The "100th Night Show," as it became known, involved songs, skits, poems, and readings in which the cadets poked fun at themselves, the officers, and even the Superintendent. Its popularity, of course, derived from its pointed wit and humor, and the show continues to this day. For the first few years, it was held in the Dialectic Society hall in the barracks above the sally port. But it became so popular that it was soon moved to the mess hall, where the entire corps and the officers and their wives could attend. This was certainly the case with Clemens's appearance in 1881.

In 1898, the cadets went so far in their sharp satire of Commandant of Cadets Otto L. Hein's efforts to eradicate hazing that he shut them down. "The very considerable licence permitted cadets" in entertainments, reported Hein, had been "curtailed." In the future, "all reference, either in disapprobation or praise, to commissioned officers on duty at the Academy or elsewhere" was prohibited. Hein, class of 1870, was so displeased with the Dialectic Society's performance that for a time he took away the group's meeting hall in the barracks and converted it into a cadet lounge.[7]

Beginning in the last years of the Civil War, discipline had deteriorated at West Point. In part this was because the officers who returned to West Point during this period were not inclined to enforce regulations that often appeared petty in light of their recent wartime experiences. But this laxity also reflected the attitudes or capabilities of the Superintendents. Lieutenant Colonel George W. Cullum—who had long served as Henry Halleck's chief of staff before being shunted to West Point in 1864 when Halleck was replaced by Grant—was unable or unwilling to overcome the reluctance of his officers to enforce discipline. Cullum left little mark as Superintendent and is better known for his *Biographical Register of the Officers and Graduates of the United States Military Academy*, his work on behalf of the Association of Graduates, and his bequest for a memorial hall named in his honor. Cullum was followed in 1866 by an even more ineffectual officer, Colonel Thomas Gamble Pitcher, class of 1845. As John Schofield later noted, wartime requirements in the field for the most capable officers had proven "prejudicial to the interests of the military academy"—a difficulty, he added, that "continued some time after the close of the war."[8] Pitcher, an infantry officer, was the first nonengineer chosen to supervise the United States Military Academy under provisions of the Act of July 13, 1866, which provided that the Superintendent might be chosen from any branch of the service. His tenure was so undistinguished that it is tempting to suggest that he was appointed to demonstrate the imprudence of this departure from tradition. Pitcher had little to recommend him for the position, and he added nothing to his reputation while there. He had graduated fortieth of forty-one in the class of 1845 and had subsequently enjoyed a largely unremarkable career.

Under Pitcher, discipline suffered so markedly that, in 1871, even the board of visitors remarked on its decline.[9] The most striking manifestation of this failure of administrative control was the dramatic increase in hazing. This tradition, even in more innocent forms, had not always been a feature of West Point life. Albert E. Church, the longtime professor of mathematics, recalled that when he arrived in 1824, "there was nothing in the Corps of Cadets approaching what is now called 'hazing.'"[10] It began as mere deviling. This occasional annoying of the plebes, however, led in only a few years to a well-developed system of torment, which became common practice by the mid-1830s. By the Civil War, it was thought a custom of the Academy, but it was still a custom of largely harmless pranks inflicted on new cadets during their first summer encampment.

After the Civil War, however, hazing took on a more sinister character. Now, throughout the year, upperclassmen forced plebes to do exhausting physical exercises that sometimes resulted in serious injuries, or to eat or drink unpalatable foods or beverages, or to humiliate themselves in any number of ways. This change was concomitant with, if not caused by, the practice begun under Cullum of segregating the plebes for some weeks in the barracks when they first arrived—a period that soon became known as "Beast Barracks." No longer were plebes introduced directly into the corps during the summer encampment, as had been the custom previously. The ostensible purpose of this new practice was to let a few upperclassmen teach the new cadets saluting, marching, and other basics of military life at the Academy. Instead, it produced a form of "official hazing" in which upperclassmen attempted to drive all sense of self-importance from the plebes and to teach them unquestioning and instant obedience. Day and night they were harassed, called "Beast," "Animal," "Thing," or "Mr. Dumbjohn." They were braced, double-timed, and ordered to do impossible tasks. Heads back, chests out, stomachs in—they were constantly ordered about, berated and harassed. This official segregation of the plebes by the West Point administration led almost immediately to their continued isolation by the other cadets when they left Beast Barracks. Now they were not fully integrated into the corps—were not *recognized* by the upperclassmen—until they became third classmen.

As a result of the lax discipline, hazing in Beast Barracks got out of hand almost immediately. Unable to curtail the practice any other way, Cullum threatened to hold a court of inquiry. Instead, the third class, which had produced the hazers, took a voluntary pledge to abstain from committing such offenses in the future. But in 1867 hazing again broke out. Pitcher, who had relieved Cullum, was equally unable to stop it. He was finally instructed to extract an oath of obedience from the cadets. In the spring of 1868 and again in 1869, all members of the plebe class—just months before they became third classmen—were required to swear that they would not interfere with, harass, molest, or injure any entering cadets nor demand menial services of any sort from the new plebes, or even accept voluntary services from them.

In 1871, President Grant personally selected Colonel Thomas Howard Ruger, class of 1854, to replace Pitcher as Superintendent. Ruger was a good choice. He had graduated high in his class and had a brilliant record in the Civil War as a division commander. More to the point, Grant knew him to be a strict disciplinarian. When the father of a cadet whom Ruger had disciplined for misconduct sought to have the new Superintendent transferred, alleging that he was too strict, Grant simply sent the letter to Ruger with the remark "It may amuse you—do with it as you please."[11]

"The present 'Supe,' who is a most rigid martinet, has instituted a good many reforms and tightened all the loose 'screws,'" wrote Cadet Tasker Bliss in 1872.[12] Ruger was particularly tough on hazers. When Cadet Hugh Scott was caught hazing a plebe, he was turned back a year. A few months later, when Scott rescued a fellow cadet from drowning, his classmates hoped that the Superintendent would grant a reprieve. Ruger, however, was unbending.

Not all upperclassmen approved of hazing, but opposing it openly invited retaliation from other members of the corps. In 1875, when Cadet Charles Robinson found a new cadet doing menial service for a member of the first class, he reported it. Reporting a fellow cadet for an offense committed by so many was unprecedented. Robinson was severely censured by his comrades for not having overlooked the offense. Clandestine meetings were held by the classes, and Robinson was "cut," or silenced, by both the first class and his own yearling, or third, class. When Ruger learned of this, he immediately reduced the cadet officers (first classmen) to the ranks and put much of the class under arrest, but to no real effect. Though Robinson was made a cadet lieutenant his first-class year, the cumulative pressure of the course and the cut were ultimately too much for him—simply too distracting. He was found deficient in academics at the end of his last year and dismissed.

Schofield, who was known as the worst prankster in the corps in his own cadet days, sharply criticized the newer practices. Hazing, he told the cadets, was essentially criminal—both vicious and illegal. He took particular exception to the names and epithets the hazers used: "Thirty years ago, if a new cadet had been assailed with the words [currently being used,] he would have done his best to kill his assailant on the spot. Anyone who would have addressed another in such words would have been denounced and cut even by his own class."[13]

Still, efforts to stamp out hazing proved fruitless. For one thing, the practice was concealed by a code of silence among cadets. As Robinson learned, upperclassmen simply did not report each other. Plebes kept silent for fear that their lives would be made even more miserable if they reported hazing. Moreover, the plebes often felt that withstanding the hazing proved their manhood and thus elevated their status in the eyes of their peers. When questioned, they said simply that they could not identify their assailants. Douglas MacArthur, who had been a particular target of upperclassmen in 1899, was questioned on this point by a congressional committee investigating hazing. "Was it too dark for you to recognize the faces of your hazers?" he was asked. "I do not think it would have been if I had looked at them," MacArthur answered. "But," he added, "it is generally customary for fourth classmen not to look at those people who are hazing them."[14]

As a result, almost the only cadets who could be disciplined for hazing were those caught in the act by the tactical officers or faculty. These young men were often dismissed—but almost as often they were reinstated. They quickly learned to address their appeals to sympathetic members of Congress—often Academy graduates—who believed that dismissal was too harsh for what they often viewed as no more than boyish pranks. Over the years, Superintendents had pleaded with Congress to stop this practice, but to no avail.

By the mid-1890s, hazing had reached such proportions that Commandant of Cadets O. L. Hein inaugurated new, more stringent measures. But his efforts to break up what he called a "pernicious system of underground hazing," which had come to be "akin to torture in some cases," had no long-term impact. The case of Cadet Oscar L. Booz, in 1900, demonstrated that. Booz ran afoul of an upperclassman and was called out to fight. A third classman of approximately the same height and weight as Booz was designated by the class fight committee to restore the honor of the class. When Booz caught a solid blow to his solar plexus, he went down and refused to resume the fight. Plebes and upperclassmen alike pronounced him a coward. Booz then became the target of a systematic hazing campaign, one feature of which was forcing him to drink a particularly large dose of tabasco sauce with every meal. Soon his throat was so badly inflamed that he could tolerate few beverages except water. Booz ultimately resigned, and within a year he died of tuberculosis of the larynx. His family charged that the hazing was responsible for his death. A congressional investigation followed, and though it concluded that the tabasco sauce was not responsible for Booz's death, it focused strong criticism at West Point and on the practice of hazing. Congressional investigators found that the fertile minds of the upperclassmen had devised more than one hundred methods of annoying and harassing plebes. The investigation was followed by legislation on March 2, 1901, that forbade hazing.[15]

Into this atmosphere came the first black cadets in 1870. Although these young men were not hazed in the traditional sense, the social climate among cadets ensured that African-Americans would be subjected to scorn and maltreatment during the whole of their stay at West Point. Between 1870 and 1889, twenty-three blacks were nominated to the Academy. Of these, twelve were admitted, but only three graduated: Henry O. Flipper in 1877, John H. Alexander in 1887, and Charles Young in 1889. Flipper was dismissed from the service in 1882 but went on to become a successful mining engineer in the West and in Mexico. Alexander died on duty as a second lieutenant in 1894. And Young, who attained the rank of colonel, was retired in 1917 for disability.

As early as 1865, Benjamin F. Butler of Massachusetts was reported to be seeking a young black man to accept an appointment to West Point, but he was unable to identify a willing candidate who had all the requisite qualities—the intellect, the physical ability, and the psychological makeup that would enable him to cope with the insults, taunts, and social exclusion he was sure to experience. Five years later, in 1870, James Webster Smith of South Carolina became the first black to be admitted to the Academy. He was ostracized by the white cadets from the beginning; they refused to room with him and even objected to sitting at the same table in the mess hall. Smith's first year was plagued by trouble and fights that resulted in his being turned back one year. After that, Smith seems to have struck an accommodation with the other cadets—though one that featured the frequent exchange of slurs. He struggled through four years at West Point but in 1874 was found deficient in natural philosophy and dismissed.[16]

Henry Flipper entered West Point in 1873 and roomed with Smith for one year. Where Smith had resented and openly fought against social ostracism, Flipper took the opposite approach and was involved in none of the exchanges of insults or blows that had characterized Smith's years. Still, though he seemed to have gained their grudging respect, Flipper was as completely ostracized by the cadets as Smith had been.[17]

Flipper was philosophical about and tried to rationalize his treatment by the other cadets. It is clear, however, that it required all his strength and self-control to endure the unrelenting pressure of cadet prejudice. The majority of cadets, he believed, would have preferred to treat him "with proper politeness." They were gentlemen, he insisted, who would "treat others as it becomes a gentleman to do." The fact that they would not associate with or speak to him other than officially he attributed to some control or power the lower social elements of the corps held over them. In Flipper's view this latter group came from "the very lowest classes of our population." They were "uncouth and rough in appearance" and had "little or no idea of courtesy." They used "the very worst language" and were "much inferior to the average Negro." The control this class exercised surprised him. "It seems to rule the corps by fear," he wrote. "Indeed I know there are many who would associate, who would treat me as a brother cadet, were they not held in constant dread of this class." To some degree this optimistic view may have been fostered by his experience with the officers at the Academy, who treated him with courtesy and impartiality.[18]

In a bittersweet sense, Flipper's faith may have been justified, for when he graduated, he was accorded a round of applause, in which his classmates joined heartily. As he saw it, graduation released them from the restraint of the lower class, and they were no longer hesitant to congratulate him or shake his hand. "All signs of ostracism were gone. All felt as if I were worthy of some regard, and did not fail to extend it to me," he wrote a year after graduation in his book *The Colored Cadet at West Point*, in which he outlined the philosophy that had allowed him to endure. According to Flipper, the black man's immediate need in 1878 was not continued agitation or legislation for social equality but the fullest self-development of his mental and moral potential. Flipper's views on gradualism, agitation, and social equality were strikingly similar to the ideas that Booker T. Washington would expound a few years later.[19]

The most unfortunate of the black cadets at West Point was Johnson Chestnut Whittaker, who entered the Academy in 1876. He roomed with Flipper his first year and tried to follow his example of meeting ostracism with silence. However, Whittaker clashed with one of the unwritten rules of the Academy: when a white cadet struck him, he did not fight back but rather turned him in. The pressure of the added torment he now suffered took its toll. One morning, in 1880, he was found in his room, bound to his bed, bruised and cut, and smeared with blood. Initially the authorities accepted Whittaker's story that he had been attacked by several masked men, but as the investigation progressed, they came to doubt him. In the end, they concluded that he himself was responsible and that the assault had been feigned as a way to divert attention from his academic difficulties. He was subsequently found deficient in natural philosophy and dismissed.[20]

After more than two years of investigations and trials, which thrust Whittaker and West Point into the national limelight, he was convicted of perjuring himself and of other acts unbecoming an officer or cadet. Despite the fact that these proceedings were disapproved by President Chester A. Arthur, Whittaker was dismissed from the Academy because of his prior academic deficiency. From this there was no reprieve.

A year later, in 1883, John H. Alexander joined the corps, followed the next year by Charles Young—the second and third black graduates. Both proceeded through the Academy, attracting as little attention to themselves as possible and leaving little more of a record there than any other cadets. Alexander graduated in 1887, thirty-second in a class of sixty-four. Young had more difficulty. He was turned back one year and was in serious academic trouble at the end of his first-class year.

The treatment of these black cadets' West Point experiences in official and semiofficial Academy histories is instructive. John Alexander, for instance, would have been surprised to learn from the fiftieth-anniversary history of his class that he was "well liked by his classmates and was treated by them and by the cadets of other classes of his time, with courtesy and con-

Cadet Charles Young (1865–1922), class of 1889, was the third African-American graduate of the United States Military Academy. He rose to the rank of colonel, served with the 10th Cavalry, was military attaché in Haiti and Liberia, retired for medical reasons in 1917, and was then recalled to active duty and served in Liberia until his death in 1922. United States Military Academy Archives.

sideration."[21] Charles Dudley Rhodes recalled the cadet years of his classmate Charles Young in a similar way in Young's obituary:

> It cannot be said that during his first years at the Academy Young was a
> popular cadet. Left much to himself, he had few opportunities to exhibit
> likable traits of character, and he made few friends. But it must be said
> that he gained ground each year at West Point, and in the fifth and last
> year, after having patiently shown for the past four years a dog-like per-
> severance in the face of many natural handicaps, his own class began to
> acknowledge and respect his finer traits of character; while a spirit of fair
> play induced many cadets of character and standing in the corps to treat
> Young with kindness and consideration that had long been his due.[22]

This condescending but affectionate picture of a determined young
African-American gradually winning over his white classmates by pluck
and hard work was perpetuated when Rhodes published his own cadet letters a few years later:

> Our colored classmate, Charles Young, whom we esteem highly for his
> patient perseverance in the face of discouraging conditions which have
> attended his cadetship for five years—did poorly in both Engineering
> and Ordnance; and was given a special, written examination in each
> subject. . . . We are all hoping that Young will get through; it would be
> a terrible disappointment for him to lose the coveted diploma after five
> years of intensive work.[23]

Unfortunately, Rhodes amended this letter for publication. The original manuscript of the letter gives a more blunt appraisal of his black classmate's experience: "Mr. Young did very poorly in both engineering and ordnance, and was
given a special written examination in each branch afterwards. . . . I hope that
the darkey got through. It would be a terrible disappointment to him after five
years of work to lose the coveted diploma just as he was about to grasp it, although I do not think the Academy or the Army is the place for him."[24]
    Young himself gave a far different, undoubtedly more accurate, and in-
finitely more touching and illuminating version of his West Point experiences. It has been well known that Young received critical support and
encouragement from at least one young faculty member, his engineering
instructor, Lieutenant George W. Goethals, class of 1880. When, after his
special examinations, Young was found deficient in engineering, Goethals
made a special plea on his behalf and won him a temporary reprieve. The
two men worked tirelessly that summer preparing for reexamination. This

time, Young passed by a comfortable margin. In August 1889, he was graduated and commissioned a Second Lieutenant of Cavalry.

But Goethals had not been Young's only source of moral support at West Point. Years later, Young wrote of his cadet years to Delamere Skerrett, one of the classmates who had shown him friendship and sympathy:

> [Y]ou know for me the Academy has, even to this day, heart-aches in spite of the many advantages I derived there. The sole bright things that come to my heart are the friendship and sympathy from men like you, [Walter A.] Bethel [1889], [Frank D.] Webster [1889], [Edward F.] McGlachlin [Jr.] [1889], [Ralph] Harrison [1889], [James M.] Lambdin [x1889], [George T.] Langhorn [1886], [Malvern Hill] Barnum [1886], and [Harry H.] Bandholtz [1890]. Yes, I must mention the disinterested help of Col. W. B. Gordon [1877] and General Goethals—I can never forget them; and have tried to pass along to others the kindness of you all, both in America, the Philippines, the West Indies and Africa. So you see you can not always tell the wide reaching influence of a word of cheer to even a black man. God knows how many white ones I have helped because you all helped me. Simply trying to pay the interest on a debt of gratitude, I owe you, that's all. The world is better and only worth living in perhaps, because it has its Skerretts, Bethels, Goethals, Gordons, Barnums, Haans [William G. Haan, 1888] and Langhornes with the others of that stripe. May they live long.[25]

Not unexpectedly, the list of classmates who aided Cadet Charles Young did not include Rhodes.

Charles Young was the last African-American to attend or graduate from the Military Academy in the nineteenth century. Outside West Point, times had changed: Reconstruction had ended, and Jim Crow laws sanctified racial segregation and discrimination. No more black cadets were admitted to West Point until after World War I, and no more were graduated until 1936.

General John M. Schofield replaced Ruger as Superintendent on September 1, 1876. It was "the mistake of my life," he later wrote.[26] Sherman assured him that his "rank and history [would] elevate [the Military Academy] and solve all trouble."[27] But when Schofield arrived, he found that Ruger had left the Academy in a very acceptable state, and there was little, if any, foundation to Sherman's assertion that the Military Academy required the assignment of such a senior officer as Superintendent. Sherman's motive in this is somewhat obscure, but Schofield was convinced that it was political.

John M. Schofield was the
Superintendent of the United
States Military Academy from
1876 to 1881. United States
Military Academy Archives.

To his dismay, Schofield discovered that despite his senior rank, he stood
in no stronger a position with respect to the powers of the Academic Board
than those who preceded him. He bridled at the limitations placed upon him
by the regulations governing the Military Academy, where his direct authority was limited to those areas of cadet, Academy, and post life dealing with
military matters in the strictest and most limited meaning. He could not
influence the curriculum or other educational concerns except in his capacity as member of the Academic Board, where his was but one of many votes.
Unlike his predecessors, however, Schofield could never accept a position
subordinate in any manner to the board. Thus he battled the professors
throughout his tenure in an effort to gain the upper hand.[28]

The Academic Board of 1870 was a familiar assemblage—led by Mahan,
Church, and Bartlett, who had assumed that leadership in the 1830s. One of
the more recent additions to the board, John W. French, the chaplain and
head of the Department of Geography, History, and Ethics, had been appointed in 1856; four of the seven academic chiefs had taken over their departments in the 1830s. But the makeup of the board changed quickly. In
1871, Bartlett retired, and Mahan and Hyacinthe R. Agnel, Professor of
French, died. The next year, 1872, Chaplain French died. In just two years,
over half the board was gone.

The last three departed within the decade. Weir, the professor of drawing, retired in 1876. Albert Church, who had taught mathematics at the Academy for fifty years, died in 1878. Henry Lane Kendrick, or "Old Hanks," as he was affectionately known to several generations of cadets, had joined the faculty upon graduation in 1835 and became professor of chemistry in 1857. A lifelong bachelor, and for years the senior member of the officers' mess, "Old Hanks" was popular with officers and cadets alike, with a reputation for being exceptionally kind to new plebes. He retired in 1880.

The leading light of this new Academic Board was Peter Smith Michie, class of 1863. He had been an assistant professor of engineering from 1867 until 1871, when he was chosen to replace Bartlett as professor of natural and experimental philosophy—a position he held until his death in 1901. Michie had a laugh that was natural and infectious, yet cadets thought him stuffy, even dour, and he was never popular among his students. During his years at the Academy, Michie wrote extensively: an elementary text on mechanics, a history of the Army of the Potomac (in which he had fought), and biographies of George McClellan and Emory Upton. Michie was a deeply religious man and insisted that his explanation of the laws of matter and force proved the existence of "a Creator who set the hosts of the skies and determined their motions." He threatened to find deficient any cadet who did not agree.

Charles W. Larned, class of 1870, who became the professor of drawing in 1876, was another member of the new faculty leadership. Unlike his predecessors in the department, Larned was not an artist, having spent his years since graduation on frontier duty with the cavalry. Where Weir had concentrated on landscape painting, Larned emphasized mathematical drawing and topographical work. On the Academic Board, he was a steadying influence and an effective spokesman.

Other members of the new Academic Board included George L. Andrews, John Forsyth, and Junius Brutus Wheeler. Andrews had graduated first in his class in 1851 and was chosen professor of French in 1871. When the French and Spanish departments were merged in 1882, he was made professor of modern languages, serving in that capacity until his retirement in 1892. Forsyth, the chaplain and professor of ethics from 1871 to 1881, was a tall, portly, Falstaffian figure, with a reputation for indifference to study. Still, cadets appreciated him for his short sermons and his pontificating on the importance of ethics—grasping his lapels and rising on his toes as he did so. Wheeler, class of 1855, was first assigned to the cavalry and then to the topographic engineers. He served as an assistant professor of mathematics from 1859 to 1863 and was selected professor of engineering in 1871. He retired in 1884.

Schofield spent the early months of his superintendency in a concerted effort to strengthen his position vis-à-vis the Academic Board. At his insistence, West Point was made a military department, a command more befitting his rank. He then set about drafting revisions to the regulations. First he attacked the tenure of the professors. "It would be beneficial, both to the officer and the public service, although the officer be one of the most efficient, to allow him to return to his corps in the Army after a certain period of service at the Academy; his place there to be filled by a younger man." Then he attacked the powers of the Academic Board directly, proposing a permanent board of visitors, made up of the Superintendent, members of Congress, and representatives of the War Department. This entity would be able "to initiate all changes necessary to be made in the Academic Board"—usurping key powers of the Academic Board.[29]

Though the War Department simply ignored these proposals, the enemy camps at West Point continued to snipe at one another. An illustration was the case of two cadets reported to the Academic Board in January 1880 for having received demerits in excess of the number allowed. The Academic Board declared the cadets deficient and recommended their dismissal. Schofield had not wanted to deal so harshly with the two, intending only to give them a stern warning. He appealed to the War Department and won the cadets a reprieve. In June, however, the Academic Board again declared them deficient—though their total demerits for the year were by then within allowable limits. Schofield angrily protested; he should have "sole jurisdiction to decide all individual questions of discipline," he argued. Both Sherman and Secretary of War Alexander Ramsey agreed. At the next Academic Board meeting, Schofield read the opinion of the Secretary of War to this effect. To his chagrin, the professors simply ordered the communication held for consideration at a later meeting. Ultimately, a compromise was worked out. The minutes reveal that the board decided the Superintendent would withdraw his report concerning the cadets. With no report of deficiency to act upon, the board's earlier dismissal of the students was withdrawn. Schofield had won a very shallow victory—the right to decide whether or not a deficiency in discipline should be reported to the board for its vote and recommendation—and no more.[30]

In these contests the Superintendent relied primarily on the support of the Army hierarchy in Washington—the Commanding General and the Secretary of War. The members of the Academic Board also wrote directly to the Commanding General and Secretary, but they reinforced this privilege through their own networks of connections in Washington and throughout the Army to press their cases. Most kept up a steady correspondence with both members of Congress and the Army's senior officers—many, in both categories, who had been former students or colleagues at West Point. As the contest boiled over in 1880, the Academic Board's supporters used Schofield's inept handling of the Whittaker case as leverage to bring pressure for his relief. Senator Augustus Hill Garland went so far as to propose that in the future "no officer above the rank of colonel" should be "assigned to duty at the Academy."[31] Under attack by the Democrats, who had regained control of the Congress, President Rutherford B. Hayes was sensitive to charges that Schofield had mishandled affairs at West Point. In August 1880, he called Schofield to Washington and informed him that he would soon be replaced.

On January 21, 1881, Brigadier General Oliver Otis Howard, class of 1854, best known as commissioner of the Freedmen's Bureau (1865–1872), took up the reins as Superintendent of the Military Academy. Howard's reputation, it was hoped, would help deflect further criticism of the institution (and the administration) in the midst of the Whittaker investigation and trial. His assignment, however, seemed to promise even more. "It is an open secret," reported the *Army and Navy Journal,* that Howard was appointed because of "his disposition to effect a radical reform" that would "lower or break down the wall of caste separation" at West Point.[32] Some reports noted that Howard himself had been ostracized by other cadets for his views on slavery and for treating as a social equal a sergeant who was a family friend. As Howard headed toward West Point, he was asked by reporters what he planned to do about the black cadets. "I think that Gen. Washington's 'hearty politeness' is about as good a thing as can be introduced anywhere," Howard answered, "or the golden rule, 'Do unto others as you would have them do to you!'"[33]

He applied a similar philosophy in his relations with the Academic Board. Shortly after assuming the superintendency, Howard raised one of the issues that had deadlocked Schofield and the board, asking "whether it would be preferable that the Superintendent should have sole power to declare a Cadet proficient or deficient in discipline or that this proficiency or deficiency should be declared by the Academic Board."[34] Not surprisingly, the professors concluded that this role should fall to them and that they should "consider and act upon such a deficiency as in cases of deficiency in studies." The unanimous vote of the board on this issue indicates that Howard concurred. The Academic Board was a "body of able men," he noted, and "every interest of the Academy is carefully weighed" by them. "In my judgement," he continued, "it is, the most powerful agent at work here. It is my earnest desire while Superintendent to work in harmony with the board as presently constituted."[35] With the arrival of Howard, another period of confrontation between the Superintendent and the Academic Board passed.

Other difficulties surrounding Schofield's assignment to West Point remained. "Because the Superintendent is a General and has all his staff officers with him," wrote Lieutenant Tasker Bliss, "there are many more officers here than ever before. The consequence is that while the older ones are barely able to secure accommodation, the junior ones may as well go begging for a roof to cover them."[36] Their arrival had created a good deal of commotion and turbulence. As a general rule, the senior officer had the right to choose the quarters he preferred. In practice, this meant that an officer could select any set of quarters that was vacant or that was occupied by officers junior to him, though at West Point the Superintendent excluded from this process the quarters assigned to the permanent professors. Lieutenant Tully McCrea described the process thus: "Perhaps you have seen boys playing near a brick pile, by placing a long row of bricks on end, just close enough so that when you knock down the brick at the end, it knocks down its neighbor, and so on throughout the whole row. It happens that this is just the case with the officers here, who are the bricks, but instead of being knocked down, they are in turn turned out of their houses, to turn out someone else." The process was particularly hard on the wives. Though McCrea was a bachelor, he had compassion for the women on whom this policy fell most harshly. "I am very sorry," he wrote, "for one lady, for she has just moved this week, and she took it quite *manfully,* and was in a very good humor about it. But today another officer makes his appearance and chooses, which necessitates the removal of this lady again."[37]

The process of assigning quarters could not have been better designed to produce conflict and hard feelings. Dissatisfaction was a constant. There were never enough quarters, and those that were available were often inadequate to the needs of the officer or family that occupied them. The turmoil created by the method of assigning quarters only added to the hardship. Noting that most of the officers arrived or departed in August of each year, Superintendent John M. Wilson, class of 1860, established a new procedure in 1891. All the officers reporting for duty at the beginning of the new term, as well as those remaining on duty at the Academy who wished to change their housing, were to make their selections at a single drawing. With the most senior officer drawing first, they would choose from among the quarters vacated by the departing officers or from those thrown in by officers who hoped to better their situation. After each set of quarters was selected, it was immediately assigned and afterward was "not again subject to selection so long as occupied by assignee, no matter what may be the rank of any officer subsequently reporting for duty." Officers arriving at other times during the year were assigned quarters as they became available.[38] No longer were officers at the Military Academy bumped over and forced to move. This solution proved so satisfactory that it persists at West Point to this day.

New quarters were added throughout the period, but there were never enough to satisfy the demand, for the number of officers brought to West

Point also increased. The "embarrassment of doubling up families in unsuitable quarters," wrote Superintendent Albert L. Mills in 1900, "will be bound to cause dissatisfaction." This, he concluded, would translate into an "impairment of the value of the services the officer would otherwise give." Neither the War Department nor Congress was moved by his argument.[39]

The situation for the unmarried officers was, if anything, worse. Although a few sets of quarters for these officers were added, there was a great need by the end of the century for both bachelor officer quarters and a new mess. The only substantial gain in housing was the long-overdue construction of some thirty sets of quarters for the senior enlisted men with families in the early 1890s.

Housing aside, most officers, wives, and families found the assignment at the Military Academy pleasant. "I never had a more agreeable tour of duty than my four years at West Point," wrote James Parker, who served as a tactical officer from 1894 to 1898. "Socially it was delightful; we had many charming acquaintances there, and many visitors; my children went to good schools; the two eldest became young ladies, danced and rode with the cadets, with whom they were great favorites, and made among them many lifelong friends."[40]

The Hudson River provided a highway to the society and hospitality of the fine houses up and down its shores. At Garrison lived the Hamilton and Stuyvesant Fishes and their cousins the Rogerses and Benjamins and many others, while at Cold Springs were the Haldanes, Fitzgeralds, and deRhams. On the west bank of the river, south of Highland Falls, lived a coterie of families, the John Bigelows, Clarence Pells, and Pierpont Morgans. The officers assigned to the Academy were frequent guests in these homes and, in turn, entertained these well-to-do civilians at West Point. "One of our favorite visiting places was the John Bigelow villa near Highland Falls," recalled Hein, "where we were often most agreeably entertained by Mrs. Bigelow and Miss Grace Bigelow." "Sammy" Tillman, then an assistant professor of chemistry and later head of that department, took Grace Bigelow to her first officers' hop.[41]

New York City also proved a magnet. Even before the West Shore Railroad linked West Point directly with Manhattan in 1883, frequent riverboats and the ferry connecting West Point's south dock with the New York Central Railroad on the east shore of the Hudson provided convenient transportation to the city. Many of the officers were widely acquainted among New York's social elite. The city was a particularly attractive haunt of the bachelors. On weekend forays they mingled with the social elite, with literary, artistic, and theatrical celebrities, and with foreign dignitaries, government officials, and the new giants of American industry.

At West Point, novelty and invention rather than high society spiced the social life. One example was a Valentine's Day party given in 1876 by Lieutenant Sam M. Mills, a tactical officer, and his wife. Before the party, each officer and lady invited was required to compose a poem in honor of another guest of the opposite sex; the person to whom the lines were to be dedicated was determined by drawing slips from a hat. Some of the verses turned out highly complimentary, and some contained witty ridicule; regardless, it produced a hilarious evening. The enterprising hosts were not finished, however. They gathered up these literary gems, published them, and provided a copy to each author.[42]

At West Point, there were also Saturday evening poker parties, moonlight excursions on the Hudson, and occasional amateur theatrical performances. In 1879, some of the younger officers put on a performance of Gilbert and Sullivan's new *H.M.S. Pinafore*, which had opened in New York earlier that year. All the parts, including the female roles, were played by the officers, who borrowed sailor costumes from friends at the Brooklyn Navy Yard and the female apparel from the ladies of the garrison. The instrumental music was furnished by the band. Sam Mills, an obviously versatile talent, played the role of Little Buttercup; George Harrison, assistant professor of French, portrayed the pompous Sir Joseph Porter, K.C.B.; and John G. D. Knight, of the mathematics department, was Dick Deadeye. Ignorance of music was only a minor obstacle; frequent rehearsals and much practice produced a "creditable amateur rendition" of the show, which gained "the entire approval" of the audience.[43]

For more cerebral diversions there was still the officers' Napoleon Club, which had been guided by Mahan since he founded it years earlier. With his death in 1871, the group floundered, but its activities were soon absorbed by the new Thayer Club, organized in 1873 to honor the recently deceased "Father of the Military Academy" and to "promote professional, scientific and literary culture." In turn, in 1878, the Thayer Club became the West Point branch of the new United States Military Service Institute.

In 1894, a group of the officers' wives formed the Ladies Reading Club, which met weekly, November through May. At the first meetings in November 1894, the topic was "Travel," but the members investigated and reported on a wide variety of subjects. Over the next few years topics included "Modern Architecture in England and the United States," "Landscape and Marine Painters of 19th Century America," "Muscular Development in Women," "Coxeyism and the Tyranny of Socialism," "Home Rule for Ireland," "The Right of Suffrage for Women," "Evolution and Man's Place in Nature," "The Dreyfus Case," "Historic Houses of Washington," "[Edward

Bellamy's] 'Looking Backwards,'" the "Bi-centennial of Yale," and "Is It Womans' First Duty to Be Attractive?"[44]

Having shepherded West Point through the Whittaker affair, Howard was replaced by Colonel Wesley Merritt in September 1882. Merritt, who had graduated in 1860, had commanded a cavalry division in the Civil War and had been breveted for gallantry in every grade from major to major general. He brought the same dash to the affairs at West Point that he had displayed in the war—and in the postwar South and West. Among his continuing concerns was the school's aging physical plant. Little major construction had taken place at West Point since the mess hall and riding hall were completed in the mid-1850s, though a new administration building had been completed in 1871. The latter was a gray stone structure with a mansard slate roof surmounted by wrought-iron grillwork—somewhat resembling a French Renaissance château. It harmonized with none of the other buildings. The balance of the buildings dated from a much earlier period, with the library and academic building dating from the late 1830s, and the barracks from the late 1840s and early 1850s.

Under Merritt's superintendence, a new although abbreviated round of construction began. A much-needed new cadet hospital was constructed just south of the mess hall and completed in 1884. In 1887, the mess hall was renovated and rededicated as Grant Hall—the first formal memorialization of a building at West Point. Then came a gymnasium completed in 1891 and a new academic building, conceived in 1885, approved in 1889, and finally occupied in 1895. Merritt, however, did not bring the same degree of conceptual power to the projects that had characterized Delafield's efforts a half century earlier. As a result, these structures lacked any central architectural theme.

In August 1887, Merritt was succeeded by Colonel John G. Parke. A member of the class of 1849 and one of the Army's senior engineers, Parke was the first of that branch to be appointed Superintendent since that position had been opened to line officers in 1866. Parke introduced telephone service to the Academy in 1887 and considerably enlarged the post by purchasing the Kinsley estate, which lay to the south between the post and the town of Highland Falls.

Perhaps Parke's brief (two-year) superintendency was best remembered for the great blizzard of March 12, 1888. Snowdrifts stood so high that they covered the fronts of the stone houses of Professors' Row and reached to the windows of the Dialectic Society Hall in the barracks, closing both entrances to the sally port. Parke resigned from the army in June 1889 in a fit of pique because he was not selected Chief of Engineers. He was succeeded by Lieutenant Colonel John M. Wilson, who had most recently supervised completion of the Washington Monument in Washington, D.C.

In 1893, Wilson was succeeded by Major Oswald Herbert Ernst, class of 1864. That same year, the Academy received a bequest of $250,000 from the estate of former Superintendent George W. Cullum for the erection of a building to house trophies of war and "statues, busts, mural tablets and por-traits of distinguished deceased officers and graduates of the Military Acad-emy." After a limited competition, the trustees of the memorial hall selected the architectural firm of McKim, Mead and White to design the building. Stanford White undertook the project. Prominently located on the east edge of the Plain, overlooking the river, this structure has a cold, austere quality. Its Classical style is emphasized on the principal front by four colossal half-engaged Ionic columns, Greek entablature, a pediment-capped entrance, and ornamented decorations at the roof edge. Extending that influence, White was also chosen to design the West Point Army Mess constructed next to the Cullum Memorial beginning in 1900. But both the Cullum edifice and the mess were in stylistic conflict with everything that had been erected in the previous sixty years—blending only with the old chapel, which, as such things went, was about to be removed.

In the meantime, in May 1896 Ernst, as president of the Academic Board, appointed Professors Charles Larned (drawing), Edgar Wales Bass (mathe-matics), and Samuel Tillman (chemistry) to design a device, or coat of arms, and motto for the Academy. The committee agreed in advance that the design should typify four things: the institution's national character, its military function, its educational mission, and its characteristic spirit and motivat-ing principles. In January 1898, after almost two years of effort, the three professors made their recommendation. The device was to be a shield bear-ing the arms of the United States, surmounted by a helmet of Pallas, the Greek goddess of wisdom and learning, over a Greek sword—the latter two symbolizing the double mission of the Academy. Above the shield was the American bald eagle, wings displayed, and a scroll bearing the words "West Point," the date 1802 in roman numerals, and the initials "U.S.M.A." The motto to be displayed on the scroll had simplicity yet grandeur—"Duty, Honor, Country."[45]

Throughout the spring of 1898, the United States had moved steadily toward war with Spain, and the Academy class was to be graduated early. On April 22, the Congress authorized a volunteer force of 200,000 men. On the twenty-sixth, it approved an increase in the regular army to 60,000 men. On the same day at West Point, Superintendent Ernst handed diplomas to the first class and then sent them off to the war. Events had moved so fast that there had been no time to incorporate the newly designed coat of arms into their diplomas.

Historians have variously characterized the period at West Point between the Civil War and the Spanish-American War as one of stagnation, isolation, or uncertainty—a time when the Military Academy was either unwilling or unable to consider the new ideas, new methods, and new organizational structures that had begun to characterize modern American colleges and universities. For the same reasons, they have concluded, West Point lost its scientific and engineering preeminence.[46]

Without question this was a period of unparalleled activity in American colleges, and the fundamental reason was the accelerating advance in man's knowledge. No longer could a person know everything worth knowing; no longer could the classically trained gentleman hope to compete. Modern universities now prepared students for a variety of careers, but in making the transition from the classical to the modern curriculum, they found themselves unable to agree about what knowledge students should imbibe. They solved the problem by adopting the system of elective courses, which threw onto the student the burden the faculties would not or could not accept.

At West Point, however, the process was very different. The decision to abandon the classical tradition had been made at the beginning. Political motives aside, Jefferson created the school to provide select young men the education necessary to prepare them as Army officers. Swift and Thayer had expanded on that foundation, establishing what, in its time, was the finest engineering school in the country. But they did so because they concluded that a mathematical and scientific education was the best preparation for future Army officers. Despite the pressures from Congress and elsewhere that forced an increased emphasis on civil engineering to support other national objectives, the production of competent civil engineers was always secondary to the making of sound military officers.

West Point's emphasis on mathematics and the sciences developed mental discipline—the key to success regardless of what difficulties the future officer might encounter. At the same time, the Thayer system of daily recitation and grading produced habits of regularity and preparedness. Military discipline netted still other benefits—habits of order, obedience, and respect to authority—and these passed directly into the Army.

If the United States Military Academy seemed to bask in the glory of its graduates' accomplishments, it was not the result of any isolation from the world of education or any uncertainty of purpose, but rather the conscious and considered conclusion of those in charge that at West Point they were already on the right course. Superintendent Thomas Ruger only echoed the sentiments of the majority of the faculty in 1872 when he reported that "the subjects of study at the Military Academy embrace all that is essential and nearly all that is necessary to the education of an officer of the Army."[47] Still, West Point did not ignore the movements in the world around it. Later that same year, the board sent Professors Michie and Kendrick to visit a number of colleges and universities in the United States and directed them to examine the newer schemes. "It is with pleasure," wrote Michie, "that I have to report that so far as the Military Academy is concerned, the character, scope and method of its instruction considering the end in view, is much superior to that of any institution either technical, special, or general." He was convinced that, even in comparison with other technical programs, the methods employed at West Point "display the best results." In conclusion, he said, "I think we may safely challenge any institution either in this country or in Europe to display results of study as favorable as those exhibited in the careers of our graduate cadets."[48]

The instrument of change at the Military Academy was the Academic Board, but it was change of an evolutionary nature. When Albert Church died (1878) and Henry Kendrick retired (1880), the transition of the Academic Board, which had begun ten years earlier, was complete. Church, who had taught at the Military Academy since 1828, was succeeded as professor of mathematics by Edgar Wales Bass, class of 1864. Bass had served four years as an engineer officer before returning to West Point as an assistant professor of natural philosophy. Like Church, Bass was not particularly popular with the cadets. Bass continued as professor of mathematics until 1898, when failing eyesight caused him to retire. He, in turn, was succeeded by Wright Prescott Edgerton, class of 1874, who joined the department in 1882 as an assistant professor and had been the associate professor since the creation of that position in 1893. Kendrick, who had served almost as many years in the chemistry department (beginning in 1835) as Church had in mathematics, was succeeded in 1880 by Samuel Tillman, class of 1869, who had already served four and a half years as assistant professor of chemistry and a year as assistant professor of natural philosophy. Tillman remained until 1911, when he retired, but he was called back to active duty as Superintendent from 1917 to 1919.

In explaining the nature of the Academic Board, Charles Larned said: "There is a disposition to make haste slowly in all matters involving change; to hold fast to what is good, and prove all things; but the authorities of the Academy are not blind nor indifferent to the value of new methods where they can be safely applied to a system which, whatever its defects, has won the applause of the world for its thoroughness and remarkable achievements."[49]

In April 1883, Tillman and George L. Andrews, Professor of Modern Languages, made a second tour of academic institutions to compare their

Samuel E. Tillman and family. Tillman served as professor of chemistry from 1880 until his retirement in 1911. He was called back to active duty as Superintendent of the United States Military Academy from 1917 to 1919. United States Military Academy Archives.

methods of instruction with those at the Military Academy. Among others, they visited Massachusetts Institute of Technology, Harvard, Yale, and Dartmouth, where they observed recitations, laboratory exercises, and conferences. Upon their return to West Point, Andrews reported that although "the course at the Academy is susceptible of improvement," just what those improvements should be "is not easy to say." Still, he warned the Academic Board that "in this age of progress, not to advance is to retrograde."[50]

Professor Tillman came back with more concrete measures in mind. He had long harbored concerns about the inadequacies of West Point's "physical teaching facilities" or laboratories, and upon returning trom this junket, he was more convinced than ever that West Point must begin to move its students out of the lecture hall and into the laboratory. In 1885, Tillman led the way in proposing a new academic building that would remedy this problem and also allow the Department of Natural Philosophy to move from the library building. A couple of years were spent in an unsuccessful attempt to

Charles W. Larned was professor of drawing from 1876
to 1911. Painted by James Carroll Beckwith (1852–
1917). West Point Museum Collection, United States
Military Academy.

remodel the old Academy building, but in 1889 appropriations were made
for a new structure. The old academic hall was pulled down in 1891 to make
room, and the new structure was completed in 1895, finally making possible
the laboratory method of teaching the sciences.

The years after 1871—after the beginning of the generational change in
the Academic Board—were a time of revision, adjustment, and change in
all the courses taught at the Military Academy. New knowledge dictated new
texts. Michie introduced his first revisions of Bartlett's texts in 1874 and
successively replaced the older works on sound and light, analytical mechanics, and hydraulics between 1882 and 1887. In engineering, Mahan's
texts were revised repeatedly from 1882 to 1894 to reflect modern engineering practice and advances in the science and art of war. This work was begun
by Wheeler, who replaced Mahan in 1871, and was completed by James
Mercur, who served from 1884 until his death in 1896.

In mathematics Bass had not only introduced new texts but also completely restructured the curriculum. Surveying, which had been taught for years by that department, was changed from a theoretical to a practical course and then transferred to the Department of Practical Engineering. Likewise, mathematical drawing was given over to the drawing department, which under Larned had also assumed a more utilitarian stance.

But the most dramatic changes in the Academy's curriculum came in the expansion of the humanities. Though there had been a Department of Geography, History, and Ethics since 1818, the professorial duties were performed by the chaplain. For years the course consisted largely of the study of ethics and of the elements of constitutional or international law. Geography, history, and rhetoric were taught only occasionally, and then only for brief periods. The expansion of the humanities began in 1874 with the creation of the Department of Law. Instruction in English was added in 1877, although it was soon placed under the Department of French (and, in 1882, under a new Department of Modern Languages). History was added in 1883 after the patient and persistent endeavors of Rev. Dr. William M. Postlethwaite, who had succeeded Forsyth in the chaplaincy and as professor of history, geography, and ethics in 1881. Upon Postlethwaite's death in 1896, history was transferred to the new Department of Law and History, and the chaplain's old department was dissolved. This increased emphasis on the humanities proved a lasting development, though mathematics and the sciences continued to dominate the curriculum. And, as events would prove, it was only the beginning of an evolution of the curriculum and an expansion of the humanities that would continue through the whole of the next century.

Neither these changes nor any other could have kept the Military Academy at the forefront of the institutions of science and engineering. Its leadership, in the years before the Civil War, had been largely serendipitous —falling to the Academy because its uniquely practical course in mathematics and military engineering positioned it advantageously. Just as the set of knowledge that defined basic engineering began to expand, and as the demand for engineers began to grow, West Point was ready with a uniquely utilitarian brand of engineering education. However, as growth in scientific knowledge began to exceed that which was necessary for practical application in the military and civil realms, the Academy was displaced by institutions whose primary function was to push back the frontiers of knowledge —universities with expanding laboratory facilities and growing postgraduate programs. The absence of a graduate school of engineering at West Point—and there was no rationale for having one—meant that the Academy would surrender its leadership in these areas to the nation's other technological institutions.

Some saw this as evidence of the Academy's decline, but the faculty who constituted the Academic Board were rightly unconcerned. They understood better than their critics—contemporary and modern—the purpose and role of the United States Military Academy. In 1900, they could point with pride to the most recent *Who's Who in America,* which listed more than one in every twenty of West Point's living graduates—a proportion higher than that of any other American college or university.

In 1902, when Professors Tillman and Edgerton visited Yale, Harvard, and Massachusetts Institute of Technology, they concluded that West Point cadets were receiving the same breadth of subject matter offered engineering students at these schools. There was a problem, however: West Point students spent nearly twice as much time as the rest on mathematics. Much of this excess was devoted to algebra and geometry, elementary subjects that should have been mastered in high schools. The culprit here was the Academy's lax requirements for admission.

Admission standards were the one area in which the Academic Board had long sought reform—and where it had repeatedly been rebuffed. In 1866, the Congress had rigidly fixed admission standards to a knowledge of reading, writing, arithmetic, English grammar, and United States history. The oral examination gave way to a written one in 1870, and, as the general educational level of the country rose, the examinations became more searching and in-depth. Yet the standards demanded of West Point plebes continued to be more elementary than those of freshmen at Harvard, Yale, Massachusetts Institute of Technology, Columbia School of Mines, Rensselaer Polytechnic, or even the United States Naval Academy. The result was a particularly high percentage of failures in the course and an overcrowded curriculum. The poor academic preparation of entering students meant that the Academy spent almost a year bringing the cadets up to the level of average college freshmen. But substantive change in the admissions standard could come only if the law of 1866 was changed. Repeated efforts to raise the standards were made by the Academic Board and by the annual reports of the boards of visitors, but Congress had not been amenable to the idea.

For years, calls for higher standards were met with essentially the same response. If West Point was to be a perfectly republican, perfectly democratic institution, the standards of admission would have to allow the son of the poorest to enter with the son of the richest. To ensure that, these young men would have to be allowed to enter the Academy even if they were barely able to read and write and were capable of only simple mathematics.

It was not until 1901 that Congress changed the law and allowed the Secretary of War (in effect the Academic Board) to establish admission requirements. Incrementally, over the next few years, the board raised admission standards to an educational level commensurate with that attained by graduates of the nation's public and private high schools.

By 1890, there was a long tradition of informal and intramural athletics at the Military Academy—field sports, baseball, sculling, tennis, and gymnastics. But nothing had prepared the institution for what happened when football was introduced—or, more precisely, when the naval cadets from Annapolis were invited to West Point in November 1890 for a friendly game. Navy had fielded a football team for several years, but only two West Point cadets, Dennis Mahan Michie and Leonard M. Prince, had ever played the game. Michie, the son of Professor Peter Smith Michie, undertook to coach the team, but Superintendent John M. Wilson allowed the cadets to practice only on rainy Saturday afternoons when parades could not be held. Predictably, Navy won by a lopsided 24 to 0.[51]

The next year, Army had a schedule of five home games: Rutgers, Tufts, Stevens Institute, Fordham, and Princeton (winning only one of these). But, already, only the Navy game counted. At Annapolis in 1891, the cadets revenged the defeat of the year before by a score of 32 to 16.

The Army-Navy game immediately become an obsession at both academies, and more particularly with their graduates. Contributions to hire a coach and buy uniforms for the team poured in from every regiment, and the Army Officers' Athletic Association was founded to support athletics at West Point. In 1892, the game returned to West Point, and in 1893 it was played again at Annapolis; the midshipmen won both. Scores and play-by-play accounts of the games were printed in the *Army and Navy Journal,* and the contest was the only topic of conversation at officers' clubs around the country for months before and after. The game in 1893 led to such a heated argument between an Army brigadier general and a Navy rear admiral at the Army-Navy Club in New York that a duel was threatened. Superintendent Oswald H. Ernst, though amenable to football generally, was concerned about this growing rivalry. "The excitement attending it exceeds all reasonable limits," he reported after the 1893 incident. He was concerned that the excitement and rivalry would continue to grow and that the game would be marked by even more bitterness. He recommended, therefore, that the series with Navy be discontinued.[52] The Secretary of War and Secretary of the Navy agreed and, in 1894, canceled future games by the simple expedient of ruling that neither team could leave its grounds for a game.

Despite that condition, Army continued to build its football program, soon scheduling the giants of the East—Harvard, Yale, and Princeton—and winning regularly. By 1897, Army ranked fourth in the nation, and two years later the Army-Navy game was revived—beginning an annual series that is still in progress. The 1899 game produced Army's second victory over the Middies. Two more victories, in 1901 and 1902, brought the series to a 4-to-4 tie. A century later, as the teams ended their 2001 seasons, Army held a bare three-game edge.

The year 1902 marked the completion of the first century of the Military Academy's life. The close of the academic year was designated as the most suitable time for commemorating the anniversary. The four days of celebration began with Alumni Day, June 9, when the oldest graduate present, General John S. McCalmont, class of 1842, opened the events in Cullum Memorial Hall.

Centennial Day, June 11, was marked by the arrival of President Theodore Roosevelt. Escorted by a detachment of cavalry, he rode up from the train station to the Plain and received the salute of the Corps of Cadets while the cannon boomed a twenty-one-gun salute. He then rode on to the Superintendent's house, descended from the carriage, joined the assembled crowd of dignitaries, and led them across the Plain to the reviewing stand. Later he spoke to the cadets and to the assembled guests. "During [the Academy's first] century," the president told them,

> no other educational institution in the land has contributed as many names as West Point has contributed to the honor roll of the nation's greatest citizens. . . . And of all the institutions in the country, none is more absolutely American; none, in the proper sense of the word, more absolutely democratic than this. Here we care nothing for the boy's birth-

President Theodore Roosevelt arrives at the Academy's Centennial Celebration, 1902. *Harper's Weekly,* June 21, 1904.

place, nor his creed, nor his social standing. . . . Here you represent, with almost mathematical exactness, all the country geographically. You are drawn from every walk of life by a method of choice made to insure . . . that heed shall be paid to nothing save the boy's aptitude for the profession into which he seeks entrance. Here you come together as representatives of America in a higher and more peculiar sense than can possibly be true of any other institution in the land, save your sister college [the Naval Academy].[53]

That evening West Point glittered. There was a graduation parade, a centennial banquet, and a fireworks display. The next day, the President handed each member of the class of 1902 his diploma. With that, the centennial celebration came to a close. Within hours, President Roosevelt had entrained, and the galaxy of ambassadors, university presidents, congressmen, and senior military officers had departed. West Point resumed its long-familiar routine. It "became again," wrote historian Roger Hurless Nye, "the eyrie of its duly-appointed oligarchs, the Superintendent, the Commandant, and the seven Professors of the Academic Board."[54]

CHAPTER SEVEN

A New Age, 1903–1931

In many ways, West Point redefined itself in the first decades of the new century. A massive construction effort provided a bold and extensive new interpretation of the nineteenth-century Gothic designs of Diaper and Delafield. At the same time, the creation of the Department of English and then the Department of Economics, Government, and History broadened the curriculum and initiated a debate about the school's proper academic pursuits—a debate that continues yet.[1]

In October 1902, invitations to participate in a limited architectural competition were mailed by Superintendent Albert L. Mills, class of 1879, who had succeeded Ernst in 1898. The winner of the competition would create, in effect, a new West Point. It was to be the most massive construction effort yet undertaken there. Ten architectural firms were invited to compete: Cope and Stewardson; Hines and LaFarge; Carrere and Hastings; Peabody and Stearns; Armes and Young; Charles C. Haight; Daniel H. Burnham; Cram, Goodhue and Ferguson; McKim, Mead and White; and Frost and Granger.[2] The work was to include a cadet barracks, an academic building, a post headquarters, headquarters for the corps of cadets, a riding hall, an artillery barracks with stable and gun shed, a cavalry barracks and stable, bachelor officers' quarters, and a hotel.

To the architects the project presented both an opportunity and a challenge; few had ever undertaken the execution of such a large scheme—one that embraced not only the structures but also the related roads, utilities, and landscaping. Moreover, their plan had to both meet the practical requirements of the Military Academy and "provide a treatment worthy of the historic associations and natural beauties of the site."

The seeds of this competition were sown in June 1899 when the Board of Visitors, reflecting on the nation's unpreparedness for the war it was then engaged in, insisted that the usefulness of the Academy should be increased by expanding the number of cadets from 381 to 500.[3] In July, Mills directed Charles W. Larned, Professor of Drawing, to examine the impact of such an expansion and determine "the necessary modifications, enlargement and increase of the public buildings" and other required "changes in the existing establishment." Mills, however, specified that Larned should contemplate an increase in the number of cadets of up to 600, and should include the maps, drawings, and estimates necessary to "make a full and explicit presentation of the subject as a basis for the action of Congress."[4]

Larned submitted this report on August 10, 1899, suggesting the enlargement of the chapel, cadet hospital, gymnasium, and mess hall and the construction of a new officers' mess and more quarters for both married and bachelor officers. He also pointed out the need for a new hotel, a central heating plant, a new facility to generate electricity, and alterations and additions to the sewers. The overall cost of these improvements, he estimated, was just over $2,200,000.[5] The only item in Larned's proposal that stirred any immediate controversy was the location he suggested for the new cadet barracks. Larned suggested placing it on the west edge of the Plain, north of the existing barracks—even though this would require removing some of the old brick professors' quarters. Mills preferred placing it behind the existing barracks, forming a quadrangle in the midst of the barracks and the academic building, and he won the acquiescence of the Academic Board.[6]

In 1900, Congress, acting on the Board of Visitors' recommendation, increased the size of the corp of cadets by 100, bringing the total to 481, but made no further provision for them. In June, the Board of Visitors acknowledged Congress's enlargement of the corp of cadets but reminded the lawmakers of the need for additional facilities as well. Mills endorsed the board's new report but warned against halfway or temporary measures. These would, he said, be "destructive to the convenience and to the dignity and beauty of the institution as an architectural whole" and also "more wasteful and extravagant in the long run."[7]

In June 1901, the Board of Visitors renewed its plea of the year before for an expansion of the Academy's facilities, but this time, led by John M. Schofield, the former Superintendent, the board went further. Taking its cue from Mills's endorsement of their prior year's report, it argued: "It would be the part of wisdom and good business to place the Military Academy, with all its natural advantages and physical imperfections, in the hands of an architect of recognized ability." If that approach was not taken, the board warned, "almost every dollar spent in the future for 'enlarging here and altering and patching there' is so much money thrown away."[8]

In October 1901, Mills ordered Larned back to his drawing board and asked him for a new plan. This time the professor produced a much more ambitious program. He warned against "temporary expediency," saying that such an arrangement was "so expensive to keep in repair" that the more comprehensive plan of new construction would be "economical in the long run." On December 21, he presented his new plan. In addition to a new cadet barracks, he called for a second academic building, a new chapel, a new riding hall, a new post headquarters, a new headquarters for the corps of cadets, and a new hotel; and he renewed his call for additional officers' quarters. His estimate of the cost was approximately $6.5 million.[9]

In 1902 Congress appropriated $5.5 million for the project. At West Point, Mills quickly appointed a board of officers to examine Larned's work and draw up requirements on which an architectural competition could be based. To that board he named Larned, Professor of Chemistry Samuel Tillman, Professor of Modern Languages Edward E. Wood, Professor of Engineering Gustav J. Fiebeger, and Captain Frank E. Hobbs, instructor of ordnance and gunnery. Though there were some differences of opinion within the board, its report to the Superintendent largely reflected Larned's most recent proposal. Still, since Congress had appropriated only $5.5 million, instead of the $6.6 million that Larned thought necessary, the board dropped the new hotel. Mills forwarded this report to Washington but expressed some reservations about its recommendations. His greatest concern was that the report was not sufficiently forward-looking. "In the scheme for the new improvements," he wrote, "the broadest view should be taken so that no work done now would have to be undone in the future." The architects, he added, should "be given the freest scope in making their studies without regard to the plans or to the particular locations recommended by the members of the Board."[10]

Things now moved rapidly. Within days the Secretary of War approved the report and directed that invitations asking firms to participate in the architectural competition be issued. In February 1903, the formal rules governing the competition were circulated to the ten firms that had chosen to compete, and the jury was identified: Schofield, Mills, and three distinguished architects, George B. Post, Walter Cook, and Cass Gilbert.[11]

The question of architectural style was ostensibly left to the firms in the competition, but there was a clear local predisposition toward the Gothic. In 1899, Larned had noted that the Tudor-Gothic style of the cadet barracks and library had, "to a certain extent, determined the character of some of the more important neighbors."[12] In 1901, he had been even more direct. "It is not desirable, that any scheme should attempt to sweep the field clean and destroy architectural associations made honorable by generations of great men, while it is of the highest importance to preserve intact the structural sentiment which gives character and individuality to the Academy."[13] The board of officers that had reviewed Larned's proposal advised quite explicitly that "the design of the principal new public buildings should conform to the prevailing Gothic."[14] Still, in his letter of invitation to the architects, Mills assured them all that the board's views "either as to location or character of buildings or as to the treatment of the subject" were not binding upon them.[15]

That said, however, there was a clear bias in favor of the Gothic. All the firms that were well known for their Gothic designs were invited to enter the competition. Since there were so few of these, however, other leading architects were also included. Still, when the Gothic designs of Cram, Goodhue and Ferguson of Boston seemed to meet all the requirements of the competition, and fit so masterfully the peculiarities of the site, the judges were unanimous in choosing their submission.[16]

In most respects, the firm's plans followed the board's recommendations of 1902 regarding the location of structures. The riding hall was to sit on the ground then occupied by the stables, the old riding hall, and the cavalry barracks. The new headquarters building was to be located across from the cadet mess. The new academic building was to occupy the site of the existing chapel and administration building, the new chapel was to be located on a hillside overlooking the parade ground, and the additional cadet barracks would create a quadrangle behind the current barracks. The jury concurred in all of this except the location of the new barracks; the majority favored Larned's proposal of placing it on the west edge of the Plain to the north of the existing barracks. The architect's plan made only two other important departures from the earlier recommendations. The first was the razing of the hotel and the construction of a new one on the hillside above the cadet hospital. Second, having cleared Trophy Point, the architects proposed to build there a massive residence for the Superintendent that would also contain reception rooms and suites of apartments for distinguished visitors. "We feel very strongly," wrote the architects, "that the main avenue as it prolongs itself across the Military Plain demands a focal point of considerable importance."[17] At first, the only concern with these two additions was cost. Later the issue became wrapped in a broader conflict between the officers of the board—essentially the Academic Board—and the Superintendent. The opposition then took on a very different tone.

In developing this new West Point, it was the aim of the architects, both in their general plan and in the design of individual buildings, to preserve the natural features that gave such distinction to the site. They sought to make their style "harmonize with the majority of the existing buildings" and to make it "emphasize rather than antagonize the picturesque natural surroundings of rocks, cliffs, mountains, and forests."[18] This was most evident in the design of the riding hall, chapel, and headquarters building. The natural appearance of these buildings was enhanced by using stone quarried from the hill immediately behind the Superintendent's quarters. The huge bulk of the riding hall made it impressive, and its broad buttresses gave it a distinctly Gothic character. It seemed to grow out of the granite cliff to which it clung. Similarly, the new headquarters or administration building, with its buttressed granite walls and tower rising 160 feet above the ground, stood like a Gothic castle.

The chapel, though, was the crown of the general plan. Situated high above the plain, with its lofty bell tower seemingly seeking the heavens, it overlooked the barracks and dominated the Plain and academic area in a physical sense that suggested an even greater moral presence and purview.

Mills met privately with the architects at West Point in late June 1903.[19] He presented the revisions that the jury had recommended and instructed the architects to consider in their plans the provisions necessary if the corps were to expand to 1,200 cadets.[20] Mills did not include any of the permanent professors in the meetings—nor did he, at the time, share either the plan or the jury's comments with them, or solicit their views. "It did not seem advisable to authorize *ad libitum* conferences between the Advisory Board and the architects," he later wrote, adding that "it has seemed both wise and proper to require both parties to present their cases to the Superintendent."[21]

A few months later, in September 1903, Mills reconvened the board of officers as an advisory board to consider the architects' plans. In its first session the board applauded the work of the architects, suggesting only that in

North Barracks (1909) and Cadet Chapel (1910). White Collection, United States Military Academy Archives.

replacing the officers' quarters lost to the new barracks, the architects should group "the houses of the professors and of the Commandant of Cadets in the [same] neighborhood, so as to keep the heads of departments in close contact with the Academy and barracks."[22] It passed without comment the plan to construct new quarters for the Superintendent on Trophy Point.

In December, however, the board members learned that the architects recommended increasing the mass of the structures on Trophy Point and had proposed grouping several additional quarters near the Superintendent. Mills, they were informed, had chosen to gather around his quarters the residences of his military staff—the Commandant of Cadets, the adjutant, the quartermaster, and the surgeon—rather than the academic staff. The advisory board immediately objected. This complex should house the Superintendent, the Commandant of Cadets, and "the permanent officers of the Academic Board," it argued. They would not be relegated to second importance.[23] Mills ignored the board and forwarded his plan to Secretary of War Elihu Root, who approved it in late January 1904—one of his last acts as Secretary.

Mills's deliberate snub of the Academic Board in this matter was symptomatic of an underlying conflict between himself and the permanent professors. When appointed in 1898, Mills, a first lieutenant, was the most junior officer ever to be made Superintendent—though he immediately assumed the local rank of colonel. His appointment as Superintendent had startled the West Point community and the Army. Mills was forty-four years old when appointed (several officers had been made Superintendent at a younger age), but he seemed young in comparison to his predecessor, and young relative to much of the faculty.[24] Michie and Larned had been full professors, and Wood, an instructor, while Mills was a cadet. His junior rank and his comparative youth seemed to befit him better for a subordinate position. In fact, Major Otto L. Hein, the Commandant of Cadets, had suggested as much to him. "I wrote to . . . Mills of my regiment, who had been seriously wounded . . . , expressing my sympathy, and offering to apply for his detail as Adjutant of the Military Academy," he later noted.[25] Imagine Hein's chagrin when, only weeks later, it was announced that Mills was to be made Superintendent.

This rather extraordinary appointment came at the personal initiative of President William McKinley and had been made over the opposition of many in Washington. Mills had lost an eye when he was shot through the head in the battle for San Juan Hill. Barely a month later, while convalescing in Washington, he was introduced to the President. McKinley was quite affected by Mills and his ordeal and was determined to reward him. At the time, McKinley had before him a slate of officers recommended to replace Ernst, the current Superintendent.[26] Finding promotion impracticable as a means to reward Mills, he fixed on making him Superintendent of the Military Academy. Both Nelson A. Miles, the Commanding General, and Secretary of War Russell Alger objected, but without effect—the recent debacle in Cuba had undercut their ability to press the issue.

To the faculty, Mills soon came to be viewed as an enfant terrible—impertinent, abrasive, and vindictive—for in his zeal he often deliberately trod on turf the academics had long since staked out as their own. His snub regarding the new quarters became a cause célèbre. The fight it engendered illustrates both the nature and the mode of the conflicts that periodically occurred between the permanent faculty and transient, but strong-minded, Superintendents. Though on the surface these often seemed trivial and spiteful, they had a significance beyond the issues in debate. In fact, they decided the broader questions of province and prerogative—questions that decided who would define the nature of the institution.

The advisory board responded formally to Mills's action on May 5, 1904. It now objected to removing the hotel from Trophy Point; that was only necessary as "a consequence of the carrying out of the proposed location of the Superintendent's quarters and other buildings at or near Trophy Point," it insisted. The board urged that further consideration of a new hotel (and, by implication, the new Superintendent's quarters) should be postponed.[27] Mills, again, simply dismissed these arguments and informed the board that he intended to erect all the principal buildings "under the present appropriation."[28]

At that, members of the advisory board composed a letter to the War Department, complaining that Mills was ignoring their concerns that the plans, as they stood, could not be executed "within the limits of the appropriation." They also objected that they were not being shown all the plans. "The issues involved," they insisted, "are such that if decided unwisely would detrimentally and permanently affect the efficiency of the institution and the comfort and welfare of its personnel."[29] As was appropriate, this letter was submitted first to Mills, but when he did not forward it to the War Department, one of the board members took the issue to the *Army and Navy Journal*, prompting an editorial critical of Mills's handling of the affair. "We have reason to believe that there is dissatisfaction with the plan of leaving so important a matter within the control of any one man [Mills]," wrote the editor. "Questions are being settled 'by authority,' which should be open to free discussion by those to whom the interests of the Military Academy are subjects of vital concern."[30]

Thus prodded, Mills forwarded the letter to the War Department but complained that the advisory board "wants power and authority over the work equal to that exercised by the Superintendent." This was, Mills insisted, "but the first step in an attempt to upset the general plan." He recommended that the board's letter not even be shown to the new Secretary of War, William Howard Taft. He also solicited a statement from the War Department to the effect that "there is no intention to alter in any material respect the general plan" that had already been approved.

Fred Ainsworth, the Military Secretary at the War Office in Washington, had no intention of getting entangled in this issue and forwarded the whole package to the new Secretary of War. Taft's response took something of a middle position. The plan approved by Root would be followed, he announced, but subject to those changes necessary "to bring the cost of the work within the amount appropriated therefore by Congress."[31] Mills sent Taft's response to Larned and the board but tried to stifle further dissent by ordering that the contents "not be made public."[32]

Undaunted, the advisory board returned to the assault in October 1904—complaining this time that the architects seemed "exceedingly anxious to economize" in the construction of the academic building and were doing so "in order to preserve the integrity of plans of other buildings which the Board regards as of less vital importance to the institution." The reference, of course, was to the complex of quarters for the Superintendent and his military staff.[33]

Mills returned the board's communication, insisting that "no grounds exist to justify [the board's assertions]," and that the tone and wording of the report were both "unmilitary and unnecessary." In the future, he instructed the board, its views should "be expressed more effectively in less objectionable language."[34] The advisory board answered him the same day. The letter had been respectful, the board members insisted, and in any case the remarks were directed to the architects and not to the Superintendent. Moreover, they wanted direct access to the architects and wished to have their views made known to the Secretary of War. They were not opposed to the general plan, they said, and had raised only a few objections, including, of course, "the grouping of military rather than Academic Staff about the Superintendent."[35]

With that, the attention of all parties was diverted by the start of construction, and for a time the issue of the Superintendent's quarters receded into the background. Construction at the south end of the post began in 1905 with barracks and stables for the artillery and cavalry troops. These were completed in 1908. In the summer of 1906, work began on the new administration building (completed 1910) and on the heating and generating plant that was to be located adjacent to the new riding hall (completed 1909).

In August 1906, Mills departed, and Major Hugh L. Scott, class of 1876, became Superintendent. "One of the pressing questions found on my arrival," wrote Scott some years later, "was the location of the new chapel. One faction wanted it at the lower end of the post, while another demanded the northern end, where it would mask the view up the Hudson, one of the glories of West Point." Scott favored the hillside site that had been selected by the architects and approved by Mills. To settle the issue, he ordered Colonel J. M. Carlson, the quartermaster who supervised the construction, "to dig a hole where the chapel now stands, blast some rock, and what would still be more convincing, spend some money." This done, "it was generally recognized that the matter was settled, and the clamor ceased."[36] The chapel was completed and dedicated in 1910.

The issue of the complex of quarters at Trophy Point was raised again in December 1906, this time by the architects, who perhaps believed that Scott would act in this case with the same resolve he had shown concerning the chapel. This "mass of buildings," they argued, "is imperative at the termination of the axis of the main Avenue . . . which is the principal and most important line of vision." In the meantime, opposition to this "mass of buildings" had grown among the graduates and friends of the Academy who feared that these structures would block the north view of the river. This sentiment was voiced forcefully in 1906 by the Board of Visitors, which made "a very earnest protest . . . against the construction of any buildings in this neighborhood."[37]

New plans for the complex arrived from Cram, Goodhue and Ferguson in February 1907. The advisory board now joined the chorus of opposition, insisting that "the intrusion upon the Plain of an extensive group of buildings . . . will necessarily intercept the view at this end of the Post and remove from the public use a large part of the most picturesque portion of the general parade."[38] The flood of letters from graduates that appeared in the *Army and Navy Journal* indicated the extent of the opposition. "To shut off the slightest portion of it would seem a useless act of vandalism and would cause more ill feeling among officers, professors and all graduates than anything that could happen," wrote Horace Porter, president of the Association of Graduates, to Secretary of War Taft.[39]

The issue took on a new sense of drama when President Theodore Roosevelt became involved in February 1907. Letters from Mrs. Henry Cabot Lodge and Mrs. C. F. LaFarge had asked him to intervene and save the renowned north view from West Point, and he did. "Indeed," wrote Scott to the architects, "the positive instructions of the President of the United States on this point are that this view shall in no manner or way be impaired."[40] The question then to be answered was whether or not the new buildings would obstruct the view.

In early March 1907, a hasty meeting was arranged between Scott and the architects. Before the conference, the architects asked that a pole be erected thirty feet high at the site that would be the southwest corner of the proposed structures. "This will enable us at once to see . . . just how much of the view is cut off from any portion of the Plain," they wrote.[41] Scott and the architects came away from this meeting convinced that the buildings would neither obstruct the view nor encroach on the Plain. The Superintendent took the report of this investigation personally to the President. Roosevelt was satisfied. "It shall be carried out exactly as recommended," he instructed.[42]

With the President's personal approval of the project, the advisory board was informed that "the question . . . is therefore definitely settled."[43] Two days later, the board forwarded to the Superintendent its study of the latest plans concerning the project. Dutifully it recommended "that the location of the buildings and their general arrangement be in conformity with the wishes of the architects." In the specifics, however, the board members raised new issues. They called attention to the areas devoted to official entertainment and functions and to two large suites of rooms—one for the President and another for the Secretary of War. These, they pointed out, would necessitate "a fully equipped kitchen," a "permanent staff" of domestics, and accommodations for them, despite the fact that "a large portion of the time there will be no use for [their] services." In addition, the board noted that the quarters proposed for the Superintendent's military staff were "considerably in excess of that designed elsewhere for officers of corresponding rank."[44]

Based on the advisory board's latest report, Scott asked Cram, Goodhue and Ferguson to "restudy and replan this whole group." There should be a "material reduction" in the "official [guest] quarters," and he ordered a significant reduction as well in the size of the staff officers' quarters.[45] The architects obliged and forwarded new plans to Scott for his approval. By this time, however, Scott had discovered that the opposition of the old grads had not been calmed by Roosevelt's approval, and he deferred final approval of the plans.

At that, the issue again receded into the background. For almost four years, the attention of the Superintendent and the architects was occupied otherwise. North Barracks was finished in 1909—the first building on the level of the Plain to be completed. The new gymnasium was begun in 1908 and completed two years later. Work on the riding hall proper began in 1909 and was finished in 1911. When the administration building and chapel were occupied in 1910, the old chapel and administration buildings could be removed to make room for the east academic building, which was under construction from 1911 to 1914. Later the old chapel was rebuilt, stone by stone, in the post cemetery, where it stands today.

In 1911, Cram, Goodhue and Ferguson once again raised the issue of the quarters complex at Trophy Point, this time to a new Superintendent, Major

General Thomas H. Barry, of the class of 1877, who had arrived in 1910. Barry, however, was not sympathetic to the project. "This group of buildings has been a burning question from the beginning," he wrote and then listed his objections: a separate set of quarters for distinguished visitors was unnecessary; and the quarters for the Superintendent and military staff would be expensive and extravagant. Moreover, he added, "there is some sentiment connected with these old buildings"—meaning the existing quarters of the Superintendent and Commandant. "I am satisfied," Barry wrote, that "the best interests of the Academy and economy do not warrant the construction of this group of buildings."[46] And so the matter was finally resolved.

Superintendent Barry departed West Point in 1912, leaving the completion of construction to his successor, Colonel Clarence Page Townsley, class of 1881. The work, which had begun in 1904, was finally completed in 1914. But, hardly had the last stone been laid before Townsley began planning for still further construction to accommodate another expansion of the corps of cadets. From 1900 to 1914, the total number of cadets authorized had grown from 481 to 748. In 1916, in response to the nation's growing commitment in the Caribbean and Pacific and to the war in Europe, the number was almost doubled, to 1,332. In 1918, when the entry of the United States into the war made growth obligatory, construction was begun on facilities to accommodate the larger number of cadets. A new barracks completed the quadrangle behind the 1851 edifice and followed the architectural lines of the Delafield barracks. It was completed in 1921. At about the same time, a new cadet hospital designed by Arnold W. Brunner was begun. It was finished in 1923. The old (1884) hospital was converted to other purposes and pulled down section by section as new buildings crowded in.

In 1920, with peace restored, the new Superintendent, Douglas MacArthur, class of 1903, called attention to the fact that although the recent reorganization of the Army had nearly doubled the prewar size of the officer corps, the authorized strength of the corps of cadets at West Point had remained at 1,334. Noting that the size of the brigade of midshipmen at Annapolis had recently been increased to an authorized strength ceiling of over 3,000, MacArthur called for an expansion at West Point to 2,500.[47] The next year he submitted plans for construction to accommodate this number. Prominent in his plan was a sports stadium or coliseum at Gee's Point and, once again, new quarters for the Superintendent at the edge of the Plain at Trophy Point.[48] MacArthur estimated the cost of the project to be $6 million, including the construction of a new hotel.

Although nothing came of the plan, piecemeal construction continued. A new stadium was built in 1924, but not at Gee's Point. Rather, it was nestled in a natural amphitheater just to the west of Lusk Reservoir—possibly the loveliest setting in all of collegiate football. A new hotel was finally built in 1925 at the south end of the post—overlooking the river—at approximately the site proposed by Larned in 1899.[49] The old hotel sat vacant for several years and was finally demolished in 1932.

The earlier construction of North Barracks on the western edge of the Plain made a more centrally located cadet dining facility very desirable, and with the completion of the new gymnasium, the site of the old gym (1891) directly between the two barracks areas became available. In 1924, the venerable structure was pulled down, and the next year a new mess hall was begun. Washington Hall, as it soon became known, was completed in 1926. William Gehron, with Arnold W. Brunner and Associates, was the architect, and his design, with strongly built buttresses fronting the structure, conformed handsomely to the Gothic character of the barracks on either side.

The construction of Washington Hall, in turn, made possible the destruction of the old Grant Hall and the erection, in its place, of a new Barracks—designed by Gehron and Sidney F. Ross. Begun in 1930, it was completed the next year. Like the old mess hall it replaced, it was called Grant Hall. The battlements, the rough-cut stone, and the entrances and windows of the cadet reception room on the first floor allowed it to blend effectively with the adjutant buildings adjoining it.

Debate over curriculum reform was virtually continuous at West Point from 1901 to 1911. By the beginning of that period, a consensus had developed among members of the Academic Board for a number of changes. One clear goal was having Army officers who were fluent in Spanish. The United States had only recently acquired important Spanish-speaking territories, and, for a time, the Army was to administer them. In response, the Academic Board increased the regular Spanish course from 78 to 160 lessons in 1902. The board also increased the number of lessons in English, chemistry, and electricity and introduced instruction in military hygiene. This was accomplished by making cuts in mathematics and natural philosophy and reducing instruction in French from four semesters to three.

Mills, who had encouraged the 1902 reforms—the "New Curriculum," as he called it—soon began to press for further changes.[50] In a letter to the War Department in March 1904, he challenged two of the pillars of the Military Academy's academic program—the emphasis on mathematics and science and the single curriculum for all cadets. The use of "scientific studies for the mental development of the students" had gone too far, he asserted. To remedy this, he suggested that "some of the courses taught might perhaps be omitted" and that the time thus gained be allotted to other subjects and other departments. Next he dismissed the argument that "every cadet who graduates from the Military Academy should pursue exactly the same course," pointing out that "in more than one department of instruction Cadets in the upper portion of the class are now carried further in their studies than those in the lower portion."[51]

Larned answered for the board in an article that appeared in the August 1904 issue of *Churchman*. The cornerstone of the curriculum, he argued, was mathematics, and the bulk of the structure was necessarily made up of the sciences. West Point shunned "the liberty of *laissez faire* in intellectual attainment" and offered instead a "well-balanced development of the mechanism of thinking based upon a through understanding of elementary principles"— the stuff of "mental discipline." The "genius of West Point," Larned argued, lay in the "three fundamentals" on which its curriculum was based: "Every man in every subject—Every man proficient in everything—Every man every day." The West Point system required that every cadet take the whole program, that every cadet attain the required standard of proficiency in every subject, and that every cadet be prepared to recite each day in each class.

By September, the conflict had reached the point that even the *Army and Navy Journal* reported the increasing "friction" at West Point. An editorial charged that at West Point issues were too often settled by "a mere exercise of military authority." "Utmost weight" should be given to the permanent professors, the paper insisted, particularly "when questions of change" were considered. "Superintendents come and go," it continued, "but the academic staff remain as the inheritors and exponents of the ideas which have made the Academy what it is."[52]

Mills, who was already at loggerheads with the professors over details of construction and physical expansion, called a meeting of the board at once and demanded to know what "friction" existed. The members were polite but explicit in outlining their grievances. Mills was not moved. He brushed aside the complaints and ordered the board to undertake a new curriculum study aimed toward providing instruction in French and Spanish throughout the cadets' last two years and accommodating physical education in each of the four years.

The committee's response in February 1905 showed its exasperation clearly. It met Mills's demand for a new schedule in languages and physical education by abolishing the English course but without touching the core of mathematics and sciences. Mills's displeasure at this result—in particular at the failure of the board to reduce or restructure the course in mathematics—was compounded when the new Professor of Mathematics, Charles P. Echols, declared 40 percent of the third class deficient. Echols, who had graduated in 1891, had replaced Professor Wright Edgerton in 1904. Mills

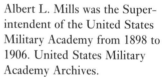

Albert L. Mills was the Superintendent of the United States
Military Academy from 1898 to
1906. United States Military
Academy Archives.

retaliated by ordering Echols away on a year's sabbatical to study the Euro-
pean military schools. Echols protested but without effect.[53]

Though Mills had few allies at the Military Academy, he could usually
count on support from the War Department. On this occasion, Washington
responded by giving him three votes on the Academic Board (following the
precedent of the Naval Academy).[54] Thus armed, he returned to the curriculum issue in the late spring of 1905. He also brought a directive from the
Secretary of War to increase the number of hours of physical education. He
instructed the Academic Board to reconsider the plan it had put forward in
February. Mills cautioned the board members that if they were not more
responsive this time, change would be prescribed from the outside, "with
results certainly less satisfactory to themselves and perhaps less prolific of
good to the institution."[55] From his perspective, however, their next report
was only marginally better than the one before. Still, this plan was implemented on a one-year trial basis in the fall of 1905 while the board continued to explore other solutions.[56]

By the end of 1905, however, Mills's base of support in Washington had
begun to erode. His contest with the permanent faculty over construction

issues began to cost him backers, as did his open warfare with Echols. Mills not only had sent the mathematics professor on an unwanted sabbatical but also had written a scathing report on the professor's conduct, questioning Echols's "attitude toward his immediate responsibilities" and charging that he had "taken a critical rather than helpful attitude" toward proposed reforms. These charges proved counterproductive. Echols protested and won the support of then Acting Chief of Staff John C. Bates and, through him, Secretary of War Taft. When Mills attacked Bates, saying that he had shown poor judgment and had improperly advised the Secretary, he further undercut his standing in Washington.[57]

Discussion of various curriculum proposals filled the winter and spring of 1906.[58] In all the board produced "eight minor reports bearing upon special points of the curriculum" and "four full reports" with "proposed schedules." Finally, in the summer of 1906, two events helped move the board toward a compromise: Professor Echols's return from his imposed sabbatical and Mills's departure. Even then, the only concession it made was the creation of the Department of English and History and the Department of Military Hygiene. The Academic Board still refused to carve hours out of the old curriculum and instead added courses by voting to extend the four-year program by three months—requiring new cadets to enroll in March rather than June. Neither Hugh Scott, the new Superintendent, nor the board was pleased with this plan, but the issue was taken out of their hands unexpectedly. George B. Davis, who had been professor of law a few years earlier and was now Judge Advocate General of the Army, learned of the board's proposal and took it upon himself to promote it in Washington. He discussed it with the Chief of Staff, the Secretary of War, and the Chairman of the House Committee on Military Affairs and obtained the endorsement of each. Finding the Academy already committed in Washington, Scott and the board had little choice but to send the proposal forward for approval.

In January 1908, just before this new plan was put into effect, President Theodore Roosevelt threatened to undo the compromise. "It seems to me a very great misfortune," he wrote to his Secretary of War, William Taft, "to lay so much stress upon mathematics in the curriculum at West Point and fail to have languages taught in accordance with the best modern conversational methods. I have several times called attention to it, but nothing has been done." He demanded "a full report on the matter."[59] The curriculum committee responded immediately. Its members reported that they had spent considerable time addressing just these problems, and the new curriculum to be introduced in March addressed many of Roosevelt's concerns. Still, they held fast to the view that mathematics was "basic in the curriculum of the Academy" and that "the habit of exact thought which has been developed by mathematical training" had utility even for officers of the line. Though they might curtail "the ground to be covered in mathematical study," they insisted that the time gained be spent achieving "a more thorough mastery of the simple fundamental principles through further practical application and more detailed instruction." Concerning languages, they pointed out that a considerable addition had already been made to the time devoted to instruction in conversational Spanish, but they held the line on French. Attaining a "mastery of the colloquial form" in French, they argued, was beyond the capability of the average student in the time that could be made available. The board ended its report by insisting that, while some changes might be necessary, there were "interests which cannot in justice be set aside." Pointing to the new curriculum that was about to be introduced, it "respectfully" asked "for a trial of [that] scheme."[60]

The President conceded, and the new curriculum was implemented in March 1908. Roosevelt left office a year later without further inquiry into the subject. The new program, with its March entry date, proved so unworkable that in 1911 the board voted unanimously to return to the regular four-year curriculum. At about the same time, another lingering symbol of the Mills reform era disappeared as quietly as the recent curriculum changes: a committee established to revise the regulations of the Academy proposed restricting the Superintendent to one vote on the Academic Board. Scott opposed this move but was about to depart, and he left the matter to Barry, his successor, who chose not to make an issue of it. The *Regulations, 1911* restored the equality of all board members in voting matters.

Discussions of curriculum change then lapsed for several years. In the meantime, the Academic Board underwent some significant membership changes. Edward Edgar Wood, who had served at West Point as a teacher of French almost continuously since 1872 and had been professor of foreign languages since 1892, retired in 1910. Two other key members of the old guard departed in 1911— Charles Larned, Professor of Drawing, died, and Samuel Tillman, Professor of Chemistry, retired. Wood was replaced by Cornelius DeWitt Willcox, class of 1885, who had been an assistant professor at West Point since 1892—first in natural philosophy and then in French. Larned was succeeded by Edwin R. Stuart, class of 1896, who had already spent nine of his fourteen years in service on the faculty. Wirt Robinson, who took Tillman's chair, was a member of the class of 1887; he had been assigned at West Point off and on since 1890. In most respects Willcox, Stuart, and Robinson were more like the men they replaced than they were different. They were military men who had served the bulk of their careers at West Point and were deeply imbued with the traditions of the Academy.

Another new member of the board, however, was not a military man at all. Lucius H. Holt, a Yale Ph.D. with no military experience, was hired in 1910 to head the Department of English and History. His predecessor, John C. Adams, also of Yale, had been hired just two years earlier when the department was first created, but Adams had not been a propitious choice. He had stunned the other members of the faculty by dropping Thayer's system of instruction and lecturing to all the classes himself. Holt restored the instructor system and broadened the history curriculum by adding a textbook on political science.

With the departure of Larned, Tillman, and Wood, seniority on the Academic Board devolved to Gustav Joseph Fiebeger, Professor of Engineering; William Brandon Gordon, Professor of Natural Philosophy; and Charles Patton Echols, Professor of Mathematics. Fiebeger, class of 1879, had been picked to succeed James Mercur when the latter died in 1896. Fiebeger had served a number of years in the field as an engineer officer but had been an assistant professor of engineering at the Academy from 1883 to 1888.[61] Gordon, class of 1877, had assumed Michie's chair in natural philosophy when the latter died in 1901. In subsequent years, Gordon authored a number of texts that replaced those written by his predecessor. Echols, who had run afoul of Mills shortly after being appointed professor of mathematics in 1904, weathered that trial only to cross swords a few years later with another "youngster" appointed as Superintendent—Douglas MacArthur.

The war that began in Europe in 1914 hardly touched West Point until 1917, but the next two years were a wrenching period. It began when Colonel John Biddle, appointed Superintendent in 1916, was ordered off to the war. To replace him, Colonel Samuel Tillman, who had retired as professor of chemistry in 1911, was recalled and made Superintendent.

The first class—the class of April 1917—was graduated on April 20, 1917, only days after the United States entered the conflict. A month later, the next class, which had entered the Academy in 1914, started an abbreviated version of the first-class course of studies. Intensive military training was added in June, and ten weeks later these cadets were graduated as the class of August 1917. A second three-year emergency class was graduated in June 1918. The following month, Tillman obtained War Department approval of a fixed three-year course for all cadets. He soon found, however, that what the War Department could give, it could also take away.

Tillman's leadership at West Point in these years was dauntless in the face of War Department demands that often smacked of the absurd.[62] Paradoxically, the most trying period was the weeks just before and after the fighting stopped in November 1918.[63] "On the 3rd of October," Tillman recalled,

"I got a telephone message from the Adjutant General at half past 10 o'clock at night telling me we were to graduate two classes on the 1st of November."[64] Further, he was informed, for the balance of the wartime emergency, the course of instruction at West Point would last just one year.[65] "Why, this means there will be no upper classmen in the Corps," Tillman protested. "The regime and traditions, which have take a century to develop, can never be restored."[66] The next day, the Superintendent went to Washington, but to no avail. In France, the Meuse-Argonne offensive, which began in September, generated massive American casualties—many of them officers. There was now a critical shortage of trained officers, and to Peyton March, class of 1888, the Army's Chief of Staff, West Point was one obvious means of addressing that situation. Nothing could be done to change the order, Tillman was told.

The news numbed the post. There had been disruptions before, but now the long gray line seemed threatened. The "delicate, intangible impulses for conduct and honor, instilled and developed in hearts and minds over past decades," could only be handed down from one cadet class to another.[67] But what if there were only one class? The question hung in the air. The timing of the affair gave it a surreal character, for by all accounts the Germans were retreating, and the war would soon be over. If that were true, they asked at West Point, why was Washington perpetrating this "absurd crime"?[68] The best Tillman could do was to extract a promise from the Washington bureaucracy that, should the war end before January 1920, members of the last class (which had been at West Point for less than sixteen months) would be returned to the Academy to complete their education.

On November 1, 1918, the classes that had entered the Academy in 1916 and 1917 were graduated and commissioned. This left only the class that had entered in June 1918—barely five months earlier. The next day, 360 new cadets were sworn in, all believing that they would be graduated within eighteen months. (The class that entered in June 1918 soon became known as fourth class "A"; the November class, fourth class "B".) On November 11, an armistice effectively ended the war. The recent graduates had not yet even reported to training camps. Barely four weeks after they had departed West Point, the more junior of the two recently graduated classes was ordered back to the Academy, but as student officers, not cadets.[69]

With the end of the war, Tillman and the Academic Board faced an array of challenges. The first was how to deal with the unique relationship between the two classes still at the Academy and the class that had entered in 1917 and had been graduated prematurely in November 1918. The latter returned to West Point uniformed as officers, but they were not given officers' privileges. They were quartered separately in South Barracks and were

Officer class of 1919. This photo appears to show them arriving at their final graduation, June 1919. White Collection, United States Military Academy Archives.

isolated at meals and ceremonies. And they agitated from the beginning to be released. For the other two classes (those admitted in June and November 1918), tactical officers furnished the guidance and leadership usually provided by the upper classes. The distinction between the two groups was emphasized in the beginning because for several months cadet gray uniforms were not available for fourth class "B." Instead, these cadets were issued the olive drab enlisted uniform, but with a distinguishing orange hat band—and were forthwith dubbed "the Orioles."[70]

For the Academic Board, however, the problem went far beyond a matter of uniforms. The board also had to devise unique academic programs for each class: a six-month program for the student officers; an additional eighteen months for fourth class "A"; and a thirty-month curriculum for fourth class "B." The student officers were graduated again in June 1919 after six months of additional schooling; the classes that had entered the Academy in June (fourth class "A") and November 1918 (fourth class "B") were to be graduated in 1920 and 1921, respectively—after courses of roughly twenty-four and thirty months.[71] By the end of June 1919, with the admission of a new plebe class and the elevation of the fourth classes "A" and "B" to the upper classes as first and second classes, respectively (there was no third class until the four-year curriculum was restored), some sense of normalcy returned.

Finally the Academic Board was faced with the challenge of reestablish-ing a fixed curriculum. In November 1918, Peyton March, the Army's Chief of Staff, directed the Academic Board to submit a three-year course of stud-ies—it might be four years, he noted, only if it included a broader offering of "cultural subjects."[72]

In mid-December, instead of the report that March had requested, the board forwarded an eight-page defense of the prewar four-year course and of its emphasis on producing mental discipline. "The course of study at the Military Academy has been mathematical and scientific and it should con-tinue so," the board insisted. "The power and habit of clear, exact and logi-cal thought engendered by the proper study" of mathematics and science "are the best assets that can be provided our graduates."[73] So far as the board was concerned, it could not abbreviate the course. The only acceptable three-year solution was to require remarkably more mathematics, French, English, and history prior to matriculation—in effect eliminating the need for those subjects that usually constituted the fourth-class year. As to a broader offer-ing of "cultural subjects," the board insisted that "no Engineering school would think of substituting cultural for necessary scientific studies."[74]

General March, however, was not receptive to this response, and in mid-May 1919, without consulting the Academy further, he recommended to Secretary of War Newton Baker that "the course of instruction at the United States Military Academy be fixed at three years." Baker approved, and the Academic Board was ordered to prepare a three-year curriculum.[75] At the same time, March also selected a new Superintendent, Brigadier General Douglas MacArthur, and ordered him to West Point immediately.[76]

Douglas MacArthur assumed command at West Point in June 1919, just after graduation. The thirty-nine-year-old officer was one of the youngest Superintendents since Thayer.[77] The new Superintendent had not been there long before many on the board were convinced that their worst fears had been realized—they were being led by another boy-Superintendent, inexperienced in educational matters yet energetic and, above all else, ambitious. The older members could not help but draw parallels with the earlier enfant terrible, Mills.

MacArthur had been instructed by March to establish a three-year cur-riculum and to put it into place at West Point. But at the first working meet-ing of the Academic Board on June 26, 1919, he found that the curriculum committee had already acted. Two curriculum reports were presented that day: the first, a math-heavy, engineering-oriented program proposed by the curriculum committee; and the second, a two-tracked curriculum championed by Professor Lucius Holt. Holt's plan offered both an engineering track and a track that emphasized economics and civil government—with no engineering. To no one's surprise, the board approved the former.[78] On June 28, 1919, MacArthur forwarded this recommendation to Washington. Secretary Baker approved, and this curriculum was implemented in September 1919.

At the same time, the board began to lobby for the restoration of a four-year curriculum. It found a willing supporter in Congressman John M. Morin of Pennsylvania, who chaired the subcommittee on Military Academy appropriations and had been president of the Board of Visitors in 1919. In February 1920, Morin opened the hearings on the Academy's appropriation by declaring his intent to reestablish the four-year course. Morin called on MacArthur to support his fight for the additional year, but the general demurred.[79] It was Tillman who took up the standard in retirement and, with Morin, persuaded Congress to restore the four-year program.[80]

At that, the curriculum committee went back to work, but after an extended debate it had done little more than restore the courses of the old four-year curriculum, curtailing them only enough to allow for a new course in economics and government.[81] Holt, the professor of English and history, had been promoting such a course since 1911, and its adoption a decade later was a typical example of the workings of the Academic Board. Though MacArthur backed Holt at this juncture and is often credited with

Lucius H. Holt was professor of English and history from 1910 to 1926 and professor of economics, government, and history from 1926 to 1930. West Point Museum Collection, United States Military Academy.

this "liberalization" of the curriculum, his support was not instrumental in the outcome.

The process of achieving lasting, substantive change at West Point in the areas where the Academic Board had cognizance was one of consensus building, and it often took years. Tillman illustrated it thus:

> In 1884, I submitted to the Academic Board [a new proposal]. This proposition involved the change of a long-established system; when first suggested, the Board simply referred it for "further consideration." Several times at intervals, I again submitted the plan, accompanied by results in its application in my own Department. In May, 1894, ten years after the new method had first been brought forward by me, the other Departments were directed to give it "careful consideration." In 1895, a committee appointed to "test the method" reported in favor of adopting it; in 1896, it was finally adopted.[82]

The process, at times, moved so slowly that outsiders—including Superintendents and nonpermanent faculty—failed to perceive any change at all. Slow as it was, however, the process did have significant advantages. It seldom admitted poor ideas, for their disadvantages became apparent before sufficient support had been mustered to pass them. And it kept curriculum turmoil to a minimum. "The Board," wrote Tillman, was "the continuing, developing and stabilizing factor of the Academy."[83]

On July 20, 1920, MacArthur forwarded the board's recommendation for a four-year program to the War Department, where it was approved and ordered into effect for all classes still at the Academy. The class that had entered in November 1918 (fourth class "B") had expected to be commissioned within a year—by late 1919. With the end of the war—just days after these cadets had been admitted—their graduation had immediately been extended to June 1921. Now, they were told, they would not graduate until June 1922. To ease the dissatisfaction among some members of this class and among the class that had joined the corps in 1919, both groups were offered the opportunity to choose between the three- and four-year curriculums. Most opted for the longer course. Only 17 of the November 1918 entrants chose the three-year program, and they became the class of 1921. The balance of that group, 102 cadets, were graduated as the class of 1922. A day later, thirty of the 1919 matriculants, who had opted for the three-year program, were graduated—becoming the class of June 14, 1922. The balance of that group chose the four-year path and were graduated the next year as the class of 1923.

MacArthur, for the most part, made little effort to win the support of the Academic Board. Though he could reasonably have written off most of the old guard, he might have been able to woo support from some of the newer and younger members. Clifton Carroll Carter was one possibility. A member of the class of 1899, he had taken William Gordon's chair of natural philosophy upon the latter's retirement in 1917. Roger Gordon Alexander, class of 1907, was an even more likely candidate. Alexander, who had become professor of drawing since Edwin Stuart's death in 1920, had only recently returned from service in France with the American Expeditionary Force. But the Superintendent made no move in that direction.

Instead, he seemed to go out of his way to intrude on the board's domain. He quizzed professors concerning the courses taught by other departments, inspected their instructors in the classroom, and commandeered their officers for nonacademic purposes. In time he turned on the professors directly, charging that they were narrow, smug, and too satisfied with their traditional way of doing business.[84] He told his adjutant, "[T]hey deliver the same schedule year after year with the blessed unction that they have reached the zenith in education."[85]

Even when MacArthur was right, his lack of tact and discretion further alienated the board. When Echols chose to protest the cuts made to his course in mathematics by reporting 95 of 572 plebes deficient, MacArthur immediately (and quite correctly) appointed a committee of the board to investigate. The committee, after concluding that Echols's course was too "intensive" and "theoretical," that the assignments were too long, and that his instructors spent too much time grading recitations and too little teaching, proposed a whole new mathematics program. Echols was incensed, but his colleagues, who had little sympathy with his tactics, voted with the committee, though they did soften the report's criticism somewhat. Echols was humiliated. MacArthur, however, was not satisfied. He transformed the board's enjoinder into a military order: the board's resolutions "will be carried out by you"; the number of deficiencies among the "good potential officer material" were to be reduced by at least 50 percent; and Echols was to make periodic progress reports to the Superintendent.[86] In this MacArthur overreached his authority. He not only had insulted Echols unnecessarily but also had inserted himself into the internal affairs of a department—a privileged sanctum where by regulation the Academic Board, not the Superintendent, had cognizance.

By now the rumblings in the Academic Board room had begun to involve the alumni. Word of MacArthur's innovations reached them through faculty letters, the *Army and Navy Journal,* and the grapevine that naturally entwines such an institution. They resented his efforts at reform—both on the academic side and in the area of cadet life. They feared that, in his efforts to codify the fourth-class system and in his more liberal pass policy, for example, MacArthur was unduly pampering cadets. Hugh Scott seems to have been thinking of MacArthur (and Mills) when he wrote in 1927: "West Point is not a subject for [drastic] reform. . . . It goes forward on its majestic course from year to year toward the fulfillment of its destiny, . . . improved from time to time to keep it abreast of the age, but without need of radical alteration."[87]

However much the life of cadets in the early years of the twentieth century resembled that of their predecessors, there were areas in which it had begun to change. One was announced in the fall of 1919. "With this the first publication of 'THE BRAY,' the Corps enters a new field—Journalism," announced the editors of a new weekly paper to be published by and for the corps of cadets.[88]

The Bray first appeared in November 1919 under the editorial direction of Cadet A. C. Spalding and was supervised by an officer who had personally been instructed by MacArthur that he would "be responsible, wholly and solely so, for every word that goes into this paper."[89] Although it would be permitted "to set forth freely and unreservedly the Cadet viewpoint on all matters," wrote the Commandant, Robert M. Danford, class of 1904, the paper was expected to be "loyal always, as a good soldier, to official decisions rendered."[90] It was to be "the organ of the entire corps" and to reflect "both the humorous and the serious side of cadet life."[91]

All went well for about six months. Then, in the issue of May 11, 1920, an editorial complained that MacArthur's efforts to reshape the fourth-class system were making the plebe year "a bed of roses." It opened bluntly: "We don't agree with the Superintendent's policies."[92] When he was shown the article, MacArthur was furious. That edition was confiscated and destroyed.[93] The publication was suspended immediately, and the officer-in-charge was summoned before the Superintendent and dismissed. "I am wiring Washington this very hour for your relief from the Academy," MacArthur told the officer curtly. "You will be off this Post without delay."[94]

In the fall of 1923, after MacArthur had departed and the class that published The Bray had graduated, the cadets again requested permission to begin their own publication. After some negotiation (during which the student editors agreed to an English department demand that at least half of each issue would be devoted to content of a literary nature), a bimonthly magazine was approved by Superintendent Fred Sladen. The Pointer, as the new publication was named, was an immediate and continuing success.[95]

Among the staples of life at West Point since the time of Thayer was the summer encampment—traditionally established at the end of June on the Plain just south of the ruins of Fort Clinton and closed on August 28 when the

Inspection, summer encampment of 1896. Summer mornings were spent in military training; afternoons were spent in relaxation and social activities. United States Military Academy Archives.

cadets returned to the barracks. Here cadets lived under canvas and took a respite from academic work. They spent their mornings training in artillery gun exercises, tactical movements, and drill. In the afternoons they lounged about camp, resting and chatting. The evenings were occasions for concerts and entertainments, with hops and balls on the weekends. Summer was the social season at West Point, and young ladies went there from the South, New York City, and elsewhere to escape the heat—and possibly to meet a young man with prospects. The season began with a celebration on the Fourth of July and climaxed at the end of the encampment with a grand ball.

The summer encampment followed much the same routine until the late 1890s, when Commandant of Cadets Otto L. Hein instituted a number of changes designed to prepare cadets better for actual field duty with troops. First he issued the cadets field service uniforms and field equipment. Then he expanded the course of practical military instruction, adding tactical exercises of infantry and cavalry and practice marches of infantry, cavalry, and light artillery. Finally, he introduced the cadets to cavalry and artillery stable duties and instituted a series of lectures on military hygiene.[96] Still, these changes did not dramatically alter the summer camp life of the cadets.

In 1920, Douglas MacArthur abolished the summer encampment at Fort Clinton, saying that it was "a ludicrous caricature of life in the field."[97] Instead, MacArthur ordered the cadets to report for summer training at Camp

Dix, New Jersey. This abrupt uprooting of the encampment—and with it the summer social season—engendered such resentment among the Academy's officers and their wives and among the old graduates that the traditional policy was reinstated by the War Department in 1922, even before MacArthur left West Point for the Philippines.[98] "The return to the traditional practice of establishing a summer camp at West Point proved an unqualified success," reported MacArthur's successor, Brigadier General Fred W. Sladen, class of 1890.[99] Although field training increased over the years, the cadets continued to encamp at Fort Clinton until 1942.

"By the summer of 1921, MacArthur had so completely drained the faculty and alumni of good will that he could no longer innovate, and was instead waging a defense of all that he had changed," wrote Roger H. Nye, a later professor of history at West Point.[100] The disenchantment with MacArthur at West Point was matched by a similar mood in Washington. Secretary of War Newton Baker, who had supported him, was replaced by John W. Weeks when President Warren Harding assumed office in March 1920. In July, Peyton March retired and was replaced as Chief of Staff by General John J. Pershing. Neither Weeks nor Pershing was sympathetic to MacArthur's plight. MacArthur had proven, in the words of biographer C. Clayton James, "a refractory individualist who created difficulties and embarrassments for the War Department in its relations with Congress, the White House, and the conservative alumni of West Point."[101]

On November 22, 1921, Pershing informed MacArthur that he was to be replaced: "I am writing now to advise you that at the end of the present school year you will be available for a tour of service beyond the limits of the United States. The selection of your successor will be made shortly."[102] At the end of January 1922, Pershing announced the appointment of Brigadier General Fred Winchester Sladen, who had earlier been Commandant of Cadets, as MacArthur's successor. "I fancy [that Sladen's appointment] means a reversal of many of the progressive policies which we inaugurated," MacArthur prophesied correctly. Within days after his departure, work was begun to restore the encampment area near Fort Clinton.[103] Likewise, the Academic Board began a review of the curriculum and soon restored Echols's mathematics course to its prewar eminence.

Within eighteen months of MacArthur's departure, the board had cut the time devoted to English, French, Spanish, history, law, economics, and government by 20 percent. But it only reduced these courses; it did not eliminate them.[104] In fact, in 1926, the board sought and obtained congressional approval to divide English and history into two departments—the Department of Economics, Government, and History, and the Department of English—officially blessing an earlier de facto arrangement. These departmental shifts, along with normal retirements, meant changes on the Academic Board. Holt, the former professor of English and history, took over the Department of Economics, Government, and History, while Clayton E. "Buck" Wheat, chaplain since 1918, was appointed professor of English. Earlier, in 1922, the scholarly William Augustus Mitchell, class of 1902, had replaced Professor of Engineering Gustav Fiebeger, who retired. And, in 1925, William Eric Morrison, class of 1907, became Willcox's successor in the Department of Modern Languages.

By contrast to the MacArthur years, the balance of the decade was a period of quiet but steady movement forward. In 1926, shortly before he left West Point, Superintendent Fred Sladen petitioned for the Academy's admission into the Association of American Universities—a necessary step toward the granting of baccalaureate degrees. Full admission to the association was granted the next year, and in 1933 congressional action authorized the United States Military Academy to award the degree of bachelor of science. Sladen was replaced in 1926 by Brigadier General Merch Bradt Stewart, class of 1896, who had been Commandant of Cadets since 1923. Stewart soon became ill, however, and surrendered the superintendency in 1927. Major General William Ruthven Smith, class of 1892, was chosen to succeed him but was not immediately available for reassignment. In the interim, Major General Edwin Baruch Winans, class of 1891, assumed command of the post. Smith arrived just four months later, in February 1928. Neither Stewart nor Winans served long enough to make any significant mark on the Academy.

After the expansion of the Academy in the first decade of the century, and the demolition of most of the old brick quarters along Jefferson Road, the three old stone doubles became the primary residences of the permanent professors. Then, as later, their social life centered on their own small group. They might find occasional diversion in the great homes along the Hudson or among New York City's elite, but at West Point they were an essentially closed society. At frequent dinners and parties they entertained one another, but few others from among the West Point community. Most professors had a maid and a gardener; some had cooks and other help, though the time was approaching when domestic servants would become a rarity. The Ladies Reading Club may have sensed this change, for its 1918–1919 program included one discussion titled "Evolution of the Hired Girl" among its more traditional fare such as "The League of Nations" and "The Irish Question."[105]

Professor Charles Patton Echols had, by this time, become the old man of the Academic Board—a lifelong bachelor and now in his early sixties, he was reminiscent of "Old Hanks" Kendrick of a half century before. Like Kendrick, Echols lived alone in one of the large stone doubles that by then was known as Professors' Row. Echols led a highly structured life and, even when alone, dined formally by candlelight. The old professor, who had repeatedly been in conflict with the Superintendents and their staffs at West Point, enjoyed seeing a mistake emanate from the headquarters. One day he emerged from his office waving the most recent communication. "Look at that," he exulted. "They have misspelled 'mispelled.'"[106]

For the officers there were numerous amusements. The Thayer Club had become moribund in the late nineteenth century, but it was revived briefly during Scott's superintendency. An officers' polo club was formed, and its members played both civilian and military teams from up and down the East Coast. But that was essentially a young man's sport. Many of the professors preferred quieter diversions. Chess was a favorite, and games went on evening after evening. After dinner, the professors would stroll in and out of each other's quarters by the back doors to take part in a match or kibitz. One night, it is said, Gustav Fiebeger, Professor of Engineering, tired of the game and decided to retire. "Well, it's my bedtime. Goodnight, gentlemen," he said, and wandered out into the night. Where he went was a bit of a mystery, for the game that night was at his own home.

The location of Professors' Row, just off the Plain, was a mixed blessing. As roads improved and as the American public obtained automobiles in the 1920s, West Point became a major attraction. The resultant wholesale use of the reservation as a picnic ground so worried the administration in 1927 that traffic was restricted through the grounds.[107] One Saturday, a group of visitors spread their blankets and picnic lunch on the broad porch of Professor Clifton Carter's quarters. That was more than Carter was willing to tolerate, but when he protested, the visitors informed him that this was public property. "We are tax-payers," they said, "and we intend to stay." Carter turned about and left without further comment, but he reappeared shortly with a hose and started washing down the porch. When his unwanted guests objected, he rejoined, "I am charged with the maintenance of this property, and I always wash down the tax-payers' porch on Saturday."[108]

Among their other duties, the permanent professors selected the instructors who would be detailed to them. In general the selections were made on the basis of the officer's academic record as a cadet and what the professors could learn of his subsequent performance in the service. Each relied on his own method. Professor William Mitchell, head of the Department of Engineering from 1922 to 1938, kept a "little black book" in which he inscribed information on potential instructors and their wives. In it he recorded notes under four columns: "aim," "name," "dame," and "fame."[109]

These instructors had usually been detailed to the Academy for four years, but between 1912 and the end of World War I, those tours were often very much curtailed. In 1912, Congress, against the advice of the War Department, prescribed that officers who had been away from their regiments for more than four years of the last six must be reassigned to them immediately. Twelve of the twenty instructors in the Department of Mathematics departed in November and December of that year. In varying degrees, the same thing happened in all the departments.[110] In 1913, Superintendent Clarence Townsley estimated that as a result of the so-called Manchu Law, none of the officers the Academy intended to request would be able to serve a four-year tour. Many would be allowed to stay just one year. The difficulty was that the officers West Point wanted were also in demand elsewhere, and often came to the Academy from other details. The result, he added, "is that we are compelled to ask for officers as instructors who, without this detached service law, would not have been considered for such duty." Townsley's request that West Point be exempted from the impact of this law was denied.[111] Relief did not come until after World War I, when the regimental system was abolished.

Over the years, instructors reported very similar experiences when they first joined the faculty—they were unprepared and had to work day and night just to stay ahead of the cadets. "On the first day of September as my cadets marched into the recitation room," reported Captain John McAuley Palmer, who joined the faculty in 1901, "I was deeply conscious of my limitations as an instructor." "During the whole of my first year," he added, "I was hard put to it to keep ahead of my cadets."[112] "I study a great deal harder than when I was a cadet," wrote Tasker Bliss in 1876, "for now I feel as though I were honor bound to know as much as I can."[113] Tully McCrea wrote in a similar vein in 1864: "I have three hours duty every day, hearing my sections. Nearly all the rest of the day, and a great deal of the night is taken up in hard study. I have to study harder now than I did when I was a cadet."[114] John Schofield, who had taught natural philosophy in 1855 and 1856, likewise recalled that as an instructor he had "formed for the first time the habit of earnest, hard mental work to the limit of my capacity for endurance, and sometimes a little beyond."[115] It required from one to two years' experience and hard work for even the best of the officers selected to become really proficient and effective instructors.

In 1911, in an effort to alleviate some of that difficulty, Professor Holt began sending some of his officers to the summer session at Yale. In 1915,

Professor Edward A. Kreger, of the law department, began sending an instructor each year to attend a summer session at the Columbia University School of Law.[116] These experiments proved so successful that in 1921 the Academic Board, with MacArthur's strong endorsement, recommended that instructors should spend one year, before reporting to the Academy, in a civilian university to prepare for their work at West Point.

MacArthur went further and attempted to persuade the Academic Board to take civilian college graduates as instructors. It was "a step backward," a "dangerous" and "problematical venture," the professors replied. MacArthur tried again to convince them, going on at length about the details that had led to his recommendation. In the midst of this, one of the professors began to interrupt. Finally, his interruptions became so annoying that MacArthur banged his fist on the table and commanded, "Sit down sir. I am the Superintendent!" A hush followed, and he added, "Even if I weren't, I should be treated in a gentlemanly manner."[117] Though he sent lists of such officers with their qualifications to the departments, only Holt made any sustained effort to recruit these men. It was not until some years after World War II that any significant number of "nongraduates" were brought to the faculty on anything other than an emergency basis.

In one area, however, the life of junior faculty at the Academy hit a high point in the first quarter of the twentieth century. For a brief period, from about 1901 through the early 1920s, there was a rare abundance of excellent quarters for officers at West Point. The bulk of these were built to the south of the academic area along Wilson and Thayer Roads. The first quarters here had been small frame cottages built in the 1850s just south of the hospital. More such housing was added in the 1870s. But in the first decade of the twentieth century, this area fairly exploded with new officers' quarters. The first were five brick duplexes built in 1901 to standardized designs of the office of the Quartermaster General. In August 1901, Captain John M. Palmer and his wife moved into one of these newly built duplexes. They were immediately among friends. The other half of the house was assigned to a classmate, and two other classmates had quarters in the same row. Mrs. Palmer "was delighted with her brand new house," her husband wrote. Typical of army wives, she was settled "in a few days"—the "curtains were up," the "rugs down," the "furniture in place," and she had found an excellent cook.[118]

In 1904, plans drawn by Cram, Goodhue and Ferguson were approved for additional quarters, which were begun the next year. The buildings' Tudor-Gothic character and varied brick facades placed them among the most attractive quarters on post. The interior spaces are also remarkable, for they contain fine examples of Craftsman and American Art Nouveau designs. Seldom have officers' quarters received a design so elegant and satisfactory. The quarters contained a parlor, dining room, library, and kitchen on the first floor; on the second and third floors were four bedrooms and two baths, plus a suite of two bedrooms and a bath for servants. Designed originally for married lieutenants who returned to teach only a few years after graduation, they are now occupied by senior permanent professors. Six sets of these triples were completed in 1908, with a seventh set added in 1910. Four other similar sets were built in 1909 along Washington Road to the north of Professors' Row and the Catholic chapel—anticipating the direction of future growth in officers' housing.

Slow but steady growth through the early years of the century had brought the authorized number of cadets to 748 by 1914, though the actual number enrolled was always somewhat smaller. Two years later, the authorized number of cadets was nearly doubled, to 1,332. The number of cadets grew as rapidly as barracks and other facilities were built to accommodate them, but it was not until the early 1930s that the corps of cadets reached its new authorization level. More cadets, of course, meant more officers, and once again officers' quarters became scarce. In 1917, two new apartment buildings— North and South Apartments—were begun; they were completed in 1919. Though the plans were drawn by the Quartermaster General's office, the designs followed closely those that had been prepared earlier by Cram, Goodhue and Ferguson. As usual, however, the number of quarters did not keep pace with the requirement. By 1927, over fifty junior officers and their families were forced to live in the neighboring towns of Highland Falls, Cornwall, and Newburgh. In 1929, a third apartment complex—Central Apartments—was constructed just south of the hospital, but this could handle only a fraction of those who needed quarters.

As the 1930s approached, a few key changes in the senior faculty again redefined the character of the Academic Board and brought to it new leaders who would see the Academy through the depression, another world war, and on to midcentury. Professor Wirt Robinson died in 1928, and Chauncey Lee Fenton, class of 1904, took charge of the recently redesignated Department of Chemistry and Electricity.[119] In 1931, Harris Jones, class of April 1917, replaced the eccentric Echols in mathematics, and Gerald Alfred Counts, class of August 1917, took charge of the new Department of Physics.

Even among this host of talented men, however, Herman Beukema, class of 1915, was remarkable. Beukema was chosen in 1930 to replace the retiring Lucius Holt, who for some years was second only to Echols in seniority on the Academic Board. Beukema was only the second head of the still new Department of Economics, Government, and History, and in a very real sense its future was in his hands. He had served on the Mexican frontier and had commanded an artillery battalion in France. He had attended the Field Artillery School and the Army Command and General Staff School, and had joined the West Point faculty as an assistant to Holt in 1928. Beukema was a soldier-scholar, who would lead the department until 1954. He was an archetype of those who would lead the Academy through World War II.

CHAPTER EIGHT

The Long Gray Line, 1930–1960

The story of West Point in the middle of the twentieth century begins with a debate that pitted formal education against military training. It ends with a second debate—this one about West Point's philosophy of formal education. This debate would keep the Academy in turmoil for the balance of the century. In the middle years, however, the Academy turned to the lighter side—possibly to escape for a moment the realities of a horrific war and the difficult peace that followed. During these years, the Military Academy flirted brazenly with America's popular culture. In the 1940s it was Army football, when Coach Earl "Red" Blaik provided West Point with some of the finest college football teams of all time. In the 1950s it was Hollywood—most remarkably, *The Long Gray Line,* starring Tyrone Power, Maureen O'Hara, Ward Bond, and West Point itself.[1]

In 1930, Superintendent William R. Smith proposed this restatement of the Military Academy's mission:

> The mission of the Military Academy is to train a cadet to think clearly and logically and to do so habitually; to teach him discipline and the basic principles applicable to the various arms in the Military Service; to develop his physique and above all his character; and to teach him to approach all of his problems with an attitude of intellectual honesty, to be sensible to the rights of others, to be inspired by a high sense of duty and honor, and unhesitatingly to lay down his life in the service of his country should the occasion arise.[2]

Smith's new delineation of the Academy's mission reignited a debate that had erupted on several earlier occasions concerning the relative emphasis on formal education on the one hand and military training on the other. One element in the Army held that the West Point graduate should be ready to take over all the responsibilities of a second lieutenant when reporting for duty—including both technical proficiency and leadership skills. Douglas MacArthur's 1920 removal of the summer camp from the Plain to Fort Dix, where the cadets would train with active Army forces, responded to this impulse. Another segment of the Army—including the Academy's Academic Board—felt that the Academy would best serve by providing a basic general and technical education that would ensure an adequate foundation for growth in the cadet's subsequent professional career. John P. Lovell, writing in the late 1970s, explained this recurring tension as "the contradictions between Athenian and Spartan goals."[3]

Superintendent Fred Sladen pushed the Academy back in the direction of academics in 1925, when he convinced the Association of American Universities to list the Military Academy as an "approved technological institution." Another step in the same direction was made in 1927, with the admission of the Academy to the Association of American Colleges.

In 1933, Superintendent William D. Connor, class of 1897, convinced Congress to confirm the emphasis on academics by authorizing the Academy to confer the degree of bachelor of science upon its graduates. Likewise, President Franklin Delano Roosevelt endorsed that goal in 1934 but went further, proposing the addition of a year to the curriculum during which the cadets of the Military Academy would join with the midshipmen of the Naval Academy for a yearlong "finishing" cruise. In their floating academy they would visit all the key countries of the world. "The end in view should be to enable student officers, during their formative years, to develop a broad outlook, a cultural background and a sympathetic understanding of world conditions."[4] When both academies proved cool to the idea, Roosevelt dropped it.

Brigadier General Jay L. Benedict, class of 1904, replaced Connor as Superintendent in 1938. In 1939, Benedict proposed a new and briefer statement of the Academy's mission: "The Mission of the United States Military Academy is to produce officers of the Army having the qualities and attributes essential to their progressive and continuing development, throughout their careers as officers and leaders."[5] Smith's admonition that the Academy should teach "the basic principles applicable to the various arms in the Military Service" was deleted. War Department approval seemed to resolve the issue in favor of academics.

This restatement of the Academy's mission reflected simply one element in the continuing evolution of its academic program. On one front, the social sciences and humanities achieved a new maturity. Herman Beukema, Professor of Economics, Government, and History, strove to integrate the study of geography, international relations, and the economics of national security. Building on a subcourse begun by Lucius Holt in 1929 entitled "Resources for War of the Great Powers," Beukema had created a full course in international relations by 1934. In history, he began to concentrate on the two areas of potential American involvement in war: Europe and the Far East. In 1938, he expanded the government course from one dealing exclusively with the United States to one that compared the governments of the major powers. Beukema's courses expanded the horizons of the cadets. "I have seldom, if ever, encountered a group of students who struck me as having been better disciplined intellectually for the study of international relations," wrote Sir Alfred Zimmern of Oxford after lecturing at West Point. "I am forced to confess that I had not expected to find in a military institution such intellectual keenness, such an open-minded and critical interest in problems lying outside what used to be considered . . . the sphere of the professional soldier."[6]

Likewise, the Department of English underwent a transformation under Clayton Wheat. Teaching methods became more liberal, and classroom discussion and teaching began to supplant recitation. Cadets engaged in a healthy give-and-take among themselves and with the instructor. At the same time, an increased emphasis on literature began to balance an earlier concentration on verbal expression.

On another front, the science and engineering courses were also evolving. In 1931, physics instruction, which had been taught in various subcourses by the Department of Natural and Experimental Philosophy and the Department of Chemistry, was brought together in a new Department of Physics. Captain Gerald A. Counts, class of August 1917, became the first departmental head. Immediately after World War II, chemistry was separated from the subject of electricity (which became a department unto itself) and merged with physics into a new Department of Physics and Chemistry under Counts.[7]

In 1934, the Department of Natural and Experimental Philosophy, which over the years had given up control over most of the physical sciences, began to gather under its auspices the various components of the science of mechanics—including the mechanical engineering course that had previously been offered by the Department of Civil and Military Engineering. Taught for years almost exclusively by analytical methods, the course emphasis changed under Professor Clifton Carter to laboratory courses in hydraulics and thermodynamics, utilizing hydraulic pumps and turbines, internal combustion and steam engines, and a wind tunnel. This process was continued by Professor Oscar J. Gatchell, class of 1912, who replaced Carter in 1940.[8] Gatchell had a natural bent for scientific and engineering studies but understood that not all his students shared that gift. Cadets insisted that he could simplify the most difficult problem and had the ability to penetrate the "goat mind."[9] In 1942, under Gatchell, the department was redesignated the Department of Mechanics.

With the transfer of work in mechanical engineering out of the Department of Civil and Military Engineering, Professor William Mitchel and his successor (in 1938), Professor Thomas D. Stamps, class of August 1917, were able to expand their course in the history of military art. By 1938, it was given more classroom hours than either civil or military engineering. In recognition of this development, the department was redesignated the Department of Military Art and Engineering in 1942. The anomalous conjunction of these two subjects continued until 1969, when military history was shifted to a new Department of History.

Mathematics, now under Colonel Harris Jones, class of April 1917, who had replaced Charles Echols in 1931, continued to be the foundation of the curriculum. (Jones became dean in 1947 and continued in that capacity until 1956.) The course itself changed little in this period, but on at least one occasion the cadets were shown the practical benefits mathematics could bestow. In 1935, a department store in nearby Newburgh offered a new Ford automobile to the person who came closest to guessing the number of pennies in a large glass bowl in the store's window. Charles Nicholas, class of 1925, then an assistant professor and later professor and head of the Department of Mathematics, measured the bowl from the sidewalk in front of the store using precision surveying equipment. Later, at West Point, Nicholas transformed the survey data into the internal volume of the bowl. Then, using calculus and statistical analysis (and a pile of copper pennies) he determined the statistical probability of distribution of pennies, poured at random into the bowl. Combining this information, he calculated the number of pennies in the container, submitted his "guess," and won the car.

In 1939, after securing a revision of the mission statement, Benedict asked the Academic Board to review the curriculum once again. Following a yearlong study, the board recommended that no changes be made. "The curriculum of the Military Academy leads to a degree of Bachelor of Science and is framed for the purpose of giving the cadet a basic general education, but at the same time training him for one and only one purpose—for success in the military profession," wrote the committee. "Of necessity [the curriculum] must include the basic technical subjects essential to a general engineering education, certain professional subjects of special importance to all Army officers, and cultural subjects of general educational value and sufficient in number to give proper balance to the curriculum." The curriculum committee considered adding courses in logic, psychology, sociology, and philosophy but concluded that, despite their considerable value, they could not be introduced without displacing subjects currently being taught—courses that were "of more practical and cultural value to the Army officers."[10]

Benedict was not pleased, but he departed for a new assignment before he could challenge the board. Still, in an exit report he called for an outside study board of civilian educators to report on the Academy, "including its objectives, curriculum, procedure and methods." Wrote Benedict, "It is my belief that the pattern of the curriculum is still too much determined by the Engineer influence of former days."[11]

The 1930s had been a period of natural, if not radical, development in the curriculum and seemed to call for the evolution of all institutions at the Academy; the West Point Army Mess was one of these. It had continued through the 1920s as a haven for the unmarried officers, but as the 1930s wore on, the number of bachelors on duty at the Academy began to decline. Still, they dined in formal elegance at a forty-foot-long table lined with massive silver pieces and candlesticks. Their meals were served by white-jacketed Filipino waiters and prepared by a chef who had been hired away from the old Astor Hotel.[12] Although a small tea room at the north end of the building and a few rooms upstairs had been made available for their use, women were seldom allowed more than a peek at the splendor of the resident mess.

But times were changing. It had become an increasingly common practice in the Army for commanders to expect officers, both married and single, to become members of the mess. The married officers and their wives soon began to argue that they received little benefit from club memberships and, in fact, were being required to support the bachelors. More than one wife at West Point thought it was about time she had a right to use all the facilities of the mess. For a few years in the mid-1930s the mess was shielded from attack by General Connor, the Superintendent from 1932 to 1935, who had little sympathy with the wives' view. As a married man, Connor may have particularly valued the sanctity of that male bastion and its solitude. He had been known, for example, to shanghai the chaplain when going fishing and to insist that the cleric take the boat with Mrs. Connor—who would talk incessantly—while Connor and his aide escaped in another to the far side of the lake.[13] The mess was safe so long as Connor remained.

The controversy came to a head almost immediately upon Connor's retirement in January 1938. Just a month later, a meeting was held in the old chemistry lecture hall in the East Academic Building to discuss changing the constitution of the mess.[14] The married officers turned out in droves, but there were only a dozen or so bachelors—all that remained of their dwindling numbers. It had become common knowledge that Benedict, the new Superintendent, was behind the married officers and that the bachelors were going to lose.[15]

Chauncey Fenton, professor of physics and chemistry and president of the mess, allowed a brief debate and then put the question: "Shall the Mess be opened to everyone and not be restricted to the bachelors?" There was a thunderous "yea" from the married side. The "nay" from the bachelors could scarcely be heard. Fenton drew himself up from his chair and announced: "The Nays have it. The meeting is adjourned." He put on his cap and started for the door. There was a moment of stunned silence, then, suddenly, laughter, whereupon Fenton returned to the chair and reversed the decision.[16] Though the facility continued to restrict access during certain hours, thus allowing the mess to be maintained for the single officers, its fundamental character had been changed forever.

In 1946, the bachelors made a last effort to maintain the traditional identity of the West Point Army Mess by proposing a separate officers' club, but they failed. Soon thereafter, the formal bachelor mess that had been established by Lieutenant Irvin McDowell more than a century before was abandoned. The long table disappeared in favor of restaurant-style dining, and the club was thrown open at all hours to the full membership and their families.[17]

By late 1940, the war clouds that had brought storms to Europe and Asia were clearly visible on America's horizon. Brigadier General Robert L. Eichelberger, class of 1909, who succeeded Jay Benedict, arrived in November committed to increasing the emphasis on military training. Eichelberger opened with a warning for the Academic Board. There were "many criticisms" being leveled at our young graduates, he advised the board, and some of the officers who had expressed "unfavorable opinions" were in a position "to influence or to take what appears to them corrective action" if they were inclined to do so. "We must recognize that time brings changes, therefore we cannot permit our curriculum to remain static," he warned. "The attitude which we take during this academic year may determine what harmful decisions will be made to govern the Military Academy next year." But that alone was not enough: "We must keep the War Department, and through it, the people, informed that we are keenly aware of the existing state of flux in military matters, that we are meeting these changes as they occur, and that we shall continue to meet them."[18]

Specifically, Eichelberger wanted to terminate the academic work of the first class in late April and give the cadets some intensive military training in the branches they had chosen. In addition, he suggested evening lectures "on leadership, soldier psychology, mess management, and kindred subjects which must be met by the young officer on joining his first command."[19] The Academic Board concurred and, except for instruction in military law, course work ended for the first class on May 14, 1941. The period of intensive branch instruction that followed was so successful that Eichelberger indicated plans to do the same the next year.[20]

At the same time, the threat of war caused the Academy to institute a number of changes in its military training program for all the cadets: increases in summer training time, branch instruction, the amount of physical training during the winter months, and motor vehicle instruction at the expense of equitation.

For many years, summer training had been restricted to the morning, with the afternoons normally being kept free for the cadets' relaxation and recreation. Beginning in the summer of 1941, however, Eichelberger ordered additional afternoon training and added specialized branch instruction for the first classmen.

In its war mobilization planning during the 1930s, West Point had insisted that "except for the early graduation of the then 1st Class, no change in the present four year curriculum is contemplated." It did suggest, however, that "tentative branch assignments" might be determined at the beginning of the first-class year to allow additional branch training.[21] When war did come, however, that plan was scrapped and new planning undertaken.

On January 12, 1942, Major General Francis B. Wilby, class of 1905, succeeded Eichelberger, who was soon sent to the South Pacific. Eichelberger wrote Wilby shortly thereafter: "My major mission [was] to save West Point from its sad lot of World War I. All our publicity, the changes in the curriculum, the increase of hours for military training, the refresher course, etc., and particularly the new air program were based in no small part on my desire for the preservation of West Point."[22] A week after taking over, Wilby initiated the first of a series of studies to determine the advantages and disadvantages of a curriculum of three years or less. The curriculum committee submitted its report on January 24, recommending a three-year course of instruction, if some shortening of the program was essential.

On January 27, Wilby was summoned to Washington for a meeting with President Roosevelt. The President's instructions were simple and straightforward. He expected the Superintendent to minimize the discharge of cadets due to deficiencies in their studies and to bring the Academy up to date in everything—particularly in air corps and tank instruction. The President also directed the continuation of intercollegiate football until instructed otherwise.

In March, the Army staff wrote, requesting views of the Academic Board on reducing the course of instruction. The board responded with a report that outlined one-, two-, and three-year plans but that recommended retaining the four-year course. The War Department decided on the three-year option and, in late August, asked Congress to authorize the President to effect the reduction for the duration of the wartime emergency. "We do not like to have West Point become subject to the criticism of being a place of refuge, where boys can go for 4 years and not be shot at," the military told the lawmakers, "particularly when all the young men within that age group at other colleges are subject to the draft, and are going to be sent out after being trained and are going to be shot at."[23] Congress obliged, though earlier in the summer it had increased the authorized size of the corps of cadets from 1,960 to 2,496. On October 1, 1942, President Roosevelt ordered the course reduced to three years.

The original class of 1943 was thus graduated early, as the class of January 1943. The original class of 1944 received abbreviated versions of both the second-class and first-class courses and became the class of June 1943. The programs of subsequent classes were modified in order to graduate them after three years.

The war naturally gave a tremendous impetus to military training at the Academy. Summer furloughs were reduced so drastically that there was almost as much training time in the new three-year program as in the prewar years. What is more, the new training area at Popolopen allowed a vastly expanded military training program.

The expansion of this training area at West Point had begun in the 1930s. In 1931, Congress authorized the purchase of some 15,135 acres to the west and south of West Point to ensure the post an adequate water supply. In the previous three years, the post had experienced acute water shortages during the dry season. By constructing a dam to control Popolopen Lake, it was possible to store sufficient water to meet West Point's demands at all times. The land also provided room for needed facilities for military training— particularly small arms, machine gun, and artillery ranges.[24] However, no money was appropriated for the purchase until 1936, and then litigation so delayed the process that by mid-1939 only 528 acres had been acquired. The pace picked up in 1940 and 1941 and was further accelerated in early 1942, when wartime condemnation procedures were employed wherever negotiations broke down. By the summer of 1942, the government had acquired a 10,300-acre tract of land. A new cadet camp was opened at Lake Popolopen in late July 1942, and the summer encampment on the Plain was abandoned for good.[25] By the next summer, the facility boasted twenty-four target ranges, a cleared artillery impact area, pillboxes, moving target ranges, a pontoon and amphibious training area, and assault courses.[26] The construction of facilities at Camp Popolopen made possible tactical training and instruction in the use of combat weapons far beyond anything that had ever been done at West Point.

The most far-reaching change at West Point during the war years, however, was the introduction of pilot training.[27] As early as 1915, there were attempts to insert aviation observer training into the curriculum, but then the best that the facilities would allow was a lecture on air service organization and supply. In 1927, a seaplane hanger and ramp were completed on the Hudson, but no change was made in cadet instruction. Rather, the facility served only to allow flying officers stationed at West Point to maintain their flying proficiency. Once Congress authorized the Popolopen purchase in 1931, plans were made to construct an airfield, but the lack of appropriations and delays in acquiring land prevented it. Again, lectures on aircraft, their construction, types, and capabilities were the only alternative. However, the Academy did begin to include, in the summer itinerary, visits to Langley, Wright, and Mitchell Fields, where cadets got a firsthand look at the Air Corps. Beginning in 1936, each cadet was given twenty hours of "air experience," but no flight training.[28]

The first formal proposal to add flight training to the curriculum was made in July 1941 by Oscar Gatchell, Professor of Natural and Experimental Philosophy, who suggested "a course in primary flying" for the first classmen who successfully passed the flight physical and indicated a preference for the Air Corps.[29] The facility where such training could be conducted came into the Academy's hands just three months later when Stewart Field, on the outskirts of nearby Newburgh, became a part of West Point.

In January 1942, the War Department authorized the Military Academy to commission up to 60 percent of its graduates in the Air Corps. Cadets who were qualified for pilot training and who desired to enter the Air Corps were designated air cadets after their second year at West Point. These cadets went away to civilian facilities to receive their flight training, although, as facilities were completed at Stewart Field, they began receiving their basic and advanced training there. Members of the class of January 1943 were the first to graduate with their "wings"; those of the class of 1946 were the last. In these years, a total of 1,033 cadets were commissioned into the Air Corps from West Point.

Over the years, outside lecturers had become an important adjunct for many courses. In the 1930s, a program of general lectures was instituted under the direction of a lecture committee of the Academic Board. Prior to the war, lecturers were chosen with an eye to broadening the cadets' knowledge of world affairs. As war became imminent, however, attention was focused on the world military situation, and—during the war—on the organization, training, and operations of the United States Army.

Academic training was hampered, but not halted, by the loss of regular officers in the early months of 1942. In fact, the exodus began in February 1941, when ten officers were relieved from duty, and their places taken by first classmen who taught halftime. Within weeks of the attack on Pearl Harbor, however, the process of recalling retired officers and commissioning civilian scholars was in full operation. By June 1944, more than two-thirds of the officers on duty at West Point were "non-graduates"—as West Pointers were inclined to call anyone who did not graduate from the United States Military Academy. The number of "non-graduates" grew so large that some, in jest, suggested forming an "Association of Non-Graduates."[30] Though they had to be familiarized with the West Point system, these "non-grads" were often outstanding scholars and fine teachers. They demonstrated the advantage of specialized graduate training for officers detailed to duty in the academic departments. One of the civilians recruited in this era, Sumner Willard, later returned to West Point as professor and head of the Department of Foreign Languages.

Cutting the curriculum to three years meant a change in scope of many courses and the deletion of a number of subcourses. In some departments, such as social sciences, it meant the elimination of entire courses. The Department of Foreign Languages was one of the few to add courses—German in 1941 and Portuguese (the language of Brazil, our principal ally in South America) in 1942. Russian was added in 1945. Still, the number of hours of language instruction was reduced. Previously, cadets spent three years in language training—two years in Spanish and one year in French. Now cadets studied a single language for two years and were allowed to choose from among the languages offered. More significantly, under the guidance of Professor William Morrison, language training moved from the traditional concentration on formal grammar to an animated and predominantly oral approach.[31]

The law that had established the wartime three-year course mandated the return to the four-year course at the return of peace. To plan for that eventuality, Wilby directed the Academic Board to study the return to the longer course in December 1943. In January 1944, the curriculum committee submitted its first report, recommending that the plebe class that matriculated in 1943 (then scheduled for graduation in 1946, after three years) be designated the first four-year class. In effect, it was recommending an immediate return to the four-year program. Wilby sent this recommendation along to Washington, but the War Department replied that it was premature. In October 1944, buoyed by the Allies' successes in Europe, Wilby again raised the issue, but once more the War Department disapproved. This time, however, he was directed to resubmit the request upon the defeat of Germany or in July 1945, whichever date was earlier.

In May 1945, coinciding with the victory in Europe, the board again pressed for a return to a four-year curriculum. This time the War Department agreed but suggested that the class that was to enter in July 1945 should be the first four-year class. The Academic Board balked at such a slow transition. Instead, it proposed splitting the class that had entered in 1943 and was scheduled to graduate (after three years) in 1946—half to graduate as scheduled, and half to be given a four-year course. The War Department, however, pointed out that retaining half the class at West Point for an additional year would limit the number of cadets that could be admitted in 1946. That was a sensitive matter because many congressmen had already committed themselves to appointments for July 1946. It was decided instead to divide the class that had entered in 1944; half would continue in the three-year program, becoming the class of 1947, and the other would become the first postwar four-year class—the class of 1948. All subsequent classes would follow four-year programs. The plan was approved and put into effect in September 1945.

In the meantime, the curriculum committee finished its work and made its report. The prewar curriculum had been carefully and thoroughly revised and modernized. Chemistry and electricity were split, creating the Department of Electricity, and joining physics and chemistry. Colonel Boyd W. Bartlett, class of 1919, became the first professor of electricity. Under his direction, and with the aid of the chief of the Signal Corps, laboratory equipment and facilities for the new department were much enlarged. At the same time, Beukema's Department of Economics, Government, and History was renamed the Department of Social Sciences.

The Academic Board also recommended the appointment of a Dean who would be responsible for coordinating academic courses, schedules, and instructional facilities and would also serve as a representative of the academic departments and an adviser to the Superintendent on academic matters. In addition, the board called for the appointment of a second permanent professor for each department and suggested that all officers selected for duty as instructors should be designated in advance and detailed to civilian universities for one year's postgraduate work. Finally, it recommended that special boards of consultants be appointed occasionally to examine the curriculum, the individual courses of study, and the methods of instruction at West Point.

On September 4, 1945, Major General Maxwell D. Taylor, class of 1922, succeeded Wilby as Superintendent and immediately implemented the several recommendations of the board. Roger Alexander, Professor of Topography and Graphics, was appointed Dean, and a number of the officers scheduled to join the faculty in 1946 were instead diverted to graduate school for a year's study before coming to the Academy.

Meanwhile, at West Point, the Academic Board found that Taylor had an agenda of his own. Shortly after his arrival, he gave the officers at West

Point a preview of his plans and policies. "Many progressive additions and revisions in the academic program and organization are contemplated," they were informed.[32] Like MacArthur, who had been the first Superintendent after World War I, Taylor was a brilliant young officer with a dazzling wartime record as both a commander and a staff officer. The similarities did not end there. Taylor, like MacArthur (and Mills and Schofield) before him, soon earned the enmity of many of the senior members of the faculty. The transition from active campaigning—where both the responsibility and the authority they had assumed were absolute—to the more limited role of the superintendency seems to have been a difficult one for such men. But it is also worth noting that as Superintendents they emulated the models they had known. Taylor's years as a cadet largely coincided with MacArthur's superintendency; similarly, MacArthur's cadet years were served under Mills, and Mills's were served under Schofield.

Taylor soon let it be known that, having created the office of Dean, he planned to limit his meetings with the Academic Board. Many matters of administration could now be handled without the board's formal input. "The Superintendent . . . will no longer have to deal with fourteen heads of departments over small details of academic administration either individual or through the Academic Board," his office reported.[33] To members of the

Maxwell D. Taylor was the Superintendent of the United States Military Academy from 1945 to 1949. Painted in 1948 by Dewitt M. Lockman (1870–1957). West Point Museum Collection, United States Military Academy.

Academic Board, this revealed Taylor's intention to reduce, if not usurp, their power and influence at West Point.

Though the ink had hardly dried on the Academic Board's new four-year curriculum study, Taylor immediately appointed a board of consultants to reexamine it. After careful scrutiny, that group expressed its approval. "The Board unanimously and most emphatically believes that the [Military Academy] should be an undergraduate institution on the collegiate level, giving a common four-year course to all cadets."[34] The curriculum, the consultants felt, provided a satisfactory balance between military and academic instruction, and between scientific and liberal subjects. They also endorsed the Academic Board's recommendation of the appointment of a Dean, of additional permanent professors, and of graduate-level training at civilian schools for prospective instructors. Though the consultants were somewhat critical of the inadequate leisure afforded the cadets (they suggested cutting military instruction), they heartily commended the Academic Board's curriculum study.

Taylor, however, was not satisfied. Even before arriving at West Point, he had sent letters to many of the Army's senior officers requesting their advice. Dwight D. Eisenhower, then Chief of Staff of the Army, urged Taylor to ensure "a profound respect for the Honor System" and strongly suggested that he include in the curriculum "a course in practical or applied psychology." Learning to deal with human problems on a human basis would, Eisenhower suggested, "do much to improve leadership and personnel handling in the Army at large."[35]

In response, Taylor sought to create a Department of Military Psychology and Leadership. The Dean and the Academic Board, however, were unsympathetic to this change. They had repeatedly considered additions to the curriculum, including psychology, and as often had concluded that these were less important to future officers than the material that already crowded the curriculum. They were not inclined to alter that position merely to accommodate the new Superintendent or even Eisenhower; no department head wished to give up hours he had fought time and again to win or protect.

Taylor would not be put off. If the Academic Board would not carve out hours for psychology in its portion of the curriculum, he would initiate the course under the auspices of the Commandant of Cadets. Under this arrangement, approximately ninety hours that had formerly been devoted to specialized branch training in the cadet's first class year were now devoted to the course in applied psychology. The Academic Board had been outmaneuvered; lacking any grounds to do otherwise, its members gave their grudging approval to this arrangement, but it only added to their determination to resist other inroads.[36]

Taylor was only beginning, however. Despite his consulting board's general approval of the mix of courses, Taylor remained critical of the curriculum. He felt that all offerings should be assessed "to verify their relevance to the whole officer corps." The curriculum, he insisted, retained an "engineering flavor" that was no longer appropriate. Math, science, and engineering, however, were not his only concerns. He took a particular interest in English instruction and "was determined to pay personal attention to the teaching of the subject." He particularly scrutinized the selection of the permanent professors of that department and personally checked on instruction in the classroom. His invasion of this privileged preserve was no more welcome than had been MacArthur's. Nor did the Academic Board take kindly his efforts to hire teachers from civilian life—in his view, a means to reduce "excessive inbreeding and homogeneity in the faculty."[37]

The Academic Board now felt compelled to respond. To some members, Taylor's efforts appeared revolutionary. Others saw him as little more than a meddler, intruding in areas in which he had no business. All recognized, however, that the board's ability to respond was somewhat hampered because a substantial proportion of its members had taken their seats only recently. Three of the seven permanent heads of the academic departments had joined since 1945 and, as yet, exercised little influence outside their own departments. There was Bartlett in the Department of Electricity; Colonel Lawrence E. Schick, class of 1920, who had taken over the Department of Military Topography and Graphics in 1946; and George R. Stephens, a Princeton graduate with a Ph.D. from Pennsylvania, who had been selected to head the English department after ten years of service at the Naval Academy.

Still, the board was not without influence. Herman Beukema, Professor of Social Sciences, had sat on the board since 1930 and was a classmate of Dwight Eisenhower's, the new Chief of Staff of the Army. When other means proved inadequate, Beukema went to Ike. "You tame him," he is said to have told the future President concerning Taylor, "or we will."[38]

Taylor, to the relief of the board, soon turned his attention to areas more traditionally reserved for the Superintendent—among them, the honor system and plebe training. In 1948, he drafted an honor pamphlet for cadets and in it coined the phrase that became synonymous with the honor code—"a cadet will neither lie, cheat nor steal."[39]

He also made a complete review of the fourth-class system and appealed to the senior cadet officers in the same manner, he said, "as MacArthur had to my class twenty-five years before, to root out any practice which could not be directly related to making a better cadet out of the plebes undergoing training." He also found an affinity with Schofield on this subject. Quoting him, Taylor wrote, "The discipline which makes the soldiers of a free country reliable in battle is not to be gained by harsh or tyrannical treatment. On the contrary, such treatment is far more likely to destroy than to make an Army."[40]

Soon, however, West Point's reputation for "honor" would be tarnished by a scandal far worse than any of those concerning plebes. Over the years, West Point had come to participate in almost the entire repertoire of intercollegiate sports, but football always remained preeminent, and Army rose steadily into the ranks of the major teams. Through the 1920s and 1930s, it won many more games than it lost; in 1933, under the coaching of Lieutenant Garrison "Gar" Davidson, class of 1927, an otherwise perfect season was spoiled only by a 13-to-12 loss to Notre Dame. By the late 1930s, however, Army's fortunes had turned. The cadets won only three games in 1939 and only a single game in 1940. So, the next year, the Academy hired a new head coach, Earl "Red" Blaik, class of 1920. By 1944, Blaik had turned the Army program around. Over the next three years, Army went undefeated, though many opponents—particularly Notre Dame—insisted that this was only because the best opposing players were in the service.

Possibly the most famous game in Army history was played against Notre Dame at New York's Yankee Stadium in 1946. Army had won games against Notre Dame in 1944 and 1945 by lopsided scores. In 1946, with its players now back from the service, Notre Dame was determined to turn the tables. The game, however, ended in an indecisive 0-to-0 tie. Billed as the "game of the century," the contest became the subject of excessive hype—end-zone seats were being scalped for as much as $300, and huge amounts of money were being bet on the game. As a result, the two schools agreed to end the series after the 1947 season.

Army was finally defeated in 1947—by Columbia and Notre Dame—but otherwise continued to pile up victories and belie the claim that its wartime success had been a fluke. It did not lose another game until 1950. From 1944 through the end of 1950, Red Blaik's teams won seventy games and lost only three. By all indications, the Army team would be even better in 1951.

Then, in April 1951, the Commandant of Cadets learned of widespread cheating among a group of football players and cadets who were assisting them. In most classes, identical written examinations were given to successive groups, even though as many as half the cadets in the course might take the examination a full day after it was first given. Clearly violating the honor code, members of the cheating ring who took such written tests early in the succession passed along the questions that were being asked to associates who had not yet been examined.

The Commandant's board of inquiry reported that approximately ninety cadets were guilty and recommended their separation from the service. The

Academic Board concurred. Before making a final decision, however, the Secretary of the Army, Frank Pace, Jr., appointed a board to review the investigation and pass on the recommendations. The board, chaired by Judge Learned Hand, concurred in the finding that the cadets had violated the honor code and unanimously supported the recommendations of the Academy authorities. Much of the team was dismissed, and Army lost seven of its nine games in 1951. Ninety cadets were ultimately offered the opportunity to resign. Most did so; those who did not were administratively separated.

This scandal brought worldwide publicity to one of the Academy's most cherished traditions. The cadet honor code is rooted in the earliest years of the Academy. It was derived from the code of honor of officers and gentlemen—a code that required that their word be their bond, and their personal character and conduct make them worthy of mutual association. In 1807, the cadets attempted to "silence" one of their number (withhold social intercourse and converse only in the line of duty) for his ungentlemanly behavior toward a servant. Jonathan Williams, the first Superintendent, intervened, arguing that this case was cognizable under the law, and therefore the "silence" was inappropriate. Though Williams insisted that he would not allow these "self-erected Censors" to prevail, and that "nothing of that kind shall ever be permitted on this Ground," the concept of a cadet-enforced code of honor persisted and flourished.[41]

Infractions and other breaches of gentlemanly conduct were usually settled by a confrontation between the accused and his accuser. In the early nineteenth century, many gentlemen still felt compelled by the code to fight a duel to resolve personal affronts. In the Army, however, regulations strictly forbade that practice, so at West Point a fistfight between the two parties was usually considered sufficient to resolve such matters. Other violations, such as making a false statement, were referred to the Superintendent for administrative punishment—often dismissal. In 1816, for example, four cadets were dismissed by Superintendent Alden Partridge for lying as to their whereabouts.[42]

The code continued for years as an unwritten prohibition against lying and ungentlemanly conduct.[43] It was passed from class to class through informal mechanisms by the upperclassmen. Although the inculcation of many of these values was considered a responsibility of the chaplain and the Commandant of Cadets, the preservation of the code was largely the preserve of the corps of cadets itself.

In 1865, an informal cadet committee attempted to drum another cadet out of the corps for stealing. When Academy officials intervened and blocked their effort, the cadets resorted to the silence.[44] In this case, Academy officials made no objection. In 1871, when three fourth classmen broke regulations and then compounded their offenses by lying, a group of first classmen gave the trio some civilian clothes and money and told them to leave the post.[45] In the investigation that followed, the upperclassmen indicated that, though they had knowledge of only one other similar case, they believed such action to be traditional.[46] The affair attracted a good deal of press attention, but after a hearing, the first classmen were given only slight punishment.

At first, such actions were organized by leaders of the corps as necessary. As the years passed, however, the mechanisms became more regularized. By the 1890s, ad hoc vigilance committees conducted organized, if unofficial, investigations of suspected honor violations.[47] By 1911, the vigilance committee had become a permanent fixture whose membership included representatives from each class—though the group was still not formally recognized by Academy officials.

The first effort to capture on paper the essence of the cadet honor code was undertaken in 1907 by Charles Larned, Professor of Drawing, whose brief essay "Corps Honor" appeared in the first edition of the *West Point Hand-Book*—a publication that soon became known as *Bugle Notes*. "Corps Honor is not and should not be different from the accepted standard of honor recognized by the ethics of Christian Nations—the code of a gentleman the world over," Larned wrote. He insisted that "Corps Honor is concerned with all questions affecting the integrity of personal action." By various illustrations, Larned defined a code that encompassed a wide range of activities: a cadet would not steal, lie, cheat, or slander; he should be physically brave, sober, and chaste; he should forswear indirection, evasion, sophistry, subtlety, and guile; and he should neither "bootlick," nor take mean advantage, nor neglect his duty, nor betray a confidence. "A true code of honor," he wrote, "stands in its integrity for right doing all around." Still, he insisted, there were "different degrees of culpability, and there are certain infractions regarding which the Corps is wholly intolerant." These, he indicated, were "theft, cowardice and deliberate falsehood."[48]

Cheating—at least getting unauthorized advanced information about examinations—was not always considered an honor offense. Thayer had attempted to treat it as such, but his successors generally did not. This began to change about the turn of the century. The first evidence of a shift in attitude came in 1899, when a vigilance committee indicted a cadet for stealing examination papers. In 1907, Larned had similarly indicated that "cheating the instructor" was an honor offense, though only two years earlier the adjutant had indicated the opposite.[49] To clear up any confusion on the point, Superintendent Hugh Scott followed up Larned's piece with a memorandum confirming that "hereafter in the section-room, either at oral recitation or at written recitation, all cadets shall be considered on honor to receive no information concerning their recitations or their lessons from any unauthorized source whatever."[50]

By the end of World War I, the vigilance committee had become an elective body, with representatives from each of the twelve companies. Though it had no official standing, it had assembled informal courts to consider honor violations for a number of years.[51] In 1920, MacArthur began to move the honor system more directly under the control of Academy officials. William Ganoe, MacArthur's adjutant during that period, suggests that his action was triggered by Secretary of War Newton Baker's testimony before Congress: West Point must ensure "the inculcation of a set of virtues admirable always but indispensable in the soldier," he told them. "Men may be inexact or even untruthful in ordinary matters, and suffer as a consequence only the disesteem of their associates, or the inconveniences of unfavorable litigation, but the inexact and untruthful soldier trifles with the lives of his fellow men; and it is, therefore, no matter of idle pride, but stern disciplinary necessity that makes West Point require of her students a character of trustworthiness which knows no evasions."[52] After discussing the problem with Commandant Robert Danford, MacArthur decided to dissolve the vigilance committee. "Select a few cadets of the highest, all-round character, who are most respected and influential in the Corps," he told Danford. "Let them be called an Honor Committee."[53] In 1922, he formally recognized the committee and charged it with the administration of the honor code.

In 1923, the new honor committee worked with the administration to define the "guiding principles" of the honor system. First, "no intentional breach of honor is excusable." Second, "everyone, offender or not, is honor bound to report any breach of honor which comes to his attention." Third, there will be no "second chance." Fourth, questions as to interpretation should be taken to a member of the honor committee. Fifth, "quibbling" and "evasive statements" to "shield guilt" would not be tolerated. And, sixth, if in doubt, errors should be made on the side of caution—"always be on the safe side."[54] These were amplified by specific examples of their application to academic work and everyday cadet life.

By 1924, it appeared that the new honor committee was exercising too much power—believing that all infractions of discipline that involved questions of honor "could be handled by them without any reference to the military machinery provided for enforcing discipline." Merch Stewart, the Commandant of Cadets, reined in the committee by carefully delineating its duties, which were to assure that cadets understood the system, guard against the birth of practices inconsistent with the stated principles, consult with the Commandant when the principles required interpretation, inquire into all suspected honor violations, and report the facts of its investigations to the Commandant.[55]

In 1926, the Academic Board reviewed the "general code of rules that has been evolved by the Cadet Honor Committee" and suggested a rewording of the portion dealing with academic work. "No cadet shall impart or receive any unauthorized assistance, either outside or inside the section room or examination room, which would tend to give any cadet an unfair advantage," the board wrote, adding a number of examples to clarify specific cases.[56]

In 1931, Superintendent William Smith reduced the statement of the code to a single sentence. "Honor . . . is a fundamental principle of character—a virtue which implies loyalty and courage, truthfulness and self-respect, justice and generosity." Smith also further defined the operation of the honor system. Violations detected by cadets and reported to the honor committee, he directed, were to be investigated by that committee, but violations discovered by officers or otherwise reported to the Commandant of Cadets were to be investigated by the Commandant. In the aftermath of such investigations, a cadet found guilty of an honor violation could demand a court-martial, though few did. Most simply resigned. Even if acquitted or given a punishment short of dismissal by the court, cadets found guilty by their peers were likely to be silenced.

In 1948, Maxwell Taylor subjected the honor code and system to a detailed review. MacArthur's recognition of the honor committee had soon led to the codification of the honor system. Taylor's reforms carried that process one step further, defining the process more and more in judicial terms. The honor committee was described "as a grand jury reporting possible violations to the Commandant of Cadets," and, from 1946 to 1953, at least, honor hearings were formalized and conducted essentially as court-martial proceedings.[57]

One outcome of the codification of the honor system was the problem created by the inevitable close relationship between honor issues and regulations—the oft-heard charge that the Academy uses honor to enforce regulations. That issue is a continuing source of cadet frustration. In 1899, in an effort to stop hazing, Superintendent Albert Mills ordered cadet company commanders to sign statements "on their honor" that they were not permitting hazing in their units. Cadets so resented this and a chain of similar demands that they responded by towing the reveille cannon to the Superintendent's quarters and pointing it at Mills's front door in 1901. A similar directive in the 1920s demanded that the cadet officer of the day and the cadet officer of the guard sign statements that they had reported all violations of all regulations. This time, cadets responded with a campaign of evasion and passive resistance. Those exercising these duties loudly jangled key chains against their swords to warn other cadets of their approach and dined with their heads lowered lest they observe infractions in the dining hall.

In the 1930s and 1940s, the honor committees argued vainly for an end to the "poop sheets," which listed what was and was not an honor violation, in favor of cadets' obeying the simpler demands of the code itself. In an effort to defuse this argument and to distinguish better between honor and regulations, in 1948, Taylor created the cadet duty committee, which was designed to aid the administration in dealing with issues of duties and regulations—separating them from honor issues. It soon lapsed due to a lack of support within the corps. The poop sheets persisted, and the complaints against them continued. Not only were they long, but they were subject to dramatic reversals. For example, the cadets' practice of stuffing their beds with pillows to avoid detection during an unauthorized late-night absence was judged to be a violation of regulations in 1921, 1948, and 1963; on other occasions, it was labeled an honor violation. Increasingly, cadets complained that the spirit of the honor code was being subordinated to a "laundry list of do's and don't's."

In 1962, the cadet honor committee formally protested the use of honor to enforce regulations. In response, West Point made some significant changes during the 1963–1964 academic year. The most important of these dealt with the "all right" and the handling of officer-reported violations. Previously, the response "all right" to a challenge signified that a cadet (1) had been within authorized geographic limits, (2) was not hazing, (3) did not possess either liquor or drugs, and (4) was not gambling. The new policy changed the "all right" to mean simply that the cadet had not violated the authorized limits. In the late 1980s, the "all right" was abolished altogether.

In the early 1970s, the nontoleration clause was again included in the statement of the code: "A cadet will not lie, cheat or steal nor tolerate those who do."[58] This change, of course, was more apparent than real. Nontoleration had long been an implicit element of the code, and on occasion it had been an explicit part. Its significance lay more in its symbology—an Academy effort to deal with a growing cadet frustration with the honor system (though not with the honor code itself) at the beginning of what was to prove a very troubled decade.

Given the expanded size of the corps of cadets in the 1930s and 1940s, it seemed axiomatic that physical expansion would follow. As the corps inched toward its authorized size of 1,374 in the early 1930s, many of the Academy's facilities were already taxed. The further enlargement of the corps beginning in 1936—reaching toward a new authorized strength of 1,960—necessitated added barracks and classroom space and the expansion of the gymnasium. To plan this expansion, the Academy chose one of America's foremost architects, Paul Cret. Begun in 1936, his work was done in two years. Cret's Scott Barracks, nestled against the hill behind North Barracks, was the first at West Point to be built of reinforced concrete, though it was faced in gray stone. Cret gave this structure the clean simplicity of modern-day functionalism, yet its towers, battlements, and buttresses established a definite sense of the Gothic. His addition to the East Academic Building displayed the extent of his talent even more fully. Though sandwiched between three buildings, the East Academic Building extension matched the site while remaining remarkable for its individuality and visual impact. Its uneven outcroppings of gray stone, large pseudo-buttresses, and huge Gothic openings—achieved by massing the windows of several floors—assured harmony with its surroundings while giving it a distinct character.

In 1942, the Academy's strength was once more increased—to a maximum of 2,496. The war soon filled the Academy to bursting. Three men to a room rather than two became the norm. This large increase, coupled with needs that had accumulated gradually over many years, prompted Academy officials to reconsider the sort of massive overhaul of facilities that had occurred forty years before.

A new competition was held in 1943. Design requirements included a new academic building within the walls of the existing riding hall, a new memorial hall supplementing the facilities of Cullum Hall, and an additional barracks. The winner was the firm of Delano and Aldrich of New York City, but competing wartime and postwar demands for funds doomed the project. In the end, the work was limited to additions to the gymnasium and mess hall, which were completed in 1946.

In 1955, continuing the piecemeal approach, the firm of Gehron and Seltzer was chosen to convert the riding hall into an academic building. The structure was to be gutted and then rebuilt to house the Departments of Mathematics, Military Art and Engineering, Social Sciences, Law, Ordnance, Foreign Languages, and English, and the office of Military Psychology and Leadership, as well as the museum, bookstore, and computer center. Construction of the new academic facility—named Thayer Hall—began in 1956 and was completed in 1958. Gehron and Seltzer also converted the old academic building (1895) into a modern barracks (1959). Two additional barracks—Lee and Sherman Barracks—were begun on the site of the old hospital in 1960 and completed in 1962, under the direction of the architectural firm of O'Connor and Kilham.

The pressure on facilities caused by the growth of the Academy in the 1930s and 1940s was mirrored in the demand for faculty quarters. Already inadequate by the late 1920s, housing was a high priority when the passage of the National Industrial Recovery Act made public works funds available. Foremost among the projects undertaken were fifty sets of officers' quarters built at the north end of the post. These quarters were especially designed for the young married officers, and the area was soon tagged "Looeyville."[59] (Today lieutenant colonels, not lieutenants, inhabit the neighborhood—now known as "Lee" area.) Economies of the depression era ensured that these new quarters would not match the lavish sets built by Cram, Goodhue and Ferguson at the turn of the century, but these quartermaster-designed brick doubles still possessed a quiet dignity and graciousness enhanced by the thoughtful and attractive plan for the area as a whole. These and some additional sets of new officers' quarters in tasteful brick row houses, also in Lee area, were expected to accommodate all the married officers assigned to the post. The new expansion of the corps of cadets that same year, of course, meant that quarters would soon be in short supply again. This situation persisted throughout the war and into the late 1940s.

In 1946 and 1947, faced with a critical nationwide housing shortage, the Congress limited the cost and size of Army-built family units. At West Point, however, the rough, rocky terrain meant inordinately high building costs. As a result, when Congress authorized 133 new sets to be built (less than half of what was needed), there were funds enough for only shoddily built, clapboard row houses that soon acquired the name "Grey Ghost."

Major General Bryant E. Moore, class of August 1917, who succeeded Maxwell Taylor in the superintendency, renewed West Point's request in 1949, asking specifically for eighty three-bedroom officers' quarters with 1,250 square feet of living area—tiny in comparison with the older quarters but in excess of the postwar allowance. He justified this exception to the current square-footage cap by pointing out that officers at West Point had a greater need for guest facilities, that instructors needed a study, and that "the type of officer selected for duty at the Military Academy would, almost without exception, occupy a dwelling with three or more bedrooms if he were doing similar work in a civilian institution."[60] Assigned a low priority by the Department of the Army, this request was never approved. Moore's successor, Major General Frederick A. Irving, class of April 1917, was equally unsuccessful, and the critical housing shortage at West Point continued.

Finally, in 1960, with no relief in sight, West Point authorities accepted the proposition that even inadequate housing was better than none, and they accepted a parcel of brick duplexes, providing roughly 130 sets of tiny (1,050-square-feet) quarters that became known as "New Brick." Tightly packed on the site, devoid of ornament, and without either basements or garages, these units had all the architectural charm of low-income tract housing.

The officers and their wives, however, did not allow their surroundings to impede the active social life to which they were accustomed. The more senior, of course, drew the older, more pleasant quarters. Many of the new additional professors allowed to each department at the end of World War II settled in the turn-of-the-century quarters at the south end of the post. Among them were George Lincoln, class of 1929, and Vincent Esposito, class of 1925. They organized themselves into the South End Officers Protective Association, which was soon famous for its exclusive New Year's Eve party and springtime masquerade. The latter, the Magnolia Festival that celebrated the annual blooming of Esposito's magnolia tree, was a costumed affair at which the members were required to read verses they had composed for the occasion.

In the years immediately after Taylor's departure, there had been few significant programmatic reforms at West Point, although pressures were building for change by the mid-1950s. In 1954, Lieutenant General Blackshear M. Bryan, class of June 14, 1922, succeeded Frederick Irving as Superintendent. Bryan faced a challenge that was novel to West Point—a threat to enrollments. In 1954, the Academy filled only 67 percent of available vacancies, continuing a downward trend that had begun in the first year of the Korean War, when only 82 percent of the vacancies had been filled. The opening of the Air Force Academy in 1955 compounded recruitment difficulties. Bryan poured time, energy, and resources into the recruiting effort and public relations. He promoted cadet speaking tours and expanded contacts with high school counselors, educators, and any group that might yield candidates—even the Boy Scouts. In the meantime, the public relations people redoubled their efforts. Colonel Russell "Red" Reeder, then employed by the Army Athletic Association, undertook his popular West Point book series: *West Point Plebe* in 1955; *West Point Yearling* and *The West Point Story* in 1956; *West Point Second Classman* in 1957; and finally *West Point First Classmen* the next year. Hollywood got into the act in 1955 with *The Long Gray Line*—an adaptation of Marty Maher's memoir, *Bringing Up the Brass: My 55 Years at West Point*.[61] And, in September 1956, CBS began a regular dramatic series entitled simply *West Point* and produced a total of thirty-nine shows. The Academy was a willing subject in this publicity barrage: cadets, faculties, and families were the eager extras, and the gray stone walls and rocky hills a ready backdrop.

"Gar" Davidson, who twenty-some years earlier had coached the Academy's football team, replaced Bryan as Superintendent in 1956 and continued to expand the recruitment effort. He organized a formal admissions division directly under his supervision and personally selected the director. He enlarged the pool of potentially acceptable candidates by shifting from exclusive reliance on the College Entrance Examination Board tests to a "whole man" selection procedure that supplemented academic achievement tests with evidence of character, leadership potential, and physical fitness. Davidson also attempted to persuade members of Congress to permit the Academic Board to rank the names of candidates in order of predicted probable success in the Army—in effect, to allow the Academy to suggest their principal appointees. In 1957, only three congressmen availed themselves of this offer, but by 1960, 128 were doing so, and the number continued to increase. However, important as recruitment was, it constituted only a sideshow to the new Superintendent's primary objectives.

Davidson had long sought the assignment to West Point and arrived with a considered plan of reform. But Davidson, unlike most of his reform-oriented predecessors, was mindful of the politics and process of change at the institution; he had been well served by his prior tour as commandant at the Army's Command and General Staff College at Fort Leavenworth.

Davidson spent much of the first year refining his goals and carefully formulating a strategy for achieving them—a scheme that provides insight into the institutional imperatives of successful reform at West Point.[62] His strategy began with an elaborate curriculum review that harnessed the tal-

Garrison H. Davidson, Superintendent of the United States Military Academy from 1956 to 1960. West Point Museum Collection, United States Military Academy.

ents (and ultimately gained the support) of many of the staff and faculty to the project; a variety of opinion surveys first tapped (and then co-opted) other important constituencies. He disarmed many potential opponents of change simply by seeking their advice and by framing questions in a way that encouraged them to consider problems from a perspective that Davidson himself had established.

Never before had such a substantial portion of the staff, faculty, student body, and alumni been engaged in contributing to a critical review of the Military Academy's programs. And never, since Thayer, had a reforming Superintendent enjoyed such esteem among the many constituencies concerned with West Point—most particularly, from his colleagues on the Academic Board.

Davidson could and did effect some reforms by decree. He announced that henceforth all officers who were appointed to permanent professorships were expected to obtain their doctorate; he established a program of sabbatical leaves; and he urged all the faculty to write for professional and scholarly journals.

Curriculum reform, of course, required the assent of the Academic Board—the venerable institution that had managed to frustrate Taylor and earlier reform-minded Superintendents. Since the Taylor years, however, the complexion of that institution had changed in important ways. Colonel Charles West, class of 1920, had been named the first permanent professor of law in 1947. Colonel William W. Bessell, Jr., a classmate of West's, had succeeded Harris Jones as professor of mathematics when the latter was made Dean in 1947. Colonel Charles J. Barrett, class of 1922, had replaced William Morrison as professor of foreign languages in 1948. And Colonel Elvin R. "Vald" Heiberg, class of 1926, had become professor of mechanics when Oscar Gatchell retired in 1953. Heiberg's selection was particularly important in changing the makeup of the board, for he was a strong advocate of electives—the first such on the mathematics-science-engineering side. His own prescription for academic reform—contained in an article, "A BS or BA Election for Cadets," published in 1953—had been soundly criticized by his colleagues, although in time his views had gained support.

In 1954, upon Herman Beukema's retirement, Colonel George A. Lincoln became professor and head of the Department of Social Sciences. Two years later, Colonel Vincent "Mike" Esposito succeeded Thomas Stamps in the Department of Military Art and Engineering. Both Lincoln and Esposito had enjoyed brilliant careers on George Marshall's staff in World War II. Lincoln had served in the Operations Division of the War Department General Staff and as a member of the Joint Planners Committee of the Combined Chiefs of Staff. Esposito had served with Lincoln in the Operations

Division and had been a War Department representative at the Quebec, Malta, Yalta, and Potsdam Conferences. Both had been promoted to brigadier general in 1945. But they were scholars and surrendered their stars at war's end in order to return to West Point. Lincoln's *Economics of National Security* was an outstanding and widely adopted textbook. Esposito's two-volume *West Point Atlas of American Wars* was based on numerous instructional atlases whose preparation he had overseen in the years just after the war. Said one critic, "These two volumes are at once a thing of art and a scholarly enlargement of our knowledge in the field of military affairs."[63] Largely unheralded was the careful research of two of Esposito's junior faculty—John Elting and Thomas E. Griess, class of January 1943, who later became the first professor of history. Also unheralded was the brilliant cartographic work of Edward J. Krasnoborski, whose handsome campaign maps had long been a fixture of West Point's classrooms and atlases. Krasnoborski, a man whose modesty only served to highlight his enormous talent, celebrated fifty years of service at West Point in 1985 but continued to preside over his studio in the Department of History until 1996, a year before his death.

The Academic Board's curriculum study was completed in November 1958, but proved something of a disappointment to Davidson. Although it advanced the concept of electives he favored, it suggested only a single elective—which was to be taken in the first-class year. The study also did nothing to alter the emphasis on mathematics, science, and engineering that had always characterized West Point curricula. To provide time for the one elective, the board proposed reducing the law course from two semesters to one.

Davidson passed the report to an outside curriculum review board in December, telling it that in his view the report's recommendations "had not gone far enough in proposing modifications to our curriculum."[64] He then gave the board his own "somewhat more radical" recommendations. In particular, he called for fifteen hours of electives, substantially more than the committee had envisioned—gaining time for these by converting some of the first-class engineering and law courses to electives and shifting some tactics instruction to the summer.

The curriculum review board attempted to reconcile the two sets of recommendations. It concurred in the prescribed curriculum in general but did call for six hours of electives (two courses) to be taken in the first-class year. To make room for the six hours of electives for all cadets, it proposed reductions in engineering, law, and tactics and military hygiene. The review board recommended an additional six hours of electives for "particularly able cadets by accelerating their progress through the required courses of earlier years."[65]

The struggle for academic reform now moved into the arena of the Academic Board. In March 1959, Davidson appointed an ad hoc curriculum committee to consider the recommendations and suggest a solution to the Academic Board. In April, when this report was completed, it was debated by the board as a whole. Those opposed to the elective program argued that "the only reason advanced for electives is that they will provide an opportunity in their final year for cadets to abandon studies which are distasteful to them and to concentrate to some extent in the fields of their primary interest or aptitude." Still, they conceded, "it appears that we must give it a trial."[66] Even many who favored reform preferred a cautious approach, expressing concern over large-scale changes.[67] Still others saw little alternative to slow progress. "We might as well recognize," wrote George Lincoln, "that the Academic Board of the Military Academy on most issues and the General Committee overwhelmingly on all issues is abdominally as well as cerebrally committed to the overriding priority of mathematics and science."[68]

In late April 1959, however, when the issues were formally presented to the board, the very first vote revealed the evolution of opinion taking place on the most fundamental issue. When asked whether the Academy should be under a single, completely prescribed curriculum, the board voted in the affirmative by only eight to seven—preserving that sacred tradition by only one vote.[69] It then proceeded to approve elective courses for all first-class cadets on a trial basis, making room for them by reducing the courses in civil and ordnance engineering, and in law—the trial period to be a four-year period beginning in the 1959–1960 academic year.[70]

Throughout the autumn of 1959, the Academic Board continued to agonize over possible changes in the curriculum. Finally, the board agreed to allow cadets with advanced preparation to validate introductory courses and accelerate their program—allowing additional electives in their first-class year. But Davidson once more pressed the board to increase the number of electives to four. He again recommended that the two semesters of civil engineering be moved out of the core curriculum and offered as electives. Feelings ran high against the proposal until Professor Heiberg, of the Department of Mechanics, proposed a compromise that would retain one semester of civil engineering in the core curriculum and allow three electives. After considerable debate, Heiberg's compromise was adopted. Heiberg told Davidson, "You shouldn't feel bad; you're going to get 92 percent of what you want."[71]

In the minds of many, what was at stake was not merely the preservation of local "fiefdoms" but also the very preservation of the integrity of the Thayer system. It was, as one observer put it, the era of "the Great Debate."[72] Said General Davidson, "The discussions in the Academic

Board meetings were intense to say the least—but friendly. Blood was drawn but the wounded lived."[73]

Davidson forwarded the Academic Board's recommendation to General Lemnitzer, the Army Chief of Staff, but he enclosed with it a long minority report expressing his own preference for a fourth elective at the expense of the one remaining semester of civil engineering. Lemnitzer, however, sided with the board (which included four of his 1920 classmates, including the Dean) and approved the three-elective program. Two years later, the Academic Board restored the excised semester of civil engineering to the prescribed curriculum and cut the number of electives to two. But this setback was temporary; only a few years later, the board again reversed itself.

As events would prove, Davidson had initiated an extended era of curriculum debate and revision. Not since Thayer had a Superintendent's efforts at academic reform had such enduring effect. Though Davidson's designs for upgrading the academic program were by no means fulfilled during his own tenure, the debate over academic reform would become a dominant theme in the decades ahead—decades that would torment and challenge the Long Gray Line and its alma mater.

CHAPTER NINE

The Years of Turmoil, 1960–2001

The last four decades of the twentieth century were a time of near-constant turmoil at West Point. The early years of the period saw dramatic changes in the demographics of the corp of cadets: a doubling of the corps size, beginning in 1964; the increased recruitment of minority students; and the admission of women in 1976. Then, also in 1976, a cheating scandal caused unprecedented scrutiny of the institution. Finally, there was a new pattern of governance and a series of superintendents who renewed the ancient contest between themselves and the Academic Board. As troublesome as these issues alone might have been, however, their impact was heightened because they were layered on a continuing and fundamental curriculum debate. Changes to the course of instruction in this period included the most radical curriculum evolution yet to take place at the Military Academy—the introduction of electives, in 1959, and majors, in 1982. More fundamentally, however, this was a debate about the content of the core curriculum and the importance of mathematics and engineering—the bedrock of West Point's educational philosophy.

Major General William C. Westmoreland, class of 1936, became Superintendent on July 1, 1960. "I was anxious to carry on the good work of my predecessor, Lieutenant General Garrison Davidson, in modernizing [the Academy]," wrote Westmoreland. "One of my goals as superintendent was to increase the size of the Corps from approximately 2,400 cadets to 4,400, roughly the strength of the Brigade of Midshipmen at the Naval Academy."[1] Expansion was an issue he had considered while a member of the Army staff before coming to West Point; it became the central focus of his superintendency.

At West Point throughout the 1950s, expansion plans had been drawn and redrawn. Using these, Westmoreland was ready to take the question to the Department of the Army by the early months of 1961. There he secured permission "to plan for and make recommendations concerning an incremental expansion of existing facilities or provision of new facilities in proximity of existing ones to accommodate an increase in the size of the Corps to about 4,250 cadets."[2]

"As I prepared to get the expansion bill started in the long trek through the bureaucracy," wrote Westmoreland, "a discussion with President Kennedy at the Army-Navy football game in December 1962 gave me an opportunity to make my point in person to the Commander in Chief." The President spent the first half of the game on the Navy side, then, at halftime, joined General Westmoreland and the cadets. During the second half, as Navy punished Army, President Kennedy turned to Westmoreland and asked, "General, why are there so many more midshipmen at the game than cadets?" Westmoreland pointed out that the two academies operated under separate statutes, and that the Naval Academy was allowed two thousand more men— adding that it meant two thousand more men to draw from for a football team. "That," he told the President with a smile, "is one of the reasons we are getting the hell kicked out of us today."[3]

By that time, Westmoreland had already established a full-time expansion planning group under the chairmanship of Colonel Charles R. Broshous, class of 1933 and professor of earth, space, and graphic sciences.[4] Broshous was an ideal choice. He fussed over every detail of the construction from concept to completion, and he strongly resisted efforts to cut corners.

As the planning progressed, a new library, approved earlier, was begun on the site of Delafield's 1838 library. The new structure was designed by the architectural firm of Gehron and Seltzer and begun in 1962. Broad, pointed arch windows divided by delicate tracery, a massive tower, and pseudo-buttresses maintained the Gothic motif. Adorning the face of the tower over the main entrance was an eighteen-foot-high relief statue of Athena, the patroness of the Military Academy, mythological protectress of the brave and valorous, and symbol of supreme wisdom—both in the sciences of peace and in the arts of war. The new library was completed and occupied in 1964.[5]

In February 1963, a preliminary expansion plan was approved by the post planning board and forwarded to the Pentagon.[6] At the same time, Westmoreland briefed the former Superintendents and the leadership of the Association of Graduates on the plan; shortly thereafter, he took the issue to a number of key alumni, including MacArthur, Eisenhower, and Lucius Clay, class of June 1918.[7]

Westmoreland and Broshous were determined that the new plan would provide a single integrated facility in the immediate vicinity of the existing structures on the Plain, and they promised worried alumni that it would entail only a "minimal encroachment upon the Plain." Moreover, they believed it essential to adhere to West Point's traditional aesthetic and construction standards. The Academy would continue to be gray stone and Gothic. The new arrangements would preserve the scene across the Plain now familiar to graduates and visitors—barracks extending along the southern and western boundaries of the Plain, the mess hall at their intersection, and the cadet chapel crowning the view.

Broshous's studies indicated that the existing mess hall could be expanded, but that the Central Barracks (completed in 1851 along lines laid out by Delafield and added to in later years) and North Barracks (Cram, Goodhue and Ferguson, 1909) could not be renovated effectively. It was decided that they should be replaced with two new structures similar to the Academy's more recently completed barracks—particularly Cret's Scott Barracks. By placing the first floor of the new barracks on the street level and reducing ceiling height, it would be possible to get six floors into the vertical space that four had previously occupied. The new plans would provide billets for over 2,550 cadets where only 824 were then housed. Broshous estimated that the projects would take some eight and a half years to complete.[8] The two new barracks would be named after Generals MacArthur and Eisenhower, and they would flank Washington Hall, the newly enlarged

The Corps of Cadets Parade before MacArthur Barracks (1972). Above and behind MacArthur Barracks is the Cadet Chapel (1910). United States Military Academy Archives.

mess, on the north and east, respectively, forming an angle that opened onto the Plain.

By June 1963, when the House Armed Services Committee began hearings on the expansion bill, Westmoreland and Broshous had built a strong base of support for the project. Even President Kennedy personally lobbied for its passage.[9] Westmoreland, however, had new orders reassigning him, and he left the further development of the project in the hands of his successor, Major General James B. Lampert, class of 1936. Lampert had married the daughter of William A. Mitchell, who was the professor of civil and military engineering when Lampert was a cadet at West Point. Lampert, an engineer, had been a trailblazer in the development of nuclear engineering and may have been selected at this juncture because of his extensive construction experience.

In February 1964, Congress authorized both the increase of the corps from 2,529 to 4,417 and the construction necessary to accommodate the additional cadets. The next month, the architect-engineering firm of O'Connor and Kilham of New York City was hired to design the Washington Hall–Barracks complex and to supervise preliminary planning of the overall expansion program.

The ground breaking for the expansion took place during graduation week in June 1965.[10] In excavating for the eastern wing of the new complex (Eisenhower Barracks), workers soon discovered the foundations of the old Academy building that Swift had built in 1815 and that had been destroyed by fire in 1838. "It is interesting to note," wrote Lampert, "that the new building will represent a return to the general line on the Plain" occupied by the earliest permanent Academy structures.[11] In August 1967, Lampert's replacement, Major General Donald V. Bennett, class of 1940, opened the first new wing of the mess hall. A year later, his successor, Major General Samuel W. Koster, class of 1942, ordered the cadets into the newly completed Eisenhower Barracks.

The mess hall expansion was completed later in the fall. Its Gothic facade, designed by O'Connor and Kilham, may have lacked some of the vitality of the older Gehron structure, but the similarities in design and exterior finish were striking, and its imposing mass made it the most prominent building on the Plain. In its visual impression, the new Washington Hall was very much a part of the continuum of the architectural tradition at West Point that had begun with Richard Delafield and Frederick Diaper.

The 1926 facade, with its elevated "poop deck," was retained as the centerpiece of the new structure from which six dining wings now radiated— three new wings now mirroring the three of the old structure. The interior finishes of the new wings matched the old as closely as possible—in particular, the slate flooring and wood paneling of the old were repeated in the new. As much as possible of the old was preserved. The grotesques depicting the evolution of warfare, which had been removed from North Barracks when it was demolished, were incorporated into the interior architectural treatment of the new wings. Carved into the granite and limestone facade of this massive structure were Washington's coat of arms and scenes depicting his genius. Surmounting all that was the Great Seal of the United States—known to the corps as "Foundation Eagle." Tradition states that any cadet who looks at it during parade will be "found deficient."

Construction on a new academic building, Mahan Hall, was begun in late 1968. Situated on the steep slopes that thrust up from the river, the building seemed to grow out of the hillside, much like the nearby headquarters building and Thayer Hall. Unexpectedly high bids forced the Academy to reexamine the project, and when construction finally began, difficulties in pouring the foundation on the near-vertical site further delayed the project. The building was not ready for occupancy until the spring of 1972, nearly two years behind schedule, and it proved difficult and expensive to maintain over the years.

In their design of Mahan Hall, the architects O'Connor and Kilham followed the precedent established in the other principal academic buildings. While the architectural details were less pronounced in Mahan Hall than in surrounding structures, the building's strong vertical lines, its very mass, and the hint of buttresses at the base and battlements at the upper reaches gave it a decidedly Gothic character.

In April 1969, the north barracks wing—MacArthur Barracks—was completed and occupied. Shortly thereafter, Central Barracks was pulled down to make room for what would become known as Bradley Barracks, the third and last of the new barracks called for in the plan. Only the venerable and historic first division of the old Central Barracks was preserved. Its special significance as the billet of many of the old corps' first captains and other illustrious graduates saved it, but it survives as a lasting link to West Point's architectural heritage. In the summer of 1972, Bradley Barracks was completed and occupied.

In January 1971, construction of Eisenhower Hall, a cadet activities center, was begun. The facility was completed and opened in 1974. Its 4,500-seat auditorium could seat the entire corps. It also contained a ballroom accommodating 1,000 persons, a snack bar to seat 1,000 cadets and their guests, a reception hall for 150 persons, and numerous activity rooms. Built below the level of the Plain, the building was allowed to be constructed of red brick rather than the gray stone so prominent in the other structures that define the cadet area.

To round out the expansion program, a number of other projects were undertaken beyond the limits of the Plain. Beginning in 1969, Michie Stadium was expanded to an ultimate capacity of 39,929. Keller Army Hospital, a four-story, sixty-five-bed facility, was begun near Washington Gate in July 1974 and completed in November 1977. In the spring of 1983, construction began on a Jewish chapel and on the Holleder Multipurpose Sports Complex, the new home of Army basketball and hockey.

In the two decades following the expansion of the 1960s and 1970s, only two projects of note were undertaken. In 1995, Herbert Hall, the new home of the Association of Graduates, was completed and dedicated. Built on the site of the old ice rink, to the south of Michie Stadium, it is a brick structure in the Tudor-Gothic style—possibly the most handsome single building at West Point. And, in 2001, construction began on the Kimsey Athletic Center, a state-of-the art intercollegiate athletic facility located at the south end of Michie Stadium. Both projects were privately funded, part of a $150 million Association of Graduates bicentennial campaign.

As expeditiously as the construction of facilities would allow, the strength of the corps was incrementally increased to its maximum authorized number of just over 4,400. Beginning with the class that entered the Academy in July 1964, the corps was enlarged by between 200 and 275 cadets per year until the new authorized strength was achieved in 1972.

As the corps grew, so did the need for additional faculty. The Academy sought an increasingly large number of instructors from among the officers who had done their undergraduate work somewhere other than West Point. By 1966, these officers constituted almost one-fourth of the faculty. In time that number reached (and has remained) approximately one-third—on average, more in the humanities and public affairs departments, and less in mathematics, science, and engineering.

Bringing officers to West Point for a teaching assignment was planned well in advance, for by now it typically entailed two years at graduate school prior to the assignment at the Academy. West Point attracted many of the best and brightest officers of the Army, and the mere assignment to the faculty was seen as a mark of approbation. The sudden demand for an increased number of faculty during the expansion occurred just as the Academy was being forced to compete with increasing demands for officers in Vietnam. This compelled the Academy to draw upon a pool of reserve officers who had deferred their two-year active duty commitment in order to attend graduate school. Many of them now had doctorates, and a number were ordered to West Point.

It was a marriage of convenience, but one in which neither party was completely comfortable. On the one hand, the senior faculty often found these short-term officers less deferential and polished than those of the regular establishment. On the other hand, the new officers sometimes resented and resisted the discipline that West Point imposed on them, and they rebelled at the term "non-graduate" that was unthinkingly applied to those who had not graduated from the Military Academy. They quickly resurrected the idea of an "Association of Non-Graduates" and suggested that its journal should be called *Disassembly*, mocking the Association of Graduates' *Assembly*. Still, the Academy profited from the many talents they brought to their assignments.

With the completion of the expansion and the end of the United States' involvement in Vietnam in the early 1970s, the faculty recruiting issue receded. It reemerged in 1991, in response to a published General Accounting Office report that criticized the high proportion of military officers on the faculty—which meant high turnover, a lack of teaching experience, and fewer doctorates. The Academy responded that military instructors provided role models for cadets and that budgetary limits precluded it from sending more officers to graduate school to earn doctorates.[12] Despite Academy resistance, Congress required in 1992 that the number of civilian faculty be increased to 25 percent by 2002.[13] Approximately half of the positions to be civilianized were to come from the permanent military faculty, with the remainder coming from rotating faculty.[14]

There had been civilian faculty at West Point for many years, but they had been largely confined to the Department of Physical Education, the Department of Foreign Languages, and visiting professors. The latter program was begun in 1972 by Colonel Thomas E. Griess, head of the Department of History, and soon spread throughout the academic establishment. By 1999, the number of civilian faculty had reached 21 percent and, due to funding constraints, had stalled there with congressional acquiescence. A larger problem, however, loomed on the horizon. A new officer personnel management system, devised to support the Army's twenty-first-century requirements (OPMS XXI), seemed almost certain to limit opportunities for many officers to attend graduate school and teach at West Point—in fact, it seemed actively to discourage them from seeking such assignments. The Academy was concerned both that the system would hamper recruiting of rotating military faculty and that it "might also deny cadets the opportunity to be taught and mentored by officers from the 'war fighting functions of the Army.'"[15]

In 1968, construction of new housing units for the expanded faculty was begun in the Stony Lonesome area, on the high ground behind Michie Stadium; it was completed two years later. Rising costs, however, forced the Academy to reconsider its original plans. The Superintendent, Major General William A. Knowlton, class of January 1943, chose to scale back the designs in order to build as many units as possible. As had been done repeatedly since World War II, he decided that marginally adequate housing was preferable to none. When the Air Force's housing units at Stewart Air Force Base in nearby Newburgh, New York, were made available to the Academy, a second stage of construction in Stony Lonesome was deferred.

Faculty housing, however, continued to be an issue. In 1979, it topped the list of officers' complaints.[16] With the units at Stewart, there were now sufficient quarters available, but the long and sometimes treacherous commute across Storm King Mountain put a premium on the housing located at West Point itself. And there, the relative inadequacy of the post–World War II quarters made competition for the remaining older sets keen.

In 1978, when the housing office attempted to abandon the old quarters drawing policy and allow newly arriving officers to draw on the basis of family size rather than seniority, a senior major, returning for a second teaching tour, appealed to the Superintendent. After noting how pleased he was to be coming back, he added, "I am a bit perplexed, however, by the new housing assignment policy that seems likely to relegate us to quarters less desirable than those we occupied five years ago. I fear another perquisite of seniority, one both traditional and functional at West Point, has been stripped away."[17] The Superintendent directed a review of the new policy and then ordered revisions that essentially restored the old procedures. "This subject has received a thorough review," the officer was told in reply. "The net result is that you are now at the top of the Majors' list and will have the choice of . . . [available] quarters at West Point."[18]

It was not until the 1990s that more quarters were built. In 1995, Lieutenant General Howard D. Graves, class of 1961, who had become Superintendent in 1991, obtained approval to build 118 new units in Stony Lonesome. A few years later, the shoddily built, postwar "Grey Ghost" structures were razed and replaced with seventy-seven new, larger units. This new construction conformed to the revised Army-wide requirement that 5 percent of new quarters provide access for the handicapped—finally recognizing that able-bodied soldiers could have spouses, children, or dependent parents with disabilities. With the addition of these, the Academy gave up the quarters it had been using at Stewart Field. In 2001, West Point obtained approval to renovate the dreary "new brick" units from the 1960s—enlarging them, rationalizing the floor plans, and providing a much needed face-lift to the exteriors.

In 1974, the Association of Graduates' alumni magazine, *Assembly,* reported that less than a decade before "there were so few blacks at USMA that they were inconspicuous"—not so much because they blended in but because "they were simply overshadowed." That had changed. "Now the black is conspicuous. He is 161-strong. He holds more rank. He's a varsity team captain. He's involved in every aspect of cadet life."[19]

During the four decades after Charles Young graduated in 1889, only two black cadets had entered the Academy.[20] Each stayed for less than six months. In 1932, however, another young black man arrived at West Point, Benjamin Oliver Davis, Jr., the son of Brigadier General Benjamin O. Davis, the Army's first black general. An excellent student, he had spent a year at Western Reserve University and two at the University of Chicago before his father could convince Congressman Oscar DePriest of Illinois to nominate him to West Point.

Even in the 1930s, however, Davis's experiences were not remarkably different than those of Henry Flipper, the Academy's first black graduate more than a half century earlier. The corps was still openly hostile, and the social ostracism that had prevailed in the nineteenth century continued. Davis was essentially "silenced" for the full four years he was at West Point. "It is true," he wrote, "that at the end of plebe year, at the recognition ceremony at Company M, large numbers of upperclass cadets from all over the corps came up to me, recognized me, and congratulated me. But after that I reverted to my status as an invisible man." Davis recalled the kind words of a couple of fellow plebes and a yearling early in Beast Barracks. They were, he said, "some of the few kind words ever spoken to me at West Point." Davis coped with his isolation by making no effort to fight it. He made no friends at West Point. He was never invited to an officer's home. And, despite numerous trips to visit him at West Point, the woman he would marry never met another cadet.[21]

Davis graduated in 1936, thirty-fifth in a class of 276, and ultimately joined the Air Corps and then the U.S. Air Force. In 1965, he became the first black to attain the rank of lieutenant general in the military service of the United States. In 1999, Davis, who had retired in 1970, was promoted once more—giving him the fourth star that many felt had been denied because of his race during his active career.

James D. Fowler followed Davis to West Point in 1937. He, too, was silenced. One white cadet was forced out of the corps by his classmates because of a rumor that he had "recognized" Fowler. But, like Davis, Fowler persevered and graduated in 1941.[22] From 1932 to 1947, twenty-one black cadets were admitted to the Academy, and seventeen graduated. However, they continued to be badly treated by the other cadets.

Beginning in 1948, however, the black experience at West Point began to change. For one thing, there were now African-American cadets in every incoming class after that year; for another, the Army itself had been ordered to integrate.[23] The result was some lessening of the open hostility that had characterized the black experience in earlier years, although racist attitudes persisted among many of the white cadets.

With the rise of the civil rights movement, the 1960s and 1970s witnessed the most significant changes yet. And, as incidents of overt racism and discrimination began to wane, the number of black cadets began slowly to grow. Among these young men were two sons of James D. Fowler, class of 1941: James D. Fowler, Jr., class of 1967, and David L. Fowler, class of 1974. Their arrival at West Point, although largely unheralded, said much about the progress that had been made.

Still, as late as 1968, there were only thirty blacks at the Military Academy. That year, however, a black officer was assigned to the admissions office and charged with the responsibility of identifying and attracting minority men who possessed the requisite intellectual and physical qualifications. Almost immediately, the number of black cadets began to increase.[24] By the end of 1971, there were almost one hundred. At the same time, other minority groups—Hispanics, Asians, and Native Americans—began to score important gains. In 1971, minorities as a group accounted for only about 5 percent of all admissions, but that number was growing. By 1990, they accounted for almost 15 percent, and by 2001, minorities accounted for almost 23 percent of total admissions. Equally as important, during the 1970s and 1980s, black officers increased in number on the staff and faculty of the Academy, and in 1987, Brigadier General Fred A. Gorden, class of 1962, became the first black Commandant of Cadets. By 1999, 4 percent of the faculty were African-Americans—a rate that compared favorably with other major universities but was just half that in the cadet population.[25]

While blacks and other minorities were making strides at the Military Academy, another group was entirely excluded. Allowing women to attend West Point was simply a notion that had never seemed to deserve serious consideration. The *Howitzer* staff in 1900 had depicted an unlikely-looking female cadet of the year 2000—with the traditional tar bucket hat and tight-fitting, high-collared gray tunic, but with a bustle and high-buttoned shoes. In 1964, Elvin R. "Vald" Heiberg, Professor of Mechanics, also took a tongue-in-cheek look ahead to the year 2000. He found the female element of the corps billeted in isolation on Constitution Island. Heiberg's "trimly-clad, glamorous young ladies in gray skirts, blouses, and berets" were known as the "Codettes." His year 2000 corps was divided into three separate brigades: engineering and science majors, public affairs majors, and physical education majors. The "Codettes" were members of the physical education brigade: they provided the Rabble Rousers (the cheerleading squad) and "lovely-to-look-at" women's teams that were nicknamed the "Black Knighties."[26]

But even as Heiberg was writing, American women were growing more vocal in their demands for equality. Soon such citadels of masculinity as Yale and Princeton were opening their doors to women, and the service academies were warned that, in refusing to admit women, they were opposing the inevitable.

In 1973, Congressman Pierre DuPont of Delaware introduced a bill in the House of Representatives designed to permit the admission of women to the service academies. Hearings on the bill began before the House Military Personnel Subcommittee the following spring. Secretary of the Army Martin R. Hoffmann and Superintendent William Knowlton testified against the bill. Their opposition was based primarily on two points. First, they said, the Academy's mission was to train combat leaders. Because the American public would never accept women in combat leadership roles and because only a limited number of cadets could be accommodated at the Military Academy, the available appointments should be reserved for men. Second, they argued, women would not be able to meet West Point's rigorous, demanding, highly disciplined training standards, either physically or emotionally, and their admission would lower standards and weaken discipline.

Those supporting the bill made a simple rebuttal: the academies were no longer educating just combat leaders. In the branch drawings, cadets were regularly allowed to choose an assignment to military intelligence, adjutant general, chemical, military police, medical service corps, ordnance, quartermaster, or transportation—as well as infantry, armor, artillery, engineer, and signal. In fact, the lower reaches of the classes were regularly "ranked" into the combat arms just to fill the minimum quotas. In reality, they argued, the Academy was educating young men to be career military officers, not just combat leaders, and on that basis there was no rationale for discriminating against women. Furthermore, the proponents of the bill pointed out, women were already being admitted to the Merchant Marine Academy, and applications from women were being accepted by the Coast Guard Academy.

In May 1975, the House of Representatives passed—by better than a three-to-one margin—a bill mandating the admission of women to the nation's service academies. The Military Academy began immediately to plan for their arrival in 1976. Senate approval came in June, and President Gerald Ford signed the legislation into law in October. Knowlton's successor, Major General Sidney B. Berry, class of 1948, launched a series of studies to establish standards and procedures for everything from the folding of brassieres to dealing with menstrual periods in the field. Berry reserved to himself the approval of any policy that would establish different standards for women. Should female cadets be permitted to wear makeup or perfume? Yes, he said, but in "tasteful" moderation. Boxing and wrestling had long been mandatory physical education courses. Should female cadets be required to take them? No, because of possible breast injuries. Instead, they would take a two-semester course in the martial arts.[27] In November the Academy's plans were submitted to the Department of the Army and approved.

"I think it is a disgrace for women to be here," remarked one male cadet, echoing the feeling of the majority of cadets—and the majority of alumni. In an effort to lessen the hostility, Berry, Dean Frederick A. Smith, Jr., and Commandant Walter F. Ulmer, Jr.—West Point's three generals—met with large groups of the cadets in question-and-answer sessions that instantly became known as "Stump the Stars." Although the questions were often ludicrous, even taunting, the generals tried to respond in reasoned tones. But sometimes reason was not enough. Once, after Berry had explained that women would be allowed to wear their hair to the collar, a cadet asked why, if they were going to have the same standards for everyone, he could not do the same. Before Berry could answer, Ulmer jumped up and shouted, "Because I say so!" The cadets applauded the Commandant's frank outburst, but these sessions did little to change cadet attitudes. "I feel it is my duty to the alumni and the entire Army," wrote one cadet, "to run out as many females as possible."[28]

In June 1976, the first female cadets were admitted to the United States Military Academy.[29] As soon as the bill authorizing women to attend the service academies had become law, the admissions office had sent letters to thousands of high school counselors, to hundreds of women who had applied for ROTC scholarships, and to others who had been identified in a student search conducted through a College Entrance Examination Board program. Six hundred thirty-one women were among the 6,761 candidates ultimately nominated and examined for the class of 1980.[30] Of these, 176 were found qualified, 148 were offered admission, and 116 became members of the class of 1980.

In cadet basic training—as the plebe summer had come to be called—these women were fully integrated into the new cadet organizational structure. After the summer training, groups of eight to ten women were assigned to twelve of the thirty-six cadet companies. By late the following year, as modifications to all the barracks were completed, and as the number of women increased, they were assigned to all thirty-six cadet companies. From the beginning, they were housed in rooms on the same corridors with their male counterparts—and none of the doors had locks, although that changed a few years later.

Academy officials hoped that the presence of women in each of the cadet companies would remove some of the stereotypical attitudes many males held toward the female cadets, but they were disappointed. "Male cadets continued to be more influenced by the attitudes of their male peers, cadet leaders, and officers than by the presence of women," the Academy reported.[31] The class of 1979—which reveled in the dubious distinction of being the last all-male class—was the most chauvinistic of all. It was not until after this class had graduated that the attitudes of male cadets began to shift. "We had imagined West Point to be this potentially wonderful experience with superior people who were models of society," wrote Carol Barkalow, class of 1980, the first graduating class with women, "but the harassment and chauvinism we encountered on a daily basis were demoralizing."[32]

Women's teams, at the club level, were organized immediately in a number of sports, and in some sports women successfully competed on men's club teams. The women, however, fielded a varsity basketball team, known formally as the Lady Knights, not the "Black Knighties" as Heiberg had predicted. The team was almost immediately nicknamed the "Sugar Smacks"; plebes were sometimes called "smacks," and this was an all-plebe team. The team closed its first season with a strong record, winning eighteen games and losing only five. Its first intercollegiate contest had been against Skidmore, which it defeated handily, 73 to 48. The Skidmore coach said afterward that it was a culture shock for her team to play Army's "group of Amazons." The Skidmore captain said, "Gee, they're rough!"[33] Barkalow agreed: "It was true—we played like brutes."[34] The team's classmates loved it, however, and packed the stands for each game. It was the first broad stamp of approval the women had received. In 1978, the Academy fielded nine women's intercollegiate teams—basketball, cross country, gymnastics, softball, swimming, tennis, indoor track, outdoor track, and volleyball—and all nine turned in winning seasons.

Due to the senior-subordinate nature of the fourth-class system, the Academy established a nonfraternization policy that prohibited upperclassmen (male or female) from dating or socializing with plebes, although there is ample evidence to show that this prohibition was often ignored.[35] Dating among cadets of the upper classes or among cadets of the fourth class was permitted. However, dating someone after having shared a soggy foxhole did not have universal appeal. "I think it's a lonely world for these girls while they are here," said Mrs. Caroline Gaspard, the Cadet Hostess, "because they do want to be accepted as 'just one of the guys,' but they want to feel attractive, too. Before a dance the boys will ask me, 'When are the girls coming up?' And I'll say, 'dance with your classmates.' And they'll say, 'Oh, them. We see them all the time.'"[36]

West Point, of course, drew up regulations to govern this male-female behavior that read a lot like the Hays Office Movie Codes of the 1930s. When a man and a woman were in a room together, the door had to be left open; at

West Point's "Sugar Smacks" vs. Skidmore, 1976. This was the first game of the new women's basketball program at the Academy. All of the members of the West Point team were plebes. United States Military Academy Archives.

least one tactical officer used masking tape to mark just how far. If they were sitting on a bed together, each of them had to keep at least one foot resting on the floor. And there were more.[37]

When cadets ran afoul of these rules, the Academy dealt with them in the same straight-faced manner with which it handled all infractions. One report cited a male cadet for having a female cadet in his room (with the door closed) and in his bed—engaged in acts of affection prejudicial to discipline and good order in the corps. His partner in the escapade was not identified. The next item on the same "gig-sheet," however, was the report of a female cadet who had been caught in the room of a male cadet (with the door closed) and in his bed—likewise engaged in acts of affection prejudicial to discipline and good order in the corps. Her partner was not identified either, but the juxtaposition of these reports was suggestive. The two cadets' indiscretion netted them demerits, confinement, and long hours "on the area."[38]

In January 1994, the General Accounting Office produced a report that criticized the service academies for significant instances of sexual harassment.[39] General Graves responded that "the GAO report significantly over-states the magnitude of the sexual harassment problem [and] completely fails to recognize the success of efforts to produce a climate which affords men and women the opportunity to realize their full potential to develop as leaders of character."[40] That fall, during a spirit run in which cadets sprinted past a cordon of football players, three members of the team groped the breasts of a number of women cadets. Both female and male cadets reported the affair through cadet and officer channels, and the Academy reacted swiftly. The three team members were punished by being restricted for the balance of the season. The Superintendent briefed the press shortly after the incident. There was an immediate flood of media interest, but a *New York Times* editorial opined that the Academy had moved "quickly, decisively and wisely."[41]

Both women and minorities could look with pride at their accomplishments. They had led the corps at every level—from squad leader to cadet first captain—and they had produced scholars of note and All-American athletes. At every echelon they had earned their places within the corps. By 1991, over a thousand women and over a thousand black cadets had graduated from the Military Academy. And in the next decade, both groups made further progress. Still, the Academy reflected many of the biases of the society it served, and both women and minorities could point to barriers that sometimes prevented their full participation in and enjoyment of the cadet experience at West Point.

As dramatic as the arrival of women at West Point was in the summer of 1976, it was nearly overshadowed by an honor crisis that had begun a few months earlier. This incident plunged the Academy into an agonizing period of analysis and reevaluation, both internal and external.

The tipoff was a statement acknowledging unauthorized assistance, jotted at the end of a cadet's solution to a graded take-home assignment in an electrical engineering course. "This computer project does not represent all my own work. Due to the fact that I was unable to complete it on my own I received help towards its completion. I am stating this so as to avoid an unfair advantage over my classmates," the cadet wrote.[42] Written instructions issued with the assignment had specifically stated that collaboration was not permitted on that particular problem, although it was permitted on two other problems on the same assignment and had been allowed, even encouraged, on earlier homework assignments.[43]

The course, Electrical Engineering 304 (EE304)—"Electronics," known to cadets as "juice"—was required of all second classmen, but it was unpopular.[44] It was widely viewed by the cadets as one of the most difficult courses in the core curriculum. The department knew of the cadet attitude toward the course and made allowances, of which collaboration on homework assignments was one example. Unfortunately, as the investigations revealed, to some cadets collaboration had come to mean simply copying the homework of brighter or more industrious cadets. By the time of the assignment in question, the habit of collaboration in this course had become widespread.[45]

A quick check by instructors of the work turned in for this assignment uncovered similarities, such as the same misspelled words and duplicate computation errors, on a number of papers. The department then compared all the papers, checking in detail the papers of cadets assigned to the same companies. When that was completed, the electrical engineering department forwarded the papers of 117 cadets suspected of cheating to the cadet honor committee for investigation. On April 12, 1976, 102 of the 117 cases were placed before the full honor board. Fifty of these were found to have violated the honor code. Two cadets immediately resigned, but the remaining 48 requested that their cases be heard before a board of officers.[46]

The EE304 scandal involved even more cadets than had the 1951 affair, although, unlike the earlier case, this was not the product of an organized ring. Rather, those who collaborated did so in small groups ranging from roommates to small circles of classmates and friends. On April 7, even before the preliminary investigations were completed, the press carried its first stories on the alleged cheating—stories prompted by a cadet who called the *New York Times* with the message: "I don't cheat. Why should they?"

On May 3, the military counsels representing the accused cadets wrote to Secretary of the Army Hoffmann charging that upwards of 300 cadets were implicated by sworn affidavits—including members of the honor committee and captains of several athletic teams. They requested the convening of an external board of inquiry.[47] Superintendent Berry endorsed their request, indicating that an independent board of inquiry might be useful. Although the request for a review board was denied at this time, Berry did direct a second review of all 821 EE304 papers. This effort identified another 150 collaborators. Eighteen of these cadets resigned, and another 102 were found guilty by an officer board that had supplanted the honor committee during the course of the continuing investigation. In the end, a total of 152 cadets either resigned or were otherwise separated from the Academy in connection with the scandal.

Even as the scope of the affair was unfolding, Berry drafted the most compelling statement made about contributing causes of the affair: "My basic assumption is pessimistic: That the EE304 cheating episode is more than simply an isolated instance and is a reflection of a more endemic set of conditions, developments and circumstances affecting the Honor Code and supporting Honor System at West Point." It was, he concluded, the result both of a "shift of values in American society" and of "structural changes at West Point which have made it increasingly difficult to grapple with these value shifts." He spoke of changes within American society in the 1960s and 1970s—a shift from group to individual values, from moral absolutes to situation ethics, of legalistic solutions that substitute for moral and duty imperatives, of an increase in the general level of cynicism about institutions and the people who run them, and of the erosion of the commitment to any permanent values or traditional standards. "Nothing," said Berry, "is absolute; everything is relative."[48]

A study in 1966 had warned about the need "of keeping the Academy properly in tune with the changing viewpoints of youth." It warned of "the rapid and revolutionary advances in science and technology and to equally rapid and revolutionary social and political changes." The problem "might even arise in regard to such basics as the Honor System, the motivational receptivity of the future cadet, or in the esteem with which the motto 'Duty, Honor, Country' is held," the report had warned.[49]

Berry concluded in 1976 that the Military Academy had inadequately addressed these issues, and he listed some of the structural changes at West Point that had exacerbated the problem. The first was the expansion of the corps from 2,529 to 4,417 cadets. "The turbulent decade from 1964 to 1973," wrote Berry, "may have been the worst possible time to increase significantly and rapidly the size of the Corps of Cadets." But other changes had disrupted the old norms, and their impact had not yet been absorbed or fully worked out: the admission of significantly larger numbers of minorities (and soon women), who increased the diversity of the corps; increased supervisory and administrative responsibilities for cadets that aggravated the overload problem; the abolition of compulsory chapel; even the design of the new barracks (whose horizontal lines dictated many rooms along long corridors instead of a few rooms on each floor in traditional vertical "divisions") had blurred old lines of community. "The environment of West Point changed," he wrote, "from the homogeneous intimacy of a small town toward the diversified impersonality of a city." Berry was not being critical of these changes (with the possible exception of the timing of the expansion) but merely pointing out that the Academy had not yet accommodated itself to them.[50] He believed they helped explain how, as would soon be revealed, some cadets had become "cool on honor."

All the while, pressure on the Academy and on the Secretary of the Army continued to build. One cadet who had been implicated filed a suit in U.S. District Court in early June, seeking an injunction against the enforcement of the honor code and system. Although that injunction was denied, seven other similar suits were filed in the civil and military appeals courts. On Capitol Hill, Senator Sam Nunn of Georgia announced that his Senate Armed Services subcommittee would hold hearings on the service academies, and Representative Thomas J. Downey of New York convened an "informal public forum" to discuss the honor issue. A total of 173 congressmen joined to ask Secretary of the Army Hoffmann to intervene, stating their belief that "punishment should be something short of expulsion from the Academy."[51]

By August, the issue was no longer "How would the crisis be resolved?" but "Who would resolve it?" Secretary Hoffmann settled both issues on August 23 when he testified before Nunn's subcommittee. First, he revealed that a special commission on the Academy would be empowered to make an in-depth assessment of the honor situation and its underlying causes. Second, bowing to pressure from Congress, he announced that the cadets involved in the EE304 affair who had resigned or been found guilty of honor violations and expelled would be eligible for readmission the next year, and the affair would be expunged from their records. For those who had left the Academy and did not wish to return, the active duty service normally demanded of first and second classmen who leave West Point would be waived.

The Secretary's Committee on the United States Military Academy was appointed on September 9. Former astronaut Frank Borman, a member of the class of 1950, headed the group, which soon became known as the Borman Commission. The commission swiftly set up offices in the Academy's library, where its members sifted through the mountain of materials generated in the earlier investigations and interviewed hundreds of officers and cadets. After several months of intensive work, the commission released its report. There was, it said, a degree of disaffection with the honor code in the corps that bordered on contempt: "cool on honor" was the cadet expression. Further, it had heard allegations of corruption in the honor committee—one cadet, for example, supposedly had been acquitted eight times of various honor violations, always protected by friends on the committee who could stymie action with a single vote. Although West Point's leadership had been aware of major inadequacies in the honor system, the report alleged, "no decisive action was taken."

In January 1977, Hoffmann directed that the Academy's regulations be changed to read that a "cadet who violates the Cadet Honor Code shall normally be separated from the Military Academy"—adding the word "normally" and giving the Superintendent greater latitude in his dealings with honor cases.[52] Of the 152 cadets who had left West Point as a result of the EE304 affair, 148 were found eligible for readmission. Of these, 105 completed their applications and were offered readmission. In June 1977, 98 actually reentered the Academy—most as first classmen in the class of 1978. As penance they had lost a year's seniority on their former classmates.

The EE304 incident demonstrated how dire the consequences of a failure of honor could be, and it called attention once again to the honor issue. In the years that followed the scandal, a number of procedural changes were made to the honor system, but little was done to solve the problem most often identified by cadets—the use of honor to enforce regulations. In 1988, Wesley W. Posvar, class of 1946 and president of the University of Pittsburgh, was asked to head an outside examination of the honor system. The Posvar panel praised the honor code, saying it "represents a standard of ethical behavior that functions effectively for cadets, to which all American professionals can aspire, and which all citizens should appreciate as a national asset." Still, the panel charged the Academy with trivializing the code—a charge that echoed many earlier studies—by intermingling honor and regulations. It argued that matters such as rapid-fire, or "pop-off," answers, bed stuffing, or the hiding of articles in a laundry bag ought not to be elevated to the status of breaches of personal integrity. "The serious issue," it reported, "is that such misuse of the System has been a repeated source of antagonism, misunderstanding, grievous injustice to cadets, and harm to the repute and regard for the honor code itself."[53]

Most of the Posvar Commission's recommendations were adopted, and many of these changes were designed to disentangle honor and the enforcement of regulations. For one thing, a new question-and-answer policy was established that allowed cadets to correct or amend unthinking responses. For another, the use of the "absence card" was eliminated. In one form or another the absence card had existed since the nineteenth century. At first, it was a heavy paper card—hence the name. Later it took on other forms, including one device with slides that could be moved from "marked" to "unmarked." Each cadet's "card" was located near the door and was used during those hours when cadets were required to be in their rooms. "Marking" the card upon leaving the room indicated that the cadet was authorized to be absent and was within the prescribed territorial limits. To "mark" the card and then violate limits was interpreted as an honor violation—for which one could be dismissed. Cadets had long complained that the absence card unfairly used honor to enforce regulations.[54]

In 1977, the Superintendent was given some discretion in dismissing cadets for honor violations. In 1992, the Secretary of the Army provided specific guidance on the issue, directing the Superintendent to evaluate honor cases using the following criteria: intent, manner reported, resolve to live honorably, severity of the violation, and unusual duress at the time of the violation. Cadets receiving discretion were generally either turned back an entire class year, or their graduation was delayed. In some cases, cadets would be sent to the Army, where they would serve as enlisted soldiers in a "line" unit under a commanding officer who would act as a mentor and then make a recommendation regarding their readmission.[55]

Beginning in the early 1970s, the honor system grew increasingly legalistic, a response, for the most part, to concerns about individuals' rights to due process. By the 1990s, the Staff Judge Advocate reviewed honor cases and advised the Commandant on them even before they were scheduled for an honor hearing. If a hearing was scheduled, it was run jointly by the cadet board president and a hearing officer from the Judge Advocate's office. As a 2000 White Paper tried to explain, a "critical balance" had to "be struck between time-honored principles and the need to adapt certain procedural aspects to meet the demands of changing conditions."[56] Finding a cadet in violation of the honor code was made easier by requiring a vote of only six of the nine members of the board, and the standard of proof was "more likely than not" for each element of the allegation. Making that finding stick was another issue.

Many both in and out of uniform feared that the EE304 scandal had shaken the nation's confidence in West Point. In the years just preceding the incident, critics in the press and in Congress multiplied, paralleling the growth of a troublesome, strongly antimilitary sentiment, which had become widespread beginning in 1968 as the war in Southeast Asia dragged on with mounting casualties and no end in sight. This had already resulted in increasing intrusion into the governance of the Academy—by the Congress, the courts, and the Department of the Army.

Those intrusions began in the late 1960s when Congress started to press for increased minority recruiting. In the early 1970s, it was the courts. Three cadets dismissed for "deficiencies in their military conduct" obtained help from the American Civil Liberties Union in securing an injunction against the Academy in 1972, arguing that the procedures employed to dismiss them had violated their right to due process.

The year 1973 was a particularly difficult one. It was a year in which the Supreme Court ruled that requiring attendance at chapel violated the cadets' constitutional right to religious freedom. This year also saw the "silencing" of Cadet James Pelosi, which subjected the Military Academy to an unwelcome barrage of criticism, and Simon and Schuster's publication of *West Point, America's Power Fraternity*, by K. Bruce Galloway and Robert B. Johnson, Jr.—the most scathing critique of West Point since Partridge's attack in 1830 and, like Partridge's work, so bitter in tone that many dismissed it.

The year 1973 also brought two major outside reviews of the Academy. The growing attention focused on West Point by the Congress, the courts, and the media prompted increased scrutiny by both the Department of the Army and the Department of Defense. In December 1973, Deputy Secretary of Defense William P. Clements established the Committee on Excellence in Education, whose membership included the service secretaries. It was tasked to investigate the programs of the various service schools, including the service academies. A more comprehensive study of the service academies by the General Accounting Office was also begun in 1973 and entailed a much more critical review of Academy programs than the Clements Committee. This study focused on three issues—attrition, curriculum, and financial management—that provided a rationale for probing into virtually all facets of the academic environment.[57]

And, in 1973, the football team lost its first nine games and then lost to Navy—a record season with no wins and ten losses. It was indeed a bad year for West Point.

The EE304 crisis, just three years later, refocused attention on the Academy. Secretary of the Army Hoffmann spent much of his time during the spring and summer of 1976 trying to diagnose and remedy the problems that had come to light in the wake of that scandal.

The findings of the Borman Commission, issued in December 1976, seemed to suggest that the foundations on which the Academy stood had been badly undermined. "The Academy," the commission wrote, "must now acknowledge the causes of the breakdown and devote its full energies to rebuilding an improved and strengthened institution."[58] It highlighted criticism it had heard from the junior members of the faculty that the Academic Board was "unduly resistant to change" and that some board members had "stacked arms" and were no longer effective.[59] This may have been true in isolated cases, but on what basis had Borman and his colleagues evaluated the testimony? Without even interviewing the members of the Academic Board they attacked, the commission's members recommended that the authority of the Superintendent be redefined: "The Superintendent should have responsibility for all aspects of the internal administration of the academy," and the permanent professors should be forced to retire after thirty years of active service "unless requested to continue on a term basis by the Superintendent."[60] The professors were incensed and offended. "I have been insulted personally, as has the Corps of Professors and the Academic Board as corporate bodies," wrote one professor to Borman.[61]

Theodore Ropp, Visiting Professor of Military History, sent a strongly worded critique of the attack on the Academy's professors to his Duke colleague A. Kenneth Pye, a member of the commission. He took "strong exception," he said, to the recommendation that would "place all of our [the Academy's] permanent professors on conditional tenure after thirty years of active service." This would cause "educational discontinuities," he argued, "in a situation in which you . . . [need] greater continuity. If academic matters are to have those higher priorities suggested by your recommendations, . . . a proposal to put the tenure of your most experienced people at the mercy of the Superintendent seems wholly counterproductive."[62]

Secretary of the Army Hoffmann and Army Chief of Staff Bernard W. Rogers (the former Commandant of Cadets) were under pressure from the Academy's friends everywhere to protect the institution—to save it from itself, if necessary. Rogers immediately appointed a special action group drawn largely from the Army staff to respond to the commission's recommendations. That group went even further than the Borman Commission, recommending that the authority of the Superintendent be significantly increased at the expense of the Academic Board.[63]

"The scope and pace of these changes are unprecedented," the department heads protested. "Those initiatives which derogate the role of the academic board to matters purely academic, greatly reducing its influence over related aspects of the USMA program, are bound to lead to a progressive weakening of the cadet's education." The proposed changes were certain "to have the most adverse long run consequences." Although there had been some "slippage in the priority accorded to academic excellence," the professors blamed "a continual temptation" to pursue "more tangible short-term goals—a better athletic record, lower costs, lower attrition, [or] more technically qualified 2d lieutenants." Even so, attacking the Academic Board was not the solution, they argued: "If one agrees that academic excellence must be restored to first priority, it would seem appropriate to strengthen the voice of those elements of the organization with responsibility for and commitment to academic excellence. Yet the changes contemplated are in the opposite direction."[64]

The Academic Board objected to the "composition of the [Army staff] committee and the tone of its charter" and asserted that "the primacy of education" had never "been fully understood" by the Army staff. "This raises the issue of the extent to which USMA will govern its affairs and to what extent it will be governed by direction from Washington." Congress, the Department of Defense, and the Department of the Army all had the prerogative to establish rules of operation for the Academy, the board acknowledged, but, it argued, there must be "a willingness to permit the institution to govern itself in a mode comparable to that which occurs in any reputable institution of higher learning." This included "the teacher in the classroom in his exercise of academic freedom" and "the Academic Board in deciding questions such as design of the curriculum."[65]

Chief of Staff Rogers then appointed three new study committees, known collectively as the West Point Study Group, to conduct an even more intensive examination of the Academy: a military professional development committee, an academic committee, and an environment committee. The Academic Board's fears were hardly diminished by the focus of this new group. Thomas E. Griess, Professor of History, was the senior member of an Academy group providing liaison to the study group's academic committee. After the first meeting of that committee, he told his West Point colleagues, "It became clear to me that the authority and role of the Academic Board will be a major area of study." Griess warned that "the questions asked in the briefings reflected some skepticism about the functions of the Academic Board" and that at least two of the consultants to the board had "observed that the Board may be the major problem in the institution's ability to govern itself and accomplish reforms."[66]

Charles H. Schilling, class of 1941, who had succeeded Vincent Esposito and was now the professor of engineering, argued strongly for an Academic Board arrangement that would provide sufficient checks and balances to "preserve the stability required in an academic institution." He stressed that an individual Superintendent "should not be able to completely scrap an existing or initiate a new curriculum or policy based upon his own personal decision." Still, Schilling cautioned his colleagues against seeking "an exact 'status quo.'"[67]

He pointed particularly to the increased number of permanent faculty—both the "not Head" professors and the new permanent associate professors. The development of the elective program begun in 1960 under Davidson and the growth in the number of courses offered as electives that followed carried with them the requirement for more permanent faculty. As a result, in 1963 the Academy began to appoint permanent associate professors who would serve the balance of their thirty-year army careers at West Point. This program soon doubled and then tripled the size of the "tenured" faculty.[68]

These officers had both "considerable service and talent," Schilling noted. In the past, the Academic Board had been collectively the memory of the Academy; now, he pointed out, "*all* tenured people comprise that body of institutional knowledge." Then he cautioned the board that these other tenured members would soon want a voice in the governance of the institution. "Those who cannot input to or influence the decision making body are prone to call that body 'obstructionist.'"[69] But Schilling's warning came too late; the frank views of a number of such tenured individuals (and other nontenured instructors) had already biased the Borman Commission and the committees of the West Point Study Group against the Academic Board. The study group was particularly susceptible to such views; seven of the nine members of its academic committee had once been voiceless faculty at West Point and shared many of their convictions.

Meanwhile, on February 15, 1977, Superintendent Berry had convened his own internal study group to examine the Academy's governance structure and submit recommendations regarding the Academic Board's authority. From that point forward, governance became a continuing topic of discussion both at the Academy and within the West Point Study Group.[70] The group noted the charge of obstructionism but argued that "a more reasonable assessment" of the operation of the Academic Board "is that it is conservative" and that "there are compelling reasons for its conservatism." The Academic Board, the study group argued, was "firmly rooted in the history of the Military Academy." It ensured stability. "Without the bulwark of the Academic Board," the report suggested, "each Superintendent could redesign the curriculum as he chose."[71]

Berry's internal study group submitted its recommendations in early June. "Any institutional governance proposal," it noted, "must grapple with one central fact: West Point's governance is essentially a collegial decision-making process imbedded in a military hierarchial authority structure." The study group acknowledged the recent criticism of the Academic Board but rejected the "radical surgery" approach. In fact, it suggested that the Academic Board, "more than any other group or individual," deserved credit for bringing the Academy through "the turbulent late sixties and early seventies." As to the EE304 scandal, the group accepted Berry's analysis of the year before: developments in the honor system, the leadership evaluation system, the conduct system, and the incursion upon cadet time by activities over which the Academic Board had no control had caused the problem. These factors "fostered an impression that academic pursuits and academic excellence were secondary to other concerns, and in turn, contributed to the EE304 situation."[72]

In opposing a strengthening of the superintendency at the expense of the Academic Board, the internal study group quoted Thayer's 1865 advice:

Nor can the desired work [of curriculum reform] be done by the Superintendent alone for reasons too obvious to need pointing out, but, granting it could be done by him, the work would not be likely to endure[;] every new Superintendent would wish to ride his own hobby, not that of his predecessor. Besides, there could scarcely fail to result a deplorable antagonism between the Superintendent and Professors. The programs once fixed in the best manner should not be changed to suit the whims of anybody. Better to 'leave well enough alone' than to try hazardous experiments.[73]

In the end, however, the internal study group acknowledged the realities of the situation: the Army staff and the West Point Study Group had already concluded that radical surgery was necessary. Moreover, the internal group agreed with Schilling's suggestion that "a Superintendent or a Commandant or a Chief of Staff would feel most comfortable operating in an environment that is similar to that of the military command structure from which he has just come." Traditional checks and balances and the sanctity of the collegial decision-making process were surrendered as the internal study group recommended to Berry a new structure in which "board decisions would be clearly advisory and could be overturned at any time by the Superintendent."[74] Berry departed, however, before any substantive action could be taken on the report.

In Washington, Bernard Rogers had already become convinced that dramatic action was necessary. Also convinced that the power of the Superintendent must be increased (and the power of the Academic Board decreased) was General Andrew Jackson Goodpaster, class of 1939, who had been an early consultant to the West Point Study Group. Many West Point graduates whose association with the Academy had been limited to their cadet days or to a brief tour as instructor or tactical officer also believed that the Academic Board had played too dominant and too conservative a role. Their number included former Superintendents and former Commandants such as Rogers. In their view, the board seemed only to obstruct change. Few appreciated the importance of the board's stabilizing role in a military institution whose leadership was, by its very nature, autocratic and ever-changing. In resisting the sometimes overzealous Superintendents (and an occasional overzealous colleague), the Academic Board had generally preserved stability and ensured continuity. Still, over the years, it had gradually yielded ground to reasoned and measured change. Unmindful of this, the outsiders who dominated the West Point Study Group and the Army hierarchy were determined to reduce the power of the Academic Board. General Goodpaster shared the outsiders' view that the influence of the Academic Board over affairs at West Point was too extensive.[75]

Goodpaster was one of the Army's foremost elder statesmen. He had retired in 1974 after five years as the Supreme Allied Commander of NATO's forces in Europe but had remained active in Washington affairs. At Rogers's urging, he agreed to return to active duty and accept the post at West Point, although this meant giving up one star and reverting, for the time being, to the three-star rank of lieutenant general. In the Chief of Staff's view, Goodpaster was the one man who could revitalize the Academy at West Point, and he was given free rein to do so. Goodpaster succeeded Sidney Berry in June 1977.

In July, after nearly seven months of investigation and analysis, the West Point Study Group's final report was completed and given to Rogers. He forwarded it to Goodpaster, saying only that the new Superintendent should take whatever action on its recommendations he deemed appropriate.[76] Goodpaster, however, was in substantial agreement with the report and most of its recommendations. "From this day forward," he replied, "we will make the Report our own."[77]

Goodpaster established a number of new committees to address the study group's recommendations.[78] One of the most important of these was the governance committee, whose first task was to review the recent recommendations in this area. The Borman Commission had charged the Military Academy's top officials and senior faculty members with failure to remain abreast of changing values and attitudes, not only among cadets but also among junior faculty.[79] The West Point Study Group had recommended a major restructuring of the Academy's governance. It was essential, they believed, to alter the power relationships at the Academy—in effect, to increase the power of the Superintendent in relation to the Academic Board. Even Berry's internal study group had agreed, in part at least, with that conclusion.

The new governance committee, after more months of study and argument, recommended changes along lines that had been proposed by the West Point Study Group. Goodpaster approved. Most significant was the creation of the "policy board," which was to be the Superintendent's main source of advice and counsel on all matters having general significance to the Academy. It supplanted the Academic Board in many of the latter's traditional advisory functions. The West Point Study Group had recommended that four tenured faculty members sit on the policy board "to magnify the influence of the faculty in the central governance of the Academy and to increase the emphasis on education," but Goodpaster opted for just two (in addition to the Dean), and the influence of the academic community was further reduced.[80]

"Now, I know there was some mumbling that I was diminishing the role of the Academic Board," Goodpaster recalled. "I never saw it that way. I felt that in the academic area I was really strengthening their role through the process of making it very clear that they would be responsible for giving the academic direction needed at the Military Academy, and they would not be allowed to evade it. They would not be allowed to fail to see what was

Andrew J. Goodpaster was the Superintendent of the United States Military Academy from 1977 to 1981. United States Military Academy Archives.

going on as it happened."[81] Prior to 1977, the regulations applicable to the Academy directed the Academic Board to report its recommendations concerning the curriculum to the Secretary of the Army—sending them *through*, not *to*, the Superintendent. The Superintendent could append any comments he might wish to the board's recommendations, but he could not overrule or block them. This bulwark prevented the Superintendent from redesigning the curriculum by fiat.[82] Under Goodpaster that changed. The primary responsibility of the Academic Board now was to advise the Superintendent on academic matters—narrowly defined. Future curriculum recommendations would be addressed *to* the Superintendent.[83]

The Academic Board realized the full meaning of this change when Goodpaster trotted out the "hobby" he wished to ride. At Princeton, where Goodpaster had completed a master's degree and a doctorate degree, he had become enamored of interdisciplinary courses. When he arrived at West Point in 1977, he suggested and championed such a course—"American Institutions." In fact, he had already sold the West Point Study Group on such a course, and the idea found its way into the group's final curricular recommendations. Though skeptical, the Academic Board could do little but comply. In 1978, the course was offered to one section on a trial basis, and the next year it became a part of the curriculum. To make room for it, the

History Department had to give up one semester of its venerable "History of Military Art." The process was deeply disturbing to many on the board.[84] Shortly after Goodpaster departed, the Academic Board dropped "American Institutions" and restored "History of Military Art" to two semesters.

Quite naturally, the members of the Academic Board took a dim view of the changes in the governance structure and the more restricted role they would now play. In the summer of 1977, five department heads retired: Colonel Elliott C. Cutler, class of 1942, Department of Electrical Engineering; Colonel Donald G. MacWilliams, class of 1944, Department of Chemistry; Colonel Edwin Van V. Sutherland, class of 1936, Department of English; Colonel Walter J. Renfroe, Jr., class of 1934, Department of Foreign Languages; and Colonel Frederick C. Lough, class of 1938, Department of Law. Renfroe and Sutherland had reached mandatory retirement age and would have departed anyway, but that was not the case with Cutler, MacWilliams, and Lough. Never before had so many department heads left in a single year. Upon his departure, Sutherland commended the West Point community on its ability "to put a cheerful countenance in the face of whatever aggravation or adversity." But he warned his colleagues who remained not to allow "our reasoned recognition of West Point's virtues and strengths to be translated into a defensive abatis, turning aside all criticism." Said Sutherland, "Ritual self approval leads to complacency and can end in disaster."[85]

The power of the academic community was further eroded in 1984 when Army Chief of Staff General John A. Wickham instructed Superintendent Willard W. Scott, Jr., class of 1948, who had succeeded Goodpaster, to implement a plan of "faculty development" that seemed intended to undermine the tenure of the permanent professors. Since World War II, professors had served beyond thirty years' active service (to age sixty-four) at the pleasure of the Secretary of the Army, but no one could recall a professor being forced out. The Borman Commission, in 1976, had recommended that permanent professors should be allowed to continue beyond thirty years of service only with the approval of the Superintendent, but that recommendation had never been acted upon.

When Wickham visited West Point in November 1983, he had taken note of the poor turnout of officers—particularly the senior permanent faculty—at the lecture he delivered and saw it as a sign that they had lost touch with the modern Army. The permanent faculty, he told Scott, needed to be "regreened," and he directed that they begin to participate in activities that would enhance their knowledge of the operations of the Army in the field.[86] After some reflection, the Chief of Staff decided that even more needed to be done to ensure that the tenured faculty not be allowed to stagnate or become too isolated. The Army staff worked out the details. In June 1984, Wickham summoned Scott to Washington, where he was briefed on a new procedure to be used in the selection of permanent academic faculty, and for the periodic review of faculty tenure—including the provision for a representative of the Army staff to sit on future selection and review panels that dealt with Professors USMA.[87]

Under Wickham's plan, the permanent faculty would be required to spend one summer of every three (or one year of every seven) with the Army in the field or at army schools. In addition, the performance of senior tenured faculty members would be reviewed upon their reaching thirty years' service and at five-year intervals thereafter. They would be "confirmed in the position or retired" based on the judgment of a review panel made up of the Superintendent, the Army's Deputy Chief of Staff for Personnel, and the director of the Army staff.[88] Scott and the staff at West Point drew up plans to implement Wickham's new directive but deferred development of the "criteria for continuation" for the locally unpopular tenure review process. When they were not pressed on the matter, they prudently let it drop.[89]

Scott left West Point in 1986 and was replaced by Lieutenant General Dave R. Palmer, class of 1956. Palmer was more of a scholar than most of his predecessors. His *River and the Rock* (1969), a history of West Point during the Revolution, was an eminently readable work, and his study of Washington in the Revolution, *Way of the Fox* (1975), although too often neglected by academic historians, is the only analysis of the general's thinking by someone who really understood what the term "strategy" means. Those who looked forward to the arrival of a scholar-educator as Superintendent, however, were disappointed. Palmer turned out to be more a Schofield than a Davidson. The brief interlude in the turmoil at West Point that Scott's superintendency had afforded was soon ended. Palmer represented everything the Academic Board abhorred and feared: a Superintendent who would *command* West Point and run roughshod over the academic staff and the academic program. In fact, in these terms, Palmer largely succeeded where Schofield had failed.[90]

"I came [to West Point] with the belief . . . that this was a military academy and we would follow the military decision-making process," said Palmer. When the members of the Academic Board would not follow willingly where he led, there were difficulties. "A lot of the problems we had and a lot of the friction that we had to work through and a lot of the unhappiness and the bitterness and the misinformation, both inside and outside West Point, came from a fairly small number of people," Palmer recalled. "Well, they were prima donnas. The planning didn't go to suit them so they did their dead-level best to undermine the results." It took him about two years, he said, to "recognize the peculiarity of some people who find themselves at West Point for a long time. There's an arrogance that develops and they begin to believe they have all knowledge. . . . Now that I recognize the problems of communicating at West Point are different, I'm a wiser person. And I would put that wisdom to work and I would have fired a few people earlier rather than tolerate them."[91]

In the beginning, in fact, Palmer did not have an effective mechanism to "fire" members of the Academic Board. But it did not take him long to find one. In the summer of 1987, he resurrected the issue of faculty tenure review. Possibly Wickham brought up the issue when he visited West Point in late May of that year—shortly before his retirement. In any case, Palmer presented his proposal to Wickham's successor as Chief of Staff, General Carl E. Vuono, class of 1957.[92] Under Palmer's plan, the first review—after

Generals Wickham and Palmer. John A. Wickham, Jr., Chief of Staff, United States Army (standing) and Dave R. Palmer, Superintendent of the United States Military Academy, 1986–1991, at the graduation ceremony of the class of 1987, May 27, 1987. United States Military Academy Archives.

thirty years' service—would be made by the Dean and the Superintendent. Thereafter, at five-year intervals, the panel proposed earlier by Wickham (with the addition of the Dean) would determine the fate of the academicians. The criteria for the professors' review of tenure included consistent academic growth and a commitment to academic excellence, an "outstanding manner of performance of military duties," and high standards of military bearing. In addition, the professor must "work constructively with colleagues in routine coordination and on committees and study groups" and "demonstrate a distinctively moral lifestyle characterized by integrity and intellectual honesty." Vuono approved the plan, and after final approval of the Secretary of the Army, the new policy was put into effect in January 1988. The first of the faculty tenure reviews were held early that year.[93] The official outcome of these reviews remains carefully guarded, but colleagues must have wondered at unexpected departures made years ahead of mandatory retirement dates. The professors were incensed by the process, but they had no one to turn to. Some simply awaited their own reviews; for others, it was just one more reason to consider an early departure themselves.[94]

Palmer did not stop there, however. In the fall of 1987, he already had begun a reorganization of the Military Academy staff that would prove a potentially more far-reaching revolution in the governance of the Academy than anything Goodpaster had been able to accomplish. Palmer assembled around himself a coterie of colonels to whom he looked for advice—isolating himself not only from the Academic Board but also, to a degree, from the Dean and the Commandant. "General Palmer had about seven or eight colonels around him that were his principal advisors," noted his successor, Howard Graves, "and they were resented very badly."[95]

The creation of this Superintendent's staff had actually begun under General Goodpaster, with the creation of the Special Assistant to the Superintendent for Plans and Policy in 1977. The title was changed, under Palmer, to the Special Assistant for Strategic Planning. The next step was the creation of the Executive for Academy Initiatives—a new staff element designed to facilitate the implementation of new initiatives. This organization was designed "to overcome normal organization inertia which resists changes to routines"—which meant the inertia and resistance of the Academic Board. To this group was added the Office of Institutional Research, the Director of Academy Relations (Public Affairs), and the Director of Academy Advancement (Alumni Affairs). It was this group and their staffs that Palmer turned to for advice, and it was this group to which he entrusted the implementation of his designs.[96] The Academic Board, which had once reached out to embrace many of the affairs of the Academy that touched on the academic experience, found itself able to influence events only in those few areas prescribed to them by law or regulation. This was not a change to which the board acceded easily.

When Howard Graves replaced Palmer in 1991, he "ran right into the buzz saw." He heard complaints from all sides. "Faculty morale was completely shot," he was told. "You know Palmer did all of this and never asked anybody," others complained. There was the perception, recalled Graves, "that even though he [Palmer] had had these committees, he already knew what he was going to do and the committees were a charade."[97]

Graves's leadership style was different. "There [were] too many common goals and too many interactions for us not to be fully coordinated," he said. "I also needed, in my own opinion, a very close advisory relationship with the Commandant, the Dean, and the Chief of Staff. And I did not want to make decisions without their full participation. Now, that was in contrast with General Palmer's technique."[98] This, however, did not result in any restoration of the power of the Academic Board. The well-meaning Graves was as distant from the academic staff as Palmer ever had been. One long-time department head recalled seeing Graves at the post exchange just before the latter finished his tour at West Point: "We were both in civilian clothes. I stood just behind him in the check-out line. He said 'hello' to me, but he didn't recognize me. He had no idea who I was."[99] The isolation of the Superintendent from the traditional corporate memory of the Academy was essentially complete.

Lieutenant General Daniel W. Christman, class of 1965, moved into the Superintendent's quarters in 1996. The gregarious Christman was very popular at West Point—and with many among the senior faculty. Still he did little, if anything, to engage the Academic Board on any topic other than curriculum, and even there his first instinct was to impose his own solutions.

In the years since 1977, governance changes—under Goodpaster and Palmer, in particular—had progressively reduced the scope of activity of the board. Those who had experienced the power of the board before 1977, or even those who had been brought up in its shadow, increasingly felt that they had been cut out of the decision-making process. It was a reasoned conclusion that did little to keep them at the helm.

Frustrated by their growing inability to influence events or bring order, permanent faculty members (in particular the department heads) departed from the Academy earlier and earlier. Retirements among the Academy's traditional leadership had surged, beginning in 1977, and reached epoch proportions during Palmer's five-year tour of duty. When one examines the data concerning the departure of department heads from West Point in the twentieth century, the number departing in the last quarter of the century stand out starkly (see Appendix 2). The rate of departures for that period is nearly twice that of any other quarter.

As former history department head, Thomas Griess assessed the situation, "The Board knew exactly what had happened [during the EE304 affair] and resented that it had taken the biggest hit when most of the problems singled out as major contributors to the debacle were in areas over which they had little influence (e.g., honor and the honor system, the leadership evaluation system, concept of duty, and its relation to honor, the adverse effect of non-academic activity [on] cadet time)."[100] Some of the professors were unhappy enough with this situation to decide on immediate retirement; for others, the new conditions merely pushed them toward the edge. Eight retired during Goodpaster's tenure (1977–1981). Only once before (in the early 1960s) had so many department heads left West Point in a like period.

This, however, was only the beginning. Even the periods of "calm" in this storm saw an unusually high turnover of senior faculty—under Scott, six departed, and under Graves, another eight. But, under Palmer, thirteen left or were forced out—far more than during any other five-year period in the Academy's nearly two centuries of experience. The arrival of new faces at Academic Board meetings was such a regular occurrence that one member complained that little work got done because at each meeting there was a newcomer who had to be briefed on everything that was under consideration.[101]

The turmoil resulting from changing demographics, the cheating scandal, and the resulting governance changes was exacerbated by an underlying current of discontent related to the curriculum. The Davidson reforms of 1959 had ended the wholly prescribed curriculum and introduced electives—if only on a trial basis. This was the first important curriculum change in more than twenty years, and the most fundamental since Thayer. Between 1965 and 2000, there were nine additional curriculum debates, and all except that of 1976 resulted in important curriculum changes; most recast the core curriculum itself. But what really counted—what was really radical—was that these debates, at their base, were about the continued relevance of the core curriculum itself and about the cardinal importance of its mathematics and engineering elements.

In 1965, the Academic Board reviewed the elective policy it had established in 1959. After a lengthy but otherwise unremarkable debate, two additional electives were added by trimming the courses in mechanics and electricity. This brought to four the number of electives a cadet could take.

Two years later, Superintendent Donald Bennett pressed the academic community for a commitment to curriculum changes that would extend the

Davidson reforms and allow "specialization in a chosen field."[102] The majority of the Academic Board agreed, with only three members dissenting: Charles Schilling in engineering, Elliott Cutler in electricity, and Colonel John S. B. Dick, class of 1935, in mathematics. In April 1968, the board approved the new curriculum, which increased the number of electives to six. In addition, cadets who wished to do so could choose their electives from a specific field within one of four areas of concentration—basic sciences, applied sciences and engineering, humanities, or national security and public affairs. Still, the curriculum continued to be a largely prescribed one, with only a limited potential for specialization.

Those opposed to the new curriculum warned that the Academy was poised "at a watershed on the trace of curriculum development." They predicted:

> Henceforth there will be three academic categories of cadets, . . . "social science" cadets; "engineering" cadets; and "science" cadets. . . . The core will soon start to be differentiated for cadets pursuing the various major tracks. The elementary drive toward optimization will force this differentiation. . . . Cadets pursuing the public affairs concentration will hardly regard themselves as possible selectees for later graduate schooling in engineering . . . and will increasingly regard their already emasculated engineering component as a useless imposition. . . . The arguments in favor of free cadet choice which have brought the majority of the Academic Board this far will then apply with redoubled vigor to the further reduction in the core.[103]

The growth in the number of courses offered as electives by the various departments seemed to confirm critics' fears. The elective program "contains powerful seeds of self-acceleration," they had warned—correctly, it proved.[104] In fact, the growth of electives (from 20 in 1960 to over 150 in 1971 and over 380 by 1988) became a force unto itself. Indeed, it changed the nature of the academic departments. Those once small fiefdoms, ruled by a usually benevolent head, in which all members taught well-defined segments of a well-defined curriculum, were fast becoming polyglot empires with diverse and sometimes conflicting interests, and with increasingly independent and vocal subcultures championed by members of the growing permanent faculty.

In 1972, Superintendent William Knowlton asked an outside review board to examine the curriculum. Although this board found the academic program to be essentially sound and properly oriented, it did recommend a reduction in the overall course load and a reduction in plebe mathematics.

The cadets, it said, were overscheduled. The debates that followed were lengthy and often heated.

Finally, in late 1973, the Academic Board voted to reduce the number of class meetings. It could not agree on which courses to drop, for every department viewed its own courses as essential. Moreover, regular cuts had been made in the past dozen years, and each department head felt that he had nothing more to give up. In the end, a compromise born of paralysis yielded what was called a "lesson drop plan," which levied an across-the-board 10 percent cut in almost every department's core course hours.[105] It was a solution that all recognized as unsatisfactory, and one that caused many to question the ability of the Academic Board to govern responsibly.

In January 1976, still another new curricular study group was created. Its proposal to the Academic Board reduced the number of courses from forty-eight to forty-two—cutting the number of courses cadets would take from six to five in all but two semesters. What opposition there was to the plan came from the math-science-engineering side, for it was largely these courses that had given way. Still, the consensus was that the proposal maintained a strong balanced core curriculum. To compensate for what had been lost, the proposal called for an increase in the depth and quality of the courses that had been retained. The Academic Board approved the proposal by a vote of twelve to three, and Berry pronounced it a "creditable piece of work." It provided, he said, "a curriculum appreciably better than the current curriculum." Final approval of this change, however, was derailed by the EE304 cheating incident of 1976. In the immediate aftermath of the Borman Commission work, Berry suggested that the Army had three options relative to curriculum change: "to conduct a hasty curricular study to get some change under way in AY 1977–78; to commission a deliberate curricular study to begin fundamental curricular change in AY 1978–79; or to approve [the plan that the Academic Board had developed in 1976]."[106] The Army opted for a hasty, new study.

In the wake of the EE304 affair, the curriculum was one area that came under close scrutiny. Both the Borman Commission (in 1976) and the West Point Study Group (in 1977) looked hard at the issue, but it was the second group that most concerned those at West Point. Berry pleaded that its recommendations "be general in nature and deal with objectives and policy rather than specific details." "Any detailed curriculum presented . . . , even when intended only as a descriptive example, can be an albatross around the institution's neck long after any potential usefulness has been overtaken by events," wrote Berry.[107] Responding to recommendations that emerged, the Academic Board approved a curriculum that set the number of required courses at forty: thirty core courses and ten electives, plus military science and physical education. Once again, however, change came largely at the expense of the math-science-engineering sector. The overwhelming majority of the members of the Academic Board believed that their 1976 effort was a better solution, but like so much else at West Point, it was overcome by the events of those years.[108]

Also in 1977, in response to a recommendation from the West Point Study Group, the Department of Behavioral Sciences and Leadership was created from the Office of Military Leadership, which had remained under the Commandant since its creation by Maxwell Taylor. Lieutenant Colonel Howard T. Prince II, class of 1962, was selected to head the new department.

In 1980, the science and engineering faculty, led by Schilling of engineering and Saunders of physics, expressed two serious concerns about the changes that were being made.[109] First, in recent years it had been the science and engineering curriculum that had given ground to make room for electives. The faculty feared that they had given up too much. Schilling argued strongly that "the engineering design process [was] a paradigm of the rational decision process" and that this way of conceptualizing problems was essential in a military career.[110] Second, they had begun to experience resistance from some of the better engineering schools to the admission of West Point graduates into advanced degree programs. More and more schools were admitting only students who had come from programs accredited by the Accreditation Board of Engineering and Technology (ABET). West Point had not yet sought that credential.

In early 1981, a new curriculum committee chaired by Saunders proposed a fundamental change in the Academy's academic program—two tracks, one in math-science-engineering and a second in humanities and public affairs. Under this plan, cadets would be required to select one of the two academic tracks at the end of their plebe year. That decision would determine the cadet's curriculum. This change would allow the math-science-engineering community to strengthen its core curriculum as a preliminary to seeking ABET accreditation—a move that would vastly enhance future graduates' engineering credentials. The new curriculum did not eliminate the mathematics, science, or engineering course from the nonengineering tracks but did offer these cadets a somewhat less intense engineering course. Following the board's favorable action, Superintendent Goodpaster approved the new program in May 1981.[111]

It was a short step from the tracking provided in the 1981 curriculum to majors—or so it seemed. Army Chief of Staff Edward C. Meyer, class of 1951, told Willard Scott, who had just arrived to replace Goodpaster, that "the time may be right to move forward with the 'majors' concept." In August 1981, Scott directed the Dean to proceed with the development of a program of optional majors.[112]

The Academic Board, however, found the transition difficult. Finally, in September 1982, after sometimes rancorous debates, the board approved an optional majors program: sixteen majors, with eight in the math-science-engineering disciplines and eight in the humanities and public affairs area. Two arguments proved most persuasive. First, as a result of the earlier decision to allow cadets to concentrate upon a particular field of study and the recent move toward ABET-accredited engineering programs, the Academy was already offering majors in all but name. Second, virtually all the reputable American colleges and universities, as well as the other service academies, were offering majors—including ABET-accredited engineering majors. That affected recruiting. If the Military Academy was to continue to attract high-quality students, it had few options. In October, Superintendent Scott forwarded the proposal to Meyer, together with a minority report representing the view of four dissenting members of the Academic Board.

It is interesting that two of the newest members of the Academic Board—Berry (law) and Flint (history)—were among those opposed to majors. And it is noteworthy that all three of the members of the Academic Board who were not West Point graduates—Flint, Berry, and William Hoff (chemistry)—were opposed. In their minority report, these three and Jack Pollin, in mathematics, expressed two general reservations. First, West Point's "majors"—which were still fitted around a substantial core of required courses largely in mathematics and science—were very different from majors in other schools and might be troublesome to accreditation committees. Second, the cadets' focus on a specific discipline might detract from their broad preparation for officership. These concerns, however, were not shared by their colleagues at West Point or by Meyer in Washington.

With Department of the Army approval in early 1983, the Academy proceeded with the introduction of the sixteen academic majors: chemistry, civil engineering, computer science, electrical engineering, engineering management, engineering physics, mathematical science, mechanical engineering, behavioral science, economics, foreign language (five choices), geography, history, literature, management, and political science. But majors were made optional; cadets could choose either to concentrate in a field of study or to declare a major.

Satisfaction with the new program, however, was short-lived. Soon many of the professors outside the engineering departments came to believe that the cadets who had not chosen engineering majors were getting inadequate career preparation in that field. In 1986, in what now seemed a turnaround, they began to object that the engineering elements of the core curriculum (for nonengineer majors) were no longer adequate. In 1988, the curriculum committee recommended yet another revision of the core curriculum, another fundamentally different approach—one built around what was called "the engineering thought process."

Beginning with the class of 1991, this new proposal would replace the general engineering core that cadets had been taking. Instead, each cadet, regardless of major, would choose one of six core sequences in the mathematics, science, and engineering area, for fifteen courses in all—four in mathematics, four in basic science, one in physical geography (terrain analysis), one in computer science, and finally a five-course engineering sequence (the content of which depended on which of the six engineering disciplines was chosen: civil, electrical, mechanical, systems, computer, or nuclear). All cadets would also be required to take a common core of sixteen courses in the humanities and public affairs area: law (1), history (4), English (3), leadership (2), social sciences (3), foreign language (2), and philosophy and ethics (1). The new curriculum continued the practice of exposing the mathematics-science-engineering majors to a substantial dose of humanities and public affairs courses. The change was required, explained Superintendent Palmer to Army Chief of Staff Vuono, to ensure that every cadet would have "the opportunity to experience the engineering thought process in depth."[113]

It was as if the Academy was returning to its roots. Nearly two centuries earlier, Jefferson had created a mathematical school, and Swift and Thayer had shaped it into a school of engineering—and so its emphasis had remained. In 1904, Charles Larned, then Professor of Drawing, said that the genius of West Point "is a well-balanced development of the mechanism of thinking based upon a thorough understanding of elementary principles"—elementary principles whose "corner-stone . . . is mathematics" and whose "structure is made up of exact sciences."[114] This was the model that the new curriculum reflected. That this model was still applicable would be challenged as the Academy's bicentennial approached.

Final ABET accreditation for civil, electrical, and mechanical engineering and for engineering management was granted in 1985. Four years later, a number of structural changes (many driven by that recent accreditation) were made in the engineering departments. Geography and Computer Science, and Electrical Engineering were reorganized as the Department of Electrical Engineering and Computer Science, and the Department of Geography. Similarly, the Departments of Engineering and Mechanics were restructured into the Department of Systems Engineering and the Department of Civil and Mechanical Engineering.[115] Colonel James L. Kays, class of 1962, was chosen to head the new Department of Systems Engineering. Later that same year, the new Department of Geography was redesignated the Department of Geography and Environmental Engineering.

In the summer of 1996, Daniel W. Christman, class of 1965, moved into the Superintendent's quarters at West Point. Christman, who possessed a strong intellect, had graduated first in his class and then gone on to earn an M.P.A. at Princeton and J.D. at George Washington University. He was polished but easygoing and often used self-deprecating humor to put people at ease, but he was as detached from his academic staff as any of his immediate predecessors.

In the summer of 1999, realizing that his time at West Point was growing short (he was more than three years into his five-year tour), Christman turned to an issue that had concerned him even before assuming the superintendency—the nature of the Academy's response to the changing roles of the Army. The officers the Academy would graduate, he often said, would be asked both to provide humanitarian relief and to fight and win the nation's wars. In a complex, global environment, they needed both mental agility and a comfort with ambiguity. This would require leaders broadly educated in the languages, customs, and cultures of the world and yet able to deal with technology—especially information technology—and cope with both its capabilities and its limitations.

Christman was an engineer, but he had taught in the Department of Social Sciences and had come to question whether the Academy's traditional emphasis on mathematics, science, and engineering was the answer in the twenty-first century. He was no longer convinced that the "engineering thought process"—the seeking of certainty—was appropriate in a world where ambiguity seemed the norm.

Army Secretary Louis Caldera, class of 1978, shared Christman's doubts. He was particularly concerned about the effect the heavy mathematics-science-engineering curriculum had on minority recruitment. When Christman voiced his concerns, Caldera made it clear that he was willing to effect a radical exorcism of the engineering emphasis.

This alignment of forces truly alarmed the senior academic faculty. From the perspective of the Academic Board, Caldera's strong, even enthusiastic, support for the changes Christman was considering was a serious threat. With the support of the Secretary, the Superintendent could impose radical change by fiat. In years past, the individual members of the Academic Board had maintained relationships with important members of Congress and even with the President, and these connections had sometimes been essential in resisting an overreaching Superintendent. But such ties were no longer common currency.

The Dean, Brigadier General Fletcher M. Lamkin, class of 1964, defused the situation, at least temporarily, by suggesting that the Academy conduct a strategic review to provide an in-depth examination of the issue. Christman agreed. He had become more reflective, some observers speculated, and was now concerned that Caldera might act on his own to build support in Washington for some radical solution.[116]

This strategic review, conducted between August 1999 and May 2000, resulted in the publication of *USMA Strategic Vision 2010*. The review was built, in part, on an institutional self-study completed in mid-1999 as a part of the decennial accreditation of the Academy.[117] It also drew on the continuing assessment of the curriculum that had long been the practice of the Academic Board.

In recent years, the Academic Board had made a special effort to keep apace of the changing needs of the Army. Part of this effort involved reaching out to former battalion commanders to find out how recent graduates— lieutenants and captains—had performed. The fourth such outreach project was conducted in January 2001 as a part of the strategic review. In general, the outcome of the interviews of the battalion commanders and of the strategic review itself reaffirmed the direction the Academy had been going.

Even before the 1999–2000 strategic review was completed, the Academic Board began another curriculum review. Drawing on the work of the strategic review group, the board proposed "to reformulate some of the Academic Program Goals that define the curriculum," particularly "the goals in the area of math, science, engineering, and technology."[118] Although the development of the "engineering thought process" remained one aspect of the academic program it was no longer the central feature. Christman clearly had initiated significant changes in an arena that had once been sacrosanct.

The new curriculum, approved in 2001, replaced the five-course engineering core sequence with a three-course sequence for all but the engineering majors but retained as requirements the four courses in mathematics, four in science, one in physical geography, and one in information technology. The two hours gained (for other than engineering students) were allotted to an additional course in information technology and to a course (to be specified by each department for its majors) that would enhance the study of foreign cultures. The new curriculum also called for an "integrative experience" in the last semester of the first class year that would be defined more specifically by each department but seemed to call for some multidisciplinary study or research project. The new curriculum would be put in place in the fall of 2001 for the class of 2005.

Between 1959 and 2001, there were nine important periods of curriculum debate. In the first century and a half of the Academy's history, important debates on curriculum reform had occurred every ten to twenty years. The last four decades of the twentieth century, particularly the period between 1976 and 1988, saw curricular debates followed by curriculum change every three or four years. This was a period of extraordinary turbulence for those who had to endure all or most of it as members of the Academic Board. Those who had witnessed the shift in the balance of power between the Academic Board and the Superintendent, and who understood its implications, now viewed the future with unease.

In 1969, Commandant of Cadets Bernard W. Rogers, class of June 1943, directed a major review of the fourth-class system. That system, the review found, had its roots in policies originating in the years just before the turn of the twentieth century. Beginning in the late 1890s, a consistent effort had been made by the tactical department to have all cadet officers, especially the first class, exercise increased leadership responsibilities. Although not explicitly permitted, this soon led to their assumption of authority over new cadets.[119] While this sometimes produced complaints of unnecessary harassment of plebes, the tactical department was so impressed by the soldierly results achieved that it did little to change the practice.

When Samuel Tillman was recalled from retirement in 1917 to superintend the Academy during World War I, he took a new look at the system. Although he officially authorized control of the new cadets by selected upperclassmen, he had reservations. "The success of the method now in operation," he wrote in 1918, "will depend upon whether men as young as our cadets can be given the authority outlined for them without abusing it themselves, or countenancing its abuse by their associates."[120]

When Douglas MacArthur succeeded Tillman in 1919, he immediately began to build upon his predecessor's efforts. He ordered the first classmen— the class of 1920, which had matriculated in June 1918—to formulate and reduce to writing the "customs of service of the corps." After numerous conferences with the tactical department and days of debate and argument, the class, on August 4, proposed a set of regulations that were to govern "the relationship between the upper classes and the lower class."[121] MacArthur praised the new rules and added: "I regard this as the first and in some respects the greatest safeguard of the New West Point which we are mutually evolving in the Spirit of Old West Point." He approved the regulations proposed by the class and had them published as "Traditions and Customs of the Corps of Cadets, 1920."[122]

Subsequent studies of the fourth-class system during the 1940s and 1950s produced only minor changes. Still, the system had its critics. A curriculum review board appointed by Davidson in 1958 spoke of the necessity of eliminating the abuses of the fourth-class system, and John L. Throckmorton, class of 1935 and Commandant of Cadets during that same period, reported that "in spite of numerous efforts . . . to effect beneficial changes in the Fourth Class System, . . . I do not believe, in the final analysis, that the System as now constituted serves the Military Academy and the Army as a whole to the best advantage."[123] Amos Jordan, class of 1946 and professor of social sciences, agreed. "As it now operates at the Military Academy," he wrote in 1960, "the plebe system is probably detrimental to the development of intellectual interests and to academic achievement."[124] These critics, however, had little impact. In 1963, Superintendent Westmoreland told the Academy's graduates what they wanted to hear: "Beast Barracks is little changed from what you experienced." The Academy had "studied this problem in detail," he added, and we have "reassured ourselves that it is a sound and effective training experience."[125]

The 1969 study initiated by Rogers, however, took a much less sentimental look at the system and found many elements inconsistent with fundamental Academy goals and objectives. It was little more than "an initiation process designed to place the Fourth Classmen in a subservient and dependent position to all upper classes." If it was the Academy's mission to develop mature and independent officers, the study concluded, then the system was counterproductive and in need of a major overhaul.[126] Rogers's remedy emphasized positive leadership and mitigated, for a time, the harshness of plebe life.

In 1979, in the wake of other difficulties and changes, the Academy authorities undertook yet another effort to ensure that the fourth class system was a positive experience for both plebes and the upper classes. They reduced by one-third the total amount of verbatim memorization required of fourth-class cadets, reduced the number of inspections to which plebes were subjected, and again attempted to delineate the responsibilities of upperclassmen, placing more emphasis on professionalism and positive leadership.[127] "I think we stripped out a great deal of the nonsense . . . that had grown up around the Plebe system," said Superintendent Andrew J. Goodpaster, who had returned to West Point in 1977. Still, he had concerns, if not reservations, about a system that attempted both to shape fourth classmen in accordance with the West Point mold and to teach leadership to the upperclassmen. Sounding much like Tillman six decades earlier, he said, "They're adolescents growing to early maturity, and they've got to learn how to handle authority, which is a very heady experience for them. To lord over somebody else is all very tempting to young people. You've got to raise their sights above that."[128]

In 1988, the Academy's accreditation steering committee argued that the system did not develop essential leadership attributes but instead "induces leader behavior in conflict with accepted practices in the Army."[129] Palmer agreed and launched yet another review. As was usually the case in reviews of the fourth-class system, new efforts were made to mitigate the harshness of the plebe experience. Under the new rules, requiring displays of plebe knowledge—often nonsensical definitions, poems, and songs—was allowed during Beast Barracks but was discouraged during the academic year. After Beast Barracks, only such recitations as "the days" (the events scheduled for that day and the number of days remaining until specific events), the menu, and national or world news (usually as reported in the *New York Times*) were permitted. Pinging (an erect, shoulders-back, rapid-cadence walk), hugging walls, and squaring corners were eliminated in favor of movement in an erect military manner at a normal pace. Talking outside their rooms was prohibited to plebes, except when they were performing their duties, which still included the delivery of laundry and newspapers within their companies, and, of course, academics.

The Palmer reforms, however, went further. Palmer's new Cadet Leader Development System (CLDS) or "Four Class System," as it became known, included a major component that dealt with the development of the upper classes. However, the system's new emphasis on cadet rank had implications that flew in the face of tradition. Privileges were now more associated with rank, as well as with class. First-class privates, for example, expected to enjoy all the privileges traditional to their class, including a measure of anonymity and insulation from the underclassmen who ranked them. Now they found themselves subordinated to cadet sergeants and corporals from whatever class. This rankled many in the corps, particularly the first class.[130] As a result, the program met with what General Graves later described as "*tremendous cadet resistance.*"[131]

There had been some who felt that the objectives of the fourth-class system, such as class bonding and the internalization of traditional West Point values, were achieved well before the end of the cadet's first academic year. They argued that ending the "plebe" experience as early as possible would "provide for a smoother transition from Fourth to Third Class year."[132] In 1990, in a move in that direction, Commandant of Cadets David A. Bramlett, class of 1964, suggested to the Policy Board that the date of "recognition" be advanced to the middle of the second academic term, just ahead of spring break. The board agreed.[133]

Under Christman (1995–2001), there was a new emphasis on making the cadet experience mimic that of the actual Army, and many earlier policies were reviewed and overturned. The most dramatic reversal, and a most decisive break with tradition, came in 2001, when Commandant of Cadets Eric T. Olson, class of 1972, suddenly abolished "recognition" and its associated cer-

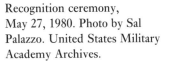

Recognition ceremony,
May 27, 1980. Photo by Sal
Palazzo. United States Military
Academy Archives.

emony. Olson explained that "the familiarity associated with being on a 'first
name basis' (after recognition) worked against the imperative to maintain a
proper senior-subordinate relationship based on rank differential that is the
hallmark of our current leader development process." Under Olson's plan, the
traditional plebe experience and its associated responsibilities ended with promotion to corporal at the end of cadet field training in the summer between
the fourth- and third-class years. With promotion to corporal, the former plebes
also gained the right to address other upperclassmen by their first names, although the Commandant did not encourage them to do so.[134] Cadets responded
to these changes with a deluge of critical, even abusive (but anonymous),
e-mail to the Commandant and Superintendent, and messages to "graduates
whom they view as having a 'sympathetic ear.'" This criticism became so pervasive that Olson had to ask the old grads not to "participate in such undermining of proper authority and the chain of command."[135]

Cadets were hardly oblivious to the many changes whirling about them—
particularly the changes in the curriculum, the honor system, the fourth-

class system, or corps demographics. Still, they were not as caught up as the staff and faculty by the intense scrutiny to which the Academy was subjected as a result of the EE304 affair, or by the resulting governance changes. In 1993, when Congress cut the size of the corps of cadets by 10 percent—to about 4,000—it caused barely a ripple among those already at West Point. If they needed distractions from the demands of the academic, physical, and military training, a myriad of well-organized extracurricular activities and recreational facilities competed for their attention. In 1962, there were 58 authorized extracurricular activities, including the debate team; the mathematics forum; the fencing club; the ski team; chess, model, and rifle clubs; the glee club; and the staffs of *Bugle Notes*, *Howitzer*, and *The Pointer*. By 2001, the number of activities had reached 106. Among the newer offerings were the mountain bike club, the scuba-diving club (which had a tradition of diving off the Florida coast during spring break), the cadet pipes and drums (with their own registered tartan), the gospel choir, and the society of women engineers. In the midst of all this growth and change, however, some traditions survived: the "100th Night Show," for example, was still written, produced, directed, and performed by cadets.

Not all cadet extracurricular activities, however, were condoned by the Academy. Consider the "great goat caper" of the class of 1966. The weekend before the Army-Navy game, a small band of conspirators drove to Annapolis determined to kidnap Navy's Billy XV. To their dismay, they learned that the goat had been moved from the Naval Academy's dairy farm to a high-security Atlantic Fleet communications center across the Severn River. Still, they did not give up. They made a reconnaissance run past the installation and found a ten-foot chain-link fence crowned with barbed wire surrounding the facility and two Marine guards manning the gate. Just beyond the guards, in a twenty-foot pen topped with more barbed wire, stood the prize. Despite these obstacles, they concluded it could be done.

That night they returned, wearing black turtlenecks, their faces darkened with burned cork. Four young women, who had been recruited as accomplices, flirted with the Marine guards, while the cadets entered the compound through an unlocked pedestrian gate and made their way to the goat's pen. There, using a crowbar wrapped in a black towel, they broke the padlock, opened the gate, and made off with the cooperative Billy. Days later, when the affair had played itself out and Billy had been returned to an embarrassed and angry Naval Academy, the culprits were called before the Commandant. "We've got to give you some punishment, so I'm going to remove your first-class privileges for two months," he told them. "But I want you to know I'd be proud to have you serve under me in the Army. Well done."[136]

Cadets have often proven to be an impish lot. In the early 1970s, they took up the newest collegiate rage—"the streak." One winter night, as the officer-in-charge left the guardhouse after taps inspection, a yell thundered from the south area barracks, and a multitude of naked bodies issued forth into the cold night air. But before the officer could reach the area, it became still and quiet—no movement anywhere. As he stood in the center of south area, however, a shout rose up in central area, and streakers rushed back and forth across that area. Into central area strode the officer, only to find it as deserted as the area he had just left. Then, another shout: south, new south, and north areas were suddenly filled with naked bodies. The officer headed for north area, but once again, all was silent. Just then, another shout went up from central area and another wave of streakers emerged. The officer-in-charge weighed the magnitude of his task, returned to the guardhouse, called out the cadet chain of command, and turned the problem over to them.

In some cases, cadet antics went beyond impishness, however. One fall evening in 1963, a mess hall rally ran amuck. It began with the firing of a cannon, which cued the plebes who had been primed to respond. They leaped onto their chairs, peeled off their uniform tunics and whirled them over their heads, shouting, "Rally! Rally! Rally!" Then in came the Rabble Rousers, and the corps took up the chant.

For reasons still not fully understood, the rally almost immediately turned into a food riot.[137] Cadets tilted their tables on end, sending china and silver crashing to the floor. "Stack tables!" someone commanded, and throughout the mess hall, cadets lifted the heavy oak tables one atop another until they were stacked three, four, five, even six tables high. Opened half-pint milk cartons sailed across the room, leaving in their wake a white liquid trail, followed by ketchup bottles and then globs of honey. Nothing since the Egg-Nog Riot of 1826 could match this frenzy. For twenty minutes the cadets persisted, the officer-in-charge all the while yelling, "Halt! This has got to stop." Then, as quickly as it had started, the riot was over, and the cadets surveyed the scene. Even they were shocked and alarmed by what they had done, and all of them scurried back to their barracks to await the inevitable reaction.

West Point's senior officials were justifiably outraged, but they could not identify any ringleaders; besides, following that rally, Army had upset Penn State, 10 to 7, spoiling, for a second year in a row, the Pennsylvania school's hopes for a national championship. When it finally came, the official reaction was surprisingly mild. Every cadet was docked $1.27 each month until the damage had been paid for. Some said, "If that was a $1.27 rally, let's have a $5.00 rally." Most cadets, however, were perfectly satisfied to have gotten off so lightly and had no intention of trying their luck again.

The tradition of cadet impishness and imaginative pranks often escaped outside observers. In 1977, the West Point Study Group's final report remarked that "a relatively humorless atmosphere seems to prevail" at the Academy. The cadets knew better—and got to the heart of the matter when the *New York Times* duly reported this finding. The next morning a hasty banner proclaimed: "How can a newspaper with no comics call us 'humorless'?"[138]

The culmination of the entire cadet year lies in graduation week. It is a milestone for everyone in the corps. For the plebe, it foretells eminent advancement into the ranks of the upper classes. For the yearlings, there is the longed-for summer furlough. For the second classmen—the cows—there is the elevation to the first class. And for the firstie, it marks the culmination of the four-year experience—graduation.

But graduation week is also a special time for former graduates, for it is impossible to spend four years at West Point without being touched by the pervasive influence of its traditions. For many "old grads" it is a time to renew friendships and strengthen the class ties and spirit that so distinguish mem-

Graduation, class of 1993. United States Military Academy Archives.

bers of the Long Gray Line. They might recall, so many years before, when they sang the words of "Army Blue":

> We've not much longer here to stay,
>   For in a month or two,
> We'll bid farewell to "Cadet Gray,"
>   And don the Army Blue.
>
> Army Blue, Army Blue,
>   Hurrah for the Army Blue
> We'll bid farewell to "Cadet Gray,"
>   And don the Army Blue.
>
> With pipe and song we'll jog along
>   Till this short time is through,
> And all among our jovial throng,
>   Have donned the Army Blue.

These words may bring a glisten to the eye of an old grad, and a cadet in gray may wonder why. But each in turn, in years to come, will understand.

On June 1, 2002, the bicentennial class performs its final rite of passage at the United States Military Academy. Diplomas in hand, there will be one final rendition, as cadets, of the "Alma Mater," a last "Dismissed!", and then a blur of white as caps are tossed high into the air, to remain where they fall—trophies for enthusiastic children who may themselves someday don the cadet gray.

Appendixes

Appendix A. Roster of Superintendents, Commandants, Deans, and Academic Department Heads

	Class	From	To	Remarks, Cullum No.*
SUPERINTENDENTS				
Williams, Jonathan	—	1801	1803†	Resigned June 20, 1803
Williams, Jonathan	—	1805	1812	Returned Apr. 19, 1805
Swift, Joseph Gardner	1802	1812	1814	1
Partridge, Alden	1806	1814	1817	From prof. of art of engineering (1812–1815), 15
Thayer, Sylvanus	1808	1817	1833	33
DeRussy, Rene Edward	1812	1833	1838	89
Delafield, Richard	1818	1838	1845	180
Brewerton, Henry	1819	1845	1852	207
Lee, Robert Edward	1829	1852	1855	542
Barnard, John Gross	1833	1855	1856	708
Delafield, Richard	1818	1856	1861	180
Beauregard, Pierre Gustave T.	1838	1861	1861	Jan. 23–Jan. 28, 1861, 942
Delafield, Richard	1818	1861	1861	Jan. 28–Mar. 1, 1861, 180
Bowman, Alexander Hamilton	1825	1861	1864	394
Tower, Zealous Bates	1841	1864	1864	July 8–Sept. 8, 1864, 1059
Cullum, George Washington	1833	1864	1866	709
Pitcher, Thomas Gamble	1845	1866	1871	1270
Ruger, Thomas Howard	1854	1871	1876	1633
Schofield, John McAllister	1853	1876	1881	1585

Source. The starting point for this work was John K. Robertson "'Who Was Who,' 1802–1990," 2d ed., April 10, 1991, typescript. I have drawn on this work, added missing material for the period before 1990, extended the work to 2001, and corrected the errors found.

*The Cullum No. is a unique, consecutive number assigned to each graduate of the United States Military Academy by the Association of Graduates. The system was created by Colonel George Washington Cullum, class of 1833.

†Williams resigned on June 21, 1803. His position was not filled in hopes that he would reconsider. He was convinced to return to service on April 19, 1805.

Appendix A *(continued)*

	Class	From	To	Remarks, Cullum No.
Howard, Oliver Otis	1854	1881	1882	1634
Merritt, Wesley	1860	1882	1887	1868
Parke, John Grubb	1849	1887	1889	1408
Wilson, John Moulder	1860	1889	1893	1858
Ernst, Oswald H.	1864	1893	1898	2025
Mills, Albert Leopold	1879	1898	1906	2796
Scott, Hugh Lenox	1876	1906	1910	2628
Barry, Thomas Henry	1877	1910	1912	2679
Townsley, Clarence Page	1881	1912	1916	2892
Biddle, John	1881	1916	1917	2880
Tillman, Samuel Escue	1869	1917	1919	From retired 1911 and prof. of chemistry, mineralogy and geology (1880–1911), 2275
MacArthur, Douglas	1903	1919	1922	4122
Sladen, Fred Winchester	1890	1922	1926	Commandant (1911– 1914), 3357
Stewart, Merch Brandt	1869	1926	1927	3715
Winans, Edwin Baruch	1891	1927	1928	3403
Smith, William Ruthven	1892	1928	1932	3459
Connor, William Dorward	1897	1932	1938	3742
Benedict, Jay Leland	1904	1938	1940	4240
Eichelberger, Robert Lawrence	1909	1940	1942	4817
Wilby, Francis Bowditch	1905	1942	1945	4314
Taylor, Maxwell Davenport	1922	1945	1949	6831
Moore, Bryand Edward	Aug. 1917	1949	1951	5845
Irving, Frederick Augustus	Apr. 1917	1951	1954	5654
Byran, Blackshear Morrison	June 14, 1922	1954	1956	6939
Davidson, Garrison Hold	1927	1956	1960	8044
Westmoreland, William Childs	1936	1960	1963	10571
Lampert, James Benjamin	1936	1963	1966	10495
Bennett, Donald Vivian	1940	1966	1968	11907
Koster, Samuel William	1942	1968	1970	12893
Knowlton, William Allen	Jan. 1943	1970	1974	13044
Berry, Sidney Bryan	1948	1974	1977	16631
Goodpaster, Andrew Jackson	1939	1977	1981	11336
Scott, Willard Warren, Jr.	1948	1981	1986	16495
Palmer, Dave Richard	1956	1986	1991	20671
Graves, Howard Dwayne	1961	1991	1996	23283
Christman, Daniel William	1965	1996	2001	25486
Lennox, William James, Jr.	1971	2001	—	29557

Appendix A *(continued)*

	Class	*From*	*To*	*Remarks, Cullum No.*
COMMANDANTS				
Gardiner, George W.	1814	1817	1818	91
Bliss, John	—	1818	1819	—
Bell, John R.	1812	1819	1820	76
Worth, William J.	—	1820	1828	—
Hitchcock, Ethan Allen	1817	1829	1833	177
Fowle, John	—	1833	1838	—
Smith, Charles Ferguson	1825	1838	1842	410
Thomas, John Addison	1833	1842	1845	721
Alden, Bradford Ripley	1831	1845	1852	653
Garnett, Robert Selden	1841	1852	1854	1085
Walker, William Henry Talbot	1837	1854	1856	936
Hardee, William Joseph	1838	1856	1860	966
Reynolds, John Fulton	1841	1860	1861	1084
Augur, Christopher Columbus	1843	1861	1861	Aug.–Dec. 1861, 1182
Garrard, Kenner	1851	1961	1862	1501
Clitz, Henry Boynton	1845	1862	1864	1267
Tidball, John Caldwell	1848	1864	1864	July–Sept. 1864, 1379
Black, Henry More	1847	1864	1870	1354
Upton, Emory	1861	1870	1875	1895
Neill, Thomas Hewston	1847	1875	1879	1357
Lazelle, Henry Martyn	1855	1879	1882	1706
Hasbrouck, Henry Conelius	May 1861	1882	1888	1708
Hawkins, Hamilton S.	—	1888	1892	—
Mills, Samuel Meyers , Jr.	1865	1892	1897	2101
Hein, Otto Louis	1870	1897	1901	2358
Treat, Charles Gould	1882	1901	1905	2944
Howze, Robert Lee	1888	1905	1909	3260
Sibley, Frederick William	1874	1909	1911	2530
Sladen, Fred Winchester	1890	1911	1914	Superintendent (1922–1926), 3357
Smith, Morton Fitz	1895	1914	1916	3646
Henry, Guy Vernor	1898	1916	1918	3853
Bugge, Jens	1895	1918	1919	3620
Danford, Robert Melville	1904	1919	1923	4247
Stewart, Merch Bradt	1809	1923	1926	3715
Hodges, Campbell Blackshear	1903	1926	1929	4177
Richardson, Robert Charlwood, Jr.	1904	1929	1933	4236
Buckner, Simon Bolivar, Jr.	1908	1933	1936	4699
McCunniff, Dennis Edward	1913	1936	1937	5177
Ryder, Charles Wolcott	1915	1937	1941	5351

Appendix A *(continued)*

	Class	From	To	Remarks, Cullum No.
Irving, Frederick Augustus	Apr. 1917	1941	1942	5654
Gallagher, Philip Edward	June 1918	1942	1943	6015
Honnen, George	1920	1943	1946	6756
Higgins, Gerald Joseph	1934	1946	1948	10113
Harkins, Paul Donal	1929	1948	1951	8620
Waters, John Knight	1931	1951	1952	9175
Michaelis, John Hersey	1936	1952	1954	10676
Messinger, Edwin John	1931	1954	1956	9197
Throckmorton, John Lathrop	1935	1956	1959	10205
Rich, Charles Wythe Gleaves	1935	1956	1961	103484
Stilwell, Richard Giles	1938	1961	1963	11046
Davidson, Michael Shannon	1939	1963	1965	11653
Scott, Richard Pressly	1941	1965	1967	12343
Rogers, Bernard William	June 1943	1967	1969	13459
Walker, Sam Sims	1946	1969	1972	15597
Feir, Philip Robert	1949	1972	1975	16988
Ulmer, Walter Francis, Jr.	1952	1975	1977	18729
Bard, John Chapman	1954	1977	1979	19532
Franklin, Joseph Powel	1955	1979	1982	20207
Moellering, John Henry	1959	1982	1984	22277
Boylan, Peter James, Jr.	1961	1984	1987	23336
Gorden, Fred Augustus	1962	1987	1989	24037
Bramlett, David Anthony	1964	1989	1992	24975
Foley, Robert Franklin	1963	1992	1994	24913
McFarren, Freddy E.	1966	1994	1995	26450
St. Onge, Robert Joseph	1969	1995	1997	28356
Abizaid, John Phllip	1973	1997	1999	31090
Olson, Eric Thorne	1972	1999	—	20262
DEANS				
Alexander, Roger Gordon	1907	1945	1947	Acting 1945–1946, 4532
Jones, Harris	Apr. 1917	1947	1956	Acting 1947, 5602
Stamps, Thomas Dodson	Aug. 1917	1956	1957	5747
Counts, Gerald Alford	Aug. 1917	1957	1959	5742
Bessell, William Weston, Jr.	1920	1959	1965	6545
Jannarone, John Robert	1938	1965	1973	11034
Smith, Frederick Adair, Jr.	1944	1974	1985	13983
Flint, Roy K.	—	1985	1990	—
Galloway, Gerald Edward, Jr.	1957	1990	1995	21148
Lamkin, Fletcher McCarthy	1964	1995	2000	25045
Kaufman, Daniel Joseph	1968	2000	—	27277

Appendix A *(continued)*

	Class	From	To	Remarks, Cullum No.
DEPARTMENT OF BEHAVIORAL SCIENCES AND LEADERSHIP				
Applied Military Psychology and Leadership* (1946–1947)				
McKinley, William Dawes	1937	1946	1947	10979
Military Psychology and Leadership (1947–1952)				
McKinley, William Dawes	1937	1947	1949	10979
Gee, Samuel Edward	1933	1949	1952	9883
Office of Military Psychology and Leadership (1952–1974)				
Exton, Hugh M.	1936	1952	1954	10253
Safford, Robert H.	1936	1954	1957	10592
Fredericks, Charles George	1939	1957	1960	11696
Tuttle, Paul Vernon, Jr.	1939	1960	1963	11495
Hauser, Auburon Paul	1941	1963	1965	12467
Hays, Samuel Hubbard	1942	1965	1969	12817
Buckley, Harry Augustine	1948	1969	1974	16734
Office of Military Leadership (1974–1977)				
Buckley, Harry Augustine	1948	1974	1977	16734
Department of Behavioral Sciences and Leadership† (1977–)				
Buckley, Harry Augustine	1948	1977	1978	Acting, 16734
Prince, Howard Taft	1962	1978	1990	23839
Wattendorf, John Martin	1965	1990	1995	Acting until Dec. 30, 1991, 25544
Hallums, James Davis	1966	1995	1996	26530
Brower, Charles Ford IV	1969	1996	2001	28079
LeBoeuf, Joseph N. G.	1974	2001	—	32096
DEPARTMENT OF CHEMISTRY				
Department of Chemistry and Mineralogy (1820–1837)				
Cutbush, James	1812	1820	1823	Acting, Post Surgeon, 87
Prescott, Jonathan	1821	1823	1824	Acting, 264
Percival, James G.	Yale, 1815	1824	1824	Acting, Asst. Surgeon
Torrey, John	College of Physicians and Surgeons, N.Y., 1818	1824	1827	Acting, Asst. Surgeon
Hopkins, William Fenn	1825	1827	1835	Acting, 402
Bailey, Jacob Whitman	1832	1835	1837	Acting, 666
Department of Chemistry, Mineralogy and Geology (1837–1943)				
Bailey, Jacob Whitman	1832	1837	1857	Acting until July 8, 1838, 666

---

*Organization created within the Department of Tactics by Order No. 30, Headquarters USCC, June 20, 1946. This organization, under various names, continued to function under the Commandant of Cadets until 1977.

†Brought under the Dean.

Appendix A *(continued)*

	Class	From	To	Remarks, Cullum No.
Kendrick, Henry Lane	1835	1857	1880	801
Tillman, Samuel Escue	1869	1880	1911	2275
Robinson, Wirt	1887	1911	1928	4229
Fenton, Chauncey Lee	1904	1928	1943	—
Department of Chemistry and Electricity (1943–1946)				
Fenton, Chauncey Lee	1904	1943	1946	4229
Bartlett, Boyd Wheeler	1919	1946	1946	To prof. of electricity, 1946–1957, 6258
Department of Physics and Chemistry (1946–1967)				
Counts, Gerald Alford	Aug 1917	1946	1957	From prof. of physics, 1931–1946, 5742
Gillette, Edward Clinton, Jr.	1920	1957	1964	6635
Jannarone, John Robert, Jr.	1938	1964	1965	To Dean, 1965–1973, 11034
Saunders, Edward A.	1946	1965	1966	Acting, to prof of physics, 1967–1984, 15299
MacWilliams, Donald Gribble	1944	1966	1967	14041
Department of Chemistry (1967–)				
MacWilliams, Donald Gribble	1944	1967	1977	14041
Hoff, Wilford J., Jr.	—	1977	1988	Acting 1977–1978
Ramsden, James Harrison	1958	1988	1990	21678
Allbee, David Clinton	1970	1990	—	28887

DEPARTMENT OF CIVIL AND MECHANICAL ENGINEERING*

	Class	From	To	Remarks, Cullum No.
Department of Natural and Experimental Philosophy (1812–1943)				
Mansfield, Jared A.	Yale	1812	1828	—
Courtenay, Edward Henry	1821	1828	1834	Acting 1828–1829, 262
Bartlett, William H. Chambers	1826	1834	1871	Acting 1834–1836, 429
Michie, Peter Smith	1863	1871	1901	From Dept. of Practical Military Engineering, 1867–1871, 1996
Gordon, William Brandon	1877	1901	1917	2646
Carter, Clifton Carroll	1899	1917	1940	3888
Gatchell, Oscar James	1912	1940	1943	From ordnance, 1938–1940, 5034
Department of Mechanics (1943–1989)				
Gatchell, Oscar James	1912	1943	1953	5034
Heiberg, Elvin Ragnvald	1926	1953	1968	7878

*In 1989 the Department of Engineering was made up of three groups—Ordnance Engineering, Civil Engineering, and Engineering Management. In July of that year the Ordnance Engineering and Civil Engineering groups were combined with the Department of Mechanics to form the Department of Civil and Mechanical Engineering. The Engineering Management group became the nucleus of the new Department of Systems Engineering.

Appendix A *(continued)*

	Class	From	To	Remarks, Cullum No
Smith, Frederick Adair, Jr.	1944	1968	1974	To Dean, 1974–1985, 13983
Wilson, Robert Maris	1950	1974	1983	17350
Carroll, William Finch	1957	1983	1985	Acting 1983–1984, 21118
Heimdahl, Peter David	1961	1985	1989	23297
Department of Civil and Mechanical Engineering (1989–)				
Heimdahl, Peter David	1961	1989	1992	23297
Lamkin, Fletcher McCarty, Jr.	1964	1992	1995	To Dean, 1995–2000, 25045
Nygren, Kip Peter	1969	1995	—	27962

DEPARTMENT OF ELECTRICAL ENGINEERING AND COMPUTER SCIENCE
Department of Chemistry and Mineralogy (1820–1837). *See* Dept. of Chemistry
Department of Chemistry, Mineralogy and Geology (1837–1943). *See* Dept. of Chemistry
Department of Chemistry and Electricity (1943–1946)

Fenton, Chauncey Lee	1904	1943	1945	4229
Bartlett, Boyd Wheeler	1919	1945	1946	6258

Department of Electricity (1946–1957)

Bartlett, Boyd Wheeler	1919	1946	1957	6258

Department of Electrical Engineering (1957–1961)

Bartlett, Boyd Wheeler	1919	1957	1961	6258

Department of Electricity (1961–1969)

Cutler, Elliott Carr, Jr.	1942	1961	1969	12668

Department of Electrical Engineering (1969–1989)

Cutler, Elliott Carr, Jr.	1942	1969	1977	12668
Reinhart, Stanley Eric, Jr.	1950	1977	1989	17352

Department of Electrical Engineering and Computer Science (1989–)

Reinhart, Stanley Eric, Jr.	1950	1989	1990	17352
Litynski, Daniel	—	1990	1996	—
Sayles, André Harding	1973	1996	—	31170

DEPARTMENT OF ENGLISH*
USMA Chaplain and Professor of Geography, History and Ethics (1814–1874). *See* Dept. of Law
Department of French Language and English Studies (1878–1882). *See* Dept. of Foreign Languages
Department of Modern Language (1882–1949). *See* Dept. of Foreign Languages
Department of English and History (1908–1926)

Adams, John C.	Yale	1908	1910	Acting

*Prior to the creation of the Department of English and History, in 1908, English was taught with other modern languages.

Appendix A *(continued)*

	Class	From	To	Remarks, Cullum No.
Holt, Lucius H.	Yale	1910	1926	Acting prof. of economics, geography, and history, 1921–1926; prof. of economics, geography, and history 1926–1930
Department of English (1926–)				
Wheat, Clayton E.	—	1926	1945	Chaplain
Stephens, George R.	Princeton	1945	1961	From Naval Academy
Alspach, Russell K.	—	1961	1965	—
Sutherland, Edwin Van V.	1936	1965	1977	10521
Capps, Jack Lee	1948	1977	1988	16721
Stromberg, Peter Leonard	1959	1988	2001	22312
Hartle, Anthony E.	1964	2001	—	244956
DEPARTMENT OF FOREIGN LANGUAGES				
Senior Teacher of French* (1803–1846)				
Masson, Francis Desere	France	1803	1810	—
Masson, Florimond	France	1810	1815	—
Berard, Claudius	France	1815	1846	—
Department of French (1846–1878)				
Berard, Claudius	France	1846	1848	—
Agnel, Hyacinthe R.	—	1848	1871	b. N.Y., studied in South America and France
Andrews, George Leonard	1851	1871	1878	To Dept. of French and English Studies (below), 1494
Department of Spanish (1857–1882)				
De Jamon, Patrice	—	1857	1863	—
Agnel, Hyacinthe R.	—	1863	1864	Acting
Platt, Edward Russell	1844	1864	1865	Acting, 1419
De Jamon, Patrice	—	1865	1882	—
Department of French Language and English Studies (1878–1882)				
Andrews, George Leonard	1851	1878	1882	1494
Department of Modern Languages (1882–1949)				
Andrews, George Leonard	1851	1882	1892	1494
Wood, Edward Edgar	1870	1892	1910	2317
Willcox, Cornelius DeWitt	1885	1910	1925	3061
Morrison, William Eric	1907	1925	1948	4571
Barrett, Charles Joseph	1922	1948	1949	6828
Department of Foreign Languages (1949–)				
Barrett, Charles Joseph	1922	1949	1963	6828
Renfroe, Walter Jackson, Jr.	1934	1963	1977	9947

*French was taught for a number of years before a professorship (and department) was created.

Appendix A *(continued)*

	Class	From	To	Remarks, Cullum No.
Willard, Sumner	—	1977	1980	—
Costa, John Joseph	1949	1980	1989	16824
Thomas, Edward J. F.	—	1989	1994	—
Held, William Gustav	1967	1994	—	Acting 1994–1995, 26976

DEPARTMENT OF GEOGRAPHY AND ENVIRONMENTAL ENGINEERING*
Teachers of Drawing (1803–1846)

Masson, Francis Desere	France	1803	1808	Also teacher of French
Zoeller, Christian	Switzerland	1808	1810	—
Zoeller, Christian	Switzerland	1812	1819	—
Gimbrede, Thomas	France	1819	1832	—
Charles, R. Leslie	England	1833	1834	—
Weir, Robert W.		1834	1846	b. U.S., studied in Italy

Department of Drawing (1846–1942)

Weir, Robert W.	—	1846	1876	—
Larned, Charles William	1870	1876	1911	2339
Stuart, Edwin Roy	—	1911	1920	—
Alexander, Roger Gordon	1907	1920	1942	2339

Department of Military Topography and Graphics (1942–1960)

Alexander, Roger Gordon	1907	1942	1945	Acting Dean 1945–1946, 4532
Schick, Lawrence Edward	1920	1946	1960	6674

Department of Earth, Space and Graphic Science (1960–1979)

Schick, Lawrence Edward	1920	1960	1961	6674
Broshous, Charles Russel	1933	1961	1972	9606
Kirby, Gilbert William, Jr.	1949	1972	1979	16869

Department of Geography and Computer Science (1979–1989)

Kirby, Gilbert William, Jr.	1949	1979	1989	16869
Galloway, Gerald Edward, Jr.	1957	1989	1989	21148

Department of Geography (1989–1990)

Galloway, Gerald Edward, Jr.	1957	1989	1990	To Dean, 1990–1995, 21148

Department of Geography and Environmental Engineering (1990–)

Reynolds, William Jerome	1964	1990	1991	Acting, 25006
Ham, Robert C.	—	1991	1991	Acting
Grubb, John Howard	1964	1991	1998	25017
King, Wendell Chris	Tenn. Tech U.	1998	—	—

*In addition to its direct lineage back to the teachers of drawing, this department also shares a history with the USMA chaplains, who taught geography, history, and ethics from 1814 to 1874. See Dept. of Law.

Appendix A *(continued)*

	Class	From	To	Remarks, Cullum No.

DEPARTMENT OF HISTORY*

History of Military Art:

Department of Civil and Military Engineering† (1813–1942). *See* Dept. of Systems Engineering

Department of Military Art and Engineering (1942–1969). *See* Dept. of Systems Engineering

Modern History:

USMA Chaplain and Professor of Geography, History and Ethics (1814–1874). *See* Dept. of Law

Department of Law and History (1896–1908). *See* Dept. of Law

Department of English and History (1908–1926). *See* Dept. of English

Department of Economics, Government and History (1926–1947). *See* Dept. of Social Sciences

Department of Social Sciences (1947–[1969]).‡ *See* Dept. of Social Sciences

Department of History (1969–)

	Class	From	To	Remarks, Cullum No.
Griess, Thomas Everett	Jan. 1943	1969	1981	13139
Flint, Roy K.	—	1981	1985	To Dean, 1985–1990
Doughty, Robert Allan	1965	1985	—	25630

DEPARTMENT OF LAW

Chaplain, USMA, and Professor of Geography, History and Ethics (1814–1874)

	Class	From	To	Remarks, Cullum No.
Empie, Adam	—	1814	1817	Chaplain, b. N.C.
Jones, Cave	—	1818	1818	Chaplain
Picton, Thomas	Wales	1818	1825	Chaplain
McIlvaine, Charles P.	Princeton, 1816	1825	1827	Chaplain
Warner, Thomas	Union College	1828	1838	Chaplain
Adams, Jasper	Brown, 1815	1838	1840	Chaplain
Parks, M. P.	—	1840	1846	Chaplain
Sprole, William T.	—	1847	1856	Chaplain, b. Nd.
French, John W.	Washington College, Hartford, Conn., ca. 1833	1856	1871	Chaplain
Forsyth, John	—	1871	1874	Chaplain, b. N.Y.
Department of Law (1874–1896)				
Gardner, Asa Bird	CCNY, 1862	1874	1878	—
Lieber, Guido Norman	U. of S.C., 1856	1878	1882	—
Curtis, Herbert P.	—	1882	1886	b. Md.
Winthrop, William	—	1886	1890	b. Conn.
Clous, John W.	—	1890	1895	—
Davis, George Breckenridge	1871	1895	1896	2379

*The Department of History shares two lines—history of military art and modern history.

†The name of this department varied over time—sometimes civil and military, sometimes military and civil. The law says merely, "the art of engineering in all its branches."

‡Modern history, which had been taught in the Department of Social Sciences, was moved in 1969 to the new Department of History. The Department of Social Sciences retained the fields of economics and government and continues to teach those subjects.

Appendix A *(continued)*

	Class	From	To	Remarks, Cullum No.
Department of Law and History (1896–1908)				
Davis, George Breckenridge	1871	1896	1901	2379
Dudley, Edgar Swartwout	1870	1901	1908	2326
Department of Law (1908–)				
Dudley, Edgar Swartwout	1870	1908	1909	2326
Bethel, Walter Augustus	1889	1909	1914	3295
Kreger, Edward A.	—	1914	1918	—
Dodds, Frank Loring	1879	1918	1919	2779
Strong, George Veazey	1904	1920	1922	4242
White, Herbert Arthur	1895	1922	1923	3624
McNeil, Edwin Calyer	1907	1923	1929	4584
Halliday, Frank W.	—	1929	1934	—
Connor, William M.	—	1934	1938	—
Betts, Edward C.	—	1938	1941	—
Connor, William M.	—	1942	1944	—
West, Charles Whitney	1920	1944	1962	6712
Lough, Frederick Charles	1938	1962	1977	11100
Berry, Robert	—	1978	1987	—
Hunt, Dennis	—	1987	1999	—
Finnegan, Patrick	1971	1999	—	29522
DEPARTMENT OF MATHEMATICAL SCIENCES				
Senior Instructor of Mathematics (1801–1812)				
Baron, George	England	1801	1802	—
Barron, William Amherst	Harvard, 1787	1802	1807	—
Hassler, Ferdinand R.	Switzerland	1807	1809	—
Partridge, Alden	1806	1809	1812	15
Department of Mathematics (1812–1989)				
Partridge, Alden	1806	1812	1813	To prof. of engineering, 15
Ellicott, Andrew	—	1813	1820	—
Douglass, David B.	—	1820	1823	To prof. of engineering
Davies, Charles	1815	1823	1837	157
Church, Albert E.	1828	1837	1878	Acting, 1837–1838, 508
Bass, Edgar Wales	1868	1878	1898	2222
Edgerton, Wright Prescott	1874	1898	1904	2522
Echols, Charles Patton	1891	1904	1931	3387
Jones, Harris	Apr. 1917	1931	1947	To Dean, 1947–1956, 5602
Bessell, William Weston, Jr.	1920	1947	1959	To Dean, 1959–1965, 6545
Nicholas, Charles Parsons	1925	1959	1967	7670
Dick, John Somers Buist	1935	1967	1974	10199

Appendix A *(continued)*

	Class	From	To	Remarks, Cullum No.
Pollin, Jack Murph	1944	1974	1985	14009
Cameron, David Herdman	1950	1985	1988	17368
Giordano, Frank Ralph	1964	1988	1989	24932
Department of Mathematical Sciences (1989–)				
Giordano, Frank Ralph	1964	1989	1994	24932
Arney, David Christopher	1971	1994	2000	29599
Krahn, Gary William	1977	2000	—	34897
DEPARTMENT OF ORDNANCE*				
Department of Ordnance and Gunnery (1857–1942)				
Benton, James Gilchrist	1842	1857	1861	1121
Benet, Stephen Vincent	1849	1861	1864	1409
Tredwell, Thomas James	1854	1864	1864	1635
Balach, George Thatcher	1851	1864	1865	1496
Mordecai, Alfred	1861	1865	1869	1941
Edson, Theodore	1860	1869	1870	1851
Bradford, Thomas Carr	June 1861	1871	1872	1938
Lyford, Stephen Carr, Jr.	June 1861	1872	1872	1943
McGinness, John Randolph	1863	1872	1874	2003
Mordecai, Alfred	1861	1874	1881	1941
Comly, Clifton	1862	1881	1886	1985
Metcalfe, Henry	1868	1886	1891	2227
Bruff, Lawrence Laurenson	1876	1891	1900	2595
Hobbs, Frank Emery	1878	1900	1904	2719
Lissak, Ormond Mitchel	1882	1904	1908	2939
O'Hein, Edward Philip	1894	1908	1908	3569
Ruggles, Colden l'Hommedieu	1890	1908	1911	3335
Tschappat, William Harvey	1869	1912	1918	Detached service 1917–1918, 3673
Mettler, Charles Gearhart	1906	1920	1924	4466
McFarland, Earl	1906	1924	1929	4474
Gillespie, Alexander Garfield	1906	1929	1933	4489
Hayes, Thomas Jay	1912	1933	1938	5037
Gatchell, Oscar James	1912	1938	1940	To Dept. of Mechanics, 5034
Leonard, Lawrence Coy	1922	1940	1942	6839
Department of Ordnance (1942–1969)				
Leonard, Lawrence Coy	1922	1942	1947	6839
Coffey, John Will	1917	1947	1951	5780

*In 1969 the Department of Ordnance was absorbed into the Department of Engineering. (See Department of Systems Engineering.)

Appendix A *(continued)*

	Class	From	To	Remarks, Cullum No.
Billingsley, John Dabney	1928	1951	1968	8341
Samz, Robert Walter	1941	1968	1969	Acting, 12305

DEPARTMENT OF PHYSICS
Department of Physics (1931–1946)

Counts, Gerald Alford	Aug. 1917	1931	1946	Acting 1931–1934, 5742

Department of Physics and Chemistry (1946–1967)

Counts, Gerald Alford	Aug. 1917	1946	1957	To Dean, 1957–1959, 5742
Gillette, Edward Clinton, Jr.	1920	1957	1964	6635
Jannarone, John Robert	1938	1964	1965	To Dean, 1965–1973, 11034
Saunders, Edward A.	1946	1965	1966	Acting, 15299
MacWilliams, Donald Gribble	1944	1966	1967	To prof. of chemistry, 1967–1977, 14041

Department of Physics (1967–)

Saunders, Edward A.	1946	1967	1984	From acting prof. of physics and chemistry, 15299
Childs, Wendell A.	1984	1987	—	
Winkel, Raymond John, Jr.	1967	1987	—	26682

DEPARTMENT OF PRACTICAL MILITARY ENGINEERING*
Department of Practical Military Engineering (1842–1922† [1925])

Swift, Alexander Joseph	1830	1842	1846	Acting 1841–1842, 587
Smith, Frederic Augustus	1833	1846	1848	707
Cullum, George Washington	1833	1848	1851	709
Bowman, Alexander Hamilton	1825	1851	1852	394
Cullum, George Washington	1833	1852	1855	709
Barnard, John Gross	1833	1855	1856	708
Donelson, Andrew Jackson, Jr.	1848	1856	1858	1370
Duane, James Chatham	1848	1858	1861	1371
Civil War				
McAlester, Miles Daniel	1856	1863	1864	1713
Craighill, William Price	1853	1864	1864	1580
Mendell, George Henry	1852	1864	1865	1538
Robert, Henry Martyn	1857	1865	1867	1763

*The department was established in 1842. During the early years of the Civil War, the functions of the department were transferred to the Department of Civil and Military Engineering. The subjects of military signaling and telegraphy were added in 1897 and then withdrawn in 1914.

†On January 1, 1923, the topics covered by this department were split between the Department of Civil and Military Engineering and the Department of Tactics. The department was formally dissolved in 1925.

Appendix A *(continued)*

	Class	From	To	Remarks, Cullum No.
Michie, Peter Smith	1863	1867	1871	To prof. of natural and experimental philosophy, 1871–1901, 1996
Ernst, Oswald H.	1864	1871	1878	Superintendent, 1893–1898, 2025
Raymond, Charles Walker	1865	1878	1881	2047
Stanton, William Sanford	1865	1881	1885	2055
Greene, Francis Vinton	1870	1885	1886	2312
Price, Phillip M., Jr.	1869	1886	1889	2276
Derby, George McClellan	1878	1889	1893	2717
Lusk, James Loring	1878	1893	1898	2718
Winslow, E. Eveleth	1889	1898	1898	3282
Goethals, George Washington	1880	1898	1900	2828
Kuhn, Joseph Ernst	1885	1900	1903	3058
Jervey, Henry	1888	1903	1905	3238
Brown, Lytle	1898	1905	1906	3812
Kutz, Charles Willaver	1893	1906	1908	3513
Wooten, William Preston	1898	1908	1910	3811
Youngberg, Gilbert Albin	1900	1910	1914	3947
Walker, Meriwether Lewis	1893	1914	1916	3514
Markham, Edward Murphy	1899	1916	1917	3872
Goethals, George Rodman	1908	1917	1918	4645
Coiner, Richard Tide	1908	1918	1918	4649
Fowler, Raymound Foster	1910	1918	1920	4861
Daley, Edmund Leo	1906	1920	1922	4457

DEPARTMENT OF SOCIAL SCIENCES

Department of Economics, Government and History [provisional] (1921–1926)

	Class	From	To	Remarks, Cullum No.
Holt, Lucius H.	Yale	1921	1926	Acting 1921–1926, also prof. of English and history, 1921–1926

Department of Economics, Government and History (1926–1947)

	Class	From	To	Remarks, Cullum No.
Holt, Lucius H.	Yale	1926	1930	—
Beukema, Herman	1915	1930	1947	5335

Department of Social Sciences (1947–)

	Class	From	To	Remarks, Cullum No.
Beukema, Herman	1915	1947	1954	5335
Lincoln, George Arthur	1929	1954	1969	8490
Jordan, Amon Azariah, Jr.	1946	1969	1972	15289
Olvey, Lee Donne	1955	1972	1989	20164
Golden, James Reed	1965	1989	1996	25489
Kaufman, Daniel Joseph	1968	1996	2000	To Dean, 2000–, 27277
Howard, Russ	San Jose State		2000	— —

Appendix A *(continued)*

	Class	From	To	Remarks, Cullum No.
DEPARTMENT OF SYSTEMS ENGINEERING*				
Professor of the Art of Engineering (1812–1820)				
Partridge, Alden	1806	1813	1816	To Superintendent, 1815–1817, 15
Crozet, Claude Ecole Polytechnic, France		1817	1820	—
Department of Engineering (1820–1827)				
Crozet, Claude Ecole Polytechnic, France		1820	1823	—
Douglass, David B.	—	1823	1827	—
Department of Civil and Military Engineering (1827–1942)†				
Douglass, David B.	—	1827	1831	—
Mahan, Dennis Hart	1824	1830	1871	Acting 1830–1832, 361
Wheeler, Junius Brutus	1855	1871	1884	1681
Mercur, James	1866	1884	1896	2116
Fiebeger, Gustav Joseph	1879	1896	1922	2764
Mitchell, William Augustus	1902	1922	1938	4068
Stamps, Thomas Dodson	Aug. 1917	1938	1942	5747
Department of Military Art and Engineering (1942–1969)				
Stamps, Thomas Dodson	Aug. 1917	1942	1956	To Dean, 1956–1957, 5747
Esposito, Vincent Joseph	1925	1956	1963	7641
Schilling, Charles Henry	1941	1963	1969	12262
Department of Engineering (1969–1989)‡				
Schilling, Charles Henry	1941	1969	1981	12262
Grum, Allen Frederick	1953	1981	1986	19026
Arbogast, Gordon Wade	1963	1986	1989	Acting, 24468
Department of Systems Engineering (1989–)				
Kays, James Lee	1962	1989	1999	Acting 1989–1990, 23824
McGinnis, Michael Luther	1977	1999	—	34726

* In 1989 the Department of Engineering was made up of three groups—Ordnance Engineering, Civil Engineering, and Engineering Management. In July of that year the Ordnance Engineering and Civil Engineering groups were combined with the Department of Mechanics to form the Department of Civil and Mechanical Engineering. The Engineering Management group became the nucleus of the new Department of Systems Engineering.

†The name of this department varied over time. I have chosen, from the various usages, titles and dates that seem to describe it best.

‡The course on the history of military art was moved to the new Department of History in 1969.

Appendix B. Rate of Departure and the Tenure of Members of the Academic Board, 1801–2000

This appendix documents the argument made in chapter 9 concerning the increasingly early departure of those members of the Academic Board who have traditionally been the Academy's corporate memory—the senior faculty of the academic departments and their Dean. This tendency toward shortened tenure of Academic Board members both reflects the turmoil among the leadership of the Academy and, at the same time, exacerbates it.

The material presented herein is drawn from the department rosters of Deans and academic department heads in Appendix A. In general, the heads of the academic departments, once selected, spent the balance of their Army careers at West Point. A few, in the nineteenth century, stayed until their deaths. More recently, the Academy's professors have been required to retire at age sixty-four, although many have left sooner. This was the pattern for most of the academic departments at the Military Academy, but the Departments of Law, Ordnance, and Practical Military Engineering were, for a long time, different in respect to the selection and tenure of their department heads. In the nineteenth century and well into the twentieth, the heads of these departments were assigned to the Military Academy by their branches for short tours of duty, usually one to three years. The Department of Practical Engineering was dissolved in the 1920s and persisted in this pattern to the end. However, at midcentury, both Ordnance and Law began selecting and treating their senior faculty in the same manner as in other academic departments. Considering this, the data concerning the departure and tenure of the heads of Practical Military Engineering have been excluded from the tables, charts, and tabulations, as had that of the Ordnance Department before 1942 and the Law Department prior to 1944. In 1969, the Department of Ordnance was absorbed by the Department of Engineering (now the Department of Systems Engineering), but the Department of Law persists to this day.

The following tables and charts reflect information on members of the Academic Board who were department heads from the following fourteen departments (and these departments' antecedents): Behavioral Sciences and Leadership, Chemistry, Civil and Mechanical Engineering, Electrical Engineering and Computer Science, English, Foreign Languages, Geography and Environmental Engineering, History, Mathematical Sciences, Physics, Social Sciences, Systems Engineering, Ordnance (1942 to 1969), and Law (beginning in 1944). Several specific aspects of the tabulation should be noted. First, as a general rule, officers assigned as "acting" heads were not included in the calculations, but exceptions to this rule were made in a few cases where the acting heads served a significant period of time. This most often occurred as departments were being created. Five acting heads were included: James Cutbush, Chemistry, 1820–1823; John Torrey, Chemistry, 1824–1827; William Fenn Hopkins, Chemistry, 1827–1835; John C. Adams, English, 1908–1910; and Gordon Wade Arbogast, Systems Engineering, 1986–1989. Second, in 1945, the position of Dean was established. Since then, eleven department heads have been selected as Dean. As Dean, of course, they continued their membership on the Academic Board, so their board tenure, which began the year they were selected as department head, actually continued to the year they retired from the deanship. Third, two department heads were selected as Superintendent: Alden Partridge (1814–1817) and Samuel Escue Tillman (1917–1919). Because the tenure of Superintendents is not considered elsewhere in these tabulations, the tenure of Partridge and Tillman was limited to that earned as department heads.

Table B.1 contains data drawn from Appendix A, including column (a), the number of department heads (or Deans) who left the Academy each year; column (b), the average tenure on the Academic Board of those who departed that year; and column (c), the number of academic departments from which data in columns (a) and (b) were drawn.

In Table B.1, at the bottom of each twenty-five-year column, the quarter-century figures in each category are calculated as follows: column (a), the sum of the number of departees of the years above; column (b), the average tenure of those departees, calculated by multiplying the annual number of departees (column a) by their average tenure (column b) and then summing those figures and dividing the result by the total number of departees for the twenty-five years; and column (c), the average number of departments for this period.

Chart B.1 displays the raw number of departees per quarter century and their average Academic Board tenure. Remarkable, on this chart, are both the rise in the number of departees and the decline in average tenure in the last half of the twentieth century, in particular in the last quarter century. The raw numbers of departees, however, are drawn from an increasing number of academic departments—six throughout most of the nineteenth century, then growing, in the twentieth century, from six to thirteen. Chart B.2 addresses the problem of comparing departure numbers when the number of departments itself changes.

Chart B.2 presents the departee numbers as the average number of board members departing per department—a figure derived simply by dividing the raw number of departees in any quarter-century period by the average number of departments for that quarter century. On chart B.2, the scale for the value of the departee information (average number of departees per department, a value from 0.67 to 3.37) is found on the left edge. The scale for the average years of tenure (values from 4.3 to 30.8) is found on the right edge. In chart B.2, as in chart B.1, the most remarkable features are the growing number of departees in the last half century (and particularly in the last twenty-five years) and the decline in tenure (which is the same in both charts).

Table B.1. Departure of Key Academic Board Members, Departees' Average Board Tenure, Number of Departments Considered
(by year and quarter century)

Year	(a)	(b)	(c)	Year	(a)	(b)	(c)	Year	(a)	(b)	(c)	Year	(a)	(b)	(c)	Year	(a)	(b)	(c)	Year	(a)	(b)	(c)	Year	(a)	(b)	(c)	Year	(a)	(b)	(c)
1801	0	0	1	1826	0	0	6	1851	0	0	6	1876	1	42	6	1901	1	30	6	1926	0	0	8	1951	1	4	11	1976	0	0	12
1802	1	1	1	1827	1	3	6	1852	0	0	6	1877	0	0	6	1902	0	0	6	1927	0	0	8	1952	0	0	11	1977	5	14	12
1803	0	0	3	1828	1	16	6	1853	0	0	6	1878	1	41	6	1903	0	0	6	1928	1	17	8	1953	1	15	11	1978	0	0	13
1804	0	0	3	1829	0	0	6	1854	0	0	6	1879	0	0	6	1904	1	6	6	1929	0	0	8	1954	1	24	11	1979	0	0	13
1805	0	0	3	1830	1	7	6	1855	0	0	6	1880	1	23	6	1905	0	0	6	1930	1	20	8	1955	0	0	11	1980	1	3	13
1806	0	0	3	1831	0	0	6	1856	0	0	6	1881	0	0	6	1906	0	0	6	1931	1	27	8	1956	1	25	11	1981	2	15	13
1807	1	5	3	1832	1	13	6	1857	1	22	6	1882	1	25	6	1907	0	0	6	1932	0	0	8	1957	1	19	11	1982	0	0	13
1808	1	5	3	1833	0	0	6	1858	0	0	6	1883	0	0	6	1908	0	0	6	1933	0	0	8	1958	0	0	11	1983	1	9	13
1809	1	2	3	1834	2	4	6	1859	0	0	6	1884	1	13	6	1909	0	0	6	1934	0	0	8	1959	1	28	11	1984	1	17	13
1810	2	5	3	1835	1	8	6	1860	0	0	6	1885	0	0	6	1910	2	10	6	1935	0	0	8	1960	0	0	11	1985	3	10	13
1811	0	0	3	1836	0	0	6	1861	0	0	6	1886	0	0	6	1911	2	33	6	1936	0	0	8	1961	3	15	11	1986	1	5	13
1812	0	0	4	1837	1	14	6	1862	0	0	6	1887	0	0	6	1912	0	0	6	1937	0	0	8	1962	1	18	11	1987	2	6	13
1813	1	4	5	1838	0	0	6	1863	0	0	6	1888	0	0	6	1913	0	0	6	1938	1	16	8	1963	2	11	11	1988	3	8	13
1814	0	0	5	1839	0	0	6	1864	0	0	6	1889	0	0	6	1914	0	0	6	1939	0	0	8	1964	1	7	11	1989	4	12	13
1815	1	5	5	1840	0	0	6	1865	0	0	6	1890	0	0	6	1915	0	0	6	1940	1	23	8	1965	2	11	11	1990	4	9	13
1816	1	3	5	1841	0	0	6	1866	0	0	6	1891	0	0	6	1916	0	0	6	1941	0	0	8	1966	0	0	11	1991	0	0	13
1817	0	0	5	1842	0	0	6	1867	0	0	6	1892	1	21	6	1917	1	16	6	1942	0	0	8	1967	1	8	12	1992	1	7	13
1818	0	0	5	1843	0	0	6	1868	0	0	6	1893	0	0	6	1918	0	0	6	1943	0	0	9	1968	2	16	12	1993	0	0	13
1819	1	7	5	1844	0	0	6	1869	0	0	6	1894	0	0	6	1919	0	0	6	1944	0	0	9	1969	1	15	12	1994	2	6	13
1820	1	7	6	1845	0	0	6	1870	0	0	6	1895	0	0	6	1920	1	9	6	1945	1	19	10	1970	0	0	12	1995	2	6	13
1821	0	0	6	1846	0	0	6	1871	3	34	6	1896	1	12	6	1921	0	0	6	1946	1	18	11	1971	0	0	12	1996	3	5	13
1822	0	0	6	1847	0	0	6	1872	0	0	6	1897	0	0	6	1922	1	26	6	1947	2	17	11	1972	2	7	12	1997	0	0	13
1823	3	4	6	1848	1	32	6	1873	0	0	6	1898	1	20	6	1923	0	0	7	1948	1	23	11	1973	2	8	12	1998	1	7	13
1824	0	0	6	1849	0	0	6	1874	0	0	6	1899	0	0	6	1924	0	0	7	1949	0	0	11	1974	0	0	12	1999	2	11	13
1825	0	0	6	1850	0	0	6	1875	0	0	6	1900	0	0	6	1925	1	15	7	1950	0	0	11	1975	0	0	12	2000	0	0	13
1st qtr	14	4.3	4	2d qtr	9	11.2	6	3d qtr	4	30.8	6	4th qtr	8	24.6	6	1st qtr	10	18.8	6	2d qtr	10	19.7	9	3d qtr	23	13.7	11	4th qtr	40	9.2	13

Column legend: (a) number of Academic Board members departing; (b) average tenure of departing Academic Board members; and (c) number of academic departments.

■ Number of Academic Board Members Departing

□ Average Tenure (years)

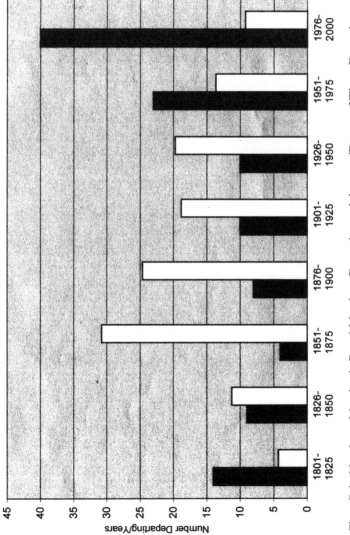

Chart B.1. Number of Academic Board Members Departing and Average Tenure of Those Departing (by quarter century)

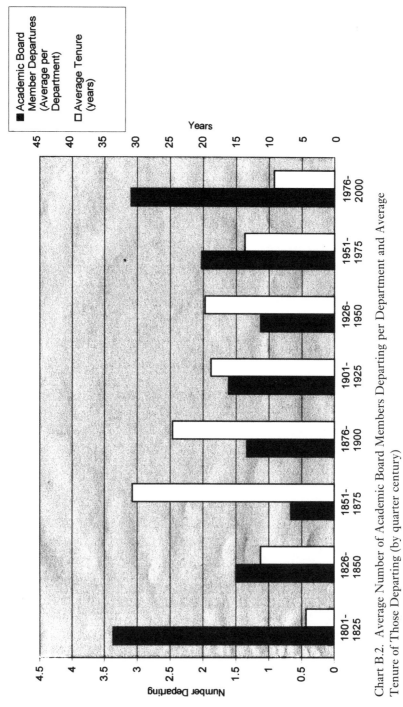

Chart B.2. Average Number of Academic Board Members Departing per Department and Average Tenure of Those Departing (by quarter century)

296

Notes

Short Titles Used Frequently in the Notes

Short titles are used throughout the notes. A full cite is provided when a source is cited for the first time; short titles are used thereafter. This list identifies those short titles that are used in the notes of more than one chapter.

Ambrose, *Duty, Honor, Country*	Stephen E. Ambrose, *Duty, Honor, Country: A History of West Point.*
ASP:MA	United States Congress, *American State Papers, Documents, Legislative and Executive, of the Congress of the United States: Military Affairs.*
Bergh, *Jefferson's Writings*	Albert Ellery Bergh, ed., *The Writings of Thomas Jefferson.*
Cappon, *Adams-Jefferson Letters*	Lester J. Cappon, ed., *The Adams-Jefferson Letters.*
Centennial History	*The Centennial of the United States Military Academy at West Point.*
Church, *Personal Reminiscences*	Albert E. Church, *Personal Reminiscences of the Military Academy from 1824 to 1831.*
Denton, "The Formative Years"	Edgar Denton, III, "The Formative Years of the United States Military Academy, 1775–1833," Ph.D. dissertation.
Forman, *West Point*	Sidney Forman, *West Point: A History of the United States Military Academy.*
Hein, *Memories of Long Ago*	Otto L. Hein, *Memories of Long Ago.*
MacArthur, *Reminiscences*	Douglas MacArthur, *Reminiscences.*
Mitchell, "Honor History"	Vance O. Mitchell, "A Brief History of the West Point and Air Force Academy Honor Codes."
Morrison, *Best School in the World*	James L. Morrison, Jr., *"The Best School in the World": West Point, the Pre–Civil War Years, 1933–1866.*

Nye, "USMA in an Era of Educational Reform" — Roger H. Nye, "The United States Military Academy in an Era of Education Reform, 1900–1925," Ph.D. dissertation.

PCC — Papers of the Continental Congress, 1774–1789, Library of Congress.

Proceedings of the Academic Board — Proceedings (Staff Records), Records of the Academic Board, RG 404, USMA Archives.

Records of the West Point Army Mess — Records of the West Point Army Mess, RG 404, USMA Archives.

Report of the Board of Visitors, [year] — *Report of the Board of Visitors, [year]*, Records of the Board of Visitors, RG 404, USMA Archives.

Supperintendents' Letterbooks — Letters Sent, Records of the Office of the Superintendent, RG 404, USMA Archives.

Swift, *Memoirs* — Joseph Gardner Swift, *The Memoirs of General Joseph Gardner Swift.*

Tillman, "Memoirs" — Samuel Tillman, "Memoirs" typescript.

USMA Annual Report, [year] — *United States Military Academy Annual Report, [year]*, Records of the Office of the Superintendent, RG 404, USMA Archives.

Wood, *West Point Scrap Book* — Oliver E. Wood, *The West Point Scrap Book.*

1. West Point in the Revolution

1. My understanding of West Point in the period of the Revolution was shaped, in large part, by a monograph on that subject created by the Department of History at the Military Academy, from which I have drawn heavily: Charles E. Miller, Jr., Donald V. Lockey, and Joseph Visconti, Jr., *Highland Fortress: The Fortification of West Point During the American Revolution* (West Point: USMA, 1988). This 1979 typescript was edited for publication in 1988 by Tom Veleker and Larry Ghormley. Unless otherwise indicated, my discussion of the fortification of the Hudson Highlands and related activities is drawn from this source. Also helpful was Dave Richard Palmer's very readable *The River and the Rock: The History of Fortress West Point, 1775–1783* (New York: Greenwood, 1969).

2. John E. Wilmolt, ed., *Journals of the Provincial Congress of New York*, 2 vols. (Albany, N.Y.: 1842), 1:723.

3. Betsy Cox, "[Reminiscences] of Miss Betsy Cox," in *Reminiscences of West Point in the Olden Time Derived from Various Sources* (East Saginaw, Mich.: Evening News Printing and Binding House, 1886).

4. Leonara Cross, "The Moores of West Point" [unpublished essay], (United States Military Academy (USMA) Library, West Point, N.Y.

5. Council of General Officers to Washington, May 17, 1777, in Philander D. Chase, ed., *The Papers of George Washington, Revolutionary War Series* (Charlottesville: University Press of Virginia, 1999).

6. John H. Bradley, "West Point and the Hudson Highlands in the American Revolution" [West Point: USMA, 1976], 9.

7. Simon Giffin, *Diary of Quartermaster Sergt Simon Giffin,* entry of January 27, 1778, is quoted in Miller et al., *Highland Fortress,* 63.

8. Samuel Parsons to Governor Clinton, February 15, 1778, quoted in Charles S. Hall, *Life and Letters of Samuel Holden Parsons: Major-General in the Continental Army and Chief Judge of the Northwestern Territory, 1737–1798* (Binghamton, N.Y.: Otseningo Publishing, 1905), 142–143.

9. Malcolm's orders are quoted in Palmer, *The River and the Rock,* 180–181.

10. An unknown author, writing from Peekskill on November 13, 1776, is quoted in Miller et al., *Highland Fortress,* 7.

11. Duportail's report of August 20, 1779, is quoted in Miller et al., *Highland Fortress,* 172.

12. On Arnold, see Willard Sterne Randall, *Benedict Arnold: Patriot and Traitor* (New York: Morrow, 1990).

13. Arnold to André, June 16, 1780, quoted in Palmer, *The River and the Rock,* 252.

14. Quoted in Palmer, *The River and the Rock,* 282.

15. The earlier Fort Clinton, near Fort Montgomery, had been abandoned when the decision was made to fortify the West Point area.

16. Washington to Lewis Nicola, June 20, 1781, in John C. Fitzpatrick, ed., *The Writings of George Washington,* 39 vols. (Washington, D.C.: GPO, [1931–1944]), 22:241–242.

17. Resolution of June 20, 1777, in *The Centennial of the United States Military Academy at West Point,* 2 vols. (Washington, D.C.: GPO, 1904; reprint, New York: Greenwood Press, 1969), 1:193.

18. John Lamb to Washington, August 10, 1781, *Centennial History,* 1:193 n.

19. Benjamin Lincoln to President of Congress, October 29, 1782, *Centennial History,* 1:194. Some chroniclers of the Military Academy have suggested that the officers of the Corps of Invalids created a school for engineers that was a precursor to the later Military Academy. That suggestion, however, derives more from the wording of the law that created the Corps than from any evidence that such a school ever existed at West Point. There had been a small detachment of Invalids at West Point before the main body of their regiment arrived, but there is no evidence that either group did any instruction there.

20. Dr. James Thacher's account, drawn from his journal, is found in Cox, "Reminiscences," 9–11.

21. Knox to Washington, July 9, 1782, Washington Papers, Library of Congress (LC).

22. Lincoln to Pickering, July 9, 1782, Document 25455, War Department Collection of Revolutionary War Records, RG 93, National Archives (NA).

23. Knox to Lincoln, July 15, 1783, Henry Knox Papers, Pierpont Morgan Library, New York.

24. John Doughty to Knox, June 30, 1784, Henry Knox Papers, Pierpont Morgan Library.

25. Benjamin Lincoln to President of Congress, March 3, 1783, Papers of the Continental Congress, 1774–1789, M247, RG 360, NA, 38:287.

26. Steuben to Washington, April 15, 1783, Washington Papers, LC.

27. Steuben to Lincoln, April 16, 1783, PCC, 38:449–465.

28. Fitzpatrick, *Writings of George Washington,* 26:396.

2. The Founding of the Military Academy

1. Report on a Military Peace Establishment, June 18, 1783, in Harold C. Syrett, ed., *The Papers of Alexander Hamilton* (New York: Columbia University Press, 1961–1979), 3:378–397.

2. Report of the Committee on the War Department, October 2, 1788, *Journals of the Continental Congress, 1774–1789,* 34 vols. (Washington, D.C.: Library of Congress, 1904–1937), 34:588–591.

3. *JCC,* 34:591.

4. Cross, "The Moores of West Point"; *JCC,* 25:614–615.

5. *JCC,* 25:616.

6. July 14, 1786, Committee report, *JCC,* 30:411–413.

7. July 31, 1786, Report of Secretary at War, *JCC,* 30:447.

8. *JCC,* 30:447.

9. *JCC,* 30:447–448.

10. Cross, "The Moores of West Point"; *Documentary History of the First Federal Congress of the United States of America,* ed. Linda Grant De Pauw and Charlene Bickford (Baltimore: Johns Hopkins University Press, 1972–), 1:2059–2062.

11. Etienne Nicholas Marie Bechat, Sieur de Rochefontaine (Stephen Rochefontaine), a French professional soldier, had served in America during the Revolutionary War. He joined his corps in June 1795 but spent the next several months inspecting fortifications and attending to the recruitment of the new companies of artillerists and engineers. He took quarters at West Point in January 1796 and remained there with the corps until his resignation in 1798.

Anne-Louis de Tousard (Louis Tousard) was born in France and had studied at the artillery school of La Père. In 1776, he was commissioned a second lieutenant in the French Royal Artillery Corps but resigned his commission to fight in the American Revolution. He gained a position on Washington's staff in June 1777 and served with some distinction during the war—losing an arm in the fighting in Rhode Island. In 1784, Tousard returned to France, but in 1794 he returned to America and, the next year, was appointed to the new Corps of Artillerists and Engineers. He returned to civilian life in 1802, when the Army was reorganized and reduced in size. In 1805, he was appointed French vice-consul in Philadelphia and later served as consul at New Orleans (1811–1815). His *American Artillerist's Companion* was published in 1808. Tousard returned to Paris in 1815 and died there in 1821.

John Jacob Ulrich Rivardi was born in Switzerland and served as an officer in the Russian army before coming to America. (Rivardi is often identified incorrectly as being French.) In early 1794, he was engaged by Henry Knox to supervise the construction of seaboard fortifications in Norfolk, Virginia, and elsewhere. The next year, he was commissioned a major in the new Corps of Artillerists and Engineers. He was discharged in 1802, when the Army was reduced, and died in 1808.

12. "An Act providing for raising and organizing a Corps of Artillerists and Engineers," May 9, 1794.

13. "Report to Military Committee, House of Representatives," February 3, 1796, in O. Pickering, *The Life of Timothy Pickering* (Boston: Little, Brown, 1867–1873), 3:136.

14. Orders of June 30 and July 6, 1795, Orderly Books of the Corps of Artillerists and Engineers, 2 vols., 1:35, 42, USMA Library.

15. Rochefontaine's order, February 10, 1796, Orderly Books of the Corps of Artillerists and Engineers, 2 vols., 2:57, USMA Library. The first "temporary engineer," Mr. C. J. Warin (often spelled "Warren"), arrived at West Point in early February 1796 and then departed the next month due to ill health. He was replaced as soon as that could be arranged, by another "temporary engineer"—a Captain Finiel. Both men were French. Rochefontaine's orders, March 28, 1796, Orderly Books of the Corps of Artillerists and Engineers, 2 vols., 2:71, USMA Library; Stephen Rochefontaine to Timothy Pickering, March 5, 1796, and C. J. Warin to Timothy Pickering, March 24, 1796, Pickering Papers, 20:134, 142, Massachusetts Historical Society (MHS), Boston.

16. Rochefontaine to Timothy Pickering, February 19, 1796, Pickering Papers, MHS.

17. Rochefontaine to Timothy Pickering, April 12, 1796, Pickering Papers, MHS. Accounts of the incident that circulated a few years later suggested that the fire was the work of disgruntled officers, but there is no other hard evidence to substantiate that claim.

18. Rochefontaine to A. Hamilton, April 28, 1796, Rochefontaine Papers, USMA Library.

19. Rochefontaine to Pickering, August 23, 1796, Pickering Papers, MHS.

20. Pickering to Knox, August 1, 1798, Pickering Papers, MHS.

21. George Washington, Eighth Annual Address, December 7, 1796, in James D. Richardson, ed., *A Compilation of the Messages and Papers of the Presidents*, 10 vols. (Washington, D.C.: GPO, 1896–1899), 1:202–203.

22. J. Steele, July 5, 1800, Letter to the Editor, *New York Spectator*, July 12, 1800.

23. Ibid.

24. John Adams to Henry Knox, November 11, 1775, in Paul H. Smith and Ronald M. Gephart, eds., *Letters of Delegates to Congress, 1774–1789*, 26 vols. (Washington, D.C.: Library of Congress, 1970–2000), 2:329. A month earlier, Adams had made a similar inquiry of William Tudor. Adams to William Tudor, October 12, 1775, in ibid., 2:170.

25. Henry Knox to John Adams, May 16, 1776, in Robert J. Taylor and Richard Ryerson, eds., *The Papers of John Adams* (Cambridge, Mass.: Belknap Press of Harvard University Press, 1977–), 4:188. Knox opens his letter by explaining why his reply to Adams's letter of November 11, 1775, was so delayed.

26. Adams to Knox, June 2, 1776, *Papers of John Adams*, 4:225.

27. Knox to Adams, September 25, 1776, *Papers of John Adams*, 5:41.

28. Knox to [Committee], September 27, 1776, PCC, 1774–1789, M247, RG360, NA, 21:29.

29. Whitfield J. Bell, Jr., *Colonel Lewis Nicola: Advocate of Monarchy, 1782*, read at the Washington Birthday Luncheon of the Pennsylvania Society of the Cincinnati, Philadelphia, February 21, 1983 (Philadelphia: Society of the Cincinnati, 1983), [4].

30. December 1793, Richardson, *Messages and Papers of the Presidents*, 1:142.

31. Alexander Hamilton to Oliver Wolcott, June 5, 1798, *Hamilton Papers*, 21:486.

32. Hamilton to Louis Le Begue Du Portail, [July 23, 1798], *Hamilton Papers*, 22:29.

33. Louis Le Begue Du Portail to Alexander Hamilton, December 9, 1798, *Hamilton Papers*, 22:339; Hamilton to McHenry, December 26, 1798, *Hamilton Papers*, 22:392; McHenry to Hamilton, December 28, 1798, *Hamilton Papers*, 22:397.

34. Norman B. Wilkinson, "The Forgotten 'Founder' of West Point," *Military Affairs* 24 (winter 1960–1961): 177–188.

35. Alexander Hamilton to James Wilkinson, October 31, 1799, *Hamilton Papers*, 23:596.

36. Hamilton to James McHenry, November 23, 1799, *Hamilton Papers*, 24:69–75.

37. Alexander Hamilton to James McHenry, November 23, 1799, *Hamilton Papers*, 23:69–75; "Military Academy, and Reorganization of the Army," January 14, 1800, United States Congress, *American State Papers: Military Affairs*, 7 vols., in *American State Papers, Documents, Legislative and Executive, of the Congress of the United States*, 38 vols. (Washington, D.C.: Gales and Seaton, 1832–1861), 1:133–135.

38. *ASP:MA*, 1:143; B. H. Latrobe, "Sketches of Proposed Military Academy," File: Architectural Drawings, USMA Library.

39. James McHenry to Harrison Gray Otis, February 11, 1800, James McHenry Papers, Clements Library, University of Michigan, Ann Arbor.

40. Manning J. Dauer (*The Adams Federalists* [Baltimore: Johns Hopkins University Press, 1953], 212–224) argues that the expansion of the Army and Hamilton's scheming to gain its command were among the most important things that defined differences between Adams and Hamilton.

41. Hamilton to Samuel Dexter, July 9, 1800, *Hamilton Papers*, 25:17–19. Jean Xavier Bureaux de Pusy (1750–1806) was a French engineer who was related, by marriage, to the Du Pont de Nemours. Bureaux de Pusy had escaped the French Revolution and had arrived in the United States only a few years earlier. In this letter Hamilton spells the Frenchman's name three different ways—De Puissy, De Pussy, and Du Pussy—all incorrect.

42. "An Act to Augment the Army of the United States, and for Other Purposes," July 16, 1798.

43. Dexter to Adams, July 16, 1800, Adams Family Papers, MHS. The correct spelling of the Frenchman's name is Bureaux de Pusy. Contemporaries managed to corrupt every element of the name on one occasion or another. See note 41.

44. John Adams to Samuel Dexter, July 25, 1800, in Charles Francis Adams, ed., *Works of John Adams, Second President of the United States,* 10 vols. (Boston: Little, Brown, 1850–1856), 9:65–66. Adams's recommendation of Barron may have stemmed from a personal acquaintance. Barron had been a Harvard classmate of John Quincy Adams. Joseph Gardner Swift, *The Memoirs of General Joseph Gardner Swift,* (privately printed, 1890), 32.

45. Arthur Pearson Wade, "Artillerists and Engineers: The Beginnings of American Seacoast Fortifications, 1794–1815" (Ph.D. diss., Kansas State University, 1977), 118.

46. John Adams to Samuel Dexter, August 13, 1800, in Adams, *Works of John Adams,* 9:79. Dexter's letter to Adams, dated August 4, is referenced in Adams's letter but was not located.

47. James Wilkinson to Jonathan Williams, 28 August, 1800, Gaff Collection, Newberry Library, Chicago.

Williams's translation of Heinrich Otto Scheel's *Treatise of Artillery [Memoires d'artillerie]* was published by the War Office in 1800, with a second volume containing tables and plates. His translation of *The Elements of Fortification* was also published by the War Office in 1800, but the first edition (500 copies) of this work was lost in the fire that destroyed the War Department offices that November. A second edition (another 500 copies) was published in 1801. Williams to Dearborn, February 6, 1802, Williams Papers, Lilly Library, Bloomington, Ind.

48. Jonathan Williams to Henry Knox, September 5, 1800, Henry Knox Papers, Pierpont Morgan Library; Jonathan Williams to Henry Knox, September 8, 1800, Williams Papers, Lilly Library.

49. Samuel Dexter to Captain Ja[me]s Taylor, November 19, 1800, Letters Sent, Secretary of War, M6, RG 107, NA.

50. Jonathan Williams to Samuel Dexter, February 24, 1801, Williams Papers, Lilly Library.

51. Albert Ellery Bergh, ed., *The Writings of Thomas Jefferson*, 20 vols. (Washington, D.C.: Thomas Jefferson Memorial Association, 1903–1904), 1:409.

52. George Baron, an Englishman, was long thought to have been a former instructor of mathematics at the Royal Military Academy at Woolwich—a colleague of Charles Hutton, Professor of Mathematics there. I have repeated this notion on a number of occasions, but in fact, it is not correct. Baron was born in England in 1769, possibly in Berwick-on-Tweed or South Shields, in the north of that country. He was the master of a mathematical academy in South Shields (Tyne and Wear) for a period in the 1790s before coming to the United States late in that decade. By mid-1798, Baron was living in Hallowell, District of Maine, where he was likely teaching mathematics. Hallowell was only a few miles from Henry Dearborn's Maine home, and it is very likely that the two men were acquainted. Baron moved from there to New York City in early 1801 and continued to teach mathematics and natural philosophy. In April 1801, he was approached by the new Jefferson administration and invited to become the instructor of mathematics at the military academy it was creating at West Point. After a brief exchange of correspondence, in which Dearborn agreed to attempt to get Baron more pay, he accepted.

The belief that Baron had taught at Woolwich seems to have originated with General Joseph Gardner Swift, who was one of Baron's first students at West Point. As Swift wrote in his memoirs, "He had been a fellow teacher with Charles Hutton on the military academy at Woolwich" (27). Swift may have come to this conclusion because Baron championed the use, at West Point, of Charles Hutton's text, which had been written by the Woolwich professor for use at that school. On Baron at West Point see Swift, *Memoirs*.

53. Henry Dearborn to George Barron [*sic* Baron], April 11, 1801, Miscellaneous Letters Sent, Secretary of War, M370, RG 107, NA. The letter to Baron was sent to Edward Livingston, who was asked to forward it. In a note to Livingston, Dearborn indicated having discussed Baron with him. This, and his belief that Livingston knew Baron's whereabouts, suggests that Dearborn had furnished the Englishman a letter of introduction. (Henry Dearborn to Edward Livingston, April 11, 1801, Miscellaneous Letters Sent, Secretary of War, M370, RG 107, NA.) Baron's appointment was for a long time attributed to John Adams, for it was mistakenly believed that Baron was appointed to the post on January 6, 1801. In fact, Baron's appointment as "Teacher of the Arts and Sciences to the Artillerists and Engineers" was dated June 6, 1801. (Dearborn to Baron, June 6, 1801, Miscellaneous Letters Sent, Secretary of War, M370, RG 107, NA.) The earliest use of the incorrect January date appears to be in Roswell Park, *A Sketch of the History and Topography of West Point and the U.S. Military Academy* (Philadelphia: Henry Perkins, 1840), 54. The mistake may

simply have come from misreading a manuscript source, where the abbreviations "Jun" and "Jan" are often difficult to distinguish. Writers for many years followed Park's lead. The January date, of course, placed his appointment in the last weeks of the Adams administration. Although there is no indication whatsoever of any correspondence between Baron and Adams or Dexter, some chroniclers may also have been confused because President Adams had suggested appointing Captain William A. Barron as an instructor in mathematics.

Baron at first rejected Dearborn's offer but later accepted it when the Secretary agreed to seek an increase in the pay. George Baron to Henry Dearborn, May 19 and June 1, 1801, Register of Letters Received, War Department, M22, RG 107, NA. Baron reported to West Point in July 1801.

54. Henry Dearborn to Commanding Officer of West Point, April 15, 1801, Letters Sent, Secretary of War, M6, RG 107, NA.

55. Williams to Jefferson, March 7, 1801, Jefferson Papers, LC.

56. James Wilkinson to Williams, April 10, 1801, Williams Papers, Lilly Library; Williams to W. W. Barrons, July 17, 1803, Williams Papers, Lilly Library; Williams to Dearborn, June 18, 1801, Williams Papers, Lilly Library.

57. [Statement of Fortifications, Public Buildings, Quartermaster Department, Manufacture of Cannon, Indian Affairs, State of the Army, and Military Bounty Lands], May 12, 1801, Jefferson Papers, LC; Henry Dearborn to James Wilkinson, May 12, 1801, Letters Sent, Secretary of War, M6, RG 107, NA; Henry Dearborn to Captain George Fleming, May 12, 1801, Letters Sent, Secretary of War, M6, RG 107, NA; Henry Dearborn to Captain George Fleming, May 26, 1801, Letters Sent, Secretary of War, M6, RG 107, NA.

58. Henry Dearborn to George Fleming, May 12, 1801, Letters Sent, Secretary of War, M6, RG 107, NA; Louis Tousard to Henry Dearborn, May 18, 1801, cited in Wilkinson, "Forgotten 'Founder,'" 185.

59. Henry Dearborn to George Fleming, May 26, 1801, Letters Sent, Secretary of War, M6, RG 107, NA.

60. Edward Lillie Pierce, *[The Life of] Major John Lillie, 1755–1801 [and] the Lillie Family of Boston, 1663–1896* (Cambridge, Mass.: John Wilson and Son, University Press, 1896), 31.

61. Henry Dearborn to Thomas H. Cushing, July 2, 1801, Letters Sent, Secretary of War, M6, RG 107, NA; Louis Tousard to Henry Burbeck, September 21, 1801, Burbeck Papers, USMA Library.

62. On the Federalist position in this debate, see Richard H. Kohn, *Eagle and Sword: The Federalists and the Creation of the Military Establishment in America, 1783–1802* (New York: Free Press, 1975). On the Jeffersonian position, see Theodore J. Crackel, *Mr. Jefferson's Army: The Political and Social Reform of the Military Establishment, 1801–1809* (New York: New York University Press, 1987).

63. Stephen E. Ambrose, *Duty, Honor, Country: A History of West Point* (Baltimore: Johns Hopkins University Press, 1966), 18. Why Jefferson should think a

military academy had a better chance of success than a civil school among Republicans who had always opposed it, Ambrose does not explain. See also Henry Adams, *History of the United States of America,* 9 vols. (New York: C. Scribner's, 1889–1891), 1:302; Thomas J. Fleming, *West Point: The Men and Times of the United States Military Academy* (New York: William Morrow, 1969), 16; Dorothy J. S. Zuersher, "Benjamin Franklin, Jonathan Williams and the United States Military Academy" (Ph.D. diss., University of North Carolina at Greensboro, 1974), 90–91.

64. Dumas Malone, *Jefferson and His Time,* vol. 5, *Jefferson the President, Second Term, 1805–1809* (Boston: Little, Brown, 1974), 510. See also James Ripley Jacobs, *The Beginning of the U.S. Army, 1783–1812* (Princeton, N.J.: Princeton University Press, 1947), 297; and Wade, "Artillerists and Engineers," 138. Sidney Forman ("Why the United States Military Academy Was Established in 1802," *Military Affairs* 29 [spring 1965]: 16–28) suggests only that it was needed to provide the practical training not available at other schools. That, however, seems to have been limited to drill and occasional lectures by Williams on fortifications. Practical experience was, for the most part, gained later "on the job."

65. See Russell F. Weigley, *Towards an American Army: Military Thought from Washington to Marshall* (New York: Columbia University Press, 1962), 27; Forest Garrett Hill, *Roads, Rails and Waterways: The Army Engineers and Early Transportation* (Norman: University of Oklahoma Press, 1957), 12–13.

66. Crackel, *Mr. Jefferson's Army.*

67. Henry Dearborn to Jonathan Williams, March 24, 1806, Letters Sent, Secretary of War, M6, RG 107, NA.

68. On these developments, see George H. Daniels, *American Science in the Age of Jackson* (New York: Columbia University Press, 1968). The United States Military Philosophical Society founded by the early faculty—once called "the first national scientific society" (G. Brown Goode, "The Origin of the National Scientific and Educational Institutions," *Annual Report of the American Historical Association for the Year 1889* [Washington, D.C.: GPO, 1890], 68)—should be viewed more as a remnant of Enlightenment science than as a precursor of the kind of professional scientific societies that came a few decades later. Despite Jefferson's formal patronage, he gave the society only token support.

69. James William Kershner, "Sylvanus Thayer: A Biography" (Ph.D. diss., West Virginia University, 1976), 10–14. Jonathan Williams ["A report on the progress and present state of the Military Academy"], March 14, 1808, in "Military Academy," *ASP:MA,* 1:229–230. See also "Statement of the examination of Cadets. . . ," 1806, Jonathan Williams Papers, USMA Library.

70. Kershner, "Sylvanus Thayer," 47; Williams, "Military Academy, 1808," 1:229.

71. Williams, "Military Academy, 1808," 1:229.

72. From an 1819 report by Colonel William McRee (USMA, 1806) and Brigadier General Simon Bernard, quoted in "Military Academy at West Point," *American*

Quarterly Review 22 (September 1837): 91–92. The increased emphasis on military engineering coincides with the arrival of Thayer (1817), and the addition of civil engineering comes with the new national interest in internal improvements. Rufus King, an early member of the Board of Visitors at West Point, recommended in 1821 that the Academy begin to teach civil engineering, thereby providing talents the nation then needed. The subject was introduced not long thereafter—but not without some resistance at West Point. King to Christopher Gore, June 22, 1821, in Charles R. King, ed., *The Life and Correspondence of Rufus King,* 6 vols. (New York: Putnam's, 1900), 6:393–394.

73. On the military aspects of this broader context, see Crackel, *Mr. Jefferson's Army.* On civil service and court reform, see Carl E. Prince, "The Passing of the Aristocracy: Jefferson's Removal of the Federalists," *Journal of American History* 51 (December 1970): 563–575.

74. Thomas Jefferson to Nathaniel Macon, May 14, 1801, in Bergh, *Jefferson's Writings,* 10:260–261. See note 57.

75. Joseph Gardner Swift, "Mss Memoirs," 34, Joseph Gardner Swift Papers, USMA Library. (This line and others were left out of the published version of these memoirs, possibly because they were considered negative or controversial. Those who use Swift's memoirs are encouraged to consult the manuscript version.)

76. See "Applicants for Military Appointments," RG 94, NA.

77. Moses Wingate to Henry Dearborn, July 18, 1806, Moses Elliott File, USMA Cadet Application Papers, 1805–1866, M688, RG 94, NA. Moses Elliott was given a cadet warrant but appears never to have gone to West Point. Based on an examination of a list of "Applicants for Military Appointments" (RG 94, NA), it appears that one-third of all cadets appointed never appear on the Academy's rolls—and can be assumed never to have enrolled at West Point.

78. Israel Smith to Henry Dearborn, December 5, 1808, John Reed File, USMA Cadet Application Papers, 1805–1866, M688, RG 94, NA. John Reed was appointed a cadet but also never seems to have enrolled at West Point. The Cadet Application Papers are very sketchy for the early years. Only a small portion of the applicants are represented for the first decade of the school's existence, and even where files are present, few seem to be complete. Still, there are enough examples to suggest a pattern of political comment, one that is even more clear in applications for other military appointments—in both the Republican and Federalist eras.

79. John Willard to Henry Dearborn, January 30, 1807, Letters Received, Adjutant General, M566, RG94, NA. This letter was in reference to Huntington Minor.

80. John Adams, *A Defence of the Constitutions of Government of the United States of America,* 3d ed., 3 vols. (Philadelphia: Budd and Bartram, 1797), 1:110.

81. Sidney H. Aronson, *Status and Kinship in the Higher Civil Service* (Cambridge, Mass.: Harvard University Press, 1964), 9.

82. Some Republicans put considerable faith in the ability of educational institu-

tions to reshape men. "I consider it is possible to convert men into republican machines," wrote Benjamin Rush in a essay first published in 1786 and reprinted in 1802. But Jefferson's aim for the Academy was made of simpler stuff. The school was not intended to politicize; it would not, as Rush might have suggested, make Republicans of Army officers. Instead, it would make Army officers of Republicans. Rush quoted in Linda K. Kerber, *Federalists in Dissent: Imagery and Ideology in Jeffersonian America* (Ithaca, N.Y.: Cornell University Press, 1970), 109.

3. The Early Years

1. Henry Dearborn to George Fleming, May 12 and 26, 1801, Letters Sent, Secretary of War, M6, RG 107, NA.

2. George Baron to Dearborn, July 24, 1801, Register of Letters Received, War Department, M22, RG 107, NA.

3. Swift, *Memoirs*, p. 27.

4. Dearborn to Baron, October 19, 1801, Miscellaneous Letters Sent, Secretary of War, M370, RG 107, NA.

5. Ibid.

6. Swift, *Memoirs*, 27–28.

7. Dearborn to Baron, October 30, 1801, Letters Sent, Secretary of War, M6, RG 107, NA; Swift, *Memoirs*, 28.

8. Dearborn to Baron, December 2, 1801, Letters Sent, Secretary of War, M6, RG 107, NA.

9. Jonathan Williams, Academy Orders, January 18, 1802, Letterbook, Williams Papers, Lilly Library.

10. Dearborn to Williams, January 19, 1802, Williams Papers, Lilly Library.

11. Dearborn to Baron, January 19, 1802, Letters Sent, Secretary of War, M6, RG 107, NA; Williams to Dearborn, February 4, 1802, Williams Papers, Lilly Library; Dearborn to Baron, February 11, 1802, Letters Sent, Secretary of War, M6, RG 107, NA.

Upon leaving West Point, Baron returned to New York City and reopened his mathematics school, adding navigation to the courses taught there. Sometime in 1803 (or shortly before), he wrote a book on navigation, which he attempted, without success, to have published. In 1804, Baron launched the *Mathematical Correspondent*, the first mathematical journal in the United States. Baron operated this publication until 1806, when he turned the magazine over to Robert Adrain, who issued one additional number and then closed it. Baron operated his mathematics school in New York until late 1809 or early 1810, when he left the city. In 1811, he published an interest chart in New York but it seems he was not living in the city at that time. Whether he remained in America or returned to England is not known, and we do not know the date or place of his death.

Baron was taciturn and difficult—not an easy man to get along with. Swift described him as "ungentlemanly and irritating" and "of rude manner." At the same time, Swift called him "an able teacher" (Swift, *Memoirs*, 27–28). His *Mathematical Correspondent* and other published works are filled with biting criticism and scorn for other mathematicians and their work. His most significant contribution was to give Adrain and other American mathematicians an opportunity to read and publish articles and problems.

On Baron and the *Mathematical Correspondent,* see Edward R. Hogan, "George Baron and the *Mathematical Correspondent," Historia Mathematica* 3 (1976): 403–415. On Baron and his school in New York City, see the annual city directories, by Longworth and others, in the Early American Imprint series published by the American Antiquarian Society, Worcester, Mass.

12. Williams to Dearborn, February 4, 1802, Williams Papers, Lilly Library; Williams to Dearborn, February 6, 1802, Williams Papers, Lilly Library.

13. "Military Peace Establishment Act of 1802," March 16, 1802.

14. "Military Academy and Reorganization of the Army," January 13, 1800, *ASP: MA,* 1:135.

15. Because of the similarity of their last names, these two men are sometimes confused. George Baron, the Englishman, was the first instructor at the Military Academy but was dismissed in early 1802. The American, Captain William Amherst Barron, whom Adams had first suggested, was ordered to West Point in mid-1802 by the Jefferson administration, also to teach mathematics.

16. Williams to Dearborn, January 19, 1802, Letterbook, Williams Papers, Lilly Library.

17. Williams to W. A. Barron, June 9, [1802], Williams Papers, Lilly Library.

18. Abraham Baldwin to Thomas Jefferson, March 29, 1802, Thomas Jefferson Papers, MHS.

19. Abraham Baldwin to Jared Mansfield, April 4, 1802, Abraham Baldwin Papers, Yale University Library, New Haven, Conn.

20. Dearborn to Jared Mansfield, May 4, 1802, Jared Mansfield Papers, USMA Library.

21. Dearborn to Williams, May 31, 1802, Letters Sent, Secretary of War, M6, RG 107, NA; Dearborn to Williams, July 8, 1802, Letters Sent, Secretary of War, M6, RG 107, NA; Williams to Mr. Dufief, July 14, 1802, Letterbook, Williams Papers, Lilly Library; Williams to Decius Wadsworth, July 14, 1802, Letterbook, Williams Papers, Lilly Library.

Williams's list *with Jefferson's notes in the margin* has not been found, although it is probably a part of or enclosed with the May 19, 1802, letter that Dearborn refers to in his letter of May 31. We cannot, therefore, be certain of the content of Jefferson's notes, or what books and instruments he may have added or deleted. However, Williams's letters to Dufief and Wadsworth, cited earlier, do seem to contain the list (or partial list) of books that were approved for purchase—Etienne Bézout's *Cours de mathématiques à l'usage de l'artillerie* (4 vols.) and the companion set, *Cours de mathématiques à l'usage de la marine* (6 vols.), and selected volumes of the expansive *Encyclopédia methodique,* in particular a selection of the multivolume *Dictionares methodique: Art militaire, Arts & métiers, Equitation l'escrime, Geographie, Marine,* and *Mathématiques* (in all, 24 vols.). It is very likely that the Bezout volumes, at least, were Jefferson's suggestion (or certainly approved by him), for he was still recommending them as texts for military schools some twenty years later. Jefferson to John Adams, September 12, 1821, in Lester J. Cappon, ed., *The Adams-Jefferson Letters,* 2 vols. (Chapel Hill: University of North Carolina Press, 1959), 2:575.

Williams apparently had difficulty locating and purchasing these precise books, but he did find another Bezout set covering much the same material. The lists of books in the library of the Military Academy in 1807 and 1810 show Bezout's *Cours de mathématiques, à l'usage des gardes du pavillon et de la marine* (6 vols.). There is no indication that the library owned any element of the *Encyclopédia methodique* prior to the catalog of the Academy's books in 1822. That copy was likely purchased by Major Sylvannus Thayer and Colonel William McRee when they were in Europe (1815–1817) to buy library materials for the Military Academy. "A list of Books belonging to the Library of the Military Academy," November 1, [1807], Williams Papers, Lilly Library; Sylvanus Thayer, "Return of Books, Instruments, Maps and other public property at the Military Academy," February 17, 1810, Williams Papers, Lilly Library; *Catalogue of Books in the Library of the Military Academy, August 1822* (Newburgh, N.Y.: Ward M. Gazlay, 1822).

22. Williams to Barron, June 9, [1802], Williams Papers, Lilly Library.

23. Williams to Dearborn, July 6, 1802, Letterbook, Williams Papers, Lilly Library.

24. Barron and Mansfield to Williams, December 1, 1802, Williams Papers, Lilly Library.

25. Williams to Dearborn, September 1, 1802, Williams Papers, Lilly Library.

26. Williams to Decius Wadsworth, August 13, 1802, Letterbook, Williams Papers, Lilly Library.

27. Wadsworth to Williams, September 5, 1802, Jonathan Williams Papers, USMA Library.

28. Williams to Dearborn, October 4, 1802, Williams Papers, Lilly Library.

29. H. Dearborn to J. Williams, February 17, 1802, Williams Papers, Lilly Library. On the process of political reform of the army, see Crackel, *Mr. Jefferson's Army,* esp. chap. 2, "A Chaste Reformation."

30. "West Point Vu en 1795 par la Rochefoucaude-Liancourt," *Revue International d'Historie Militaire* 32 (1972–1975): 495–498.

31. Swift, *Memoirs,* 27

32. Williams to Dearborn, July 19, 1802, Williams Papers, Lilly Library.

33. Edgar Denton III, "The Formative Years of the United States Military Academy, 1775–1833" (Ph.D. diss., Syracuse University, 1964), 34.

34. Williams to Dearborn, October 14, 1802, Letterbook, Williams Papers, Lilly Library; Barron to Williams, October 21, 1802, Williams Papers, Lilly Library.

35. On the activities of the United States Military Philosophical Society, see Arthur P. Wade, "A Military Offspring of the American Philosophical Society," *Military Affairs* 38 (September 1974): 103–107.

36. Wadsworth to Williams (Wadsworth's emphasis), January 17, 1803, Williams Papers, Lilly Library.

37. Swift, *Memoirs*, p. 37.

38. Ibid.

39. Williams, "Military Academy, 1808," 229.

40. Henry Dearborn, July 5, 1802, "Regulations for West Point," Williams Papers, Lilly Library.

41. Williams to Dearborn, September 8, 1802, Williams Papers, Lilly Library.

42. Williams to Barron, September 13, 1802, Williams Papers, Lilly Library; "Points" [March 1803], Williams Papers, Lilly Library; Williams to Jefferson, June 24, 1803, Daniel Parker Papers, Historical Society of Pennsylvania (HSP), Philadelphia.

43. [Jonathan Williams], Engineer Orders, June 20, 1803, Williams Papers, Lilly Library.

44. Dearborn to Wadsworth, 21 June 1803, Williams Papers, Lilly Library.

45. Elizabeth Mansfield to Miss Harriot Sisson [later Mrs. Harriot Drake], December 26, 1802, Elizabeth Mansfield Papers, USMA Library.

46. Swift, *Memoirs*, 41.

47. Alexander Macomb to Williams, October 8, 1804, Williams Papers, Lilly Library.

48. R. W. Osborn to James Wilkinson, December 9, 1804, Daniel Parker Papers, HSP.

49. James Wilkinson to Jonathan Williams, March 29, 1805, Williams Papers, Lilly Library. Wilkinson was apparently repeating information given him personally by Macomb.

50. Jonathan Williams to Henry Dearborn, May 27, 1805, Williams Papers, Lilly Library. In this letter, Williams indicates that Dearborn, in a private conversation during a journey they had made in late April, had informed him of rumors about Barron and a woman he kept in his quarters.

51. Alexander Macomb to J. Williams, March 1, 1805, Williams Papers, Lilly Library.

52. All three letters from Wilkinson to Williams, March 29, 1805, are in the Williams Papers at the Lilly Library.

53. This discussion of Barron and his women draws on Jonathan Williams, Notes on Testimony, [June 1807], Williams Papers, Lilly Library; Jonathan Williams, "Notes for the testimony of J[onathan] W[illiams]," June 15, 1807, Williams Papers, Lilly Library. Although Williams destroyed the materials generated by the inquiry in 1805, another such inquiry in 1807 reviewed the events of 1805.

54. Williams to Swift, February 8, 1805, Joseph Gardner Swift Papers, USMA Library.

55. Jonathan Williams to Alexander Macomb, November 29, 1806, Williams Papers, Lilly Library; W. A. Barron to Williams, January 20, 1807, Williams Papers, Lilly Library.

56. Williams to Dearborn, June 5, 1805, Williams Papers, Lilly Library.

57. Barron to Williams, May 5, 1805, Williams Papers, Lilly Library; Williams to Dearborn, June 8, 1805, Williams Papers, Lilly Library.

58. Williams to Dearborn, June 24, 1805, Williams Papers, Lilly Library.

59. Williams to Dearborn, June 24, 1805, Williams Papers, Lilly Library; Dearborn to Williams, July 1, 1805, Letters Sent, Secretary of War, M6, RG 107, NA; Barron to Williams, January 20, 1807, Williams Papers, Lilly Library.

60. Williams to Dearborn, June 5, 1805, Williams Papers, Lilly Library.

61. Ibid.

62. Dearborn to Williams, June 19, 1805, Williams Papers, Lilly Library.

63. William A. Barron to Jonathan Williams, May 7, 1806, Williams Papers, Lilly Library. A few months earlier, Barron had warned Williams that if the Academy was to stay at West Point, repairs would be necessary to some of the key buildings.

64. Alexander Macomb to Williams, February 6, 1806, Williams Papers, Lilly Library.

65. Jonathan Williams to Henry Dearborn, May 22, 1806, Williams Papers, Lilly Library. Again, Williams's request for musicians seems to have been ignored, but on occasion one or two musicians were sent to West Point from the garrison at Governor's Island in New York Harbor.

66. Dearborn to Fleming, May 24, 1806, Letters Sent, Secretary of War, M6, RG 107, NA.

67. Alexander Macomb to Jonathan Williams, November 7, 1806, Williams Papers, Lilly Library.

68. Williams to Alexander Macomb, November 29, 1806, Williams Papers, Lilly Library.

69. Williams to Dearborn, December 27, 1806, Williams Papers, Lilly Library.

70. Williams to Swift, March 23, 1807, Joseph Gardner Swift Papers, USMA Library.

71. Jonathan Williams to Marianne Williams (wife), February 7, 1807, Williams Manuscripts, Yale University Library.

72. Williams to Swift, March 23, 1807, Swift Papers, USMA Library.

73. Jonathan Williams, "West Point Orders," October 12, 1807, Williams Papers, Lilly Library.

74. Williams to Jefferson, March 5, 1808, Williams Papers, Lilly Library; [Dearborn] to [Jefferson], March 7, 1808, Williams Papers, Lilly Library.

75. Williams, "Military Academy, 1808." This proposal was submitted to Jefferson in draft, as was a proposal by Dearborn, who proposed two professors (military and

civil engineering, and mathematics) and four assistants. Both proposed adding ten officers and cadets to the Corps of Engineers.

76. Williams, "Military Academy, 1808."

77. Prior to the 1808 legislation, a total of between forty-four and fifty cadets (forty cadets of artillery and from four to ten of engineers) had been authorized. The wording of the Military Peace Establishment Act of 1802 had provided for the variable number. In addition to forty artillery cadets, it originally authorized ten cadets of engineers in the beginning—part of a combined total of twenty engineer officers and cadets. That total of twenty included sixteen authorized officer billets, of which only ten were to be filled immediately. By 1808, the engineer corps had its full complement of sixteen officers, leaving only four slots for cadets.

78. Williams to Mansfield (Williams's emphasis), March 20, 1809, Jared Mansfield Papers, USMA Library.

79. R. Whiley to Williams, February 2, 1809, Williams Papers, Lilly Library.

80. William Eustis to Mansfield, January 4, 1810, Jared Mansfield Papers, USMA Library.

81. My understanding of Eustis and Madison, and their relations with the Military Academy, has been much aided by Denton, "The Formative Years."

82. Eustis to James Madison, July 29, 1810, Robert A. Rutland and John C. A. Stagg, eds., Papers of James Madison, Presidential Series, 4 vols. to date (Charlottesville: University Press of Virginia, 1984–), 2:453.

83. Jonathan Williams to James Madison, June 13, 1810, Williams Papers, USMA Library.

84. Williams to Swift, October 9, 1812, Swift Manuscripts, USMA Library.

85. "An Act making further provision for the Corps of Engineers," April 29, 1812.

86. Armstrong to Swift, June 24, 1814, quoted in Denton, "The Formative Years," 95.

87. Swift to Armstrong, July 3, 1813, Letters Sent, Relating to the Military Academy, M91, RG 94, NA.

88. Swift, "Sketch of a Plan for the Conducting of a Military Academy," January 1808, Swift Manuscripts, USMA Library; on Swift's 1808 proposals, see Denton, "The Formative Years," 59–64.

89. The discussion of Swift's opposition to narrowly trained military technicians is drawn from Denton, "The Formative Years," 63ff. The Swift quotation is from his memoirs. Joseph Gardner Swift, Mss. Memoirs, 34, Joseph Gardner Swift papers, USMA Library. (The line in question was not included in the published version.)

90. War Department to Partridge, July 1, 1814, quoted in Denton, "The Formative Years," 93.

91. Warren Howe, "The Beginnings of the West Point Band," <http://www.usma.edu/band/news/99/Summer05.htm>, summer 1999.

92. Swift to John Armstrong, July 3, 1813, Letters Sent, Relating to the Military Academy, M91, RG 94, NA; Swift to Armstrong, February 16, 1814, Letters Sent, Relating to the Military Academy, M91, RG 94, NA; Swift to Monroe, December 8, 1814, Letters Sent [by the Engineer Department] Relating to the Military Academy, M91, RG 94, NA.

93. Swift to Monroe, December 30, 1815, Letters Sent, Relating to the Military Academy, M91, RG 94, NA.

94. Jared Mansfield to Swift, August 26, 1814, Sylvanus Thayer Papers, USMA Library; Mrs. Charles Davies, "Reminiscences of Colonel Jared Mansfield, Received Through His Daughter, Mrs. Davies," pts. 2 and 3 of *Reminiscences of West Point in the Olden Time Derived from Various Sources* (East Saginaw, Mich.: Evening News Printing and Binding House, 1886), 20.

95. Elizabeth Mansfield to [Daniel Drake], December 8, 1817, Elizabeth Mansfield Papers, USMA Library.

96. Elizabeth Mansfield to Daniel Drake, January 26, 1817, Elizabeth Mansfield Papers, USMA Library.

97. "Account of the National Military School of the United States of America," *[London] Quarterly Journal* 21 (April 1826): 3.

98. Jared Mansfield, Andrew Ellicott, and E.E. Zoeller to Secretary of War, January 2, 1815, Partridge Papers, USMA Library.

99. James Monroe to Partridge, January 22, 1815, quoted in Denton, "The Formative Years," 106.

100. Swift to Ellicott, February 2, 1815, quoted in Denton, "The Formative Years," 106.

101. Partridge to Swift, February 6, 1815, quoted in Denton, "The Formative Years," 107.

102. Ellicott to Swift, February 10, 1815, Thayer Papers, USMA Library.

103. Mansfield to David Dagget, February 5, 1816, David Dagget Papers, Yale University Library.

104. Swift, *Memoirs,* 141–142.

105. Thayer to Swift, March 24, 1854, Thayer Papers, USMA Library.

106. Swift to Daniel Parker, November 4, 1814, Daniel Parker Papers, HSP.

107. George Graham [Ad Interim Secretary of War] to Swift, May 19, 1817, quoted in Denton, "The Formative Years," 159.

4. Sylvanus Thayer: Father of the Military Academy

1. My understanding of the Thayer years was much aided by Edgar Denton, "The Formative Years of the United States Military Academy, 1775–1833" (Ph.D. diss., Syracuse University, 1964).

2. George Graham [Acting Secretary of War] to Thayer, August 6, 1817, Letters Sent, Secretary of War, M6, RG 107, NA.

3. Thayer, "Memorandum to the Academic Staff," [mid-]August 1817, Thayer Papers, USMA Library. Although this document is undated, the evidence very clearly suggests to me that the document was drafted in midmonth—*after* receipt of George Graham's letter of August 6, 1817, cited in note 2 above.

4. Thayer to Swift, September 10, 1817, Miscellaneous Letters Sent, Secretary of War, M370, RG 107, NA.

5. Paragraph 14 [Duties of the Academic Board], Article 78 (Military Academy), *General Regulations for the Army* (Philadelphia: M. Carey and Sons, 1821), 527. At this time the Academy's regulations were simply incorporated into the broader "Regulations for the Army."

6. Thayer to Josiah Moulton, October 17, 1817, Cullum Papers [Thayer file, Box 5], USMA Library.

7. Thayer, "Order," September 29, 1817, Thayer Papers, USMA Library.

8. Swift to George Graham, September 7, 1817, Military Academy Letters, Engineer Department, RG 77, NA.

9. Edward Deering Mansfield, *Personal Memories, Social, Political and Literary* (Cincinnati: R. Clarke and Co., 1879), 70–71.

10. Thayer to Calhoun, January 31, 1818, Letters Received, Engineer Department, RG 77, NA. This first midwinter examination was conducted over the period December 15, 1817, to January 3, 1818.

11. Rawling Lowndes to G. W. Cullum, November 29, 1872, Cullum Files, USMA Library.

12. Quoted in Robert H. Hall, "Early Discipline at the United States Military Academy," *Journal of the Military Service Institute of the United States* 2 (1882): 473.

13. [Committee of Five] to Thayer, November 24, 1818, [included as "c" in] December 27, 1819, "Complaints Against the Military Academy at West Point," *ASP:MA*, 2:12.

14. Thayer to Walker K. Armistead [Chief of Engineers], [November 1818], in Hall, "Early Discipline," 471.

15. Article 78, "Military Academy," *General Regulations for the Army.*

16. Oliver E. Wood, *West Point Scrap Book* (New York: Van Nostrand, 1871), 29.

17. The story of the Egg-Nog Riot of 1826 is best told in a historical novel about the event: James B. Agnew, *Eggnog Riot: The Christmas Mutiny at West Point* (San Rafael, Calif.: Presidio Press, 1979). Agnew draws heavily on the documentary record and stays very close to it.

18. Albert E. Church, *Personal Reminiscences of the Military Academy, from 1824 to 1831* (West Point: USMA Press, 1879), 66.

19. Swift, *Memoirs*, 151.

20. John H. B. Latrobe, "West Point Reminiscences," in *Eighteenth Annual Reunion of the Association of Graduates* (East Saginaw, Mich., 1887), 6.

21. Cozzens quoted in Church, *Personal Reminiscences,* 25.

22. Church, *Personal Reminiscences,* 17.

23. "Memorandum of agreement between Thayer and Gridley," October 26, 1820, and Thayer to Macomb, January 28, 1823, Correspondence Relating to the Military Academy, RG 94, NA. The government purchased the Gridley property in 1823 with the understanding that Gridley could continue to occupy and operate his establishment for another year.

24. Church, *Personal Reminiscences,* 19.

25. Robert J. Wood, "Early Days of Benny Havens," *The Pointer,* February 26, 1937.

26. Wood, *West Point Scrap Book,* 59–64.

27. On musical clubs, see F. A. Smith to Lewis Cass, December 9, 1832, Thayer Papers, USMA Library; on literary clubs, see Park, *History of West Point,* 117–119.

28. George Ticknor to wife, June 5, 1826, in Davies, "Jared Mansfield," 28.

29. Though commutation (monetary rather than in-kind compensation) was authorized in 1829, it was not yet being paid in January 1831. BG Charles Gratiot to Lt. Kinsley, October 1, 1829, [filed with Knowlton to Thayer, January 27, 1831], Correspondence Relating to the Military Academy, 1819–1866, RG 94, NA.

30. Church, *Personal Reminiscences,* 84.

31. L. B. Webster to Thomas S. Jessup, November 21, 1832, and December 20, 1832, "Buildings" file, USMA Library; Irwin McDowell to G. S. Anderson, February 16, 1881, in Minutes, Records of the West Point Army Mess, RG 404, USMA Archives, 3:70–74.

32. George Graham to Thayer, August 6, 1817, Letters Sent, Secretary of War, M6, RG 107, NA.

33. Thayer to Graham, August 1, 1817, Thayer Papers, USMA Library.

34. [Thayer], "Estimate of Appropriations Necessary for 1818," December 1, 1817, Thayer Papers, USMA Library. In addition to new housing, Thayer requested funds for a new hospital and moneys to enlarge the kitchen of the recently completed mess hall.

35. Calhoun to Thayer, January 8, 1818, Thayer Papers, USMA Library.

36. Thayer to Calhoun, January 19, 1818, and "Report on Public Quarters at West Point," January [19], 1818, Thayer Papers, USMA Library.

37. Thayer to W. K. Armistead, Correspondence Relating to the Military Academy, 1819–1866, RG 94, NA; Elizabeth Mansfield to Daniel Drake, January 31, 1819, Elizabeth Mansfield Papers, USMA Library.

38. The Superintendent's quarters were long considered the oldest—a tradition that extends back at least to the "Post Facilities Report" of 1889. However, a report by the post quartermaster on September 30, 1819, clearly indicates that the two professors' quarters were to be completed several months ahead of the Superintendent's quarters. James Green to Thayer, September 30, 1819, Correspondence Relating to the Military Academy, RG 94, NA.

39. Davies, "Jared Mansfield," 16. This set of quarters, the first stone doubles, has been variously known as quarters number 41, then quarters 107/108, and now 107A and B.

40. Thayer to Macomb, March 27, 1826, and April 29, 1826, Correspondence Relating to the Military Academy, RG 94, NA.

41. On the possible introduction of gas lighting and steam heat, see Gouverneur Kemble to William Kemble, May 28, 1821, Gouverneur Kemble Papers, USMA Library.

42. Elizabeth Mansfield to Daniel Drake, March 18, 1818, and January 31, 1819, Elizabeth Mansfield Papers, USMA Library. This confident, outgoing woman is barely recognizable as the shy, retiring woman we met in 1802, when the Mansfields first arrived at West Point.

43. Church, *Personal Reminiscences*, 79–80.

44. Thayer, Orders, March 12, 1818, in Hall, "Early Discipline," 466.

45. Thomas J. Cram, "Manuscript Memoirs," 15–16, Thomas J. Cram Papers, USMA Library. Cram, class of 1826, was an assistant professor at West Point from 1826 to 1836, when he resigned from the Army.

46. Francis H. Smith, *West Point Fifty Years Ago* (New York: Van Nostrand, 1879), 6–7.

47. Church, *Personal Reminiscences*, 82–83.

48. Minutes, January 15–April 19, 1819, Proceedings (Staff Records), Records of the Academic Board, RG 404, USMA Archives.

49. Minutes, June 28 and October 6, 1823, Proceedings of the Academic Board. Except for a brief period from 1859 to 1861, "Grand Tactics" or "The Science of War" remained with engineering (Department of Civil and Military Engineering, renamed the Department of Military Art and Engineering in 1942) until the Department of History was created in 1969, and the material was shifted to that department as the "History of Military Art."

50. King to Christopher Gore, June 22, 1821, in Charles R. King, ed., *Life and Correspondence of Rufus King*, 6 vols. (New York: Putnams, 1900), 6:293–294.

51. "Course of Instruction & Studies . . . Engineering," *USMA Rules 1820*, Military History Institute (MHI) Library, Carlisle Barracks, Pa. Throughout this period, the class was examined only on "the science of war and fortifications," though the first section was sometimes also examined on drawing—perspective, shades, and shadows (Proceedings of the Academic Board, vol. 1). Crozet had introduced Joseph M. Sganzin's text (*Program d'un course de construction*), which addressed civil architecture, but the text was used primarily in teaching perspective, shades, and shadows. Church, who graduated in 1828, after the civil engineering program had been installed, called Sganzin "very diffuse and with difficulty comprehended." "We had to pick up most of our knowledge in these subjects from the lectures of . . . Professor [David B. Douglass]," who replaced Crozet in 1823. Church, *Personal Reminiscences*, 51–52.

52. Thayer to Alexander Macomb, December 12, 1823, Thayer Papers, USMA Library. Thayer used this as one illustration of how excess engineers might be used, supporting the argument that the Corps of Engineers should be expanded.

53. Thayer to Macomb, December 14, 1825, Correspondence Relating to the Military Academy, 1819–1866, RG 94, NA.

54. *Debates and Proceedings in the Congress of the United States* (Washington, D.C.: Gales and Seaton, 1834–1856), 18th Cong., 1st sess., 2:3217.

55. Academic Board, January 23, 1824, Proceedings of the Academic Board, vol. 1, USMA Archives.

56. In addition to the course revision directed by the Academic Board, evidence that the course in civil engineering was introduced at this time lies in timing of examinations on this subject. In the midyear examinations of January 1823, the engineering students (first class) were examined only on the "science of war and fortifications" and "shades, shadows [and] perspective" (Academic Board, January 20 and 21, 1824, Proceedings of the Academic Board, vol. l). In June, Douglass examined only the 1st (top) Section of the 1st Class in civil engineering. The 2nd Section was examined only in military engineering (Minutes, June 8 and 9, 1824, Proceedings of the Academic Board, vol. 1, RG 404, USMA Archives).

57. *Report of the Board of Visitors, 1824*, Records of the Board of Visitors, RG 404, USMA Archives.

58. Douglass to Secretary of War James Barbour, March 1, 1827, David Douglass Papers, USMA Library.

59. On private work, see David Douglass to Professor Silliman, September 20, 1826, and Douglass to Secretary of War John Eaton, September 2, 1829, Douglass Papers, USMA Library.

60. *Report of the Board of Visitors, 1824*.

61. On the civil engineering society, see "The Cadet Life of Jacob Whitman Bailey," *Association of Graduates, Bulletin No. 4*, April 1905, 68.

62. Minutes, March 13, 1840, Proceedings of the Academic Board.

63. Minutes, April 19, 1819, Proceedings of the Academic Board.

64. Worth to Thayer, September 1821, Correspondence Relating to the Military Academy, RG 94, NA; John Adams, "Address to Cadets at Quincy," *Works of John Adams*, 10:419–420.

65. Adams to Jefferson, August 20, 1821, and Jefferson to Adams, September 12, 1821, in Cappon, *Adams-Jefferson Letters*, 2:573–576.

66. Mansfield to Jefferson, January 26, 1821, Jared Mansfield Papers, USMA Library; Jefferson to Jared Mansfield, February 13, 1821, in Bergh, *Jefferson's Writings*, 15:313–314.

67. J. Q. Adams's diary entry of July 2, 1827, in Charles Francis Adams, ed., *Memoirs of John Quincy Adams*, 12 vols. (Philadelphia: Lippincott, 1875), 7:298–300. Adams had received several complaints about the naked physical, some from highly placed Washington officials.

68. Thayer to J. G. Swift, February 29, 1832, Thayer Papers, USMA Library.

69. [Alden Partridge] Americannus, *The Military Academy, at West Point, Unmasked: or, Corruption and Military Despotism Exposed* (Washington, D.C.: J. Elliot, 1830).

70. David Crockett, February 25, 1830, *Register of Debates,* 1st sess., 21st Cong., p. 583.

71. W. A. Croffut, ed., *Fifty Years in Camp and Field: Diary of Major-General Ethan Allen Hitchcock, U.S.A.* (New York: Putnam's, 1909), 66–67.

72. Thayer to Lewis Cass, November 26, 1832, Thayer Papers, USMA Library.

73. James L. Morrison, *The Best School in the World: West Point, the Pre–Civil War Years, 1833–1866* (Kent, Ohio: Kent State University Press, 1986), 23.

74. George Woodbridge to Cullum, October 25, 1872, George Washington Cullum Papers, USMA Archives.

75. Macomb to Thayer, October 11, 1827, quoted in Denton, "The Formative Years," 228.

76. Although commonly referred to as simply the Department of Chemistry, the correct name was Department of Chemistry and Mineralogy (1820–1837) and later Department of Chemistry, Mineralogy and Geology (1837–1928).

77. Smith, *West Point Fifty Years Ago,* 6–7.

5. Years of Growth and Fulfillment

1. Dennis Hart Mahan to Thayer, November 3, 1833, Thayer Papers, USMA Library.

2. Ibid.

3. Rene E. DeRussy to Charles Gratiot, July 29, 1833, Correspondence Relating to the Military Academy, 1819–1866, RG 94, NA.

4. Weir's *Landing of the Pilgrims* hangs in the rotunda of the Capitol in Washington.

5. Andrew Jackson, [Order in relation to Cadet Hammond], December 8, 1835, Andrew Jackson Manuscripts, USMA Library.

6. Diary of John Bratt, January 1, 1837, John Bratt Papers, USMA Library.

7. Gouverneur Kemble to Thayer, July 30, 1838, Thayer Papers, USMA Library.

8. Letter of January 28, 1838, Gouverneur Kemble Papers, USMA Library.

9. Proceedings of a Board of Officers [to investigate the causes of the fire which destroyed the "Academy" on February 19, 1838], March 2, 1838, Correspondence Relating to the Military Academy, 1819–1866, RG 94, NA.

10. DeRussy to Gratiot, April 2, 1838, Correspondence Relating to the Military Academy, 1819–1866, RG 94, NA.

11. Delafield to Gratiot, September 18, 1838, Correspondence Relating to the Military Academy, 1819–1866, RG 94, NA.

12. Thayer to Delafield, September 22, 1838, Delafield Papers, USMA.

13. Morrison, *Best School in the World,* 41.

14. Delafield to Gratiot, October 8, 1838, Correspondence Relating to the Military Academy, 1819–1866, RG 94, NA.

15. Board of Officers to Delafield, February 5, 1839, Correspondence Relating to the Military Academy, 1819–1866, RG 94, NA; Delafield to Joseph Totten, November 30, 1838, Correspondence Relating to the Military Academy, 1819–1866, RG 94, NA.

16. Board of Officers to Delafield, February 5, 1839, Correspondence Relating to the Military Academy, 1819–1866, RG 94, NA.

17. Delafield to Gratiot, February 5, 1839, [a brief note signed RD], Correspondence Relating to the Military Academy, 1819–1866, RG 94, NA.

18. Frederick Diaper (1810–1906) was born in Devonshsire, England, and studied with Robert Smirke, a favored architect of the Tory establishment. Aesthetically, Diaper, like Smirke before him, was a dedicated Greek Revivalist, and most of his commercial buildings reflected that. But Diaper, like Smirke, was less confined in his designs of other structures.

The precise source of Diaper's inspiration for a Tudor-Gothic motif for the Military Academy is not known with certainty, but the Gothic Revival style was quite popular in England when he was in training with Smirke. Even Smirke was involved with some such efforts in that time, including Erskine House, Renfrewshire, of Gothic design in 1828; the addition of towers to Chalmondeley Castle, Cheshire, about 1829; and Sir Robert Peel's Elizabethan-styled Drayton Manor in Staffordshire, which was begun in 1831. Diaper may have worked on some of these projects, but even if he did not, he certainly would have been aware of them and almost as certainly would have seen sketches and drawings associated with them.

Diaper also would have been aware of the work of other architects whose designs were more dramatically Gothic. Possibly he had seen the Royal Military Academy at Woolwich, whose appearance is similar in many ways to the designs that Diaper presented to Delafield.

Diaper's arrangement with Delafield is not clear from what little correspondence survives, but he does not seem to have objected to having his plans for West Point largely appropriated by Delafield. Interestingly, Diaper lived long enough to have seen, or seen stories about, the next generation of Gothic structures built at West Point at the end of the nineteenth century, but there is no known record of his reaction.

On Smirke, see Howard Colvin, ed., *A Bibliographical Dictionary of British Architects, 1600–1840* (New Haven, Conn.: Yale University Press, 1995), 875–881. On Diaper, see Adolf K. Placzek, ed., *Macmillan Encyclopedia of Architects* (New York: Free Press, 1982), 570–571.

19. Delafield to Totten, June 3, 1839, Correspondence Relating to the Military Academy, 1819–1866, RG 94, NA. This letter is also found in Letters Sent, Records of the Office of the Superintendent, RG 404, USMA Archives.

20. Delafield to Totten, June 3, 1839, Correspondence Relating to the Military Academy, 1819–1866, RG 94, NA.

21. The choice of the Tudor-Gothic had a historical logic. The origin of the Tudor influence was essentially military; in medieval England, where the style developed, the petty conflicts of the times usually centered around the homes of the warring barons. These homes therefore took on the character of forts, possessing serrations called battlements along the tops of the walls, corner towers, sally ports, moats, and narrow windows, all features contributed to the structure's defensive strength. Later, in the Gothic Revival, these once-functional features became merely decorative. By the last years of the eighteenth century, scores of massive country homes and public buildings with battlements and turrets in the style of a castle were being built in England. "The medieval Gothic is the most militant architecture of the modern Western world," wrote Professor Charles W. Larned, who guided a later era of reconstruction at West Point, "and this has been combined with the Tudor style—which has come through Oxford to embody academic education—in such a manner as to present an imposing and massive military ensemble which blends into the academic by gradual transition." Larned quoted in Joseph Pearson Farley, *Three Rivers: The James, the Potomac, the Hudson* (New York: Neale Publishing, 1910), 184.

22. Willam Dutton to his cousin, Lucy Matthews, February 18, 1843, William Dutton Papers, USMA Library.

23. Delafield to Totten, February 5, 1839, Correspondence Relating to the Military Academy, 1819–1866, RG 94, NA. This letter can also be found in Superintendents' Letterbooks.

24. William Dutton to Miss L. J. Matthews [cousin], February 18, 1843, William Dutton Papers, USMA Library; Charles Larned, undated, "General Conditions," with Larned to Adjutant, USMA, December 21, 1901, [printed copy], Charles Larned Papers, USMA Library.

25. Lists Relating to Economic and Social Status of Cadets' Parents (Circumstance of Parents of Cadets), 1842–1910, RG 404, USMA Archives.

26. "Lists of Cadets at West Point in 1828, and Rule in Making Appointments and Filling Vacancies," *ASP:MA*, 3:794; "An Act making appropriations for the support of the army and of the military academy . . . ," March 1, 1843.

27. Irwin McDowell to S. Anderson, February 16, 1881, copied into Minutes, Records of the West Point Army Mess, 2:70–74.

28. Bylaws, 1841, Records of the West Point Army Mess, 1:1.

29. Minutes, December 20, 1843, Records of the West Point Army Mess.

30. Kendrick's remarks [concerning McDowell's letter], April 8, 1881, Records of the West Point Army Mess, 2:74.

31. Irwin McDowell to S. Anderson, February 16, 1881, copied into Records of the West Point Army Mess, 2:70–74.

32. Dabney Herndon Maury, *Recollections of a Virginian in the Mexican, Indian,*

and Civil War, 3d ed. (New York: Scribner's, 1894), 50–51; Peter S. Michie, *General McClellan* (New York: D. Appleton and Co., 1901), 24.

33. Miner Knowlton to Totten, September 16, 1841, Correspondence Relating to the Military Academy, 1819–1866, RG 94, NA.

34. Delafield to Totten, September 17, 1841, Correspondence Relating to the Military Academy, 1819–1866, RG 94, NA.

35. Brewerton to Totten, August 12, 1850, Superintendents' Letterbooks.

36. George W. Cullum to Totten, July 30, 1852, Superintendents' Letterbooks.

37. John G. Barnard to Totten, November 5, 1855, Superintendents' Letterbooks.

38. George W. C. Lee graduated with the class of 1854; Fitzhugh Lee graduated with the class of 1856.

39. Charles Dudley Rhodes, *Robert E. Lee, the West Pointer* (Richmond, Va.: Garrett and Massie, ca. 1932), 31.

40. E. R. Pennell and J. Pennell, *The Life of James McNeill Whistler* (Philadelphia: Lippincott, 1911), 23. The Pennells attributed the Mrs. Thompson story to Loomis L. Langdon, class of 1854, and the examination story to Professor Charles Larned. The Pennells had corresponded with both.

41. Dutton to Lucy Matthews, February 18, 1843, William Dutton Papers, USMA Library.

42. Tully McCrea to Belle McCrea, September 16, 1860, Tully McCrea Papers, USMA Library. Tully McCrea graduated with the class of 1862. He was wounded and returned to West Point as an assistant professor (1864–1866).

43. Samuel H. Raymond to his father, Josiah Raymond, October 1, 1842, Samuel H. Raymond Papers, USMA Library.

44. Tully McCrea to Belle McCrea, January 19, 1861, Tully McCrea Papers, USMA Library.

45. File: Dialectic Society, USMA Library.

46. Minutes, September 16, 1842, Proceedings of the Academic Board.

47. Morrison, *Best School in the World*, 75. On Grant as president of the Dialectic Society, see William B. Hesseltine, *Ulysses S. Grant, Politician* (New York: Fredrick Ungar, 1935), 9. Grant graduated with the class of 1843.

48. Wood, *West Point Scrap Book*, 289.

49. Professors were appointed at the pleasure of the President but were seldom removed. Most stayed for years.

50. The only Superintendents of this period who were not Thayer men were P. G. T. Beauregard (class of 1838), who served as Superintendent just five days in 1861, and Zealous B. Tower (class of 1841), who served only two months in 1864.

51. Wood, *West Point Scrap Book*, 67.

52. Minutes, October 3, 1843, Proceedings of the Academic Board.

53. On the five-year course, see Morrison, *Best School in the World*, 114–140.

54. *Centennial History*, 1:324–325.

55. Later in the year (1855), in his annual report, Davis recommended that the superintendency be opened to officers of all branches of service. The engineer establishment objected, however, and the proposal was defeated. Davis renewed this effort in 1860 and this time was successful.

56. Mary Elizabeth Sergent, *They Lie Forgotten: The United States Military Academy, 1856–1861* (Middletown, N.Y.: Prior King Press, 1986), 40.

57. Morris Schaff, *The Spirit of Old West Point, 1858–1862* (Boston: Houghton, Mifflin and Co., 1907), 142–143.

58. Sergent, *They Lie Forgotten,* 40. Pelham, from Alabama, would resign in 1861 and join Stuart's cavalry. He was killed in action in 1863.

59. Jane Leigh Mahan, "Random Memories," *The Pointer,* March 15, 1929, 6–7.

60. Schaff, *Spirit of Old West Point,* 145–148. Ramseur graduated with the class of 1860 but resigned his commission in 1861 and joined the Confederacy. He rose to the rank of major general in that service.

61. Ibid., 142–148. Gibbes graduated with the class of 1860 but resigned and joined the Confederate Army in 1861. He rose to the rank of major of artillery. Upton, class of May 1861, rose to the rank of major general during the Civil War. A few years after the war, he returned to West Point as Commandant of Cadets (1870–1875).

62. Ibid., 164–167.

63. Mahan, "Random Memories," 7.

64. Morrison, *Best School in the World,* 136.

65. Samuel Gibbs French, *Two Wars: An Autobiography of General Samuel G. French* (Nashville, Tenn.: Confederate Veteran, 1901), 14–15. Franklin Gardner, class of 1843, was born in New York and appointed to the Academy from Iowa, but he joined the Confederate Army in 1861 and rose therein to the rank of major general.

66. Edward Chauncey Marshall, *Are the West Point Graduates Loyal?* (New York: Van Nostrand, 1862), 6–7.

6. Basking in the Glory

1. My understanding of many aspects of this period has been aided by the thorough work done by Walter Scott Dillard, "The United States Military Academy, 1865–1900: The Uncertain Years" (Ph.D. diss., University of Washington, 1972). As the title of Dillard's work—"The Uncertain Years"—suggests, I have interpreted some of the major themes of the era in a different manner than he has. Still, his careful research and writing have been very useful.

2. Wood, *West Point Scrap Book,* 209–214.

3. Tasker Bliss to [father], January 1, 1880, Tasker Bliss Papers, MHI Library; "Discipline at West Point," June 5, 1893, *New York Times,* 5.

4. Clemens's visit was arranged by Cadet Andrew G. Hammond, the Clemenses' neighbor in Hartford. Clemens had apparently made several earlier visits to West

Point, beginning in 1876, but had not before made a formal presentation. Philip W. Leon, *Mark Twain and West Point* (Oakville, Ontario: ECW Press, 1996). Hammond's letters to Clemens about the visit (and also other correspondence with Twain about West Point visits) are published in *Mark Twain and West Point*, 220ff.

5. Ibid., 19, 38.

6. Ibid., 195–211; *Army and Navy Journal* 23 (May 1887): 815.

7. *USMA Annual Report, 1898*, 16, Records of the Office of the Superintendent, USMA Archives.

8. John M. Schofield, *Forty-six Years in the Army* (New York: Century Co., 1897), 442.

9. *Report of the Board of Visitors, 1871.*

10. Church, *Personal Reminiscences*, 13.

11. Grant quoted in Obituary, Thomas Howard Ruger, class of 1854, *Annual Reunion, June 12th, 1908* (West Point: Association of Graduates, 1908), 111.

12. Tasker Bliss to [mother], December 17, 1872, Tasker Bliss Papers, MHI Library. Bliss graduated with the class of 1875 and returned the next year as an assistant professor.

13. John McAllister Schofield, *An Address Delivered by Major General John McAllister Schofield, USMA 1853, to the Corps of Cadets* (West Point: USMA Press, 1879), 4.

14. Douglas MacArthur, *Reminiscences* (New York: McGraw-Hill, 1964), 25.

15. On the hazing scandal of 1898–1901, see Philip W. Leon, *Bullies and Cowards: The West Point Hazing Scandal, 1898–1901* (Westport, Conn.: Greenwood Press, 2000).

16. On James Webster Smith's years at West Point, see Henry O. Flipper, *The Colored Cadet at West Point* (New York: Homer Lee and Co., 1878), 288–317; and Dillard, "Military Academy," 195–203.

17. On Flipper's experiences at West Point see Flipper, *Colored Cadet*.

18. Ibid., 121.

19. Ibid., 244.

20. On the Whittaker incident and the trial, see John F. Marszalek, Jr., *Court-Martial: A Black Man in America* (New York: Scribner's, 1972).

21. Nathaniel F. McClure, ed., *Class of 1887, United States Military Academy* (Washington: D.C.: P. S. Bond, 1938), 24–25. Remarks a few paragraphs later in McClure's compilation are probably a more accurate reflection of the bigotry Alexander had to face: "Friends of the colored people of America are continually striving to have young colored men go through the Military Academy or the Naval Academy [which admitted the first black midshipman in 1872 but did not graduate an African-American until 1949]. A few of these have succeeded in graduating but to what a sad fate have they been condemned by their friends in their efforts to establish a principle which is fallacious 'ab initio.' It has been amply demonstrated that there are insuperable difficulties in the way of having white troops in the Army of the United States commanded by

colored officers. The few that graduate only prove this rule, and are condemned from the beginning to a life of loneliness. It would be much better for all concerned if they chose some other calling." The biographical sketch ends thus: "Alexander was well thought of by his Class and well treated by authorities at West Point but this did not compensate him for six years and more of lonely Army life that fell to his lot after four equally lonely years at West Point."

22. Obituary, Charles Young (1855–1922), by Charles Dudley Rhodes, *Annual Report, June 12, 1922* (West Point: Association of Graduates USMA, 1922).

23. Charles Dudley Rhodes, *Intimate Letters of a West Point Cadet: An Epic in Blank Verse of the Class of 1889, United States Military Academy*, typescript publication "for class circulation only," June 10, 1935, copy in Charles Dudley Rhodes Papers, USMA Library. Unfortunately, Rhodes's *amended* version of the letter has, up to now, been the one most quoted by historians, including this author.

24. Charles D. Rhodes to All [family], June 9, 1889, Charles Dudley Rhodes Papers, USMA Library.

25. Young to Skerrett, July 26, 1915, Charles Young Papers, USMA Library. The "x" before the class year indicates a cadet who did not graduate.

26. Schofield, *Forty-six Years*, 439.

27. Letter of March 28, 1876, in ibid.

28. Dillard, "Military Academy," 161–162.

29. J. M. Schofield to Adjutant General, April 20, 1877, No. 12 A, *Annual Report of the Secretary of War, 1877* (Washington, D.C.: GPO, 1878), 153.

30. Minutes, June 19–22, 1880, Proceedings of the Academic Board.

31. Senator Garland quoted in *Army and Navy Journal*, January 22, 1881.

32. "[Social] Revolution at West Point," *Army and Navy Journal*, January 22, 1881.

33. Howard quoted *Army and Navy Journal*, January 22, 1881.

34. Minutes, February 10, 1881, Proceedings of the Academic Board.

35. *USMA Annual Report, 1881*.

36. Tasker Bliss to his father, October 8, 1876, Tasker Bliss Papers, MHI Library.

37. Tully McCrea to Belle McCrea, March 16, 1865, Tully McCrea Papers, USMA Library.

38. John M. Wilson to Chauncey McKeever, January 7, 1891, Superintendents' Letterbooks.

39. Mills to H. G. Corbin, August 1, 1900, Superintendents' Letterbooks.

40. James Parker, *The Old Army: Memories, 1872–1918* (Philadelphia: Dorrance and Co., 1929), 205.

41. Samuel E. Tillman, "Memoirs" [typescript], p. 4:9, Samuel Tillman Papers, USMA Library (Part 4 of these memoirs appears to have been written by another faculty member after Tillman's death).

42. Otto L. Hein, *Memories of Long Ago* (New York: Putnam's, 1925), 114. See also S. M. Mills, *A Valentine Party Given by Lieut. and Mrs. S. M. Mills* (West Point: n.p., 1876).

43. Hein, *Memories of Long Ago,* 113.

44. Ladies Reading Club file, USMA Library.

45. "Report of the Committee on Device for the United States Military Academy," January 31, 1898, Proceedings of the Academic Board.

46. Sidney Forman argued that, in this period, "West Point exhibited two contradictory features. One was a sense of satisfaction with the *status quo* marked by a conservative resistance to change. . . . The opposing and contradictory feature was the stubborn fact of change itself—change which was transforming the country, the organization of the Army, military doctrine, higher education, the body of scientific knowledge and therefore the academy itself." Sidney Forman, *West Point: A History of the United States Military Academy* (New York: Columbia University Press, 1950), 134–136. Forman was not alone in his criticism of the Academy.

Stephen E. Ambrose entitles his chapter covering this period "Stagnation." "America in the Gilded Age was bold and brash, always changing, living in and for the future," Ambrose wrote. "New ideas, new methods, new organizations dominated. With few exceptions, the American college reflected this spirit as much as any other institution. The major exception was the United States Military Academy." Ambrose, *Duty, Honor, Country,* 192.

47. Thomas Ruger, "Report of the Superintendent of the U.S. Military Academy," October 5, 1872, *Annual Report of the Secretary of War, 1872,* 787.

48. Michie to Adjutant, USMA, "Report," July 25, 1873, USMA Archives.

49. Charles Larned, "Comment and Criticism" [response to a paper on the Military Academy by Elmer W. Hubbard], *Journal of the Military Service Institution of the United States* 16 (March 1895): 323. Hubbard's article, "The Military Academy and the Education of Officers," appeared in the January 1895 issue of the *Journal.*

50. Tillman, "Memoirs," 3:110; George L. Andrews, "Report on Visit to MIT, Harvard, Yale & Dartmouth," [April 1883], Proceedings of the Academic Board.

51. Cadets Michie and Prince both graduated with the class of 1892.

52. Ernst to Adjutant General, December 12, 1893, Superintendents' Letterbooks.

53. Theodore Roosevelt, Centennial Address, June 11, 1902, *Centennial History,* 20–26.

54. Roger Hurless Nye, "The United States Military Academy in an Era of Educational Reform, 1900–1925" (Ph.D. diss., Columbia University, 1968), 11.

7. A New Age

1. My understanding of this era was aided immensely by Roger Hurless Nye's dissertation, "The United States Military Academy in an Era of Educational Reform, 1900–1925."

2. Mills to [various architects and architectural firms], October 20, 1902, Letters Sent [by the Superintendent], USMA Archives. See also "Rules Governing Architectural Competition," February 3, 1903, in *United States Military Academy Annual*

Report, 1903, Apendix I, Records of the Office of the Superintendent, RG 404, USMA Archives.

3. *Report of the Board of Visitors, 1899,* 10. Although the number of cadets authorized in 1899 was 381, the actual strength of the Corps of Cadets of July 19, 1899, was just 329. Charles W. Larned, *Report . . . on the Enlargement of the Military Academy, West Point, August [10], 1899* (West Point: U.S. Military Academy Press and Bindery, 1899), 3.

4. S. C. Hazzard [Adjutant] to Larned, July 19, 1899, in Larned, *Expansion Report, 1899.*

5. Larned, *Expansion Report, 1899.*

6. Ibid., 15. Larned continued to oppose Mills's plan for the location of the barracks. In 1902, Larned, in a minority report, noted that he had been studying the problem for three years and that such an "important and architecturally impressive building . . . should face, not an area and the rear of barracks, but the parade and exterior facades of that structure, where it is not only equally accessible to cadets but much more so to all others who may have occasion to use it." Board of Officers, *Improvements at the U.S. Military Academy: Report of a Board of Officers* (West Point: USMA Press, 1902), 25.

7. *USMA Annual Report, 1900,* 14.

8. *Report of the Board of Visitors, 1901,* 7.

9. Charles W. Larned, ["Study of the reorganization of the plant of the U.S. Military Academy," December 1901], under cover of Larned to Adjutant, USMA, December 21, 1901, Samuel Tillman Papers, USMA Library.
Though this study effort is usually attributed solely to Larned, Mills insisted that Larned's work in 1901 "was accomplished in constant consultation with him [the Superintendent], and that material revisions and changes were made by him [the Superintendent] in Colonel Larned's estimates before the matter was finally forwarded to the War Department and submitted to Congress." Mills to Military Secretary [Fred Ainsworth], August 19, 1904, Samuel Tillman Papers, USMA Library.

10. A. L. Mills to Adjutant General, October 7, 1902, [letter forwarding the report of the board of officers] in Board of Officers, *Improvements Report, 1902,* 29.

11. "Rules Governing Architectural Competition," February 3, 1903, in *USMA Annual Report, 1903,* 57–60.

12. Larned, *Expansion Report, 1899,* 12.

13. Charles W. Larned, ["Study of the reorganization of the plant of the U.S. Military Academy," December 1901], under cover of Larned to Adjutant, USMA, December 21, 1901, Samuel Tillman Papers, USMA Library.

14. Board of Officers, *Improvements Report, 1902,* 18.

15. Mills to [various architects and architectural firms], October 20, 1901, Superintendents' Letterbooks.

16. Mills to Cram, Goodhue & Ferguson, June 1, 1903, Superintendents' Letterbooks.

17. Cram, Goodhue & Ferguson, "West Point Military Academy," *Architectural Review* 10, no. 6 (June 1903): 68.

18. Sylvester Baxter, "The New West Point," *Century Magazine* 68 (July 1904): 335–336.

19. Mills to Cram, Goodhue & Ferguson, June 1, 1903, USMA Library.

20. It is not wholly clear whether Mills told the architects to plan on a future expansion to 1,200 at this point or later in the fall. The timing of the architects' plan changes suggests that they were so advised in the summer of 1903. In particular, this is suggested by their shifting of the new cadet barracks, which appears to have been done before September. Report of the Advisory Board Report, September 7, 1903, Advisory Board Reports, USMA Archives. The advisory board was not told to determine the added requirements for 1,200 cadets until November 19, 1903. This is an example of how Mills kept the advisory board in the dark and out of the circle that had any direct impact on events.

21. Superintendent [Mills] to Military Secretary [Fred C. Ainsworth], November 9, 1904 [fourth endorsement to Mills to Military Secretary, August 19, 1904], Document Files, Records of the Office of the Deputy Chief of Staff for Personnel and Administration, RG 404, USMA Archives, Item 2333.

22. Report of the Advisory Board, September 7, 1903, Advisory Board Reports, USMA Archives.

23. Report of the Advisory Board, December 17, 1903, Advisory Board Reports, USMA Archives.

24. Mills's predecessor, Oswald Ernst, had graduated fifteen years ahead of him, and several members of the academic board had first arrived at West Point while Mills was but a young boy.

25. Hein, *Memories of Long Ago,* 269–270.

26. Ibid.

27. Report of the Advisory Board, May 5, 1904, and Report of the Advisory Board, June 8, 1904 [submitted to Mills, June 20, 1904], Advisory Board Reports, USMA Archives.

28. Adjutant [the Superintendent "directs me to . . ."] to Larned, June 20, 1904, Advisory Board Reports, USMA Archives.

29. Advisory Board to Military Secretary [F. C. Ainsworth], July 6, 1904, Samuel Tillman Papers, USMA Library.

30. "The New West Point," *Army and Navy Journal,* July 30, 1904.

31. Ainsworth to Mills, August 24, 1904, Samuel Tillman Papers, USMA Library.

32. Adjutant to Larned, August 30, 1904, [second endorsement to Mills's August 19, 1804, letter], Samuel Tillman Papers, USMA Library.

33. Report of the Advisory Board, October 10, 1904, Advisory Board Reports, USMA Archives.

34. Adjutant to Larned, October 12, 1904, Advisory Board Reports, USMA Archives.

35. Advisory Board to Superintendent, October 12, 1904, [third endorsement to Mills to Military Secretary, August 19, 1904], Document Files, Item 2333.

36. Hugh L. Scott, *Some Memories of a Soldier* (New York: Century Co., 1928), 426.

37. *Board of Visitors Report, 1906;* Hugh L. Scott to Cram, Goodhue & Ferguson, February 19, 1907, cited in Cram, Goodhue & Ferguson to Scott, February 23, 1907, Document Files, File 2333-6.

38. Advisory Board to Adjutant, February 21, 1907, Document Files, File 2333-10.

39. Horace Porter [AOG president and president of 1906 Board of Visitors] to William H. Taft, March 9, 1907, Document Files, File 2333-23.

40. H. L. Scott to Cram, Goodhue & Ferguson, February 27, 1907, Document Files, File 2333-9; H. L. Scott to Cram, Goodhue & Ferguson, February 28, 1907, Document Files, File 2333–11. For the Lodge and LaFarge letters to Roosevelt and Scott's correspondence with them, see Document Files, File 2333-13.

41. Cram, Goodhue & Ferguson to H. L. Scott, March 1, 1907, Document Files, File 2333-15.

42. Theodore Roosevelt to William H. Taft, March 20, 1907, Document Files, File 2333-33.

43. Adjutant to Larned, March 25, 1907, Document Files, File 2333-40.

44. Advisory Board to Adjutant, March 27, 1907, Document Files, File 2333-40.

45. H. L. Scott to Cram, Goodhue and Ferguson, April 11, 1907, Document Files, File 2333-48.

46. Memorandum, Thomas H. Barry to Adjutant General, February 2, 1911, Document Files, File 2333-75.

47. *USMA Annual Report, 1920.*

48. *USMA Annual Report, 1921.* MacArthur included drawings based on these plans with his 1921 annual report.

49. Larned, *Expansion Report, 1899,* 21.

50. Nye, "USMA in an Era of Educational Reform," 198–200.

51. Mills to Adjutant General, March 31, 1904, Samuel Tillman Papers, USMA Library.

52. *Army and Navy Journal,* September 24, 1904.

53. Nye, "USMA in an Era of Educational Reform," 205–206.

54. Ibid., 207–208.

55. Adjutant to Larned, May 4, 1905, Samuel Tillman Papers, USMA Library.

56. Committee Report, [April 1906], Samuel Tillman Papers, USMA Library. See also Nye, "USMA in an Era of Educational Reform," 210–211.

57. This affair is documented in a series of letters from August 8 through November 24, 1905, as cited in Nye, "USMA in an Era of Educational Reform," 206 n.

58. Larned later touched on this issue in Larned to E. L. Amory, March 21, 1908, Larned Papers, USMA Library.

59. Theodore Roosevelt to William H. Taft, January 11, 1908, Edward S. Holden Collection, USMA Library.

60. [Curriculum committee] to Adjutant, January 30, 1908, Edward S. Holden Collection, USMA Library.

61. *Centennial History,* 1:280.

62. Nye, "USMA in an Era of Educational Reform," 263–267.

63. By the end of 1918, the Academy lay "battered and broken," wrote William Addleman Ganoe, the adjutant. William Addleman Ganoe, *MacArthur Close-Up* (New York: Vantage Press, 1962), 13. The evidence, however, simply does not bear that out. Given the turmoil that the War Department had caused in October and November 1918, Tillman and the Academic Board seem to have managed remarkably well. By the time MacArthur arrived in June 1919, the academy had achieved a large measure of stability. The corps of cadets (after graduating the student officers) consisted of three classes, and the Academic Board had prepared a three-year curriculum, which would be implemented in September.

64. Tillman's testimony before the House Committee on Military Affairs, December 30, 1918, quoted in Nye, "USMA in an Era of Educational Reform," 285.

65. Ibid.

66. Tillman quoted in Ganoe, *MacArthur Close-Up,* 15.

67. Ganoe, *MacArthur Close-Up,* 15–16.

68. Ibid., 16.

69. The four war emergency classes were known by the month and year of their graduation—the class of April 1917, the class of August 1917, the class of June 1918, and the class of November 1918.

70. Forman, *West Point,* 194.

71. Adjutant General to Superintendent, November 16, 1918, USMA AG Files, Curriculum 1917–1920, USMA Archives. D. Clayton James (*The Years of MacArthur,* 2 vols. [Boston: Houghton Mifflin, 1970], 1:263) says that many cadets had entered the Academy in the expectation that they would graduate in one year, and that over 100 resigned.

72. Adjutant General to Superintendent, November 16, 1918, USMA AG Files, Curriculum 1917–1920, USMA Archives.

73. Academic Board to Superintendent [and forwarded to the War Department], December 13, 1918, quoted in Nye, "USMA in an Era of Educational Reform," 292.

74. General Committee to Superintendent [forwarded to War Department], December 5, 1918, quoted in Nye, "USMA in an Era of Educational Reform," 294.

75. March to Baker, May 12, 1919, Samuel Tillman Papers, USMA Library.

76. On May 13, MacArthur wrote that he had already been interviewed by March and told of his assignment to West Point. MacArthur to [?] Weller, May 13, 1919, in MacArthur, *Reminiscences,* 72–73.

77. In the years since Thayer assumed the superintendency at age thirty-two, only Thomas H. Ruger (at thirty-eight) was younger than MacArthur upon assuming the office (1871–1876). Prior to Thayer, Partridge had been thirty and Swift, before him, twenty-nine. Williams, the first Superintendent, had been somewhat older.

MacArthur seemed even younger in comparison with his predecessor, Tillman, who was over seventy when he retired from the superintendency in 1919.

78. Minutes, June 26, 1919, Proceedings of the Academic Board.

79. MacArthur later took credit for restoring the four-year curriculum, but he seems to have done little more than forward the four-year plan that the Academic Board developed. Douglas MacArthur to Herman Beukema, July 10, 1939, Roger H. Nye Papers, USMA Library; MacArthur, *Reminiscences*, 78.

80. Much of this discussion was drawn from Nye, "USMA in an Era of Educational Reform," 304–307. On Tillman's efforts, see also Chauncey L. Fenton to Tillman, July 20, 1921, Samuel Tillman Papers, USMA Library.

81. Nye, "USMA in an Era of Educational Reform," 309.

82. Tillman, "Memoirs," 3:110.

83. *USMA Annual Report, 1919*, 63.

84. Nye, "USMA in an Era of Educational Reform," 325–328; Ganoe, *MacArthur Close-Up*, 88.

85. Ganoe, *MacArthur Close-Up*, 88–89.

86. MacArthur to Echols, May 18, 1921, quoted in Nye, "USMA in an Era of Educational Reform," 324.

87. Scott, *Memories of a Soldier*, 420.

88. Editorial, *The Bray*, vol. 1, no. 1, November 26, 1919, USMA Library.

89. Ganoe, *MacArthur Close-Up*, 54. I could not determine the name of the officer placed in charge of *The Bray*.

90. Commandant [Robert Danford], [yet unnamed, mimeographed newspaper], vol. 1, no. 1, November 4, 1919, bound with *The Bray*, USMA Library.

91. Editorial, *The Bray*, November 26, 1919. Cadet Alba Carleton Spalding graduated with the class of 1922.

92. Ganoe, *MacArthur Close-Up*, 54–55; *The Bray*, November 26, 1919, to April 27, 1920, USMA Library; "The Bray" file, USMA Library.

93. *The Bray* was published weekly. Copies of each number (vol. 1, nos. 1–24) from November 26, 1919, until May 4, 1919, are on file at USMA Library. A mimeographed publication dated November 4, 1919, announced the upcoming publication and asked what it should be called. Since the editorial in the May 4 issue does not seem to match Ganoe's description of the offending piece, I have assumed that the issue that brought this establishment to a close was the next one (no. 25), which would have been dated May 11.

94. Ganoe, *MacArthur Close-Up*, 57.

95. James E. Moore to Ray Beurkey, [undated, ca. 1973], File: Pointer, USMA Library.

96. Hein, *Memories of Long Ago*, 267.

97. James, *Years of MacArthur*, 1:279.

98. Nye, "USMA in an Era of Educational Reform," 331.

99. *USMA Annual Report, 1923*, 6.

100. Nye, "USMA in an Era of Educational Reform," 330–331.

101. James, *Years of MacArthur*, 1:292.

102. Pershing to MacArthur, November 22, 1921, quoted in ibid., 1:288. Ganoe's hagiographic biography not withstanding (Ganoe, *MacArthur Close-Up*), one suspects that if MacArthur had not achieved substantial fame in World War II and the years after (well beyond that he had achieved as Chief of Staff in the 1930s), we would pay scant attention to his three years as superintendent at the Military Academy at West Point.

103. Ambrose, *Duty, Honor, Country*, 283.

104. Nye, "USMA in an Era of Educational Reform," 333.

105. File: Ladies Reading Club, USMA Library.

106. Mrs. E. R. Heiberg, "Professors' Row" (typescript), 7, 24, USMA Library.

107. Editorial, *Army and Navy Journal*, September 17, 1927. This move brought objections from the governor and local officials.

108. Heiberg, "Professors' Row," 26.

109. Ibid., 25.

110. Nye, "USMA in an Era of Educational Reform," 228.

111. *USMA Annual Report, 1913*, 10–12. Townsley repeated his appeal in each of his subsequent reports, 1914–1916.

112. I. B. Holley, Jr., *General John M. Palmer, Citizen Soldiers, and the Army of a Democracy* (Westport, Conn.: Greenwood Press, 1982), 129.

113. Tasker Bliss to Mother, October 8, 1876, Tasker Bliss Papers, MHI Library.

114. Tully McCrea to Belle McCrea, October 12, 1864, Tully McCrea Papers, USMA Library.

115. Schofield, *Forty-six Years*, 27.

116. Nye, "USMA in an Era of Educational Reform," 229.

117. Ganoe, *MacArthur Close-Up*, 98–99.

118. Holley, *General John M. Palmer*, 129.

119. On March 1, 1928, the Department of Chemistry, Mineralogy and Geology was redesignated the Department of Chemistry and Electricity. For reasons that are not clear now, the professorship was not so redesignated until February 11, 1943.

8. The Long Gray Line

1. I have found John P. Lovell's *Neither Athens nor Sparta? The American Service Academies in Transition* (Bloomington: Indiana University Press, 1979) to be very useful in coming to grips with many aspects of this period.

2. *USMA Annual Report, 1930*, 1.

3. Lovell, *Neither Athens nor Sparta?* 11.

4. Memorandum, October 9, 1934; and Memorandum, Captain Brown [Naval

Aide] to Secretary of the Navy, October 12, 1934, both filed with Minutes, November 7, 1934, Proceedings of the Academic Board.

5. Quoted in Forman, *West Point,* 197.

6. Sir Alfred Zimmern to Herman Beukema, December 28, 1938, excerpt of letter in Report to the Superintendent, 1949, George Lincoln Papers, USMA Library.

7. G. A. Counts, "The Department of Physics and Chemistry," *Assembly,* April 1954, 2f. The Department of Electricity was created in 1946, and its name went through a curious evolution. In 1957, the name was changed to the Department of Electrical Engineering; in 1960, it was returned to the Department of Electricity; then, in 1969, it was changed back once more to the Department of Electrical Engineering. In 1989, it became the Department of Electrical Engineering and Computer Science.

8. G. J. Murry, "The Department of Mechanics, USMA," *Assembly,* April 1951, 2f.

9. "Professor Gatchell Retires," *Assembly,* January 1953, 6.

10. "Consideration of New Subjects for Inclusion in the West Point Curriculum," October 7, 1940, Proceedings of the Academic Board, 52:214f.

11. Jay L. Benedict to Adjutant General, November 16, 1940, in Proceedings of the Academic Board, 53:28.

12. Louis F. Dixon, "West Point Army Mess, 1841–1963," *Assembly* 22 (spring 1963): 26–29.

13. Holt Fairfield Butt III, Mss. memoir, 32, H. F. Butt, USMA Library.

14. Chauncey Fenton, Memorandum for the Superintendent [Connor], February 25, 1938, File: Superintendent's Quarters, USMA Library.

15. Just before the meeting, Chauncey Fenton wrote Benedict to suggest that the latter might wish to discuss the proposed change in the West Point Army Mess constitution. But he added, apparently suspecting that the Superintendent had already made up his mind, "If you are thoroughly conversant with the question of course there is no need." Fenton to Superintendent, February 25, 1938, Adjutant General's Files, USMA Archives.

16. Letter of Colonel Duncan S. Somerville, USMA 1928, quoted in "Recollections of the West Point Army Mess," *Friends of the West Point Library Newsletter* 14 (February 1989): [3].

17. On hours for women in the mess, see Customs of the Mess, October 27, 1944, House Rules, Minutes of Meetings of Council of Administration 1942–1946, Records of the West Point Army Mess. On organization of separate officers' club, see Proposal of F. J. Tate, January 29, 1946, Minutes, Records of the West Point Army Mess.

18. [Confidential] Memorandum for the Academic Board [from R. L. Eichelberger], January 28, 1941, Proceedings of the Academic Board, 53:22f.

19. Ibid., 23.

20. *USMA Annual Report, 1941,* 5.

21. War Mobilization Plan, USMA, February 1, 1935, quoted in Department of Social Sciences, "Wartime History of the United States Military Academy" (typescript), [1945?], USMA Library. My information about West Point during World War II is drawn largely from this document.

22. Eichelberger Papers, MHI Library.

23. War Department request of Congress quoted in "Wartime History of the United States Military Academy," 9, USMA Archives.

24. *USMA Annual Report, 1931*, 1.

25. *USMA Annual Report, 1942*, 10.

26. *USMA Annual Report, 1943*.

27. On pilot training, see Forman, *West Point*, 203–206.

28. *USMA Annual Report, 1936*, 6.

29. Gatchell quoted in Forman, *West Point*, 205.

30. Author's conversation with Mrs. Sumner Willard, West Point, April 1990.

31. *Assembly*, July 1948, 6; Fall 1958, 4.

32. *Assembly*, October 1945, 9.

33. Ibid.

34. *Report of the Board of Consultants*, November 7, 1945, Proceedings of the Academic Board.

35. Dwight David Eisenhower to Taylor, January 2, 1946, in Alfred D. Chandler Jr., and Louis Galambos, eds., *The Papers of Dwight David Eisenhower*, 13 vols. to date (Baltimore: Johns Hopkins University Press, 1970–), 7:709–711.

36. Howard T. Prince and William L. Wilson, "The Leadership Legacy of General Maxwell D. Taylor," *Assembly*, February 1946, 14; Superintendent [Taylor] to Chief of Staff (Attn: Asst Chief of Staff, G-3), May 10, 1946, Proceedings of the Academic Board, 58:110f.

37. Maxwell D. Taylor, *Swords and Plowshares* (New York: Norton, 1972), 113–117.

38. Author's conversation with Sumner Willard, West Point, April 1990.

39. Maxwell D. Taylor, *West Point Honor System: Its Objectives and Procedures* (West Point: USMA, 1948), 5.

40. Taylor, *Swords and Plowshares*, 119.

41. Williams to Swift, March 23, 1807, Joseph Gardner Swift Papers, USMA Library.

42. On honor, see Vance O. Mitchell, "A Brief History of the West Point and Air Force Academy Honor Codes," typescript, Office of Air Force History, November 13, 1984. I have found Mitchell in error on a few points, and where that was the case, I have presented the information I believe to be correct along with the source of my data.

43. Dillard, "United States Military Academy," 79.

44. Ibid., 81.

45. For a more complete discussion of this affair, see ibid., 83–88.

46. Forman, *West Point*, 154–155.

47. Campbell B. Hodges, writing as Commandant of Cadets in 1928, recalled that when he was a cadet (1899–1903), there were no vigilance committees; rather, "leaders of the Corps generally took the matter up." Hodges to Sinclair Gannon, March 23, 1928, Campbell B. Hodges Papers, USMA Library.

48. Charles W. Larned, "Corps Honor," in *The West Point Hand-Book* (West Point: YMCA of the USMA, 1907), 27–32.

49. Adjutant to Robert M. Toms, May 9, 1905, quoted in Dillard, "United States Military Academy," 316.

50. Adjutant to Commandant of Cadets, September 4, 1907, File: "Honor Code and System, Cadet," USMA Library.

51. William W. Ford [USMA 1920], "The Long Gray Line," *Assembly*, December 1982, 22ff.

52. Ganoe, *MacArthur Close-Up*, 108; Baker quoted on 108–109.

53. Ibid., 110. The date of formation of the honor committee is usually placed in 1922. Ganoe, however, tells the story as if it were linked to the 1920 statement of Baker and is specific in saying that it occurred during his tour, which ended in the late spring of 1921. I therefore have concluded that the committee was first formed in 1920 on the same informal footing as the earlier vigilance committees and then given a more formal status in 1922. I could find nothing in the official records to indicate the exact date of either occurrence.

54. *Bugle Notes*, [1923–1924], 62–63.

55. Hodges to Gannon, March 23, 1928, Campbell B. Hodges Papers, USMA Library; Memorandum, Stewart to Superintendent, Subject: Functions, Honor Committee, July 16, 1924, File: "Honor Committee," USMA Library.

56. General Committee to Superintendent, Subject: Application of Honor System to Academic Work, May 11, 1926, File: "Honor System," USMA Library.

57. Maxwell Taylor, *West Point Honor System* (West Point: USMA, 1948), 5.

58. See above the 1923 statement of the "guiding principles" of the honor system. Mitchell says that the more recent addition of "non-toleration" occurs in 1970 (Mitchell, "Honor History," 9). An undated Academy fact sheet says the same thing; however, the new statement first appears in *Bugle Notes* in 1973.

59. "Building Construction at the Military Academy," *The Association of Graduates . . . Bulletin No. 8* (May 1, 1934), 6. On "Looeyville," see Freemont W. Bowley II, "West Point Has Grown," *Assembly*, January 1944, 2.

60. Adjutant, USMA, to Dir. of Logistics, US Army, January 17, 1949, 1st endorsement to Adjutant General to Superintendent, USMA, Subject: Sizes of family quarters, December 17, 1948, File: 620, Quarters 1948–1950, USMA Archives.

61. Marty Maher arrived at West Point in about 1897 as a young man fresh from Ireland's County Tipperary. He found a job there as a waiter at the cadet mess and then, in 1898, enlisted in the Army. The next year he was assigned to the Academy's gymnasium as a swimming instructor, though he claimed he could not swim a stroke.

He retired from the Army in 1928 as a Technical Sergeant (E-7) and became a civilian employee of the Department of Physical Education. He retired again in 1948. In his five decades at West Point, Maher and his wife earned a special place in the hearts of many, many graduates. Through his book and the film it spawned, the couple also earned a place in the hearts of countless moviegoers. Maher died in 1961, at the age of eighty-four, and is buried at West Point.

62. I found Davidson's memoir (Garrison H. Davidson, *Grandpa Gar: The Saga of One Soldier as Told to His Grandchildren* [n.p., 1974]) very helpful in sorting out this complex period.

63. Quoted in Thomas Griess, "Vincent Esposito, Soldier and Scholar," *Assembly*, winter 1964, 5.

64. Lovell, *Neither Athens nor Sparta?* 112.

65. Ibid.

66. L. E. Schick, Memorandum to: Members of the General Committee, April 16, 1959, George Lincoln Papers, USMA Library.

67. Amos A. Jordan, Jr., memo, Subject: Jordan's Remarks to the Board of Consultants, January 22, 1959, George Lincoln Papers, USMA Library. Jordan often sat in for Lincoln on the Academic Board during this period and replaced Lincoln as head of the Department of Social Sciences in 1969.

68. G. A. Lincoln, Memorandum for: Colonel Jordan, Subject: Comments on our Curriculum Proposition, April 20, 1959, George Lincoln Papers, USMA Library.

69. Minutes, April 24, 1959, Proceedings of the Academic Board.

70. Ibid.

71. Davidson, *Grandpa Gar*, 164.

72. Amos Jordan quoted in Lovell, *Neither Athens nor Sparta?* 117.

73. Davidson, *Grandpa Gar*, 163–164.

9. The Years of Turmoil

1. William C. Westmoreland, *A Soldier Reports: General William C. Westmoreland* (Garden City, N.Y.: Doubleday, 1976), 38, 43. The authorized strength of the Academy was 2,529 when Westmoreland took over and ultimately grew to 4,417. Academy officials often rounded these figures—sometimes rounding badly.

2. *Assembly*, winter 1963, 1; *USMA Annual Report, 1962*, iv. In his memoir, Westmoreland says he waited to initiate action until Eisenhower (who earlier in his administration had rejected an effort to expand the Academy) had left office. Westmoreland, *A Soldier Reports*, 43

3. Westmoreland, *A Soldier Reports*, 43–44. The conversation between Westmoreland and Kennedy was confirmed by President Kennedy to Bob Warren (class of 1940), who was then Superintendent of the Air Force Academy. *Fifty Years, Class of 1940 Memoirs* (n.p., 1990), 74. Westmoreland, in his memoir, suggested that Kennedy's military aide, Chester V. "Ted" Clifton, class of 1936, might have

prompted the President's question. Clifton told me that the President's inquiry was spontaneous, although it was his recollection that the President asked why Army was getting beaten so badly. Phone interview with Major General (retired) Chester V. Clifton, June 1990.

4. *Assembly*, winter 1963, 1.

5. *USMA Annual Report, 1963–1964*, vii.

6. *USMA Annual Report, 1962–1963*, 54; *Assembly*, winter 1963, 1.

7. *Assembly*, winter 1963, 1; *Assembly*, summer 1963, 20.

8. *Assembly*, spring 1963, 2.

9. Phone interview with Major General (retired) Chester V. Clifton, June 1990. Clifton, who was Kennedy's military aide, confirmed the Kennedy-Westmoreland conversation (see note 3), and noted Kennedy's active support of the expansion legislation.

10. *USMA Annual Report, 1964–1965*, x.

11. *USMA Annual Report, 1965–1966*, 5.

12. General Accounting Office, *DOD Service Academies: Improved Cost and Performance Monitoring Needed* (Washington, D.C.: GAO, 1991).

13. Title 10, *U.S. Code*, Public Law 102-484, Sec. 523.

14. Office of Policy, Planning, and Analysis, *Years of Continuity and Progress, 1991–1996* (West Point: USMA, June 1966), 44.

15. *Institutional Self-Study: Report of the United States Military Academy* (West Point: USMA, June 1999), 78–80.

16. "Officer and Enlisted Morale and Quality of Life," *Record of the USMA Conference on the State of the Academy*, [a Superintendent's conference held at Camp Buckner, September 7–8, 1979] [West Point: USMA, 1979], 19–20.

17. Theodore J. Crackel to Andrew J. Goodpaster, May 26, 1978, author's files.

18. Frederick A. Smith [Dean] to Theodore J. Crackel, June 6, 1978, author's files.

19. *Assembly*, June 1974, 26.

20. My discussion of African-American cadets in the twentieth-century Academy was aided by "Roots, Achievements, Projections," a USMA Black History Week pamphlet, February 1978.

21. Benjamin O. Davis, Jr., *Benjamin O. Davis, Jr., American: An Autobiography* (Washington, D.C.: Smithsonian Institution Press, 1991), 21–50.

22. Ezra Floyd Ferris, Jr., to the President [F. D. Roosevelt], September 1, 1938, Proceedings of the Academic Board.

23. Harry S. Truman, July 28, 1948, Executive Order 9981.

24. *USMA Annual Report, 1968–1969*, 7.

25. *Institutional Self-Study*, 10.

26. *Assembly*, winter 1964, 10–13.

27. Rick Atkinson, *The Long Gray Line: The American Journey of West Point's Class of 1966* (Boston: Houghton Mifflin, 1989), 408.

28. Ibid., 410.

29. Except as otherwise noted, the following discussion of the admission of women to West Point is informed by the *USMA Annual Reports* for the years 1976 to 1980.

30. *USMA Annual Report, 1976,* 20.

31. Ibid., *USMA Annual Report, 1978,* 50.

32. Carol Barkalow, *In the Men's House* (New York: Poseidon Press, 1990), 56.

33. Frederick A. Smith to William A. Knowlton, December 21, 1976, Box 21, William A. Knowlton Papers, USMA Library.

34. Barkalow, *In the Men's House,* 68. Barkalow, at five feet eight inches, was the Lady Knights' tallest player and was made center of the all-plebe team.

35. Ibid., 71.

36. Gaspard quoted in ibid., 54.

37. U.S. Corps of Cadets (USCC) Regulations (1979); *USMA Annual Report, 1980,* 56; Barkalow, *In the Men's House,* 40; Atkinson, *Long Gray Line,* 411.

38. "Gig-sheet," author's file.

39. General Accounting Office, *DOD Service Academies: More Actions Needed to Eliminate Sexual Harassment* (Washington, D.C.: GAO, January 1994).

40. OPPA, *Continuity and Progress,* 29.

41. OPPA, *Continuity and Progress,* 17; Editorial Desk, November 2, 1994, "Wisdom at West Point," *New York Times,* late edition—final, A:22. Graves took advantage of a previously scheduled meeting with the editorial board of the *New York Times* to reveal this incident.

42. *USMA Annual Report, 1977,* 34.

43. Mitchell, "Honor History," 24.

44. EE304 was the second of a two-course required sequence in electrical engineering. The first course, EE301, Electric Circuits, was described thus: "Fundamental quantities and circuit laws are introduced and applied first to resistive networks. Impedance is then introduced, and the circuit analysis extended to cover general lineal networks. Laboratory exercises included." The second course, the course in question (EE304, Electronics), was described in this manner: "Frequency selectivity in communication circuits. Characteristics and modeling of electronic devices. Diode circuits, amplifiers, oscillators, and modulation methods. Radio and other electronic systems. Laboratory exercises reinforce key points." *West Point, United States Military Academy, 1975–1976 Catalog* (West Point: USMA, 1975), 59.

45. Mitchell, "Honor History," 23–24.

46. *USMA Annual Report, 1977,* 34–35.

47. On honor representatives and athletes being involved, see Atkinson, *Long Gray Line,* 406.

48. Sidney B. Berry, June 14, 1976, "A Preliminary Analysis—Why an Honor Problem at West Point in 1976?" Memorandum for Record, Personal papers of Thomas E. Griess.

49. C. H. Bonesteel et al., April 19, 1966, *Report by the Superintendent's Curriculum Review Group, USMA,* quoted in ibid.

50. Sidney B. Berry, June 14, 1976, "A Preliminary Analysis—Why an Honor Problem at West Point in 1976?" Memorandum for Record, Personal Papers of Thomas E. Griess.

51. *USMA Annual Report, 1977,* 37.

52. Ibid., 42.

53. Posvar Commission Report quoted in Larry R. Donnithorne, "The Year of Honor at USMA—1988–1989," *Assembly,* October 1989, 15.

54. Larry R. Donnithorne, *Preparing for West Point's Third Century: A Summary of the Years of Affirmation and Change, 1986–1991* (West Point: USMA, 1991), 72–73.

55. Center for the Professional Military Ethic, "White Paper: Cadet Honor Code and Honor System," *Assembly,* May/June 2000, 60–61.

56. Ibid.

57. Lovell, *Neither Athens nor Sparta?* 237.

58. *Report to the Secretary of the Army by the Special Commission of the United States Military Academy,* December 15, 1976, 17, File: Borman Commission, USMA Archives.

59. *Report [of the Borman Commission] to the Secretary of the Army by the Special Commission of the United States Military Academy* (West Point: USMA, December 15, 1976), 72–73.

60. Ibid., 21. Brigadier General (then Colonel) Thomas E. Griess, Professor of History, had to ask to be interviewed—and then was heard only after most of the commission's work was done. Many on the Academic Board were not interviewed at all by the Borman Commission. Griess to author, February 21, 2001, [written responses to the author's questions], author's files.

61. Charles H. Schilling to Frank Borman, December 19, 1976, Schilling Papers, USMA Library.

62. Theodore Ropp to A. Kenneth Pye, December 21, 1976, Personal papers of Thomas E. Griess.

63. Army staff actions in response to the Borman Commission's recommendations are itemized in *Final Report of the West Point Study Group,* July 27, 1977, 147.

64. [Members of the Academic Board] through Superintendent to Chief of Staff, U.S. Army, January 10, 1977, Subject: Aftermath of the Borman Commission, Charles H. Schilling Papers, USMA Library.

65. Ibid.

66. Thomas E. Griess, Memorandum for [members of the Academic Board], March 9, 1977, Charles H. Schilling Papers, USMA Library.

67. Schilling to Griess, March 16, 1977, Schilling Papers, USMA Library.

68. *USMA Annual Report, 1967–1968,* 6. I have used the term "tenured faculty" because it is commonly used at West Point. It is essentially synonymous with the term "permanent faculty." Both are misnomers. In fact, there is no formal tenure

for faculty at the Military Academy. From 1947 to 1988, professors were allowed to serve (at the pleasure of the Secretary of the Army) until age sixty-four. In 1988, a tenure review was instituted for professors, which was to renew (or revoke) their "tenure" every five years, beginning at their thirtieth year of service. Associate professors—at one time called permanent associate professors, or PAPs—are allowed to remain at West Point until normal retirement at thirty years of service.

69. Charles H. Schilling to T[homas] E. Griess, March 16, 1977, Subject: Function of the Academic Board, Charles H. Schilling Papers, USMA Library.

70. Dana Mead, Memorandum for the Superintendent, June 3, 1977, Subject: USMA Governance Structure, File 1011.14, School Study File, Governance Committee (January–July 1977), USMA Archives.

71. Roger Arango, "Evolution of USMA Governing Institutions," April 1977, pp. 14–16, File 1011.04, School Study File, Governance Committee (January–July 1977), USMA Archives.

72. Dana Mead, Memorandum for the Superintendent, June 3, 1977, Subject: USMA Governance Structure, p. 15, File 1011.04, School Study File, Governance Committee (January to July 1977), USMA Archives. See also Sidney B. Berry, June 14, 1976, "A Preliminary Analysis—Why an Honor Problem at West Point in 1976?" Memorandum for Record, Personal Papers of BG Thomas E. Griess.

73. Dana Mead, Memorandum for the Superintendent, June 3, 1977, Subject: USMA Governance Structure, pp. 19–20, File 1011.04, School Study File, Governance Committee (January to July 1977), USMA Archives.

74. Ibid., p. 6.

75. Andrew J. Goodpaster, interviewed by James M. Johnson, "Andrew J. Goodpaster Oral History, March 7, 1988," USMA Library, 30.

76. Andrew J. Goodpaster to Garrison Davidson, January 5, 1978, File 1011.04, School Study File, Governance Committee, USMA Archives.

77. *USMA Annual Report, 1978,* 35.

78. Charles H. Schilling to James B. Lampert, July 15, 1977, Box 17, James B. Lampert Papers, USMA Library; *USMA Annual Report, 1978,* 35.

79. Lovell, *Neither Athens nor Sparta?* 294.

80. *Final Report of the West Point Study Group,* July 27, 1977, 147; Goodpaster, "Oral History," 44–45. It was later suggested that the two rotating department heads on the Policy Board that Goodpaster had accepted should be eliminated because academic interests were already represented by the Dean. No action was taken on this recommendation and the two department heads continue to sit on the Policy Board. Donnithorne, *Affirmation and Change,* 61.

81. Goodpaster, "Oral History," 24.

82. Roger Arango, "Evolution of USMA Governing Institutions," April 1977, pp. 14–16, File 1011.04, School Study File, Governance Committee (January–July 1977), USMA Archives. A version of this paper also appeared in *Assembly,* September 1977.

83. Regulations, USMA, 1979.

84. Griess to author, February 21, 2001, author's files.

85. Edwin Van V. Sutherland, "Thoughts of an Academic Board Member on Leaving West Point," *Assembly*, September 1977, 31f.

86. *USMA Annual Report, 1985*, 6. Wickham spoke at West Point on about November 15, 1983.

87. Ibid., 7.

88. Army Study Group briefing slide from conference between Scott and Wickham in June 1984. Copies of the three briefing slides used at this conference to describe the tenure review process were included in a 1987 memorandum from the Dean to the Superintendent. Roy K. Flint to [Dave Palmer], Subject: Implementing Procedures for Periodic Performance Reviews of Permanent Professors, September 10, 1987, author's files.

89. Scott to Wickham, Subject: United States Military Academy (USMA) Faculty Development Program, September 27, 1984, Office of the Dean, USMA.

90. It is interesting that the "official" history of Palmer's superintendency (Donnithorne, *Affirmation and Change*) portrays this period as one of "tranquility." Nothing could have been further from the truth, although a decade of perspective may have been necessary to recognize that.

91. Dave R. Palmer, interviewed by Steve Groves, "Lieutenant General Dave R. Palmer, USMA Superintendent 1986–1991, Oral Interview, June 13–July 3, 1991," USMA Historian's Office, pp. 51–52.

92. *USMA Annual Report, 1987*, 12.

93. Palmer to Carl Vuono, [September 1987]. A draft of this letter is in a 1987 memorandum from the Dean to the Superintendent. Flint to [Palmer], Subject: Implementing Procedures for Periodic Performance Reviews of Permanent Professors, September 10, 1987, Office of the Dean, USMA.

94. The number of Deans or professors at USMA whose tenure was not renewed by the review boards is unknown. For obvious reasons, these decisions were not revealed publicly. From background interviews and circumstantial evidence, however, it is clear that some officers were forced out in this way, but the number seems to have been small.

95. Howard D. Graves, interviewed by Steve Groves, "Oral History Interview with Lieutenant General Howard Graves, Superintendent, U.S. Military Academy, May 10–June 18, 1996," Office of the Historian, USMA, 20.

96. Donnithorne, *Affirmation and Change*, 61–65.

97. Graves, "Oral History," 16.

98. Ibid., 20.

99. Background interviews, author's files.

100. Thomas E. Griess to author, February 21, 2001, author's files.

101. Background interviews, author's files.

102. D. V. Bennett to C. H. Schilling, January 13, 1967, Charles H. Schilling Papers, USMA Library.

103. Cutler, Schilling, and Dick, "Minority Report, Curriculum Revision, Academic Board Actions 17–18 April, 1968," Charles H. Schilling Papers, USMA Library.

104. Ibid.

105. *USMA Annual Report, 1981*, 27.

106. Sidney B. Berry to Bernard W. Rogers, January 1, 1977, Personal papers of Thomas E. Griess.

107. Sidney B. Berry to Joseph P. Kingston, Subject: Comments on Alternative Curricular Proposals and Recommendations, June 7, 1977, Personal papers of Thomas E. Griess.

108. Griess to author, April 12, 2001, author's files.

109. *Assembly*, September 1980, 37.

110. Ibid.

111. *USMA Annual Report, 1981*, 9–12.

112. *USMA Annual Report, 1983*, 52.

113. Palmer to Vuono, August 15, 1988, quoted in *USMA Annual Report, 1988*, 10.

114. Charles W. Larned, "The Genius of West Point," *The Churchman*, August 6, 1904.

115. Roy K. Flint, "Academic Links," *Assembly*, October 1989, 32.

116. This analysis is built on a reading of the speeches of both the Superintendent and the Secretary of the Army, and of numerous background interviews of persons at West Point, in Washington, and elsewhere.

117. *USMA Strategic Vision 2010* (West Point: USMA, 2000); *Institutional Self-Study*. The Academy's sixth decennial accreditation by the Middle States Association of Colleges and Schools was conducted in November 1999. The strategic review also drew on the studies and reports that resulted from the 1996–1997 visit of the Accreditation Board for Engineering and Technology.

118. The new 2001 curriculum and supporting materials were made available in early 2001 on the Academy's Web site.

119. My understanding of the fourth-class system (now the four-class system) has been aided by the following sources: "History of the Fourth Class System," July 11, 1989, Office of the Historian, USMA; Donnithorne, *Affirmation and Change;* and OPPA, *Continuity and Progress*.

120. *USMA Annual Report, 1918*, 12.

121. William W. Ford, "The Long Gray Line," *Assembly* 41 (December 1982): 22ff; [Resolutions of the First Class (1920)], August 4, 1919, File 351.1 Cadets General 1879 and 1919–1945, Adjutant General Records, USMA Archives. (Ford, class of 1920, incorrectly recalled that this event took place in the summer of 1920.)

122. MacArthur's endorsement [August 6, 1919] to [Resolutions of the First Class (1920)], August 4, 1919, File 351.1 Cadets General 1879 and 1919–1945, AG Records, USMA Archives.

123. *Superintendent's Curriculum Study: Summary of the Report of the Evaluation Committee* [Ewell Board], November 18, 1958, USMA Archives; Throckmorton quoted in R. H. Marcrum et al., "A Preliminary Evaluation of the Fourth Class System, [1969]," Annex C, "Historical Analysis," p. 1, File: Fourth-Class System, USMA Library.

124. Amos Jordon, Memorandum, March 4, 1960, George A. Lincoln Papers, Box VI, USMA Library.

125. Westmoreland speech, June 3, 1963, in *USMA Annual Report, 1962*, ii.

126. R. H. Marcrum and W. L. Golden et al., "A Preliminary Evaluation of the Fourth Class System, [1969]," Annex C, "Historical Analysis," p. 2, File: Fourth-Class System, USMA Library.

127. *USMA Annual Report, 1979*, 33–34.

128. Goodpaster, "Oral History," 88.

129. *Interim Report of the Middle States Accreditation Steering Committee*, 3 vols. (West Point: USMA, December 20, 1988), 2:12–32 to 2:12–33.

130. Donnithorne, *Affirmation and Change, 1986–1991*, 30–32.

131. Graves, "Oral History," 15.

132. *Interim Report of the Middle States Accreditation Steering Committee*, 2:12–32 to 2:12–33.

133. Donnithorne, *Affirmation and Change*, 31. Recognition was the point at which (usually in some form of ceremony) the fourth classmen were addressed and could in turn address upperclassmen, on a first-name basis. It was the effective end of "plebe" status, although some fourth-class duties still pertained. Advancing the date of recognition caused others, on and off the Policy Board, to suggest different dates. One proposed March 16, Founders Day; another suggested the end of the Army-Navy football game, if Army won, and the beginning of Christmas leave, if Navy prevailed.

134. Author's background interview.

135. Eric T. Olson, [February 2001], "A Message from the Commandant on the Fourth Class Recognition," Commandant's Corner, <http://www.usma.edu/USCC/correspondence/feb01.htm>.

136. Ernie Webb, John D. Hart, and James E. Foley, *West Point Sketch Book* (New York: Vantage Press, 1976), 110; Atkinson, *Long Gray Line*, 130–133.

137. On the food riot, see Atkinson, *Long Gray Line*, 86–88.

138. Ibid., 416.

Bibliography

Manuscript Collections

Baldwin, Abraham. Papers. Yale University Library, New Haven, Conn.

Bliss, Tasker. Papers. United States Army Military History Institute, Carlisle Barracks, Pa.

Bratt, John. Papers. USMA Library.

Burbeck, Henry. Papers. USMA Library.

Cram, Thomas J. Papers. USMA Library.

Correspondence Relating to the Military Academy, 1819–1866. RG 94, National Archives (NA), Washington, D.C.

Document Files. Records of the Office of the Deputy Chief of Staff for Personnel and Administration. RG 404, USMA Archives.

Cullum, George Washington. Papers. USMA Library.

Dagget, David. Papers. Yale University Library.

Delafield, Richard. Papers. USMA Library.

Dialectic Society File. USMA Library.

Douglass, David. Papers. USMA Library.

Eichelberger, Robert L. Papers. U.S. Army Military History Institute, Carlisle Barracks, Pa.

Gaff Collection. Newberry Library, Chicago.

Griess, Thomas E. Personal papers. In General Griess's possession.

Hodges, Campbell B. Papers. USMA Library.

Holden, Edward S. Collection. USMA Library.

Holt, Fairfield Butt. Papers. USMA Library.

Jefferson, Thomas. Papers. Library of Congress (LC), Washington, D.C.

Kemble, Gouverneur. Papers. USMA Library.

Knowlton, William A. Papers. USMA Library.

Knox, Henry. Papers. Pierpont Morgan Library, New York.

Lampert, James B. Papers. USMA Library.

Larned, Charles. Papers. USMA Library.

Lincoln, George. Papers. USMA Library.

Mansfield, Elizabeth. Papers. USMA Library.

Mansfield, Jared. Papers. USMA Library.

Mansfield, Jared. Papers. Yale University Library.

McCrea, Tully. Papers. USMA Library.

Nye, Roger H. Papers. USMA Library.
Papers of the Continental Congress, 1774–1789. M247, RG 360, NA.
Parker, Daniel. Papers. Historical Society of Pennsylvania, Philadelphia.
Partridge, Alden. Papers. USMA Library.
Proceedings (Staff Records). Records of the Academic Board. RG 404, USMA
   Archives.
Raymond, Samuel H. Papers. USMA Library.
Records of the Board of Visitors. RG 404, USMA Archives.
Records of the West Point Army Mess. RG 404, USMA Archives.
Rhodes, Charles Dudley. Papers. USMA Library.
Schilling, Charles H. Papers. USMA Library.
Swift, Jonathan Gardner. Mss. memoirs. USMA Library.
Swift, Jonathan Gardner. Papers. USMA Library.
Thayer, Sylvanus. Papers. USMA Library.
Tillman, Samuel. Papers. USMA Library.
Washington, George. Papers. LC.
Williams, Jonathan. Papers. Lilly Library, Bloomington, Ind.
Williams, Jonathan. Papers. USMA Library.
Young, Charles. Papers. USMA Library.

Official Publications

Annual Report of the Secretary of War, [year]. Washington, D.C.: GPO, [year]. [Annual published report of the War Department.]
Board of Officers. *Improvements at the U.S. Military Academy: Report of a Board of Officers*. West Point, USMA Press, 1902.
Catalogue of Books in the Library of the Military Academy, August 1822. Newburgh, NY: Ward M. Gazlay, 1822.
Debates and Proceedings in the Congress of the United States. 42 Vols. Washington, D.C.: Gales and Seaton, 1834–1856.
Donnithorne, Larry R. *Preparing for West Point's Third Century: A Summary of the Years of Affirmation and Change, 1986–1991*. West Point: USMA, 1991.
General Accounting Office. *DOD Service Academies: Improved Cost and Performance Monitoring Needed*. Washington, D.C.: GAO, 1991.
———. *DOD Service Academies: More Actions Needed to Eliminate Sexual Harassment*. Washington, D.C.: GAO, January 1994.
General Regulations for the Army. Philadelphia: M. Carey and Sons, 1821.
Institutional Self-Study, Report of the United States Military Academy. West Point: USMA, June 1999.
Interim Report of the Middle States Accreditation Steering Committee. 3 Vols. West Point: USMA, December 20, 1988.
Journals of the Continental Congress, 1774–1789. 34 Vols. Washington, D.C.: Library of Congress, 1904–1937.

Larned, Charles W. *Report . . . on the Enlargement of the Military Academy, West Point, August [10], 1899.* West Point: U.S. Military Academy Press and Bindery, 1899.

"Military Academy and Reorganization of the Army." January 13, 1800. *American State Papers, Military Affairs* 1:135.

Office of Policy, Planning, and Analysis. *Years of Continuity and Progress, 1991–1996.* West Point: USMA, June 1966.

Record of the USMA Conference on The State of the Academy. Camp Buckner, September 7–8, 1979. West Point: USMA, 1979.

Register of Debates in Congress: Comprising the Leading Debates and Incidents of the [2nd Sess., 18th Cong. to 1st Sess., 25th Cong.]. 14 vols. in 29 covers. Washington, D.C.: Gales and Seaton, 1825–1837.

Report of the Board of Visitors, [year]. Records of the Board of Visitors, USMA Archives. [Annual reports often printed, are made to Congress or the Secretary of War or the President after the board's annual visit to West Point.]

Report to the Secretary of the Army by the Special Commission of the United States Military Academy. West Point: USMA, December 15, 1976. [The Borman Commision Report.]

Richardson, James D., ed. *A Compilation of the Messages and Papers of the Presidents.* 10 Vols. Washington, D.C.: GPO, 1896–1899.

United States Congress. *American State Papers: Military Affairs.* 7 vols. In *American State Papers, Documents, Legislative and Executive, of the Congress of the United States.* 38 vols. Washington, D.C.: Gales and Seaton, 1832–1861.

United States Military Academy. *The Centennial of the United States Military Academy at West Point.* 2 vols. Washington, D.C.: GPO, 1904. Reprint, New York: Greenwood Press, 1969.

United States Military Academy Annual Report, [year]. Records of the Office of the Superintendent, RG 404, USMA Archives. [Annual printed reports by the Superintendent concering the state and accomplishments of USMA. In the nineteenth century these were sometimes included in the War Department Annual Report. The last USMA annual report was made in 1985, after which periodic reports were prepared, usually coinciding with the tenure of the succeeding Superintendents.]

USMA Strategic Vision. West Point: USMA, 2000.

Published Documents

Adams, Charles Francis. *Works of John Adams, Second President of the United States.* 10 Vols. Boston: Little, Brown, 1850–1856.

———. *Memoirs of John Quincy Adams.* 12 Vols. Philadelphia: Lippincott, 1875.

Bergh, Albert Ellery, ed. *The Writings of Thomas Jefferson.* 20 Vols. Washington, D.C.: Thomas Jefferson Memorial Association, 1903–1904.

Cappon, Lester J., ed. *The Adams-Jefferson Letters.* 2 Vols. Chapel Hill: The University of North Carolina Press, 1959.

Chandler, Alfred D., Jr., and Louis Galambos, eds. *The Papers of Dwight David Eisenhower.* 13 Vols. to date. Baltimore: Johns Hopkins University Press, 1970–.

Chase, Philander D., ed. *The Papers of George Washington, Revolutionary War Series.* 10 Vols. to date. Charlottesville: University of Virginia Press, 1985–.

Fitzpatrick, John C., ed. *The Writings of George Washington.* 39 Vols. Washington, D.C.: GPO, 1931–1944.

Hall, Charles Samuel. *Life and Letters of Samuel Holden Parsons: Major-General in the Continental Army and Chief Judge of the Northwestern Territory, 1737.* Binghamton, N.Y.: Otseningo Publishing, 1905.

King, Charles R., ed. *The Life and Correspondence of Rufus King.* 6 Vols. New York: Putnam's, 1900.

Rhodes, Charles Dudley. *Intimate Letters of a West Point Cadet, An Epic in Blank Verse of the Class of 1889, United States Military Academy.* Typescript. June 10, 1935. Charles Dudley Rhodes Papers, USMA Library.

Rutland, Robert A., and John C. A. Stagg, eds. *Papers of James Madison, Presidential Series.* 4 Vols. to date. Charlottesville: University Press of Virginia, 1984–.

Smith, Paul H., and Ronald M. Gephart, eds. *Letters of Delegates to Congress, 1774–1789.* 26 vols. Washington, D.C.: Library of Congress, 1970–2000.

Syrett, Harold C., ed. *The Papers of Alexander Hamilton.* 27 vols. New York: Columbia University Press, 1961–1987.

Taylor, Robert J., and Richard Ryerson, eds. *The Papers of John Adams.* 10 vols. to date. Cambridge, Mass.: Belknap Press of Harvard University Press, 1977–.

Memoir Literature

Barkalow, Carol. *In the Men's House.* New York: Poseidon Press, 1990.

Church, Albert E. *Personal Reminiscences of the Military Academy, from 1824 to 1831.* West Point: USMA Press, 1879.

Croffut, W. A., ed. *Fifty Years in Camp and Field: Diary of Major-General Ethan Allen Hitchcock, U.S.A.* New York: Putnam's, 1909.

Davidson, Garrison H. *Grandpa Gar: The Saga of One Soldier as Told to His Grandchildren.* N.p., 1974.

Davis, Benjamin O., Jr. *Benjamin O. Davis, Jr., American: An Autobiography.* Washington, D.C.: Smithsonian Institution Press, 1991.

Flipper, Henry O. *The Colored Cadet at West Point.* New York: Homer Lee and Co., 1878.

French, Samuel Gibbs. *Two Wars: An Autobiography of General Samuel G. French.* Nashville, Tenn.: Confederate Veteran, 1901.

Hein, Otto L. *Memories of Long Ago.* New York: Putnam's, 1925.

MacArthur, Douglas. *Reminiscences.* New York: McGraw-Hill, 1964.

Mansfield, Edward Deering. *Personal Memories, Social, Political and Literary.* Cincinnati: R. Clarke and Co., 1879.

Maury, Dabney Herndon. *Recollections of a Virginian in the Mexican, Indian, and Civil War.* 3d ed. New York: Scribner's, 1894.

Parker, James. *The Old Army, Memories, 1872–1918.* Philadelphia: Dorrance and Co., 1929.

Reminiscences of West Point in the Olden Time Derived from Various Sources. East Saginaw, Mich.: Evening News Printing and Binding House, 1886.

Schofield, John H. *Forty-six Years in the Army.* New York: Century Co., 1897.

Scott, Hugh L. *Some Memories of a Soldier.* New York: Century Co., 1928.

Smith, Francis H. *West Point Fifty Years Ago.* New York: Van Nostrand, 1879.

Swift, Joseph Gardner. *The Memoirs of General Joseph Gardner Swift.* Privately printed, 1890.

Westmoreland, William C. *A Soldier Reports: General William C. Westmoreland.* Garden City, N.Y.: Doubleday, 1976.

Secondary Literature

BOOKS

Adams, Henry. *History of the United States of America.* 9 vols. New York: Scribner's, 1889–1891.

Adams, John. *A Defence of the Constitutions of Government of the United States of America.* 3d ed. 3 vols. Philadelphia: Budd and Bartram, 1797.

Agnew, James B. *Eggnog Riot: The Christmas Mutiny at West Point.* San Rafael, Calif.: Presidio Press, 1979.

Ambrose, Stephen E. *Duty, Honor, Country: A History of West Point.* Baltimore: Johns Hopkins Press, 1966.

Aronson, Sidney H. *Status and Kinship in the Higher Civil Service.* Cambridge, Mass.: Harvard University Press, 1964.

Atkinson, Rick. *The Long Gray Line: The American Journey of West Point's Class of 1966.* Boston: Houghton Mifflin, 1989.

Bell, Whitfield J., Jr. *Colonel Lewis Nicola: Advocate of Monarchy, 1782.* Read at the Washington Birthday Luncheon of the Pennsylvania Society of the Cincinnati, Philadelphia, February 21, 1983. Philadelphia: Society of the Cincinnati, 1983.

Blackwell, James A. *On, Brave Old Army Team: The Cheating Scandal that Rocked the Nation, West Point, 1951.* Novato, Calif.: Presidio Press, 1990.

Boynton, Edward C. *History of West Point.* New York: Van Nostrand, 1964.

Buel, Richard, Jr. *Securing the Revolution, Ideology in American Politics, 1789–1815.* Ithaca, N.Y.: Cornell University Press, 1972.

Colvin, Howard, ed. *A Biographical Dictionary of British Architects, 1600–1840.* New Haven, Conn.: Yale University Press, 1995.

Crackel, Theodore J. *Mr. Jefferson's Army: The Political and Social Reform of the Military Establishment, 1801–1809.* New York: New York University Press, 1987.

Daniels, George H. *American Science in the Age of Jackson.* New York: Columbia University Press, 1968.

Dauer, Manning J. *The Adams Federalists.* Baltimore: Johns Hopkins University Press, 1953.

Department of Social Sciences. "Wartime History of the United States Military Academy." Typescript, [1945?]. [Copy in USMA Library.]

Ellis, Joseph J., and Robert Moore. *School for Soldiers: West Point and the Profession of Arms.* New York: Oxford University Press, 1974.

Erney, Richard A. *The Public Life of Henry Dearborn.* New York: Arno Press, 1979.

Farley, Joseph Pearson. *Three Rivers: The James, the Potomac, the Hudson.* New York: The Neale Publishing, 1910.

Fleming, Thomas J. *West Point: The Men and Times of the United States Military Academy.* New York: William Morrow, 1969.

Forman, Sidney. *Cadet Life Before the Mexican War.* West Point: USMA Printing Office, 1945.

———. *West Point: A History of the United States Military Academy.* New York: Columbia University Press, 1950.

Ganoe, William Addleman. *MacArthur Close-Up.* New York: Vantage Press, 1902.

Hesseltine, William B. *Ulysses S. Grant, Politician.* New York: Fredrick Ungar, 1935.

Hill, Forest Garrett. *Roads, Rails and Waterways: The Army Engineers and Early Transportation.* Norman: University of Oklahoma Press, 1957.

Holley, I. B., Jr. *General John M. Palmer, Citizen Soldiers, and the Army of a Democracy.* Westport, Conn.: Greenwood Press, 1982.

Hunter, Robert F., and Edwin L. Dooley Jr. *Claudius Crozet, French Engineer in America, 1790–1864.* Charlottesville: University Press of Virginia, 1989.

Jacobs, James Ripley. *The Beginning of the U.S. Army, 1783–1812.* Princeton, N.J.: Princeton University Press, 1947.

James, D. Clayton. *The Years of MacArthur.* 2 vols. Boston: Houghton Mifflin, 1970.

Kerber, Linda K. *Federalists in Dissent: Imagery and Ideology in Jeffersonian America.* Ithaca, N.Y.: Cornell University Press, 1970.

Kohn, Richard H. *Eagle and Sword: The Federalists and the Creation of the Military Establishment in America, 1783–1802.* New York: The Free Press, 1975.

Leon, Philip W. *Mark Twain and West Point.* Oakville, Ontario: ECW Press, 1996.

———. *Bullies and Cowards: The West Point Hazing Scandal, 1898–1901.* Westport, Conn.: Greenwood Press, 2000.

Leslie, W. Bruce. *Gentlemen and Scholars: College and Community in the "Age of the University," 1865–1917.* University Park: Pennsylvania State University Press, 1992.

Lovell, John P. *Neither Athens nor Sparta? The American Service Academies in Transition.* Bloomington: Indiana University Press, 1979.

Marshall, Edward Chauncey. *Are the West Point Graduates Loyal?* New York: D. Van Nostrand, 1862.

Marszalek, John F., Jr. *Court-Martial: A Black Man in America*. New York: Scribner's, 1972.

McClure, Nathaniel F., ed. *Class of 1887, United States Military Academy*. Washington, D.C.: P. S. Bond, 1938.

Michie, Peter S. *General McClellan*. New York: D. Appleton and Co., 1901.

Miller, Charles E., Jr., Donald V. Lockey, and Joseph Visconti, Jr. *Highland Fortress: The Fortification of West Point During the American Revolution*. West Point: USMA, 1988.

Mills, S. M. *A Valentine Party Given by Lieut. and Mrs. S. M. Mills*. West Point: n.p., 1876.

Mitchell, Vance O. "A Brief History of the West Point and Air Force Academy Honor Codes." Typescript. Office of Air Force History, November 13, 1984. [Copy in USMA Library.]

Morrison, James L. *The Best School in the World: West Point, the Pre–Civil War Years, 1833–1866*. Kent, Ohio: Kent State University Press, 1986.

Palmer, Dave Richard. *The River and the Rock: The History of Fortress West Point, 1775–1783*. New York: Greenwood, 1969.

Park, Roswell. *A Sketch of the History and Topography of West Point and the U.S. Military Academy*. Philadelphia: Henry Perkins, 1840.

[Partridge, Alden] Americannus. *The Military Academy, at West Point, Unmasked: or, Corruption and Military Despotism Exposed*. Washington, D.C.: J. Elliot, 1830.

Pennell, E. R., and J. Pennell. *The Life of James McNeill Whistler*. Philadelphia: Lippincott, 1911.

Pierce, Edward Lillie. *[The Life of] Major John Lillie, 1755–1801 [and] The Lillie Family of Boston, 1663–1896*. Cambridge: John Wilson and Son, University Press, 1896.

Placzek, Adolf K., ed. *Macmillan Encyclopedia of Architects*. New York: The Free Press, 1982.

Randall, Willard Sterne. *Benedict Arnold: Patriot and Traitor*. New York: Morrow, 1990.

Rhodes, Charles Dudley. *Robert E. Lee, the West Pointer*. Richmond, Va.: Garrett & Massie, 1932.

Robson, David W. *Educating Republicans: The College in the Era of the American Revolution, 1750–1800*. Westport, Conn.: Greenwood Press, 1985.

Schaff, Morris. *The Spirit of Old West Point, 1858–1862*. Boston. Houghton, Mifflin and Co., 1907.

Schofield, John McAllister. *An Address Delivered by Major General John McAllister Schofield, USMA 1853, to the Corps of Cadets*. West Point: USMA Press, 1879.

Sergent, Mary Elizabeth. *They Lie Forgotten: The United States Military Academy, 1856–1861*. Middletown, N.Y.: Prior King Press, 1986.

Stagg, John C. A. *Mr. Madison's War: Politics, Diplomacy, and Warfare in the Early American Republic, 1783–1830*. Princeton, N.J.: Princeton University Press, 1983.

Taylor, Maxwell D. *West Point Honor System: Its Objectives and Procedures.* West Point: USMA, 1948.

————. *Swords and Plowshares.* New York: Norton, 1972.

Webb, Ernie, John D. Hart, and James E. Foley. *West Point Sketch Book.* New York: Vantage Press, 1976.

Weigley, Russell F. *Towards an American Army: Military Thought from Washington to Marshall.* New York: Columbia University Press, 1962.

Wilmolt, John E., ed. *Journals of the Provincial Congress of New York.* 2 vols. Albany, N.Y., 1842.

Wood, Oliver E. *West Point Scrap Book.* New York: D. Van Nostrand, 1871.

ARTICLES AND ESSAYS

"Account of the National Military School of the United States of America." *[London] Quarterly Journal* 21 (April 1826): 3.

Andrews, George L. "The Military Academy and the Education of Officers," *Journal of the Military Service Institution* 16. (March 1895): 316–343.

Baxter, Sylvester. "The New West Point." *Century Magazine* 68 (July 1904): 335–336.

Bowley, Freemont W., II. "West Point Has Grown." *Assembly,* January 1944, 2.

"Building Construction at the Military Academy." *The Association of Graduates . . . Bulletin No. 8,* May 1, 1934.

Center for the Professional Military Ethic. "White Paper: Cadet Honor Code and Honor System." *Assembly,* May/June 2000, 60–61.

Counts, G. A. "The Department of Physics and Chemistry." *Assembly,* April 1954, 2f.

Crackel, Theodore J. "The Founding of West Point: Jefferson and the Politics of Security." *Armed Forces and Society* 7 (summer 1981): 529–543.

Cram, Goodhue & Ferguson. "West Point Military Academy." *Architectural Review* 10, no. 6 (June 1903): 68.

Cross, Lenora. "The Moores of West Point." Unpublished essay. USMA Library.

Donnithorne, Larry R. "The Year of Honor at USMA—1988–1989." *Assembly,* October 1989, 15.

Dudley, Charlotte W. "Jared Mansfield: United States Surveyor General." *Ohio History* 85 (summer 1976): 231–46.

Flint, Roy K. "Academic Links." *Assembly,* October 1989, 32.

Forman, Sidney. "The First School of Engineering." *Military Engineer* 44 (March–April 1952): 109–112.

————. "Why the United States Military Academy Was Established in 1802." *Military Affairs* 29 (Spring 1965): 16–28.

Goode, G. Brown. "The Origin of the National Scientific and Educational Institutions." In *Annual Report of the American Historical Association for the Year 1889.* Washington, D.C.: GPO, 1890.

Griess, Thomas. "Vincent Esposito, Soldier and Scholar." *Assembly,* winter 1964, 5.

Hall, Robert H. "Early Discipline at the United States Military Academy." *Journal of the Military Service Institute of the United States* 2 (1882): 473.

Heiberg, Mrs. E. R. "Professors' Row." Typescript. USMA Library.

Hogan, Edward R. "George Baron and the *Mathematical Correspondent.*" *Historia Mathematica* 3 (1976): 403–415.

Hubbard, Elmer W. "The Military Academy and the Education of Officers." *Journal of the Military Service Institution of the United States* 16 (January 1895), 1–24.

Hunt, Gaillard. "Office-Seeking During Jefferson's Administration." *American Historical Review* 124 (April 1980): 91–96.

Larned, Charles. "Comment and Criticism." *Journal of the Military Service Institution of the United States* 16 (March 1895): 323.

———. "The Genius of West Point." *The Churchman*, August 6, 1904.

———. "Corps Honor." In *The West Point Hand-Book*, 27–32. West Point: YMCA of the USMA, 1907.

Latrobe, John H. B. "West Point Reminiscences." In *Eighteenth Annual Reunion of the Association of Graduates*. East Saginaw, Mich.: 1887.

Mahan, Jane Leigh. "Random Memories." *The Pointer*, March 15, 1929.

"Military Academy at West Point." *American Quarterly Review* 22 (September, 1837): 91–92.

Murry, G. J. "The Department of Mechanics, USMA." *Assembly*, April 1951, 2f.

Prince, Carl E. "The Passing of the Aristocracy: Jefferson's Removal of the Federalists." *Journal of American History* 51 (December 1970): 563–575.

Prince, Howard T., and William L. Wilson. "The Leadership Legacy of General Maxwell D. Taylor." *Assembly*, February 1946, 14.

Sutherland, Edwin Van V. "Thoughts of an Academic Board Member On Leaving West Point." *Assembly*, September 1977, 31f.

Wade, Arthur P. "A Military Offspring of the American Philosophical Society." *Military Affairs* 38 (September 1974): 103–107.

"West Point Vu en 1795 par la Rochefoucaude-Liancourt." *Revue International d'Historie Militaire* 32 (1972–1975): 495–498.

Wilkinson, Norman B. "The Forgotten 'Founder' of West Point." *Military Affairs* 24 (winter 1960–1961): 177–188.

Wood, Robert J. "Early Days of Benny Havens." *The Pointer*, February 26, 1937.

DISSERTATIONS

Carhart, Tom. "African-American West Pointers in the Nineteenth Century." Ph.D. diss., Princeton University, 1998.

Denton, Edgar, III. "The Formative Years of the United States Military Academy, 1775–1833." Ph.D. diss., Syracuse University, 1964.

Dillard, Walter Scott. "The United States Military Academy, 1865–1900: The Uncertain Years." Ph.D. diss., University of Washington, 1972.

Griess, Thomas E. "Dennis Hart Mahan: West Point Professor and Advocate of Military Professionalism, 1830–1871." Ph.D. diss., Duke University, 1968.

Janda, Robert Lance. "Stronger Than Custom: West Point and the Admission of Women, 1972–1980." Ph.D. diss., University of Oklahoma, Norman, 1998.

Kershner, James William. "Sylvanus Thayer, A Biography." Ph.D. diss., West Virginia University, 1976.

Molloy, Peter Michael. "Technical Education and the Young Republic: West Point as America's École Polytechnique, 1802–1833." Ph.D. diss., Brown University, 1975.

Nye, Roger Hurless. "The United States Military Academy in an Era of Educational Reform, 1900–1925." Ph.D. diss., Columbia University, 1968.

Shaughnessy, Thomas Elliott. "Beginnings of National Professional Military Education in America, 1775–1825." D.Ed. diss., Johns Hopkins University, 1956.

Wade, Arthur Pearson. "Artillerists and Engineers: The Beginnings of American Seacoast Fortifications, 1794–1815." Ph.D. diss., Kansas State University, 1977.

Zuersher, Dorothy J. S. "Benjamin Franklin, Jonathan Williams and the United States Military Academy." Ph.D. diss., University of North Carolina at Greensboro, 1974.

INTERVIEWS AND ORAL HISTORIES

Goodpaster, Andrew J., interviewed by James M. Johnson. "Andrew J. Goodpaster Oral History, March 7, 1988." USMA Library.

Graves, Howard D., interviewed by Steve Groves. "Oral History Interview with Lieutenant General Howard Graves, Superintendent, U.S. Military Academy, May 10–June 18, 1996." Office of the Historian, USMA.

Palmer, Dave R., interviewed by Steve Groves. "Lieutenant General Dave R. Palmer, USMA Superintendent 1986–1991, Oral Interview, June 13–July 3, 1991." Office of the Historian, USMA.

Index

Warin, C. J. (temporary engineer), 33,
301n 15
Warner, Thomas, 286
Washington, George, 14, 17, 22–29
Waters, John Knight, 280
Wattendorf, John Martin, 281
Wayne, Anthony, 9, 37
Wayne, Henry C., 117
Way of the Fox (Palmer), 257
Webster, Frank D., 149
Weeks, John W., 194
Weir, Robert W., 108, 120, 150, 151, 285
West, Charles Whitney, 225, 287
Westmoreland, William Childs, 229–232,
270, 278, 336n 2
"West Point" (CBS television series), 223
West Point, America's Power Fraternity
(Galloway and Johnson), 248
West Point, the Life of a Cadet (Engleman),
223
West Point Army Mess, 116–118, 205–206,
333nn 15, 17
West Point Atlas of American Wars
(Esposito), 226
West Point First Classman (Reeder), 223
West Point Plebe (Reeder), 223
West Point Second Classman (Reeder), 223
West Point Story, The (Reeder), 223
West Point Study Group, 251–255, 263
West Point Yearling (Reeder), 223
Wheat, Clayton E. "Buck", 195, 203, 284
Wheeler, Junius Brutus, 151, 162, 291
Whiskey Rebellion, 42
Whistler, George Washington, 120
Whistler, James Abbot McNeil, 120–121
Whistler vs. Ruskin: Art and Art Critics
(Whistler), 121

White, Herbert Arthur, 287
Whittaker, Johnson Chestnut, 146–147, 157
Wickham, John A., 256–259, *258*
Wilby, Francis Bowditch, 207, 278
Wilkinson, James, 38, 63
Willard, Sumner, 285
Willcox, Cornelius DeWitt, 184, 185, 284
Williams, Jonathan, 54–71, 277
and Baron, 54–55
and Dexter, 42–43
and Jefferson, 45, 56
Wilson, James, 58
Wilson, John Moulder, 158, 278
Wilson, Robert Maris, 283
Wilson, William, 34, 54, 58
Winans, Edwin Baruch, 195, 278
Winkel, Raymond John, Jr., 289
Winslow, E. Eveleth, 290
Winter vacations (1802–1817), 58–59
Winthrop, William, 286
Women cadets, 238–243, *242, 272, 275*
Wood, Charles E. S., 140
Wood, Edward Edgar, 171, 184, 284
Woodruff, Thomas J., 74, 75
Woolwich, Royal Military Academy at,
304n 52
Wooten, William Preston, 290
World War I, 149, 185–188, 200, 269
World War II, 200, 203, 206–211, 225, 236
Worth, William J., 86, 104, 279

Young, Charles, 145–149, *147,* 237
Youngberg, Gilbert Albin, 290

Zimmern, Sir Alfred, 202
Zoeller, Christian, 69, 72, 81, 285
Zuersher, Dorothy J. S., 305–306n 63